RITUAL IN NARRATIVE

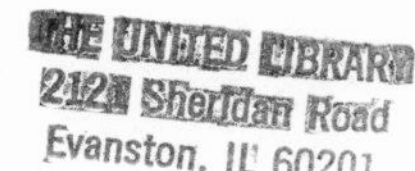

RITUAL IN NARRATIVE

*The Dynamics of
Feasting, Mourning, and Retaliation Rites
in the Ugaritic Tale of Aqhat*

David P. Wright

Winona Lake, Indiana
EISENBRAUNS

Printed in the United States of America.

Cataloging-in-Publication Data

Wright, David P. (David Pearson), 1953-
Ritual in narrative : the dynamics of feasting, mourning, and retaliation rites in the Ugaritic tale of Aqhat / by David P. Wright
p. cm.
Includes the text of Aqhat in Ugaritic (romanized) and English.
Includes bibliographical references and index.
ISBN 1-57506-046-9 (cloth : alk. paper)
1. Aqhat epic. 2. Ugarit (Extinct city)—Religion—Liturgy. 3. Fasts and feasts—Syria—Ugarit (Extinct city). I. Aqhat epic. English & Ugaritic. II. Title.

PJ4150.Z77 W75 2000
892′.67—dc21

00-021876
CIP

The paper used in this publication meets the minimum requirements of the American National Standard for Information Sciences—Permanence of Paper for Printed Library Materials, ANSI Z39.48-1984.⊗™

Contents

Preface

This book is an outgrowth of work on ritual in the Bible and ancient Near Eastern texts that I have been pursuing for a number of years. After laying a foundation in the study of prescriptive ritual texts,[1] I began to explore ritual in various narrative texts[2] and the Psalms.[3] While these later studies were mainly interested in examining ritual in the Bible and the ancient Near East at large, they indicated that the study of ritual within a tale's (or poem's) context is an invaluable aid in deciphering the meaning of the text.

At the same time, I began teaching courses on Northwest Semitic languages and texts, including Ugaritic and its texts, at Brandeis University. As I read the Aqhat, Kirta, and Baʿl legends and myths with students, it was clear that, because of the density of ritual motifs in these stories, a study of ritual in narrative context would provide insight into their meaning. The conjunction of my interest in ritual embedded in narrative and the study of the Ugaritic stories with students gave birth to the idea for this book.

This study tries to serve two audiences. It is mainly intended for scholars and students of the ancient Near East, and this intention is partly a function of the state and nature of the text and Ugaritic studies. The text is imperfectly preserved and the language is not perfectly known (especially the meanings of many words). Hence detailed philological analysis is required as part of any larger attempt at interpretation. Nevertheless, I have tried to make the work accessible to those outside of Near Eastern

---

1. See, for example, my book *The Disposal of Impurity: Elimination Rites in the Bible and in Hittite and Mesopotamian Literature* (SBLDS 101; Atlanta: Scholars Press, 1987) and the articles "Deuteronomy 21:1–9 as a Rite of Elimination," *CBQ* 49 (1987) 387–403; "The Gesture of Hand Placement in the Hebrew Bible and in Hittite Literature," *JAOS* 106 (1986) 433–46"; "The Spectrum of Priestly Impurity," in *Priesthood and Cult in Ancient Israel* (ed. G. A. Anderson and S. M. Olyan; JSOTSup 125; Sheffield: JSOT Press, 1991).

2. For example, "David autem Remansit in Hierusalem: Felix Coniunctio!" in *Pomegranates and Golden Bells: Studies in Biblical, Jewish, and Near Eastern Ritual, Law, and Literature in Honor of Jacob Milgrom* (ed. D. P. Wright, D. N. Freedman, and A. Hurvitz; Winona Lake, Ind.: Eisenbrauns, 1995) 215–30; "Holiness, Sex, and Death in the Garden of Eden," *Bib* 77 (1996) 305–29.

3. "Ritual Analogy in Psalm 109," *JBL* 113 (1994) 385–404; "Blown Away like a Bramble: The Dynamics of Analogy in Psalm 58," *RB* 102 (1996) 213–36.

studies who will have an interest in this work, especially those in disciplines such as anthropology or comparative literature, as well as educated nonprofessional readers. I have provided translations of all cited texts and, it is hoped, enough explanation to orient the latter group of readers. The reason for servicing these readers is clear: the study provides not just a reading of the Aqhat story but also elucidates a method that can be pursued in texts from any society in any period. I hope that in some small way it will prod others to ask similar questions of their texts and sources.

Over the last few years, as this study has developed, I have had the opportunity to share conclusions with others. I have read papers on ritual in Aqhat and Kirta at the American Oriental Society annual meeting (1993, 1994) and in the Ugaritic Studies and Northwest Semitic Epigraphy Group of the Society of Biblical Literature (1995, 1996). I benefited much from the comments of colleagues on these occasions; especially I would like to thank Daniel Fleming, Brian Schmidt, Edward Greenstein, Jack Sasson, and Peter Machinist.

In the preparation of this manuscript, I want to thank two graduate students: Samantha Joo, for her careful reading of preliminary drafts, questioning arguments, and finding mistakes; and Alan Lenzi, for his careful editorial eye that helped to polish the final draft and proofs. I also thank students in my Ugaritic seminar (fall 1996), who responded to several of the arguments made in this book.

I express appreciation to Brandeis University for providing the time and means necessary to complete the main draft of this study by granting a Bernstein Faculty Fellowship in the spring of 1996.

I finally thank my wife, Dianne, and children, Rebekah, Sarah, Benjamin, and Aharon, for their forbearance while I researched and wrote this study.

Abbreviations

AB	Anchor Bible
ABD	Freedman, D. N., editor. *Anchor Bible Dictionary*. 6 vols. New York: Doubleday, 1992
AHw	von Soden, W. *Akkadisches Handwörterbuch*. 3 vols. Wiesbaden: Harrassowitz, 1965–81
AJSL	*American Journal of Semitic Languages and Literatures*
ALASP(M)	Abhandlungen zur Literature Alt-Syrien-Palästina (und Mesopotamiens)
ANEP	Pritchard, J. B., editor. *The Ancient Near East in Pictures Relating to the Old Testament*. 2d ed. Princeton: Princeton University Press, 1969
ANET	Pritchard, J. B., editor. *Ancient Near Eastern Texts Relating to the Old Testament*. 3d ed. Princeton: Princeton University Press, 1969
AnOr	Analecta Orientalia
AOAT	Alter Orient und Altes Testament
AOATS	Alter Orient und Altes Testament Sonderreihe
ARTU	de Moor, J. C. *An Anthology of Religious Texts from Ugarit*. Religious Texts Translation Series: Nisaba 16. Leiden: Brill, 1987
BARev	*Biblical Archaeology Review*
BASOR	*Bulletin of the American Schools of Oriental Research*
BDB	Brown, F., S. R. Driver, and C. A. Briggs. *A Hebrew and English Lexicon of the Old Testament*. Oxford: Clarendon, 1953
Bib	*Biblica*
BO	*Bibliotheca Orientalis*
BZAW	Beiheft zur ZAW
CAD	Oppenheim, A. L., et al., editors. *The Assyrian Dictionary of the Oriental Institute of the University of Chicago*. Chicago: Oriental Institute of the University of Chicago, 1956–
CahRB	Cahiers de la Revue Biblique
CARTU	de Moor, J. C., and K. Spronk. *A Cuneiform Anthology of Religious Texts from Ugarit*. Semitic Study Series 6. Leiden: Brill, 1987
CAT	Dietrich, M., O. Loretz, and J. Sanmartín. *The Cuneiform Alphabetic Texts from Ugarit, Ras Ibn Hani and Other Places (KTU: Second, Enlarged Edition)*. ALASPM 8. Münster: Ugarit-Verlag, 1995
CBQ	*Catholic Biblical Quarterly*
CHD	Güterbock, H. G., and H. A. Hoffner, editors. *The Hittite Dictionary of the Oriental Institute of the University of Chicago*. Chicago: Oriental Instutute of the University of Chicago, 1980–
CML	Gibson, J. C. L. *Canaanite Myths and Legends*. 2d ed. Edinburgh: T. & T. Clark, 1978

CTA	Herdner, A. *Corpus des tablettes en cunéiformes alphabétiques, découvertes à Ras Shamra-Ugarit de 1929 à 1939*. Mission de Ras Shamra 10. Paris: Imprimerie Nationale / Geuthner, 1963
CTH	Laroche, E. *Catalogue des textes hittites*. 2d ed. Paris: Klincksieck, 1971
DLU	Olmo Lete, G. del, and J. Sanmartín. *Diccionario de la lengua ugarítica*. Aula Orientalis Supp. 7. Barcelona: AUSA, 1996
DMWA	Wehr, H., and J. M. Cowan. *A Dictionary of Modern Written Arabic*. Ithaca, N.Y.: Spoken Languages Services, 1976
DNWSI	Hoftijzer, J., and K. Jongeling. *The Dictionary of the North-West Semitic Inscriptions*. Handbuch der Orientalistik 1/21. 2 vols. Leiden: Brill, 1995
ErIsr	*Eretz-Israel*
FAT	Forschungen zum Alten Testament
GUL	Sivan, D. *A Grammar of the Ugaritic Language*. Handbuch der Orientalistik 1/28. Leiden: Brill, 1997
HALAT	Baumgartner, W., et al. *Hebräisches und aramäisches Lexikon zum Alten Testament*. 4 vols. Leiden: Brill, 1967–
HSM	Harvard Semitic Monographs
HSS	Harvard Semitic Studies
HUS	Watson, W. G. E., and N. Wyatt, editors. *Handbook of Ugaritic Studies*. Handbuch der Orientalistik 1/39. Leiden: Brill, 1999
HW[1]	Friedrich, J. *Hethitisches Wörterbuch: Kurzgefasste kritisches Sammlung der Deutungen hethitischer Wörter*. Heidelberg: Carl Winter, 1952
HW[2]	Friedrich, J., and A. Kammenhuber. *Hethitisches Wörterbuch*. 2d ed. Heidelberg: Carl Winter, 1975–
IBoT	Bozkurt, H., M. Çiğ, and H. G. Güterbock. *Istanbul Arkeoloji Müzelerinde bulunan Boğazköy Tabletlerinden Seçme Metinler*. 3 vols. Istanbul: Maarif Matbaası, 1944–54
IDBSup	Crim, K., editor. *The Interpreter's Dictionary of the Bible*, Supplementary Volume. Nashville: Abindon, 1976
IEJ	*Israel Exploration Journal*
JANES(CU)	*Journal of the Ancient Near Eastern Society of Columbia University*
JAOS	*Journal of the American Oriental Society*
JAOSSup	JAOS Supplement
JBL	*Journal of Biblical Literature*
JCS	*Journal of Cuneiform Studies*
JNES	*Journal of Near Eastern Studies*
JNSL	*Journal of Northwest Semitic Languages*
JSOT	*Journal for the Study of the Old Testament*
JSOTSup	JSOT Supplement
JSS	*Journal of Semitic Studies*
JSSMon	JSS Monograph Series
KAI	Donner, H., and W. Röllig. *Kanaanäische und aramäische Inschriften*. 3 vols. 3d ed. Wiesbaden: Harrassowitz, 1971–76

KBo	*Keilschrifttexte aus Boghazköi*
KTU[1]	Dietrich, M., O. Loretz, and J. Sanmartín. *Die keilalphabetischen Texte aus Ugarit.* AOAT 24. Kevelaer: Butzon & Bercker / Neukirchen-Vluyn: Neukirchener Verlag, 1976. [for KTU, 2d ed., see *CAT*]
KUB	*Keilschrifturkunden aus Boghazköi*
MLC	del Olmo Lete, G. *Mitos y leyendas de Canaan: Según la tradición de Ugarit.* Institución San Jerónimo para la Investigación Bíblica: Fuentes de la Ciencia Bíblica 1. Madrid: Ediciones Cristiandad, 1981
MSS	*Münchener Studien zur Sprachwissenschaft*
OAWS	Österreichische Akademie der Wissenschaften, Philosophisch-historische Klasse
OBO	Orbis biblicus et orientalis
Or	*Orientalia*
OTL	Old Testament Library
OTS	*Oudtestamentische Studiën*
PRU 3	Nougayrol, J. *Le Palais Royal d'Ugarit*, vol. 3: *Textes Accadiens et Hourrites des Archives Est, Ouest et Centrales.* 2 vols. Mission de Ras Shamra 6. Paris: Imprimerie Nationale / Klincksieck, 1955
PRU 4	Nougayrol, J. *Le Palais Royal d'Ugarit*, vol. 4: *Textes Accadiens des Archives Sud.* 2 vols. Mission de Ras Shamra 9. Paris: Imprimerie Nationale / Klincksieck, 1956
QS	Quaderni di Semitistica
RB	*Revue biblique*
RHA	*Revue hittite et asianique*
RHPR	*Revue d'histoire et de philosophie religieuses*
RS	Field numbers of objects excavated at Ras Shamra
RTU	Wyatt, N. *Religious Texts from Ugarit: The Words of Ilimilku and His Colleagues.* The Biblical Seminar 53. Sheffield: Sheffield Academic Press, 1998
SBLDS	Society of Biblical Literature Dissertation Series
SBLRBS	Society of Biblical Literature Resources for Biblical Study
SBLWAW	Society of Biblical Literature Writings from the Ancient World
SEL	*Studi epigrafici e linguistici*
SHCANE	Studies in the History and Culture of the Ancient Near East
SJOT	*Scandinavian Journal of the Old Testament*
SP	de Moor, J. C. *The Seasonal Pattern in the Ugaritic Myth of Baʿlu according to the Version of Ilimilku.* AOAT 16. Kevelaer: Butzon & Bercker /Neukirchen-Vluyn: Neukirchener Verlag, 1971
SSN	Studia semitica neerlandica
STBoT	Studien zu den Boğazköy-Texten
TO 1	Caquot, A., M. Sznycer, and A. Herdner. *Textes Ougaritiques, Tome I: Mythes et légendes.* Paris: du Cerf, 1974
UF	*Ugarit-Forschungen*
Ug. 5	Nougayrol, J., et al. *Ugaritica*, vol. 5: *Nouveax Textes Accadiens, Hourrites et Ugaritiques des Archives et Bibliothèques Privées d'Ugarit.*

	Mission de Ras Shamra 16. Bibliothèque Archéologique et Historique 80. Paris: Geuthner, 1968
Ug. 6	Courtois, J.-C., editor. *Ugaritica*, vol. 6. Mission de Ras Shamra 17. Bibliothèque Archéologique et Historique 81. Paris: Mission Archéologique de Ras Shamra, Collège de France / Geuthner, 1969
UNP	Parker, S., editor. *Ugaritic Narrative Poetry*. SBLWAW 9. Atlanta: Scholars Press, 1997
UPA	Margalit, B. *The Ugaritic Poem of AQHT: Text, Translation, Commentary*. BZAW 182. Berlin: de Gruyter, 1989
VBoT	Götze, A., editor. *Verstreute Boghazköi-Texte*. Marburg: A. Götze, 1930
VT	*Vetus Testamentum*
VTSup	VT Supplements
ZA	*Zeitschrift für Assyriologie*
ZAW	*Zeitschrift für die Alttestamentliche Wissenschaft*

Introduction

Ritual in the Ugaritic Texts

Since 1929, excavations at and near Ras Shamra, Syria, just off the Mediterranean coast, have yielded a large number of written records on clay tablets. Many of the documents are in the Akkadian language, the lingua franca of the ancient Near East in the fourteenth century B.C.E., the time of the majority of the texts. But documents written in other languages, including Hurrian, Hittite, Egyptian, and undeciphered Cypro-Minoan have also been discovered. The variety of languages is in part due to Ugarit's economic and geographical position and significance. The city-state was a focal point of the competing Mitannian, Egyptian, and Hittite empires that vied for power in the area.[1]

The documentary finds at Ugarit and in its vicinity, however, are most significant for the large number of tablets written in the native dialect of the area, which modern scholars have appropriately labeled "Ugaritic." This language, unknown prior to 1929, was written in a system also quite unknown before the discovery of the texts. The system used cuneiform—wedges impressed on clay tablets, similar to that used in writing Sumerian, Akkadian, Hittite, and Hurrian texts. In contrast to these systems, all of which are syllabic, Ugaritic cuneiform was alphabetic or consonantal (like Hebrew) and consisted of a short and therefore very serviceable list of thirty characters.[2]

---

1. For recent introductory summaries, see M. Yon, "Ugarit: History and Archaeology," *ABD* 6.695–706; D. Pardee and P. Bordreuil, "Ugarit: Texts and Literature," *ABD* 6.706–21; see also the comprehensive *HUS*. On basic issues in political history, commerce, and religion, see M. Astour, "Ugarit and the Great Powers," in *Ugarit in Retrospect: 50 Years of Ugarit and Ugaritic* (ed. G. D. Young; Winona Lake, Ind.: Eisenbrauns, 1981) 4–29; I. Cornelius, "A Bird's Eye View of Trade in Ancient Ugarit," *JNSL* 9 (1981) 13–31; P. D. Miller, "Ugarit and the History of Religions," *JNSL* 9 (1981) 119–28; and the articles in *HUS*.

2. For a recent study of its development and character, see M. Dietrich and O. Loretz, *Die Keilalphabete: Die phönizisch-kanaanäischen und altarabischen Alphabete in Ugarit* (ALASP 1; Münster: Ugarit-Verlag, 1988); cf. *HUS* 81–90. A few Hurrian (*CAT* 1.30, 1.32, 1.33, 1.34–37, 1.42; 1.44, 1.51, 1.52, 1.54, 1.59, 1.60, 1.66, 1.68; 1.110, 1.111, 1.116, 1.120, 1.125, 1.128, 1.131, 1.132, 1.135, 1.149, 7.40, 7.43) and Akkadian (*CAT* 1.67, 1.69, 1.70, 1.73:1–7) texts are written in the alphabetic script. [In citing Ugaritic texts throughout this work, reference will mainly be made only to *CAT* section and text numbers without explicit reference to *CAT*, as in n. 4, below.]

The Ugaritic texts in alphabetic script, of which more than 1325 have been published[3] (though many are very fragmentary), reflect several genres. They include a number of royal and non-royal letters; a few legal texts, including royal grants and contracts; many economic texts, including records of transactions and lists of persons, professions, and materials; some scribal exercises; a handful of hippiatric texts; some medical prescriptions; inscriptions on knives, axes, handles, cylinder seals, labels, stelae, weights, and ivory; omen texts; and various religious compositions, including myths, legends, and ritual texts.

The ritual texts are varied and consist of incantations, prayers, hymns, votive texts, god lists, a festival catalogue, sacrificial lists, and ritual prescriptions or descriptions.[4] These texts, to which several books and many articles have been devoted,[5] theoretically promise to reveal much

3. *CAT* lists 529 unpublished texts, pp. 569-603.

4. The other categories contain a few documents that are relevant to ritual matters: 4.15 is a list of workers at a temple; 4.216 is a record of wine for shrines. No doubt, other economic texts are related to the cult.

Incantations: 1.13, 1.23, 1.44, 1.54, 1.65?, 1.82, 1.86?, 1.96, 1.100, 1.107, 1.114, 1.128, 1.131, 1.169, 9.435 (cf. 1.20-22, 1.51).

Prayers: 1.65?, 1.93?, 1.104?, 1.123.

Hymns: 1.24, 1.101, 1.108.

Votive texts: 1.77, 1.80.

God lists: 1.47, 1.102, 1.118. It is assumed that these are not simply theological texts but had some cultic use or setting.

Festival catalogue: 1.91.

Sacrificial lists: 1.26, 1.27, 1.28, 1.29, 1.31, 1.38?, 1.39, 1.43, 1.46, 1.48, 1.49, 1.50, 1.53, 1.56?, 1.58, 1.76?, 1.79?, 1.80, 1.81?, 1.87, 1.90, 1.105, 1.106, 1.109, 1.110, 1.112, 1.115, 1.116, 1.119, 1.125, 1.126, 1.130, 1.132, 1.134, 1.135, 1.136?, 1.138, 1.139, 1.148, 1.162, 1.164, 1.168, 1.170, 1.171, 1.173.

Ritual prescriptions or *descriptions* overlap to some extent with the foregoing category. See: 1.24, 1.28, 1.29, 1.31, 1.32, 1.40, 1.41, 1.43, 1.48, 1.49, 1.50, 1.53, 1.56?, 1.57?, 1.58, 1.76?, 1.81?, 1.84, 1.86?, 1.90, 1.91?, 1.105, 1.106, 1.112, 1.113?, 1.115, 1.119, 1.121, 1.122, 1.126, 1.136?, 1.137?, 1.146?, 1.147?, 1.153?, 1.156?, 1.161, 1.162, 1.164, 1.165?, 1.166?, 1.168, 1.174?, 4.275?, 9.422 (cf. 1.20-22).

Perhaps a *liturgy* is to be found in 1.123.

For a discussion of the ritual corpus, cf. D. M. Clemens, *A Study of the Sacrificial Terminology at Ugarit: A Collection and Analysis of the Ugaritic and Akkadian Textual Data* (Ph.D. diss., University of Chicago, 1999) 52-122, 823-906.

5. Cf. J.-M. de Tarragon, *Le culte à Ugarit* (CahRB 19; Paris: Gabalda, 1980); P. Xella, *I testi rituali di Ugarit-I: Testi* (La Civiltà Fenicia e Punica 21 [Studi Semitici 54]; Rome: Consiglio Nazionale delle Ricerche, 1981); A. Caquot, and J.-M. de Tarragon. *Textes ougaritiques: Tome II: Textes religieux et rituels; correspondance* (Paris: du Cerf, 1989); *ARTU*; G. del Olmo Lete, *Canaanite Religion according to the Liturgical Texts of Ugarit* (Bethesda, Md.: CDL, 1999). See the exemplary study by B. A. Levine and J.-M. de Tarragon, "The King Proclaims the Day: Ugaritic Rites for the Vintage," *RB* 100 (1993) 76-115. See also Clemens's recent *Study of the Sacrificial Terminology at Ugarit*, which has

about ritual practice and thought in this place and time. But certain difficulties make them less informative than one would hope. In addition to problems with the state of preservation of many of the tablets–a problem with texts of all genres–many of the terms used in the ritual texts are opaque. Moreover, the syntax in some of the texts is quite difficult. If these problems were not enough, many of the texts are written laconically. Some seem to be excerpts from larger undescribed ritual performances, and others are little more than lists, perhaps records of ritual events or, in some cases, mnemonic aids for performing rituals. They thus lack a context that might help explain the use of materials and their setting. All of these difficulties combine to make it extremely difficult to formulate confident assessments of the characteristics, purposes, and significance of ritual in and around Ugarit.

There is, however, another source of ritual in the Ugaritic texts that helps remedy this problem to a certain degree, namely, the legends and myths. The three longest, Aqhat, Kirta (Keret), and the Baʿl cycle (especially the first two), are packed with descriptions of ritual activities and phenomena.[6] The ritual scenes in these texts are, to be sure, not always transparent themselves because, like actual ritual texts, syntax and the meaning of terms are not always clear, and sometimes the description is too brief. Furthermore, we cannot assume that they reflect the actual ritual practice of the kingdom of Ugarit. The composers of the texts may have incorporated archaic practices in the works, much like biblical authors, who drew on old stories when they composed Genesis and other portions of the Bible.[7] In addition, it is likely that inventive imagination played a part in formulating the scenes. As this study will show, ritual in the legends and myths of Ugarit serves the need of the larger narrative context; even the gods are written into the scenes as participants. These are some of the signs that historical ritual practices have not been simply excerpted and inserted into the stories. Nevertheless, these factors should not lead us to assume that there is no contact with contemporary

a prolegomenon to the study of Ugaritic ritual texts (pp. 1–122) and otherwise studies the ritual lexicon of Ugaritic letters, legal and administrative texts, scribal exercises, inscribed objects, unclassified and unpublished texts, and of Akkadian texts from Ugarit. These works contain useful bibliography; see also *HUS* 270–352, for an introduction to these texts with bibliography, as well as J.-L. Cunchillos, *La trouvaille épigraphique de l'Ougarit 2: Bibliographie* (Ras Shamra-Ougarit 5; Paris: Éditions Recherche sur les Civilisations, 1989).

6. For translations, see *UNP*; *RTU*; *ARTU*; *CML*; M. D. Coogan, *Stories from Ancient Canaan* (Philadelphia: Westminster, 1978); *ANET* 129–55; *TO* 1.

7. Cf. *UPA* 307–10 for the argument that archaic practices have been incorporated into the telling of the story of Aqhat. Also *SP* 245.

ceremonial reality in the texts. The authors of the stories did not intend to reinvent religion or to reform cultic performance. These texts are not programmatic, like the priestly legislation of the Torah or the description of Ezekiel's visionary temple, nor do these stories concern themselves with reform, like the biblical tales about Hezekiah and Josiah (that is, by the Deuteronomist and, later, the Chronicler). The authors of the Ugaritic narratives had other goals. To accomplish these, it is reasonable to think that the authors to some extent employed ritual practices, patterns, and motifs–albeit in a creative way–with which they and their audience were familiar. This consideration, as well as the fact that rituals appear in contexts that elucidate them and that describe them clearly enough to contribute to the sense of the story, mean that these narrative examples can aid in assessing the nature and significance of ritual in Ugarit and the larger ancient Near East.

Ritual in these narratives has been studied with two main purposes in mind. One has been to examine how these narratives as whole texts fit into or reflect larger cultic or ritual contexts. Theodor Gaster, for example, argued that the Baʿl cycle and the Aqhat story displayed a pattern found in rites that makes the transition from the end of the old year or season to the new year or season. The Baʿl cycle is at least "a seasonal myth based on the traditional ritual drama of the autumn festival" if not an accompaniment to that festival.[8] The Aqhat story "in the form in which it has come down to us . . . was never formally acted and probably not even formally recited as a liturgical chant" but is "an artistic transformation of the time-honored seasonal drama."[9] John Gray similarly associated parts of the Baʿl texts with seasonal rites and, in particular, an autumn new year festival.[10] Johannes C. de Moor has sought to define more precisely the seasonal pattern in the texts.[11] He believes that the Baʿl myth was a nature and cult myth that may have been used in the autumnal new year and wine festival, not as a script of a drama but perhaps recited as part of the performance. He has also attempted to coordinate scenes within the texts with external cultic activities. For example, he

8. T. H. Gaster, *Thespis: Ritual, Myth, and Drama in the Ancient Near East* (New York: Norton, 1977 [original 1950]) 129.

9. Ibid., 316.

10. J. Gray, *The Legacy of Canaan: The Ras Shamra Texts and Their Relevance to the Old Testament* (VTSup 5; Leiden: Brill 1965) 9–10, 17–18; "The Blood Bath of the Goddess Anat in the Ras Shamra Texts," *UF* 11 (1979) 322–24; "Baʿal's Atonement," *UF* 3 (1971) 69–70; "Social Aspects of Canaanite Religion," in *Volume du Congrès Genève, 1965* (VTSup 15; Leiden: Brill, 1966) 170–71.

11. See de Moor, *SP* 55–62, 245–49; idem, "The Seasonal Pattern in the Legend of Aqhatu," *SEL* 5 (1988) 61–77; idem, *ARTU* 1 n. 1, 236 nn. 78–81, 238–39 nn. 100–101. Cf. J. C. L. Gibson, "The Theology of the Ugaritic Baal Cycle," *Or* 53 (1984) 214.

sees the initial three offerings in the Aqhat text as reflecting characteristics of a new year festival. Meindert Dijkstra specifically suggests that the Aqhat story (which for him includes *CAT* 1.20–22, the so-called *rpum*-texts) was, "in its final form, probably intended to be recited on [the Ugaritic New Year Festival]."[12] An early speculation by Simon Parker was that Aqhat may have been a cult legend.[13] He also saw the development of the Kirta story in the context of the cult of El and concurred with K.-H. Bernhardt that the text may have been recited "on occasions of national emergency," which implies a ritual use.[14]

The frequency of ritual motifs in these stories, the appearance of mythological pericopae in Ugaritic ritual contexts (for example, 1.23), as well as the use of the Babylonian creation epic *Enuma eliš* in the Babylonian *akītu* festival of the spring new year,[15] justify explorations in these directions. But these interpretations may also be disputed because of the questionable supposition that myth is necessarily connected with ritual and, more particularly, because of the hypothetical and even arbitrary character of many of the observations and conclusions.[16]

12. M. Dijkstra, "Some Reflections on the Legend of Aqhat," *UF* 11 (1979) 210.

13. S. B. Parker, "The Feast of Rāpiu," *UF* 2 (1970) 249.

14. Idem, "The Historical Composition of *KRT* and the Cult of El," *ZAW* 89 (1977) 171–75 (on pp. 161–62 he summarizes Bernhardt's view that "the text would have been used on days of general penitence prompted by any national emergency").

15. For cautions about the significance of the reading of *Enuma eliš* in the *akītu* festival, see K. van der Toorn, "The Babylonian New Year Festival: New Insights from the Cuneiform Texts and Their Bearing on Old Testament Study," *Congress Volume: Leuven, 1989* (VTSup 43; Leiden: Brill, 1991) 337. For the argument that the Sitz im Leben of Gen 1:1–2:3 is cultic, see M. Weinfeld, "Sabbath, Temple and the Enthronement of the Lord: The Problem of the Sitz im Leben of Genesis 1:1–2:3," in *Mélanges bibliques et orientaux en l'honneur de M. Henri Cazelles* (ed. A. Caquot and M. Delcor; AOAT 212; Kevelaer: Butzon & Bercker / Neukirchen-Vluyn: Neukirchener Verlag, 1981) 501–12.

16. Critiques include: L. L. Grabbe, "The Seasonal Pattern and the 'Baal Cycle,'" *UF* 8 (1976) 57–63; M. S. Smith, "Interpreting the Baal Cycle," *UF* 18 (1986) 314–18, 329–32; idem, *The Ugaritic Baal Cycle, Volume 1: Introduction with Text, Translation and Commentary of* KTU *1.1-1.2* (VTSup 55; Leiden: Brill, 1994) 60–75; N. Wyatt, *Myths of Power: A Study of Royal Myth and Ideology in Ugaritic and Biblical Tradition* (Ugaritisch-Biblische Literature 13: Münster: Ugarit-Verlag, 1996) 144–45; N. H. Walls, *The Goddess Anat in Ugaritic Myth* (SBLDS 135; Atlanta: Scholars Press, 1992) 3–7, 162; J. C. L. Gibson, "Myth, Legend and Folk-Lore in the Ugaritic Keret and Aqhat Texts," in *Congress Volume: Edinburgh, 1974* (VTSup 28; Leiden: Brill, 1975) 60–61 and passim; de Moor also reviews some critiques in *SP* 24–28. The place where the Baʿl, Kirta, and Aqhat texts were discovered (in other words, the archive of the high priest) might suggest that these texts have a cultic connection. But A. R. Petersen ("Where Did Schaeffer Find the Clay Tablets of the Ugarit Baal-Cycle?" *SJOT* 8 [1994] 46, 51) notes that these texts were stored apart from the actual ritual texts. This might suggest they were not used for cultic purposes.

The other major purpose in studying ritual elements in the narratives has been to discover what they can say about the actual ritual practices of the time and place in which they were composed. Thus, the narratives are often studied in comparison with the actual ritual texts. An example of this type of study is J.-M. de Tarragon's examination of the Ugaritic cult.[17] De Tarragon mainly investigated the texts that manifest actual practice ("textes de la pratique"). He treats ritual features in narrative infrequently and mainly with regard to how they are similar to (or different from) the texts describing ritual practice.[18] P. Xella's study of Ugaritic ritual is similarly concerned with actual ritual texts.[19] Reference to the narrative texts is restricted to his notes, where he only makes comparisons with texts of primary interest to him. Del Olmo Lete's recent work more fully integrates narrative texts into a study of the primary ritual texts but still only briefly treats the stories of Kirta and Aqhat in a chapter on popular religion. It is more often concerned with theological and royal ideas than the details of ritual.[20]

The present study is devoted to presenting a third approach to ritual in the narrative texts: the examination of how ritual functions within the narrative context of stories. In contrast to the approaches described above–which are *externally* oriented, that is, interested in how a text relates in one way or another to actual ritual practice that exists outside the story–this approach looks at ritual *within* a story's context to see how it contributes to the development of the story, advances the plot, forges major and minor climaxes, structures and periodicizes the story, and operates to enhance the portrayal of characters. As intimated above, the ritual motifs and scenes in these stories–and any story for that matter–are not simply selections from actual ritual texts or records of practice mechanically inserted into a text. The scenes have been composed, apart from whatever relationship they have to actual practice, to serve the specific narrative context. Part of the task of understanding them, either as ritual practices per se or, ultimately, how they relate to actual practice, requires careful study of them within the narrative context.

To undertake this approach satisfactorily, it is necessary to restrict the scope of inquiry. This study will deal only with the Aqhat story (*CAT* 1.17–19).[21] It tells a story similar to stories found in the so-called patriar-

17. De Tarragon, *Culte à Ugarit*.

18. Note the index, ibid., 199, and the references to CTA 1-6, 14-16, 17-19 (and 20-22).

19. Xella, *I Testi rituali*.

20. Del Olmo Lete, *Canaanite Religion*, 325-36.

21. For a recent discussion of the themes and problems of the Aqhat text, see *HUS* 234-58. The so-called *rāpiʾūma* texts (1.20-22) are not here considered part of the Aqhat story. For the problems in making the connection, see W. Pitard, "A New Edition

chal tales of Genesis.[22] A father, whose name is Daniʾil (which is comparable to the Hebrew name Daniel and whom Israelite tradition may have actually remembered as a pious individual[23]), is childless, or at least sonless. He prays to the gods for a son by presenting an offering for six days. The high gods Baʿl and Il respond to his request and promise him a son through a blessing. After Daniʾil returns to his home, perhaps from a temple he was visiting, the Kotharat (conception and birth deities) visit him, and he feasts them for six days. They ensure the reproductive success of Daniʾil and his wife, Danatay. She soon bears a son, who is named Aqhat, hence the name of the story. When Aqhat grows up, his father is given a bow and arrows, made and delivered by the craftsman god, Kothar-wa-Ḫasis, whom Daniʾil hospitably feasts. At this occasion, Daniʾil presumably gives the bow and arrows to his son, for whom they were apparently made. He also blesses his son at this time.

Soon after these favorable events, another feast is held and the goddess Anat sees Aqhat's bow and covets it. She offers the young man riches and even eternal life for it, but he refuses these offers and offends the goddess. As a consequence, she threatens to kill him. Directly after the contentious feast, she goes to the chief god Il, apparently to receive his permission to punish Aqhat. After obtaining the god's consent, she instructs Aqhat to celebrate another feast. At this occasion, and in accordance with the suggestion of her mercenary Yaṭupan, she flies among the

of the 'Rāpiʾūma' Texts: KTU 1.20–22," *BASOR* 285 (1992) 72–74. For a recent claim of possible connection, see M. Dijkstra, "The Legend of Danel and the Rephaim," *UF* 20 (1988) 35–52. On the *rāpiʾūma* texts, see p. 77 n. 27, below.

22. On the motif of the childless hero who is blessed with a child, see S. B. Parker, "Death and Devotion: The Composition and Theme of *Aqht*," in *Love and Death in the Ancient Near East: Essays in Honor of Marvin H. Pope* (ed. J. H. Marks and R. M. Good; Guilford, Conn.: Four Quarters, 1987) 73–74. Parker compares the story to the introduction of the Egyptian *Doomed Prince*, the Hurrian-Hittite Appu story (cf. J. Siegelová, *Appu-Märchen und Ḫedammu-Mythus* [StBoT 14; Wiesbaden: Harrassowitz, 1971] 4–17 and passim); 1 Samuel 1; Gen 25:21, 30:22–23. It is a common motif, similar to one of R. Alter's type-scenes (*The Art of Biblical Narrative* [New York: Basic, 1981] 47–62), which could be reused and creatively altered. For biblical parallels, see also J. Obermann, *How Daniel Was Blessed with a Son: An Incubation Scene in Ugaritic* (JAOSSup 20; Baltimore: American Oriental Society, 1946) 28–29; E. M. Good, "Two Notes on Aqhat," *JBL* 77 (1958) 72–73.

23. Cf. Ezek 14:14, 20; H.-P. Müller, "Magisch-mantische Weisheit und die Gestalt Daniels," *UF* 1 (1969) 79–94 (cf. M. Dietrich and O. Loretz, "Die Weisheit des ugaritischen Gottes El im Kontext der altorientalischen Weisheit," *UF* 24 [1992] 35); Gibson, "Myth, Legend," 68; J. Day, "The Daniel of Ugarit and Ezekiel and the Hero of the Book of Daniel," *VT* 30 (1980) 174–84; B. Margalit, "Interpreting the Story of Aqht," *VT* 30 (1980) 361–65; H. H. P. Dressler, "The Identification of the Ugaritic Dnil with the Daniel of Ezekiel," *VT* 29 (1979) 152–61; idem, "Reading and Interpreting the Aqht Text," *VT* 34 (1984) 78–82.

vultures circling over Aqhat's feast and has Yaṭupan fly down and strike Aqhat on the head, killing him.

Anat immediately begins to lament the boy's death, and nature suffers from the effects of the murder. Daniʾil and his daughter Pughat, not knowing that Aqhat is dead, begin to mourn the drought. Daniʾil performs several rites that contain prayers for rain and the revival of the crop. Messengers then come and inform Daniʾil of his son's death. He responds to the bad news by performing rituals to recover his son's remains from scavenging vultures that are flying overhead and to curse the places near which his son was killed. Only at the end of seven years do the members of his household cease their mourning. At this point, Daniʾil can again make offerings to the gods. At his first sacrifice after the death of his son, Pughat asks her father for a blessing to help her avenge her brother. She disguises herself as Anat and then goes to Yaṭupan's camp, where she serves him wine. The extant story comes to an end at this point, but it is reasonable to assume that she gets Yaṭupan drunk by the wine she serves him and then kills him.

As can be seen from this summary, the Aqhat story is replete with ritual motifs and scenes. Of its approximately 650 extant poetic lines, about 530 deal with ritual performances or their contexts (82%). It thus is an excellent text through which to explore the dynamics of ritual in narrative. I have selected it over the Kirta story, which is equally dense with ritual elements, because, despite the Aqhat text's breaks and gaps and its missing ending, it is slightly more intelligible and readable than the Kirta story in regard to ritual matters.[24] The study of Aqhat will provide a model for this approach in the other major Ugaritic narratives as well as for the study of ritual in other Near Eastern narratives and beyond.

The Definition of Ritual

If it is clear that the story of Aqhat is an ideal starting place for the study of ritual in Ugaritic narrative, it remains to determine what ritual is and, consequently, what will be of interest in this story. Researchers have often noted that one knows ritual when one sees it but that it is otherwise difficult to define without excluding phenomena that are clearly ritual in nature and including others that are not. The difficulty of defining ritual has even raised questions about whether ritual is a real category of behavior and expression that can be separated as an object of research.

24. The Kirta text is particularly difficult in the description of the feasts held while Kirta is ill and in what his children do after these feasts but prior to his recovery.

Some have looked for a taxonomic definition of ritual based on form and content. Evan Zuesse's definition in the relatively recent *Encyclopedia of Religion* is an example.

> For our purposes, we shall understand as "ritual" those conscious and voluntary, repetitious and stylized symbolic bodily actions that are centered on cosmic structure and/or sacred presences.[25]

Victor Turner offers a similar definition:

> [Ritual is] prescribed formal behavior for occasions not given over to technological routine, having reference to beliefs in mystical beings or power.[26]

These definitions highlight formality, stylization, and repetition as well as a connection with supernatural powers, or at least "cosmic structure," as the main elements in ritual. They, and other definitions like them, grow out of an attempt to offer "objective" criteria, which might be quite mechanically applied, for setting ritual activities off, distinct from other activities. These attempts fail by either overdefining or underdefining the phenomenon. Overdefinition occurs when criteria set limits that exclude clear cases of ritual found in societies other than those originally examined when constructing the definition. For example, a modern secular wedding is clearly ritual in character but does not necessarily fit the definitions given above, because it may lack any reference to supernatural beings.[27] Underdefinition occurs when form-content definitions set the parameters of ritual so broadly that actions that are not, according to our intuition, ritual activities are included. Jack Goody, for example, found Turner's inclusion of the phrase "having reference to mystical beings" too restrictive. This left a definition of ritual as "formal behaviour in the non-technological realm." But Goody then goes on to say, "while this is (for me) acceptable, it is also of very limited significance, largely because the category is so engulfing it seems likely to block research."[28]

Other definitions have attempted to avoid the pitfalls of the form-content definition by focusing on the *function* of ritual behavior as a

25. E. M. Zuesse, "Ritual," *Encyclopedia of Religion* (New York: Macmillan, 1987) 12.405.

26. V. Turner, *Forest of Symbols* (Ithaca: Cornell University Press, 1967) 19; idem, *The Drums of Affliction* (Ithaca: Cornell University Press, 1968) 15.

27. D. I. Kertzer (*Ritual, Politics and Power* [New Haven: Yale University Press, 1988] 9) proposes a definition similar to the foregoing but leaves out the supernatural: "ritual [is] symbolic behavior that is socially standardized and repetitive."

28. J. Goody, "Against 'Ritual': Loosely Structured Thoughts on a Loosely Defined Topic," in *Secular Ritual* (ed. S. F. Moore and B. G. Myerhoff; Assen/Amsterdam: Van Gorcum, 1977) 27.

mode of communication, in the spirit of Leach's pithy summary statement that "we engage in rituals in order to transmit collective messages to ourselves."[29] Robert Wuthnow, for example, contrasts ritual as expressive activity over against quotidian instrumental activity. In formulating his definition, he compares various activities, some of which one would define as ritual and others not. Comparing two of these, a wedding and changing a flat tire, he notes,

> The difference between getting married and fixing a tire, as far as ritual is concerned, lies essentially in the fact that a wedding is structured to evoke and communicate meanings, whereas fixing a tire does not have this as one of its primary or alleged purposes. The music, physical arrangements, and preparation involved in a wedding ceremony are carefully structured to elicit and convey deep emotion, even if emotion is not naturally present. . . . These activities also communicate to the various parties involved that a redefinition of social relations has occurred, that consent has been obtained, and that good wishes are in order.[30]

He is careful to qualify this with the observation that

> The distinction between expressive and instrumental activity is not a hard-and-fast rule that can be used to divide the world into two categories. The distinction is, rather, an analytic distinction that allows activities to be arranged along a continuum. . . . Ritual is not a type of social activity that can be set off from the rest of the world for special investigation. It is a dimension of all social activity.[31]

Sally Moore and Barbara Myerhoff combine the elements of expressiveness and form in their discussion of ritual.[32] The basic formal properties include: repetition, acting (which involves doing, not just thinking or speaking), special behavior or stylization, order, evocative presentation style or staging, and a collective or social dimension. By virture of these properties, ritual is a "traditionalizing instrument," that is, it makes what is expressed thereby acceptable and common. It hides the novelty and even radicalness of new ideas and acts. It also allows those of diverse social groups, even strangers, to participate together and feel commonality and solidarity. In addition to any direct teaching it may include, ritual

29. Cf. E. Leach, *Culture and Communication* (Cambridge: Cambridge University Press, 1976) 45.

30. Wuthnow, *Meaning and Moral Order: Explorations in Cultural Analysis* (Berkeley: University of California Press, 1987) 98–99.

31. Ibid., 101.

32. S. F. Moore and B. G. Myerhoff, "Secular Ritual: Forms and Meanings," in *Secular Ritual* (ed. S. F. Moore and B. G. Myerhoff; Assen/Amsterdam: Van Gorcum, 1977) 3–24.

communicates latently about morality, authority, the legitimacy of the social order, and the nature of social reality. And not only does it reflect these social aspects, it transforms society by its performance. Because they are dealing with secular ritual, the authors avoid the problematic inclusion of the supernatural in the list of characteristic elements. But they do note how even secular ritual is connected with the notion of the sacred. The sacred may be partly defined as what is unquestionable. Ritual, and what it communicates, is similarly unquestionable, at least when it functions properly.

One of the strengths of Leach's and Wuthnow's, as well as Moore's and Myerhoff's definitions is the avoidance of a strict dichotomy between ritual and nonritual activity. Ritual is not to be set apart as a way of acting that is unrelated to other activities.[33] Nevertheless—in addition to Moore's and Myerhoff's inclusion of formal criteria—a common difficulty in these definitions is claiming that ritual is particularly characterized by its expressive capacity. The problem is that ritual does not really function like a language. True, it often involves symbols (objects and actions), but it is not entirely made up of these. Moreover, when ritual is seen to communicate, it is often described as happening latently or implicitly, not manifestly or explicitly, even to the point that often only analysts, and not the performers, consciously recognize the message. Frits Staal has observed this problem in the starkest terms by arguing that in many cases ritual does not mean anything to agents in its performance.[34] The recognition of symbols in a rite and the determination of their meaning is often something that occurs outside of the ritual context as part of secondary reflection. These objections are not to be taken to mean that ritual has no expressive capability; they do, however, indicate that it may not be a primary defining feature.

Catherine Bell objects to defining ritual as expressive behavior from a philosophical perspective. She suggests that distinguishing ritual action from nonritual action as expressive versus instrumental action (note Wuthnow's view in particular) can end up becoming a contrast between

---

33. I accepted the type of distinction that Wuthnow makes in my paper "Analogy in Biblical and Hittite Ritual," in *Internationales Symposion: Religionsgeschichtliche Beziehungen zwischen Kleinasien, Nordsyrien und dem Alten Testament im 2. und 1. vorchristlichen Jahrtausend* (ed. K. Koch, B. Janowski, and G. Wilhelm; OBO 129; Göttingen: Vandenhoeck and Ruprecht, 1993) 473–506. For a similar view of ritual, see B. Lincoln, *Discourse and the Construction of Society: Comparative Studies of Myth, Ritual, and Classification* (New York: Oxford University Press, 1989) 53.

34. See F. Staal, *Rules without Meaning: Ritual, Mantras and the Human Sciences* (New York: Peter Lang, 1989) 115–40; idem, "The Meaninglessness of Ritual," *Numen* 26 (1975) 2–22.

irrationality and rationality, between emotion and logic, a distinction that is to be avoided.[35] Moreover, she argues that viewing ritual as expressive also presupposes that the content or meaning of ritual is separable from the action itself. A major concern of her work is the rejection of this dichotomy. For Bell, if ritual "communicates" it is specifically by situating the body in a structured spatial and temporal context that ritualizes the body through the experience of various sets of hierarchically counterposed oppositions (for example, high versus low; right versus left; etc.). By these means, relationships with others are not merely reflected or expressed but actually formed. In other words, ritual does not simply communicate something about social relationships, it creates them.

Her definition of ritual, or as she prefers to call and view it, "ritualization," provides a way around the problems of the previous interpretations.[36] She describes ritualization succinctly as

> a way of acting that is designed and orchestrated to distinguish and privilege what is being done in comparison to other, usually more quotidian, activities. As such, ritualization is a matter of various culturally specific strategies for setting some activities off from others, for creating and privileging a qualitative distinction between the "sacred" and the "profane," and for ascribing such distinctions to realities thought to transcend the powers of human actors.[37]

The way ritualized activity is privileged in comparison to another activity can be seen by considering what might be esteemed a mundane version of a phenomenon alongside a ritualized version of the same basic phenomenon. Ritual and nonritual meals are good examples, not only because Bell herself discusses them to exemplify her definition,[38] but also because ritual meals (feasts and offerings) are chief among the examples of ritual activity in the Aqhat story. Ritual meals set themselves apart from mundane meals by various means, including: (a) their unusual frequency (they are usually less frequent than normal meals), (b) the involvement of participants who would not ordinarily be involved in regular meals (for example, the extended family or people outside the family; in the Aqhat story we will see the gods brought in as participants), (c) seating arrangements that vary from what is found in everyday meals, (d) the donning of different or unusual clothing, (e) the presence of too much food or too

35. C. Bell, *Ritual Theory, Ritual Practice* (New York: Oxford University, 1992) 71. For development of her ideas, see also idem, *Ritual: Perspectives and Dimensions* (New York: Oxford University Press, 1997).

36. Idem, *Ritual Theory*, 69–93; cf. *Perspectives*, 81–83, 166–69.

37. Idem, *Ritual Theory*, 74.

38. Ibid., 90–91.

little food for a normal meal and nutritional needs, (f) a connection with other elements that are ritualized (for example, prayers, sacrifice, the locus of a temple).

In Bell's understanding of ritualization, features that are prominent in the form-content definitions of ritual—formality, fixity, and repetition—are not primary. It is true that they may be ways of distinguishing certain ritual activities from mundane action of the same type. But the opposite features—informality, irregularity, and unique expression—may also be means of setting ritual activity apart. What is important is the contrast between ritualization and normal activity. This often has to be determined by the study of a particular activity within its larger sociocultural context. It should also be noted that the lack of instrumentality plays only a minor role (see [e] above). Ritual activity may in many cases have a practical goal, such as providing nourishment for participants and guests through sacrifice.[39]

Ritual in Aqhat

Using Bell's outline for what constitutes ritualization when there is any doubt (and the body of the study, below, contains justification for these cases), I have identified 20 ritual scenes or elements in the Aqhat narrative. These are the object of study in this work. The majority can be sorted into four categories: (a) feasts, (b) blessings, (c) mourning rites, and (d) retaliation rites.

The feasts include (1) the initial six-day offering that Daniʾil gives to the high gods, (2) the six-day offering that he gives to the Kotharat when they visit him before the birth of Aqhat, (3) the one-day meal that Daniʾil gives to Kothar-wa-Ḫasis when he delivers the bow to Daniʾil, (4) the feast at which Anat asks Aqhat for the bow, (5) the feast at which Aqhat is killed, (6) Daniʾil's *dbḥ* 'sacrifice' offered after his recovery from mourning for his son, and (7) Pughat's presentation of wine to Yaṭupan at the end of the extant story.

The blessings are connected with the feasts that precede them but can be separately analyzed as ritual events. They include: (8) Il's blessing of Daniʾil after the latter's initial sacrifice, (9) Daniʾil's blessing of Aqhat after receiving the bow from Kothar-wa-Ḫasis, and (10) Daniʾil's blessing of Pughat in preparation for her attack on Yaṭupan.

The mourning and retaliation rites are interconnected in that they are all responses to Aqhat's death. They form a continuous chain from the death of Aqhat to Daniʾil's *dbḥ* (which along with Pughat's wine service,

39. Ibid., 92–93.

numbers [6] and [7] above, can be considered part of the chain of recovery and retaliation rites), and there is a logical evolution from one ritual response to the next. The mourning rites include: (11) Anat's mourning, (12) Pughat's limited mourning on account of the drought, (13) Daniʾil's prayer for moisture, (14) his two prayers for plants in the field, (15) the mourning of the messengers bringing the news of Aqhat's death to Daniʾil, and (16) the seven-year mourning of Daniʾil's household. The retaliation rites include: (17) Daniʾil's conjuration and curse of the vultures and (18) his curse of the towns associated with Aqhat's death.

The two ritual elements that stand outside of the foregoing classification include (19) Anat's obeisance before Il when she complains about Aqhat and (20) the ritual activities listed among the duties that an ideal son is to perform for his father. The ritual duties in (20) are treated as a single instance because they appear in the list together and because this list stands outside the main narrative flow. They are not actions that any character performs in the course of the story.

All of the foregoing scenes and elements are distributed over the four parts into which the narrative can be divided. The first part deals with the birth and youth of Aqhat. The main ritual elements in this section are feasts that function positively in the story (1–3). Associated with these are the first two blessings and the filial duties (8–9, 20). The second part also consists mainly of feasts (4–5), but these have a negative character. This part also includes Anat's petition before Il (19). The third part of the story deals with the aftermath of the murder. It contains the mourning and retaliation rites (11–18). The fourth part (and the shortest, because the last section of the story is missing) deals with affairs after the completion of mourning for Aqhat. This section returns to feasting and blessing (6–7, 10).

The body of the study below is concerned with examining these various elements in their individual contexts and in their interaction with each other. They will be studied for the most part in series, since the earlier elements prepare for the ones that follow. This book is divided, therefore, into four parts according to the four sections of the narrative noted above. Almost every ritual scene or element is discussed in a separate chapter (see the table of contents). The few that do not have their own chapter are treated along with other related cases (Pughat's mourning is treated in chapter 13 along with Daniʾil's agricultural prayers; the mourning of the messengers is treated in chapter 14 along with the conjuration of the vulture; the mourning of Daniʾil's household is treated in chapter 16, the conclusion to part 3).

Because the Aqhat text is incomplete, damaged, and otherwise difficult to understand in regard to many linguistic (morphological, syntactic, and semantic) matters, this book devotes attention to these problems in the passages under study in order to provide a basis for analysis. Part of this includes the presentation of the relevant transliterated text with accompanying translation, annotated and with chief problems discussed in the body of the study that follows.[40] The difficulties make confident solutions and accompanying larger interpretations impossible in some cases (especially the first two filial duties [see chapter 2], Daniʾil's blessing of Aqhat, Anat's mourning, and Pughat's serving wine to Yaṭupan). I have nevertheless chosen in such cases to offer as sound an interpretation of the text as possible in order to be thorough in the pursuit of my approach to ritual in narrative and in order to gain a theoretical, if not definitive, grasp on the contextual interrelationship of the various ritual scenes and elements.

In order to facilitate this contextual analysis, I will bring data to bear from other Ugaritic and Near Eastern texts, especially the Bible. I shall also avail myself of anthropological and, more specifically, ritual theory, as I have already in dealing with the definition of ritual above. There are always risks in employing the theoretical literature. Besides the practical difficulty of not being able to be a master of all trades, the application of theoretical perspectives to ancient texts, which are often physically damaged, and the larger cultural context of which is not sufficiently known, poses difficulties.[41] The amount of data that is available for formulating modern ritual theories is not available for the ancient texts. In many cases, if a particular perspective can be applied, it can only be done in a general way. Nonetheless, the attempt can open our eyes to interpretive and analytic possibilities not otherwise visible. The gains thus outweigh the risks.

This examination, in addition to showing how texts similar to Aqhat might be studied from a ritual point of view, will contribute to understanding the Aqhat text itself. One of my concerns will be to show how ritual scenes and elements *contrast* with and *echo* one another. For example, one of the more significant contrasts is between successful and

40. The basic text used is mainly the text found in *CAT*, though attention is paid to Parker's recent reading of the text based on new photographs (*UNP* 49–80, and see the comment on the present state of the tablets, p. 51, there).

41. Note R. Gnuse's comment ("Review of J. Fager, *Land Tenure and the Biblical Jubilee*," *JBL* 113 [1994] 703–4): although "applying sociological methods directly to literary texts of a culture two millennia old is difficult and speculative, and pure sociologists might even scoff at the attempt, the method helps us reclaim past scholarship in a more nuanced presentation of the issues." Compare R. Knierim, *Text and Concept in Leviticus 1:1–9* (FAT 2; Tübingen: Mohr [Siebeck], 1992) 18, for reservations about anthropological study in programmatic texts, which, like literary texts, "differ from the description of any observed performance, or an entire system of performances."

unsuccessful or, better, felicitous and infelicitous rites. The story's first three feasts, which are specifically offerings to gods, are positive events. They are conducted in propriety, and the gods and humans are happy with the results. These are followed by two unhappy feasts: at the first, Anat asks Aqhat for the bow he had received, and at the next, Anat kills Aqhat. The felicitous feasts set up expectations about how such performances should proceed. The infelicitous feasts betray these expectations. The dissonance contributes to the dramatic effect of the story.

An example of ritual echo is found in the blessing that Daniʾil gives Pughat just after the *dbḥ* that he performs when he ceases mourning for Aqhat. This blessing is formulated similarly to the blessing that Il gives Daniʾil at the beginning of the story just after Daniʾil makes an offering to the gods. Because of the similarity in form, the feast-blessing complex at the end of the story carries with it some of the force of the feast-blessing complex at the beginning of the story. Like the first, the second marks an upswing in the fortunes of Daniʾil. The second complex also creates a sense that the story has come around more or less to where it began: a cycle has been completed. Of course, one must be attentive to differences amid similarities. A notable contrast in Pughat's blessing is that a human, not a deity, bestows the blessing. This means that it may not entirely replicate the dynamics of the blessing at the beginning of the story.

In addition to contrasts and echoes, the ritual scenes and elements in the story exhibit structures and patterns. For example, the mourning and retaliation rites performed after the death of Aqhat up to Daniʾil's *dbḥ* manifest a structure of intensification. If we look just at Daniʾil's own rites in this section, he begins with a *single* prayer for moisture followed by a *double* prayer for plants in the field. After this comes a *threefold* conjuration of the vultures who may have consumed Aqhat's remains, followed by a single capping curse of the vultures. This is followed by a *threefold* curse of towns (?) near which Aqhat was killed. A focusing of purpose accompanies this numerical increase: Daniʾil's responses evolve from diffuse mourning to retaliating against entities associated with his son's death. This structural and contextual intensification and focusing becomes an index of the depth of Daniʾil's grief and misfortune.

There are a number of other instances of ritual contrasts, echoes, and patterns (including patterns of intensification) in the story, as well as a host of other cases in which ritual contributes to the meaning and dynamic development of the story. Because ritual operates in such a wide variety of ways and because ritual scenes and elements are so abundant in the narrative, this study contributes to the comprehension of the story as a whole.

This book's interest in the contextual analysis of ritual gives it a "literary" orientation.[42] Its ultimate interest, however, is actually in the history of religious ideas and practices in the ancient Near East. As I noted in the beginning of this introduction, the texts from Ugarit that deal with actual ritual practice are quite obscure. While the study of ritual in the Aqhat story cannot necessarily be used to clarify the obscurities of those texts or supply their phenomenological and psychosocial contexts, it can cast light on views and attitudes toward ritual in the time and area where it was produced. It reflects on, for example, how practitioners viewed, at least ideally, the involvement of gods in their rites. It also provides an indirect confession that ritual situations did not always proceed effectively and properly. With this, the story hints at some of the reasons that agents might give to explain away ritual failure. The story shows, too, that ritual is not necessarily a passive experience in which subordinates simply bow to superiors. Those of lesser status, even humans, might use ritual to fulfill their particular desires when they are in opposition to the desires of the powerful.

---

42. For literary or contextual studies, though not focusing on ritual, see K. Aitken, *The Aqhat Narrative: A Study in the Narrative Structure and Composition of an Ugaritic Tale* (JSSMon 13; Manchester: University of Manchester Press, 1990); idem, "Oral Formulaic Composition and Theme in the Aqhat Narrative," *UF* 21 (1989) 1-16; J.-M. Husser, "The Birth of a Hero: Form and Meaning of KTU 1.17 i-ii," in *Ugarit, Religion and Culture: Proceedings of the International Colloquium on Ugarit, Religion and Culture–Edinburgh, July 1994* (ed. N. Wyatt, W. G. E. Watson, and J. B. Lloyd; Ugaritische-Biblische Literature 12; Münster: Ugarit-Verlag, 1996) 85-98; S. Parker, *The Pre-Biblical Narrative Tradition: Essays on the Ugaritic Poems of Keret and Aqhat* (SBLRBS 24; Atlanta: Scholars Press, 1989); idem, "Death and Devotion," 71-83. W. G. E. Watson's work is often directed to literary analysis: "Antithesis in Ugaritic Verse," *UF* 18 (1986) 413-19; "Apostrophe in the Aqhat Poem," *UF* 16 (1984) 323-26; "Delaying Devices in Ugaritic Verse," *SEL* 5 (1988) 207-18; "The Falcon Episode in the Aqhat Tale," *JNSL* 5 (1977) 69-75; "Internal Parallelism in Ugaritic Verse," *SEL* 1 (1984) 53-67; "More on Preludes to Speech in Ugaritic," *UF* 24 (1992) 361-66; "Parallels to Some Passages in Ugaritic," *UF* 10 (1978) 397-401; "Puzzling Passages in the Tale of Aqhat," *UF* 8 (1976) 371-78; "Two Similes in Aqht," *UF* 23 (1991) 359-60; "Unravelling Ugaritic *mdl*," *SEL* 3 (1986) 73-78. See on the Kirta story, G. Hens-Piazza, "Repetition and Rhetoric in Canaanite Epic: A Close Reading of KTU 1.14. III 20-49," *UF* 24 (1992) 103-12; and G. N. Knoppers, "Dissonance and Disaster in the Legend of Kirta," *JAOS* 114 (1994) 572-82. On the problem of calling ancient Near Eastern writings "literature," see M. Z. Brettler, *The Creation of History in Ancient Israel* (London: Routledge, 1995) 14-17.

Part 1

Felicitous Feasts and Offerings

The theme of feasting dominates much of the Aqhat story, either in the specific context of offerings to the gods or as more general banqueting.[1] The first part of the story up to the death of Aqhat includes five examples, although they are not all of the same "ethical" type. The first three cases—Daniʾil's six-day offering to the high gods with their blessing on the seventh; his six-day offering to the Kotharat, conception and birth goddesses; and a one-day offering to the craftsman god Kothar-wa-Ḫasis—all proceed without difficulty. They are successful, or felicitous, to use the term of Ronald Grimes, borrowed from J. L. Austin, to describe proper and effective ritual performances.[2] The remaining two feasts—the banquet at which the goddess Anat seeks possession of Aqhat's bow and the feast at which Anat kills Aqhat—are infelicitous.

The initial triad of happy feasts, which we study in part 1 of this work, sets up a paradigm for the two infelicitous feasts that follow. This group creates expectations in regard to how ritual should proceed, how agents should participate in it, and what its results might be. They also set up the relationships between the various characters. The ensuing two cases of infelicitous feasting, to be studied in part 2, run counter to the first three and cancel much of what they had achieved. This contrast allows the upset to stand out in sharp contrast and thus to have significant dramatic effect.

Interspersed among the felicitous feasts are other ritual activities or references to them: the blessings given to Daniʾil and Aqhat in the first and third feasts and the ritual activities (including cases of feasting) listed among the duties of an ideal son in the blessing of Daniʾil in the first feast. These augment the sense of success in the feasts with which they are associated. They also set up expectations about the performance and results of ritual beyond the context of feasting.

1. On feasting in Ugaritic narrative texts, see J. B. Lloyd, "The Banquet Theme in Ugaritic Narrative," *UF* 22 (1990) 169–93.

2. See R. Grimes, *Ritual Criticism: Case Studies in Its Practice, Essays on Its Theory* (Columbia: University of South Carolina Press, 1990) 191–209; a full discussion of Grimes's typology of ritual infelicity appears in chapter 8, below.

Chapter 1
Daniʾil's First Offering

About ten lines of the beginning of the story are broken away.[1] To judge from the introduction of the thematically similar Kirta text (1.14 I 1–25), these lines may have briefly noted that Daniʾil was sonless and also may have set up the context for the offering that appears at the beginning of the extant story. This offering takes place over six days and culminates on the seventh. The mechanics of the offering are not entirely clear. The evidence points to the conclusion, however, that Daniʾil is presenting food and drink to the gods while dressed in mourning clothing. A notable feature in the description of the seven-day offering is its climaxing structure. The description of the first six days never reveals the full purpose of the offering. It is only made evident on the seventh day. This structure pits ritual action against ritual word in a way that creates and sustains interest. In addition to the internal structure, an external structure obtains. This feast is one of a triad of felicitous feasts that serve as a paradigm against which ensuing infelicitous banquets play, as noted in the introduction to this section. In addition, the offering *by itself* provides a standard for all feasts that follow, including the next two, because of its elaborateness, its successful character, and the fact that it establishes the divine-human relationships that ensue.

The Nature of the Feast

The description of the offering breaks down into two parts: the presentation of the offering for six days (1.17 I 0–15a) and the gods' response on the seventh day (I 15b–II 23).[2] The text of the first part reads:

1. Cf. *CAT* 47 n. 1. It is possible that another tablet preceded this one, as Margalit indicates (*UPA* 250–51; *RTU* 250 n. 3), but the elements he would like to see recounted in the missing preceding portion could have been dealt with in the first ten lines (something about Daniʾil's wife and the birth of or at least a statement about the existence of Pughat). The beginning of the Kirta text (1.14 I 1–25) shows that a hero's personal circumstances can be briefly treated in a way that allows mourning and petition to appear near the beginning of the text (cf. lines 26ff.).

2. Margalit (*UPA* 266) assumes that offerings are made on the seventh day, but the text does not describe them. A case where activity lasts for six days with divergence on

[apnk] (1) [dnil . mt . rp]i.[3]	[So] (1) [Dani'il, the Rap]i'an,[4]
aph⟨n⟩ . ǵzr (2) [mt . hrnmy[5] .]	then, the hero, [the Harnamiyyan],
uzr . ilm . *ylḥm*.	a girded-offering he presented as food to the gods,
(3) [uzr . yšqy.] *bn* . *qdš* .	[a girded-offering he presented as drink] to the holy ones.
yd (4) [ṣth . ⟨dnil]	⟨Dani'il⟩ removed [his *ṣt*-clothing,[6]]
[yd ṣth⟩[7] yʿl .] w *yškb* .	[⟨he removed his *ṣt*-clothing,⟩ went up[8]] and lay down.
yd (5) [mizrth .] p *yln*.	He removed [his waistcloth], and so spent the night.
hn . *ym* (6) [w ṯn .]	Now, for one day [and a second,]
[uzr .] *ilm* . *dnil*	[a girded-offering,] to the gods, Dani'il,
(7) [uzr . ilm] . *ylḥm*.	[a girded-offering] he presented as food [to the gods],
uzr (8) [yšqy . b]n . *qdš* .	a girded-offering [he presented as drink to the] holy ones.

the seventh is found in the *Iliad* XIV (noted in *UPA* 291 n. 7). See the examples of seven-day activities, listed below.

3. My use of italic and roman characters in transliteration follows the custom found in recent text editions (for example, KTU 2d ed. = *CAT*). Italicized letters represent Ugaritic letters whose reading is certain; roman characters represent letters whose reading is not entirely certain or letters that are partially broken in the original text. Roman characters are also used for restorations. This latter reason explains why whole words are sometimes in roman rather than in italic type.

4. For this epithet, see p. 77 n. 27 below on the *rpum*.

5. This has generally been taken as an adjective referring to Dani'il's place of residence, often specifically connected with Egyptian *hrnm/arnm* (Hermel), in the vicinity of the Orontes (cf. W. F. Albright, "The Traditional Home of the Syrian Daniel," *BASOR* 130 [1953] 26–27; *ARTU* 225 n. 6). While the exact geographical location may be questioned, it seems, based on 1.19 IV 24, 31, that it is a geographical name (cf. M. Dijkstra and J. C. de Moor, "Problematical Passages in the Legend of Aqhâtu," *UF* 7 [1975] 172). S. B. Parker ("The Ugaritic Deity Rāpiu," *UF* 2 [1972] 97–104) suggests that it refers to the god *rpu*. Dani'il is thus the "man of the Harnamite." Margalit follows Parker's lead and argues that it is a divine name, "Rainmaker," referring to Baʿl (*UPA* 255–60; cf. *RTU* 250 n. 5). M. C. Astour ("Place Names," in *Ras Shamra Parallels: The Texts from Ugarit and the Hebrew Bible* [ed. D. E. Smith and S. Rummel; AnOr 50; Rome: Pontifical Biblical Institute, 1975] 283–84) compares *bêt hrn* (Num 32:36) in Transjordan to *Hrnm*. *Hrn* also appears in Gen 11:26, 27, 28, 29, 31; 1 Chr 23:9.

6. For etymologies, see Dijkstra and de Moor, "Passages," 174. *MLC* 616: "atuendo"; *UPA* 143: "extended *garment*."

7. Parablepsis has apparently occurred; cf. lines 13b–14; the restoration follows Margalit, *UPA* 117; idem, "Restorations and Reconstructions in the Epic of Aqht," *JNSL* 9 (1981) 77–78 (I do not accept his line division, however).

8. So *GUL* 164. *MLC* 367 has "se echó encima" ('he lay down on top').

ṯlṯ . rbʿ ym	For a third, a fourth day,
(9) [uzr . i]l*m . dnil .*	[a girded-offering, to the g]ods, Dani'il,
uzr (10) [ilm . y]l*ḥm .*	a girded-offering he presented as fo[od to the gods],
uzr . yšqy . bn (11) [qdš.]	a girded-offering he presented as drink to the [holy] ones.
ḫmš . ṯdṯ . ym .	[For a fif]th, a sixth day,
uzr (12) . [il]m *. dnil .*	a girded-offering, [to the go]ds, Dani'il,
uzr . ilm . ylḥm	a girded-offering he presented as food to the gods,
(13) [uz]r *. yšqy . bn . qdš.*	[a girded-off]ering he presented as drink to the holy ones.
yd . ṣth (14) [dn]i*l .*	Dani'il removed his *ṣt*-clothing.
yd . ṣth . yʿl . w yškb	He removed his *ṣt*-clothing, went up and lay down.
(15) [yd .] *mizrth . p yln .*	[He removed] his waistcloth, and so spent the night.
mk . b šbʿ . ymm	Then on the seventh day,
(16) [w]*yqrb . bʿl . b ḥnth*[9]	Baʿl drew near in his compassion.

Though the text is clear and the few lacunae that appear can be confidently filled in because of the repetitive structure, it is nonetheless difficult to understand. The main problem is how the verbs *ylḥm* and *yšqy* should be understood. These are not manifestly causative forms and consequently might be construed with noncausative meaning: 'he (Dani'il) ate' and 'he drank'.[10] The different language used in other cases of feeding the gods in the story may recommend this rendering. The Kotharat come to Dani'il's home to aid in the birth of his son (1.17 II 30–38; see chapter 4, below). Dani'il feasts them for six days. This is described with Š-stem (i.e., causative) verbs (*yšlḥm* 'he caused to eat'; *yššq* 'he gave drink'). Similarly when Kothar-wa-Ḫasis brings a bow as a gift to Dani'il and Aqhat, he is feasted. The verbs here are also Š-stems (1.17 V 19, 29).

9. On the form and meaning, see Dijkstra and de Moor, "Passages," 174; cf. *GUL* 173. The *ḥnt* 'compassion' is Baʿl's, not Dani'il's.

10. So *TO* 1 419–20; J. Tropper, *Der ugaritische Kausativstamm und die Kausativbildungen des Semitischen: Eine morphologisch-semantische Untersuchung zum Š-Stamm und zu den umstrittenen nichtsibilantischen Kausativstämmen des Ugaritischen* (ALASP 2; Münster: Ugarit-Verlag, 1990) 139–40; the difficulty is noted by *CML* 103 n. 1. C. H. Gordon (*Ugaritic Literature* [Rome: Pontifical Biblical Institute, 1949] 85–86) has the gods as subject of the verb. This is problematic since it cannot give a good account of the word *dnil*. He translates the repeated phrase: 'The *offerings*, the gods, Daniel! / The gods eat the *offerings*, / the deities drink the offerings'. On *lḥm* and *šqy* as a word pair, see K. T. Aitken, "Word Pairs and Tradition in an Ugaritic Tale," *UF* 21 (1989) 25.

The lack of Š-stems in the first offering of the story makes it possible to think that Daniʾil is not feeding or giving drink but doing the eating and drinking himself. What he eats and drinks is the *uzr* of the gods, which are either offerings presented to them and eaten by Daniʾil much as an Israelite would eat portions from a sacrifice given to the god (see Lev 7:15–21) or, more mystically and magically, offerings or other materials imbued with the gods' power that by eating could help Daniʾil recover from impotence.[11]

A syntactic peculiarity, however, makes this interpretation unlikely. It requires taking *uzr ilm* as a construct chain ('*uzr* of the gods'). This is thrown into doubt by the parallel line *uzr yšqy bn qdš* (lines 3a, 7b–8a, 13a, and 22, below) where the verb *yšqy* interrupts the expected construct chain **uzr bn qdš* 'the *uzr* of the holy ones'. The phrase *uzr yšqy bn qdš* could be understood as a broken or discontinuous construct chain,[12] but these are rare and usually involve smaller elements, such as an enclitic *mem*.[13] What makes this explanation especially suspect is that *yšqy* appears in the same position in all five instances in which it occurs (1.17 I 3, 7–8, 10–11, 13, 22; for line 22, see p. 39). In the last of these instances one has to suppose that an enclitic *mem* has also been interposed (*uzrm . yšqy . bn . qdš*) and that an enclitic *mem* has also been inserted in the supposed construct phrase of the preceding parallel line there (*uzrm . ilm*).

This difficulty suggests that the verbs should not be taken with a simple meaning 'to eat/drink' but with a causative sense 'to make eat/ drink'.

11. *TO* 1 419–20 and Tropper, *Kausativstamm*, 140 connect it with Arab. *ʾazr* 'power' and see Daniʾil's eating as enhancing his male potency. *TO* 1 specifically interprets Daniʾil's epithet *mt rpi* as 'homme de la guérison' (cf. *TO* 1 402–3) and translate *uzr ilm* as 'stimulant divin', which is "destiné à rendre au héros sa capacité virile" (p. 419 and note c). C. Gordon ("Poetic Legends and Myths from Ugarit," *Berytus* 25 [1977] 9) also has Daniʾil eating the offerings, though he takes the gods as the subject of the verb "drink" (contrast his solution in the previous note). *UPA* 253–55 details the difficulties of these interpretations.

12. So *TO* 1 419–20 and Tropper, *Kausativstamm*, 139–40.

13. Note C. H. Gordon, *Ugaritic Textbook* (AnOr 38; Rome: Pontifical Biblical Institute, 1965) §8.16: "F[u]rthermore, with a single exception [the enclitic *-m*], nothing can be interposed between the const[ruct] and its gen[itive]." Examples from Hebrew where nouns and even verbs appear to intervene between elements of the chain may include: *kol-mašlîkê bayʾōr ḥakkâ* 'all that throw a fishhook into the Nile' (Isa 19:8); *derek yĕraṣṣĕḥû šekmâ* 'they murder on the road to Shechem' (Hos 6:9); *kol-tiśśāʾ ʿāwōn* 'forgive all iniquity' (Hos 14:3). Cf. *GUL* 193; B. K. Waltke and M. O'Connor, *An Introduction to Biblical Hebrew Syntax* (Winona Lake, Ind.: Eisenbrauns, 1990) §§9.3c; 9.6; 9.8; 10.5; D. N. Freedman, *Pottery, Poetry, and Prophecy: Studies in Early Hebrew Poetry* (Winona Lake, Ind.: Eisenbrauns, 1980) 339–41; M. Dahood, *Psalms III: 101–150* (AB 17A; Garden City, N.Y.: Doubleday, 1970) 381–83; F. I. Andersen and D. N. Freedman, *Hosea* (AB 24; Garden City, N.Y.: Doubleday, 1980) 645.

But what are the verbs' verbal stems? It may be doubted from the beginning that they are internal causatives (C- or A-stems).[14] These patterns do not exist with certainty in Ugaritic, or if they do, they are extremely rare.[15] Hence the verbs likely employ other stems. Once this is said, however, it cannot be assumed that both employ the same stem. Each must be inspected separately.

The stem of *šqy* in our passage is relatively easy to explain, though it is not without dispute. Tropper has recently argued, following cues from Gordon and Aistleitner, that non-Š examples of the root reflect two different stems: a G (i.e., basic) stem with the simple meaning 'drink' and a D (often factitive or quasi-causative) stem with the meaning 'ein Getränk versetzen, einschenken' (this opposed to the Š-stem meaning of 'trinken lassen; veranlassen, daß jemand trinken kann').[16] The examples that he gives as cases of the D-stem include: (a) the very broken description of a feast involving Il in 1.1 IV 9: *šqy . rṯn . tnmy* 'he gives abundant mud (?) to drink';[17] (b) Baʿl's being served at the beginning of 1.3 I 8–9: *ndd yʿšr w yšqynh* '(the server) stood, made ready, and gave him (Baʿl) drink';[18] (c) Anat's promise of eternal life to Aqhat, which uses the same language as in the service to Baʿl (1.17 VI 30–31; see chapter 7); (d) Ṯitmanat's giving drink to her father, Kirta: *tšqy* [. . .] 'she gave [Kirta] drink' (1.16 II 14).

There is no argument against these examples of non-Š-stem *šqy* having a causative sense. The problem is in whether they are actually D-stems. The judgment that they are is largely dependent on the supposition of the

14. One of the scholars who sees *ylḥm* as an internal causative is S. Segert, *A Basic Grammar of the Ugaritic Language* (Berkeley: University of California Press, 1984) §54.47. Dijkstra and de Moor ("Passages," 172 n. 9) allow it as a possibility, though they say it may be a D-stem. *CARTU* (148) lists a D-stem for the root; their glossary contains no C- or A-stems. Those who see *yšqy* as an internal causative include C. Virolleaud, *La légende phénicienne de Danel, texte cunéiforme alphabétique* (Paris: Geuthner, 1936) 5; E. Hammershaimb, *Das Verbum im Dialekt von Ras Schamra* (Copenhagen: Munksgaard, 1941) 32.

15. For doubts about the existence of the stem, see Tropper, *Kausativestamm*, 128–93; E. H. Merrill, "The Aphel Causative: Does It Exist in Ugaritic?" *JNSL* 3 (1974) 40–49; D. Pardee, "The Semitic Root *mrr* and the Etymology of Ugaritic *mr(r)* || *brk*," *UF* 10 (1978) 251 n. 11 (see the previous note on the glossary in *CARTU*); A. F. Rainey, "Observations on Ugaritic Grammar," *UF* 3 (1971) 167–68; cf. *GUL* 108–9. For authors accepting this stem, see Hammershaimb, *Das Verbum*, 25–40; Segert, *Basic Grammar*, §54.47 (he notes the syllabically written *ya-aš-li-ma-* as an example); P. J. van Zijl, "A Discussion of the Words *anš* and *nšy* in the Ugaritic Texts," *UF* 7 (1975) 503–14.

16. For a similar distinction in meaning between non-Š and Š causatives, see Segert, *Basic Grammar*, 203: G(?) or D(?) 'to serve drinks' and Š 'to give to drink'.

17. M. Smith (*Baal Cycle*, 132) takes this as a *marzeaḥ* celebration and has Il drinking rather than serving ('He drinks curdled milk overflowing'), but he does not explain the usage of *šqy* (cf. pp. 146–48).

18. See the form *yšlḥmnh* 'he gave him food' in line 5.

existence of a G-stem with the simple meaning 'to drink'. The examples of this that Tropper gives from Ugaritic literature are: (a) the feast here at the beginning of the Aqhat story and (b) the drinking involved in Pughat's visit to Yaṭupan at the end of the story (1.19 IV 53–61). We have already seen evidence that makes it likely that the first example actually uses *šqy* in a causative sense. The case involving Pughat probably also displays a causative meaning of the verb (see the discussion in chapter 18). Thus, all of the cases of non-Š-stem *šqy* have a causative meaning. This means that there is most likely only one stem behind these verbs, either D or G.

It is likely, based on the use of the root in other Semitic languages, that the cases just mentioned belong to the G-stem. Akkadian *šaqû* has a G-stem with the meaning 'tränken, bewässern' and an Š-stem with the meaning 'tränken lassen', with no D attested.[19] Likewise Arabic *saqā(y)* has a pattern I (G) verb with the meaning 'to give to drink' and a pattern IV (C) verb with the same meaning, while also lacking a II (D) form.[20] The Biblical Hebrew root *šqh*, though it has the *Piel* (D) pattern noun *šiqqūy* 'beverage, drink' (attested three times), appears as a verb only in the *Hiphil* (C), lacking both the *Qal* (G) and *Piel* (D) patterns.[21] This evidence leads to the conclusion that the root *šqy* probably appears only in the G- and Š-stems in Ugaritic.

Note that in the various Semitic languages both the G- and the Š-stems of this verb basically have a causative sense (the possible nuances of the two in Ugaritic is explained below). The meaning 'to drink' is not covered by *šqy*. This meaning is mainly represented by the verb **šty* in the various languages.[22] This adds evidence to the conclusion that the occurrences of *šqy* in Daniʾil's intitial offering and in Pughat's visit to Yaṭupan are causative in sense.[23]

Determining the stem of the verb *lḥm* is a greater problem.[24] Other examples of a non-Š-stem form with a causative sense are not known. All

19. AHw 1181. Note the substantive *šāqû* 'tränkend; Mundschenk' (AHw 1182).

20. Form I in Arabic can take a double accusative (of the drink and the one who drinks), as appears to be the case in our Ugaritic passage (see *DMWA* 416).

21. As for Aramaic, *DNWSI* 1186 lists causatives with the meaning 'give drink; irrigate'.

22. Ug. *šty*; Akk. *šatû*; Heb. *šātâ*; Aram. *štā/štē*. Arabic does not attest this root but instead uses *šaraba*.

23. This agrees with the conclusions made in *SP* 72; Dijkstra and de Moor, "Passages," 172 n. 9, 173 (so also *RTU* 251 n. 7). De Moor (*SP* 72) notes that proof for the causative sense of the G pattern of *šqy* is found in the term *šqym* 'those who give drink, cup-bearers' in *CAT* 4.246:8.

24. M. Tsevat's argument ("Eating and Drinking, Hosting and Sacrificing in the Epic of Aqht," *UF* 18 [1986] 345–50) that the root is a G-stem with the gods (that is,

other non-Š-stem forms appear to have the simple meaning 'to eat'.[25] Therefore, one must posit that the verb in our texts, if not a C- or A-stem (which may not exist as noted above), is a D-stem. The problem with this supposition is that other Semitic languages do not have a D-stem of the root,[26] though it must be said at the same time that the root is not well represented among the Semitic languages as a verb for eating. It is not certain if these difficulties are enough to force us to take the verbs *lḥm* and *šqy* as having the simple meanings 'to eat/drink'. In my judgment, the syntactic difficulty, noted above, as well as the attestation of non-Š-stem forms of *šqy* with a causative sense lead to the conclusion that here we have in fact an instance of *lḥm* with a causative sense, probably a D-stem.[27]

Given this conclusion, one wonders why Š-stems are used in the feasting of Kothar-wa-Ḫasis and, in particular, in the similar six-day feasting of the Kotharat. The choice of verb stem may depend on the differences between the meals. In the feasts for the Kotharat and Kothar-wa-Hasis, the verbs for feeding and giving drink appear together in the same poetic line, whereas in the first feast they appear in different lines. The circumstances surrounding the meals are also different. The latter feasts are partly meals of hospitality, whereas here the offerings are made because of personal need and petition. Furthermore, and probably most importantly, in the latter feasts the verbs do not have objects of items offered, whereas, in the initial feast, *uzr* (on the meaning, see below) is presumably the verbal object.[28]

This last observation proves to be a significant reason when coupled with the distinctive meanings Tropper gives to the supposed D- and attested Š-stems of *šqy*.[29] As noted above, he assigns to the former the meaning 'ein Getränk vorsetzen, einshenken' and to the latter 'trinken lassen;

---

their statues) as objects, based on a Hittite idiom, is too speculative. It requires the transfer of a Hittite idiom in which the verb *eku-* 'drink' has a supernatural being as a direct object, meaning 'to toast (the deity)' (for this meaning, see J. Puhvel, *Hittite Etymological Dictionary*, vol. 1: *Words Beginning with A*; vol. 2: *Words Beginning with E and I* [Trends in Linguistics: Documentation 1; Berlin: Mouton, 1984] 262; and see O. Gurney, *Some Aspects of Hittite Religion* [Oxford: Oxford University Press for the British Academy, 1977] 34) to include the verb *lḥm*. Tsevat's argument also requires taking *šqy* with the meaning 'to drink'.

25. For example, 1.4 III 40, V 48, VI 55; 1.23:6; 1.114:2.

26. Tropper, *Kausativstamm*, 140.

27. Those who take this instance as a D-stem include: *CML* 150; *MLC* 571; *CARTU* 148; Dijkstra and de Moor, "Passages," 172 n. 9. It is not clear how Parker understands the grammar of the verbs, but he does translate the passage as referring to Dani'il's giving of food and drink to the gods (*UNP* 51-52).

28. One could also suppose that the underlying diverse traditions or differing real world cultic contexts are also responsible.

29. So also Segert, *Basic Grammar*, 203.

veranlassen, daß jemand trinken kann'.[30] The D-stem thus highlights the *presentation* of beverage, and the Š-stem the *drinking* of the guests. This distinction of meaning can apply in our estimate of the stems of *šqy*: Tropper's definition for the D-stem can be simply shifted to our G-stem. If the same modalities of meaning for the stems of *šqy* is assumed for the D- and Š-stems of *lḥm*, the differences in verbs in the different feasts in Aqhat makes sense. The story's first feast is concerned with the *presentation* of the specific mentioned object, the *uzr*. The feasts for the Kotharat and Kothar-wa-Ḫasis, which do not mention the specific objects fed to the gods (though the larger contexts say that meat is provided), are more concerned with the guests' *eating* and *drinking*.

The reason that verbal objects appear only in the first feast may be due to the central position and significance of *uzr*-offerings in the rite. To see how this is so, the meaning of *uzr* must be examined closely. Some have taken it as an adjective from the root *ʾzr* referring to Daniʾil's being clad in a *mizrt*. Thus, for example, the recurring phrase *uzr . ilm . ylḥm* could be rendered 'being girded, he offered food to the gods'.[31] In this interpretation, the word *uzr* would be a passive participle of the *qatūl* pattern. The first vowel would be explained by vowel harmony with the second vowel: /*ʾuzūr-*/ ← /**ʾazūr-*/.[32] Hence, the form does not preclude this interpretation.[33] Problematic for the interpretation of *uzr* as an adjective is Baʿl's summary of Daniʾil's activity. He says to Il: *uzrm . ilm . ylḥm* / *uzrm . yšqy . bn . qdš* (1.17 I 21b–22; see the full text and translation below). The term *uzr* in both of these cases has *-m* at the end. This may be understood as an enclitic *mem*. However, since it occurs only here in the summary of what happened over six days, and it occurs twice, one suspects that it marks a plural noun. Accordingly, *uzr* in the entire passage appears to be an object of the verbs *ylḥm/yšqy* and appears to denote what is offered to the gods.[34]

30. Tropper, *Kausativstamm*, 168–69.

31. M. Dietrich and O. Loretz, "Bemerkungen zum Aqhat-Text: Zur ugaritischen Lexikographie (XIV)," *UF* 10 (1978) 65–66; H. H. P. Dressler, "Ugaritic *uzr* and Joel 1:13," *UF* 7 (1975) 221–25; J. Sanmartín, "Ug. *uzr* und Verwandtes," *UF* 9 (1977) 369–70; *MLC* 367–68, 524; *UNP* 51–52; *UPA* 144; *RTU* 251. A related interpretation takes *uzr* as a type of clothing (Gaster, *Thespis*, 330–31; J. Aistleitner, *Wörterbuch der ugaritischen Sprache* [Berichte über die Verhandlungen der Sächsischen Akademie der Wissenschaften zu Leipzig, Philologisch-historische Klasse 106/3; Berlin: Akademie, 1963] #130).

32. So J. Huehnergard, *Ugaritic Vocabulary in Syllabic Transcription* (HSS 32; Atlanta: Scholars Press, 1987) 105; *GUL* 44, 122. Compare Gordon, *Ugaritic Textbook*, §9.24.

33. So *ARTU* 225 n. 7, referring to the apparently incomplete grammatical description of Segert, *Basic Grammar*, §54.28.

34. Dijkstra and de Moor, "Passages," 172–73 (the root is *nzr* and means something like 'consecrated food, sacrifice'); *ARTU* 225 ('consecrated oblations'); A. Jirku,

The nature of the offering can be more precisely defined. First of all, since it is the object of both *ylḥm* and *yšqy*, *uzr* must refer to all of the offering materials, solid and liquid, that are presented to the gods. It does not, in other words, refer to a specific type or cut of meat or a type of beverage.

Second, *uzr*, presumably coming from the root *ʾzr* rather than *nzr*,[35] may have a conceptual or phenomenological connection with the *mizrt* 'waistcloth' that is part of Daniʾil's clothing, because it has the same root letters *ʾ-z-r*. Reference to this item of clothing appears, together with *ṣt*-clothing, at the beginning and end of the description of the six days of offerings. The context is one of lying down and spending the night. Presumably Daniʾil is sleeping at this time, which means that the offerings are made before he goes to sleep, though it is not clear if the offerings are made in the full light of day, at dusk, or even later in the evening, just before going to bed. It appears that he removes his *mizrt* and *ṣt*-clothing before retiring. This is indicated by the term *yd*, which can be interpreted as a verb from *ndy* or *ydy* 'cast down, cast off; remove'.[36] This understanding is better than construing the term as the preposition 'with' and viewing Daniʾil as ascending his bed wearing (in other words, 'with') the clothing mentioned,[37] since elsewhere this preposition has a comitative or associative sense ('together/along with') rather than one of containment or envelopment, which would suit a reference to clothing on the body.[38]

Kanaanäische Mythen und Epen aus Ras Schamra-Ugarit (Gütersloher: Mohn, 1962) 115 ('*uzr*-[Opfer]'); *ANET* 149–50; Gordon, *Ugaritic Textbook*, 354 #125 ('food or drink offerings'). It does not appear that the Punic *ʾzrm*, which appears with the offering term *mlk* (cf. *DNWSI* 26–27; with *mlk*, 642–43), can be used as evidence for the meaning of Ugaritic *uzr* (see *CML* 103 n. 1; contra Dijkstra and de Moor, "Passages," 172–73).

35. For the latter, see J. C. de Moor, "Ugaritic Smalltalk," *UF* 17 (1986) 219, and see the previous note.

36. So J. Tropper and E. Verreet, "Ugaritisch *ndy, ydy, hdy, ndd* und *d(w)d*," *UF* 20 (1988) 340–41, 348; Dijkstra and de Moor, "Passages," 173–74; Jirku, *Mythen*, 115–16; *CML* 152; *SP* 243; *GUL* 42; *UNP* 51–52. Del Olmo Lete (*MLC* 558) takes the root as *ydy* 'quitarse, arrojar' (compare Heb. *yādâ*), noting that the root may be *ndy* with the same meaning. Obermann (*Daniel*, 5, 9) takes the verb to mean 'besprinkle' (compare Heb. *nzh*).

37. *ARTU* 225–26; *CARTU* 142 (referring to this passage); Dressler, "Ugaritic *uzr*," 224 n. 42; E. Ashley, *The "Epic of Aqht" and the "Rpum Texts": A Critical Interpretation (Parts One and Two)* (Ph.D. diss.; New York: New York University, 1977) 16–17. De Moor (*ARTU* 225–26) translates lines 3b–5a: 'In his sackcloth he went up and lay down, in his loincloth–and so he spent the night'. Other interpretations include: 'couch' (*ANET* 150; marked as questionable); 'upon' (*UPA* 143).

38. See 1.14 II 1, III 23, etc.; 3.5:7, 8, 9; 4.80:5, 15, 18, 19; 4.107:1–8 (with *npṣ* 'clothing' but in a comitative sense); 4.125:8, 9; 4.145:3, 4, 5; 4.243:41, 42, [44]; 4.363:2, 5; 4.659:2, 7. See Gordon, *Ugaritic Textbook*, 101, 409 #1072; *MLC* 558. Dijkstra and de Moor ("Passages," 173) reject the prepositional use, but see the previous note.

A small difficulty that needs attention in the wake of this interpretation is whether we are to imagine that Daniʾil removes his clothing every evening. The passage describing the six days of offering (lines 5b–13a) mentions only the making of offerings, not the removal of clothing. The latter is mentioned twice, *before* and *after* the six days of offering (3b–5a, 13b–15a). One might infer that the removal of clothing occurred only at the beginning and end of the offering week. But it is doubtful that the passage should be read in a strictly sequential fashion. The descriptions of removing clothing form an inclusio around the six days of offering. In other words, art rather than logic determined their placement. Consequently, they can be seen as conceptually applying to each of the six days. Moreover, the first mention of clothing removal follows a general introductory statement that Daniʾil presented food and drink to the gods (2b–3a). This seems to set up the pattern for the six days of offerings. One of the effects of this inclusio is to focus attention on the presentation of the offerings described in the center of the passage.

According to the foregoing considerations, Daniʾil appears to remove his clothing every evening, and the *uzr*-offering may be so denominated because it is an offering performed while wearing the *mizrt*, or, as I have rendered it, a "girded-offering" (that is, an offering made while girded).

This association of *uzr* and *mizrt* is supported by a structural feature in the passage. Either *uzr* or *yd* appears at the beginning of every poetic line in the passage except the lines that provide the larger circumstantial context (the introductory lines and the lines in which the days are counted). This distribution makes the terms appear central to the description and suggests further that they are conceptually connected. A suitable connection is provided when they are seen as referring to the conditions of wearing and laying aside requisite ritual clothing.

From Vagueness to Clarity and Climax

While the basic mechanics of the rite are now clear, its purpose is not.[39] The missing first lines of the story may have set this out to some

39. I agree with Margalit that this is not an incubation ritual in the classical sense (*UPA* 250, 260–66). The gods involved are not chthonic (the high gods Baʿl and Il are the deities that answer him), Daniʾil does not appear to receive his revelation in a dream (as opposed, for example, to Kirta, 1.14 III 50–51; but contrast T. Mullen, *The Divine Council in Canaanite and Early Hebrew Literature* [HSM 24; Chico, Calif.: Scholars Press, 1980] 248), and the goal does not seem to be for healing—all elements of the Greco-Roman incubation model. Use of this analogy obscures rather than clarifies what is going on in the performance. Dijkstra and de Moor ("Passages,"173–74) suggest its goal (specifically the goal of undressing) may have been to bring a dream-revelation but are very reserved about this conclusion.

extent, but it is surprising that the description of the six-day feast itself does not communicate it. It is only on the seventh day that the purpose and rationale of the offering are spelled out. This conceptual development along with the elaborateness of description on the seventh day create a sense of climax.

The six-day offering rite contains only hints about its purpose. The *mizrt* 'waistcloth', for example, is a sign that the rite involves an attitude and condition similar to mourning. In the Baʕl cycle, when Il hears of Baʕl's death, he puts on a *mizrt* (1.5 VI):[40]

(12) . . . yrd.l *ksi* .	He (Il) descended from (his) chair,
yṯb (13) *lhd*m .	he sat on the footstool.
w *l* . *hdm* . *yṯb* (14) *l arṣ* .	Then (descending) from the footstool, he sat on the ground.
yṣq . *ʿmr* (15) *un* . *l* rišh .	He poured straw of mourning on his head,
ʿpr . *plṯt* (16) *l* . *qdq*dh .	the dust in which he rolled, on his pate.
lpš . *yks* (17) *mizrtm* .	As clothing he covered himself with a waistcloth.
ǵr . *b abn* (18) *ydy* .	He scraped[41] (his) skin with a stone,
psltm . *b yʿ*r	with a flint as a razor.[42]
(19) *yhdy* . *lḥm* . *w* dq*n*	He cut (his) cheek and chin.
(20) *yṯlṯ* . *qn* . *ḏr*ʕh[.]	He furrowed his clavicles.
yḥrṯ (21) *k gn* . *ap lb* .	He plowed (his) breast like a garden,
*k ʿ*mq . *yṯlṯ* (22) *bmt* .	like a valley he furrowed (his) chest.
yšu . *gh*[.]*w yṣḥ*	He raised his voice and cried:
(23) *b*ʕ*l* . *mt* . *my* . *lim* .	"Baʕl is dead! What will become of the people?
bn (24) *dgn* . *my* . *hmlt* .	The son of Dagan! What will become of the multitude?
aṯr . (25) *b*ʕ*l ard* . *b arṣ*	I will descend after Baʕl to the underworld."

Anat acts similarly when immediately afterward she finds Baʕl's corpse (1.5 VI 30–1.6 I 8):

(31). . .[lpš] . *tks*. *miz*[rtm]	[As clothing] she covered herself with a waist[cloth].

40. Cf. M. Dietrich and O. Loretz, "Die Trauer Els und Anats (KTU 1.5 vi 11–22. 31–1.6 i 5)," *UF* 18 (1986) 100–110. I am in essential agreement with them on colometric issues except for lines 17b–19, which seem to be overloaded in their interpretation. For notes on the *mizrt*, see p. 107 there.

41. Tropper and Verreet, "Ugaritisch *ndy*," 343–44.

42. For a different line division at this point, see *UPA* 436 (cf. B. Margalit, *A Matter of Life and Death* [AOAT 206; Kevelaer: Butzon & Bercker / Neukirchen-Vluyn: Neukirchener Verlag, 1980] 129–30).

(2) *ǵr . b ab*⟨n⟩ *. td*	She scraped (her) skin with a stone,
psl*tm* [. byʿr]	with a flint [as a razor].
(3) *thdy . lḥm . w dqn .*	She cut (her) cheek and chin.
t[ṯ]l[ṯ] (4) *qn . d̲rʿh .*	She fu[rrowed] her clavicles.
tḥrṯ . km . gn (5) *ap lb .*	She plowed (her) breast like a garden,
k ʿmq . ṯṯlṯ . bmt	like a valley she furrowed (her) chest.
(6) *bʿl . mt . my . lim .*	"Baʿl is dead! What will become of the people?
bn dgn (7) *my . hmlt .*	The son of Dagan! What will become of the multitude?
a*ṯr . bʿl . nrd* (8) *b arṣ*	We will descend after Baʿl to the underworld."

The various actions connected with mourning here suggest that a *mizrt* in particular is an article of clothing suited to mourning, an outward symbol of this state. Presumably because of its collocation to the *mizrt*, *ṣt*-clothing also had this character. In any case, at least the presence of the *mizrt* conveys the impression that Daniʾil's performance involves mourning, lament, or complaint. We should, of course, not think that his sadness is due to the loss of children. Rather it is apparently due to the lack of a male heir. Nonetheless, in this regard a lack is similar to a loss, and it makes sense that Daniʾil employs a number of mourning customs. However, if we can say that the clothing portrays Daniʾil as mourning, we cannot specify the nature and cause of mourning.

A feature in the passages about mourning for Baʿl shows just how reserved the passage in Aqhat is in describing the offering. After Il and Anat mortify their bodies, they add an exclamation that essentially gives the reason for their actions. In contrast, the Aqhat passage does not cite any words spoken by Daniʾil that cast light on the reason for the offerings. This is surprising in view of the evidence later in the text that Daniʾil does not make his offering in silence (see below).

An index of the rite's meaning is not just the presence of the *mizrt* (and perhaps the *ṣt*) but also the way it was (they were) used. Daniʾil, as noted above, is constantly changing in and out of this clothing. Wearing the clothing is in itself significant, but having Daniʾil change in and out of it creates a flashing light that attracts attention to the clothing and consequently emphasizes the mourning character of the performance.

The concentration on the change of clothing makes sense in view of the recognition that ritual is largely concerned with, if not based in, actions performed by and upon the body. These activities orient the body within the world and create, not just reflect, the relationships and understandings they may be said to symbolize. Kneeling in prayer, for example, is not simply a sign of submission but an *act* of submission. Similarly, acts of mourning do not simply reflect this state but constitute what mourning is all about and even induce the attitude.[43] Catherine Bell, in particular, has discussed how such performances ritualize an individual, partly by the basic "schemes of binary oppositions" that are impressed on an individual in ritual.[44] This provides a clue for understanding Dani'il's clothing and unclothing. In Dani'il's ceremony, two sets of oppositions play against each other. The one is *regular* versus *austere* clothing. The other is *being clothed* versus *being unclothed*.[45] Regular clothing or being clothed in these pairs of oppositions is the normal social state. Wearing austere clothing or being unclothed marks deprivation.[46] The ritual is able to maintain and highlight an atmosphere of mourning by moving back and forth between the two modes of deprivation, without ever returning Dani'il to a normal state.

In addition to the clothing that shows that the rite involves lament, the feast seeks to engage the gods, to communicate with them, as it were, through giving them food and drink. A few theoretical considerations about the meaning of offerings help elucidate the sense of this activity. First, it should be noted that, while this is an *offering*, it is not necessarily a *sacrifice*—an offering in which the killing of the victim is ritually performed and/or in which the killing has ritual significance. It is true that meat may be included in what Dani'il gives the gods to eat, as is found in the feasts of the Kotharat and Kothar-wa-Ḫasis, but the presence of meat (or even the mention of the slaughtering of an animal, as in the last two cases) does not necessarily make an offering a sacrifice. For example, in a recent article discussing offerings made to gods in Mesopotamia, W. G. Lambert deliberately avoids calling them sacrifices.[47] In the texts describ-

43. Bell, *Ritual Theory*, 94–117. Cf. V. Turner, *Dramas, Fields, and Metaphors: Symbolic Action in Human Society* (Ithaca: Cornell University Press, 1974) 279–99; M. Douglas, *Natural Symbols: Explorations in Cosmology*. (New York: Pantheon, 1982) 65–81. On body as the basis of cognition in general, see G. Lakoff and M. Johnson, *Metaphors We Live By* (Chicago: University of Chicago Press, 1980); M. Johnson, *The Body in the Mind: The Bodily Basis of Meaning, Imagination, and Reason* (Chicago: University of Chicago Press, 1987).

44. Bell, *Ritual Theory*, 98–104.

45. It is not clear that we are to imagine Dani'il completely naked after having removed his clothing at night.

46. Thus, I would agree, for example, with Dijkstra and de Moor ("Passages," 173), who note that undressing is a sign of grief (they refer to Gilgamesh VII ii 22; Mic 1:8; *ANEP* 459, 634, 638). Margalit, on the other hand, sees the removal of clothing as merely a means to provide bedding material (*UPA* 266).

47. W. G. Lambert, "Donations of Food and Drink to the Gods in Ancient Mesopotamia," in *Ritual and Sacrifice in the Ancient Near East* (Orientalia Lovaniensia Analecta 55; ed. J. Quaegebeur; Leuven: Peeters, 1993) 191–201 (and note his first sentence). See also Oppenheim's treatment of offerings in Mesopotamia (A. L. Oppenheim and E. Reiner, *Ancient Mesopotamia: Portrait of a Dead Civilization* [Chicago: University of

ing the practice, there is no focus on killing the animal. The emphasis is on the foods–meat, breads, drinks, and so forth–presented to the gods as a meal. The same observation can be made about many offerings in the Hittite cult.[48] The present case in the Aqhat story is similar in dealing only with the presentation of food, not with an act of slaughter. In fact, the text says nothing explicitly about meat (*animal* flesh); meat is just assumed, as already noted. Therefore, one must carefully distinguish between the general category of offering and the specific and more restricted category of sacrifice. This means that theories of sacrifice, concerned to a greater or lesser extent with explaining the killing of animals, are not of much help in clarifying what is signified here, be it the idea that the animal is a substitute for the offerer, that it mediates between the profane and sacred spheres,[49] that its slaughter is a mimetic repetition of a prior killing of a human,[50] that it is a ritualization of the hunt,[51] that it is "the artificial (i.e., ritualized) killing of an artificial (i.e., domesticated) animal,"[52] or that it is a means of establishing and sustaining descent through males that is not a fact of nature and must be ritually created.[53]

Chicago Press, 1977] 183-98) and his observation that blood sacrifice such as found in the Israelite tradition is not found there. For distinguishing between blood sacrifice and offering in Ugaritic studies, see Clemens, *Sacrificial Terminology*, 1-16.

48. See Gurney, *Aspects*, 28-34. There are some other practices that use the blood of animals in a ritual way or in which the death of the victim is of importance.

49. H. Hubert and M. Mauss, *Sacrifice: Its Nature and Function* (Chicago: University of Chicago, 1964). T. P. van Baaren ("Theoretical Speculations on Sacrifice," *Numen* 11 [1964] 9) notes that, in sacrifice, killing the animal may be "little more than a technical requirement" and thus not symbolically or conceptually significant to the rite.

50. R. Girard, *Violence and the Sacred* (Baltimore: Johns Hopkins University Press, 1977); compare B. Mack, "Introduction: Religion and Ritual," in *Violent Origins: Walter Burkert, René Girard, and Jonathan Z. Smith on Ritual Killing and Cultural Formation* (ed. R. G. Hamerton-Kelly; Stanford, Calif.: Stanford University Press, 1987) 6-22.

51. W. Burkert, *Homo Necans: The Anthropology of Ancient Greek Sacrificial Ritual and Myth* (Berkeley: University of California Press, 1983); compare Mack, "Introduction," 22-32.

52. J. Z. Smith, "The Domestication of Sacrifice," in *Violent Origins: Walter Burkert, René Girard, and Jonathan Z. Smith on Ritual Killing and Cultural Formation* (ed. R. G. Hamerton-Kelly; Stanford, Calif.: Stanford University Press, 1987) 201 (see pp. 196-202). On p. 199 Smith says, "the starting point for a theory of sacrifice, that which looms largest in a redescription of sacrifice, ought no longer to be the verb 'to kill,' or the noun 'animal,' but the adjective 'domesticated.'" Nevertheless, the killing is a point of focus in his theory.

53. N. Jay, *Throughout Your Generations Forever: Sacrifice, Religion and Paternity* (Chicago: University of Chicago, 1992). Jay speaks more broadly about the consumption of sacrificial flesh and not just killing, but the killing of the animal is an integral part of her theory (see pp. 71, 149, 150; also her comments on the parallel between male and female shedding of blood). See also I. Strenski, "Between Theory and Speciality: Sacrifice in the 90s," *Religious Studies Review* 22/1 (January 1996) 10-20.

Theories that focus on the act of presentation provide more help. One explanation is to see the giving of offerings as a metaphorical or analogical act based on the presentation of gifts, food gifts in particular, to human superiors. This is reasonable, because theological constructs often arise out of metaphorical, specifically "anthropo-metaphorical," contexts; hence, for example, the description of deity in the Judeo-Christian tradition as redeemer, savior, father, and so forth. Moreover, as analysts such as S. Tambiah have shown, metaphor, though certainly not unique to ritual, is a basic component in it.[54] My own study has shown how analogical elements play an important role in biblical and Hittite ritual texts.[55] Thus it is reasonable that part of the motivation for the presentation of foods to the gods was to engage them in a way similar to the way a human superior is engaged by such gifts.[56]

Two texts from other ancient Near Eastern societies make the analogy explicit. The Hittite Temple Officials text warns people to make proper offerings to the gods with this rationale:

> Are the minds of man and the gods somehow different? No! Even here [in regard to their respective meals]? No! The(ir) minds are the same. When a servant stands up before his master he is washed and wears clean (clothing). (Then) either he gives him (the master) (something) to eat, or he give him something to drink. Then when he, his master, eats (and) drinks, he is relieved in his mind.[57]

The book of Malachi condemns the improper bringing of sacrifice with similar words (1:8):[58]

> When you offer a blind animal for sacrifice, is there nothing wrong? When you offer a lame and sick animal, is there nothing wrong? Present it to your governor; will he accept you or show you favor?

As noted already, this motif is quite explicit in the Mesopotamian offering contexts. Oppenheim's summary of the cult in Uruk during the Seleu-

---

54. S. J. Tambiah, "The Magical Power of Words," *Man* 3 (1968) 175–208; idem, "Form and Meaning of Magical Acts: A Point of View," in *Modes of Thought: Essays on Thinking in Western and Non-western Societies* (ed. R. Horton and R. Finnegan; London: Faber and Faber, 1973) 199–229.

55. D. P. Wright, "Analogy in Biblical and Hittite Ritual"; idem, "Ritual Analogy in Psalm 109," *JBL* 113 (1994) 385–404; idem, "Blown Away like a Bramble: The Dynamics of Analogy in Psalm 58," *RB* 102 (1996) 213–36.

56. This is not to deny other motivations for these gifts, such as an elaboration of a custom of providing the dead with nourishment.

57. KUB 13 i 21–26. Compare CHD L 3a. For a translation of the whole text, see *ANET* 207b.

58. P. Segal ("Nosafot le-Tiqbolot ben Sifrut ha-Kehuna le-ven ha-Hora'ot ha-Hittiyyot le-Mesharte ha-Miqdash," *Šnaton* 7–8 [1984] 265–68) has even gone as far as to suggest that Malachi reflects the Hittite Temple Officials text in some way.

cid period shows this clearly.[59] The gods' images were served two meals each day. Offerings of liquid and semiliquid foods, a main dish of meats, and also fruits were placed on a table before the images. The food was then given to the king to eat (which shows that there was no notion that the gods consumed the food in a physical way, contrary, for example, to the polemic of the apocryphal tale of Bel and the Dragon).

The Bible, in addition to the statement in Malachi noted above, manifests this analogical motif throughout. Not only meats, but breads (with oil), wine, and even salt are part of altar offerings. These are the staples of the human diet. The offerings, especially in P, provide a "sweet aroma to God." Sacrificial portions are called the deity's food.[60] The open-air altar is called Yahweh's "table" (Ezek 44:16; Mal 1:7, 12). The sanctuary or temple is set up as the divine abode, which is consistent with viewing sacrifices as the deity's meal. Ps 50:8–23 recognizes the metaphor, though denies its literal sense.[61]

The particular force of analogically feasting the gods depends on the surrounding mood and motivation. Sometimes a food gift can be brought with the positive motivations of thanksgiving or praise. It can be brought to remedy human fault by appeasing the deities. It can also be brought to make a request for blessing. This might be done in a positive context, when the continued blessing of the gods is sought, such as at harvest. It can also be brought in a dour context, when the offerer has suffered upset, defeat, or affliction. These various motivations are found, for example, in the priestly tradition in ancient Israel. Thanks and praise are rendered by the *šĕlāmîm* offering, including the special thanksgiving offering (*tôdâ*), and by the burnt offering (*ʿōlâ*). Appeasement is achieved chiefly by the purgation (*ḥaṭṭāʾt*) and reparation (*ʾāšām*) offerings and sometimes by the burnt offering. Blessing is sought by bringing the *šĕlāmîm* and burnt offerings.[62]

These purposes for offerings correlate with the various purposes of verbal communications directed to the gods (prayer, hymns, incantations, and so on). To take the biblical psalms as an example, we find there expressions of thanksgiving, praise, penitence, confession, and requests for blessing.[63] The correlation of purposes and the fact that prayer might

59. Oppenheim, *Ancient Mesopotamia*, 183–98.

60. Lev 3:11, 16; 21:6, 8, 17, 21, 22; 22:25; Num 28:2, 24; Ezek 44:7; Mal 1:7.

61. A similar denial that camel sacrifice, particularly one made on a pilgrimage to Mecca, is God's food can be found in the Qurʾān 22:37.

62. See J. Milgrom, "Sacrifices and Offerings, OT," *IDBSup* 763–71.

63. On the different genres, see H. Gunkel and J. Begrich, *Einleitung in die Psalmen: Die Gattungen der religiösen Lyrik Israels* (2d ed; Göttingen: Vandenhoeck & Ruprecht, 1966); E. Gerstenberger, "Psalms," in *Old Testament Form Criticism* (ed. J. Hayes; San Antonio: Trinity University Press, 1974) 179–223.

accompany sacrifice or even stand in its place[64] suggest that one can look at sacrifices and offerings as being, in a way, instances of concretized prayer. Certainly we should not assimilate or reduce the one phenomenon to the other. But there is nonetheless some phenomenological overlap that elucidates the significance of offerings.

These various perspectives illumine the meaning of Daniʾil's offering. Though Daniʾil is not portrayed as speaking (but see below), he nevertheless communicates with the gods: his offering is a form of prayer. At the same time, the offering is a present to the gods. It seeks to induce the gods to act on his behalf rather than to thank them for blessings received. That it is an inducement is evident in the mood accompanying the sacrifice. Daniʾil is in a state of deprivation, as marked by the clothing he wears. Further, the name of the offerings, *uzr*, if connected with *mizrt* as argued above, indicates that the offerings are brought to fill a need.

In addition to the foregoing, the elaborateness and structure of the description of the rite convey a sense of gravity and even urgency. Later on, I discuss how this initial feast is more complex than others in the story. For example, it lasts longer, contains a full range of foods, takes place presumably in a temple, has the high gods as recipients of the sacrifice, and occupies more narrative space (including the events of the seventh day) than other feasts. But even without this comparative evaluation in mind, a reader or hearer first encountering the description of the feast senses that it is elaborately described. Concerning structure, we noted above that the description has an introduction stating that Daniʾil presented food and drink to the gods, followed by the two notices about the removal of clothing that frame the central description of six days of feasting in two-day increments. The repetition and the tightly bound arrangement focus concentration and thus signal exigency. On the urgent character of the feast, see also chapter 3 below.

In sum, then, the description in 1.17 I 1–15 lets us comprehend the basic character of the feast: *it is a serious and urgent petition to rectify a lamentable condition*. But, as we have noted, specifics are lacking. The full purpose and mood of the rite is only revealed with Baʿl's response and Il's blessing. The full disclosure's placement after restrained description creates a climaxing effect.

Before looking at Baʿl's response, we should note that a movement toward climax is already underway in the description of the offerings. Seven

64. On the issue of prayer and the Israelite cult and more specifically in priestly tradition, see M. Haran, "Temple and Community in Ancient Israel," in *Temple in Society* (ed. M. V. Fox; Winona Lake, Ind.: Eisenbrauns, 1988) 23; I. Knohl, "Between Voice and Silence: The Relationship between Prayer and Temple Cult," *JBL* 115 (1996) 17–30; J. Milgrom, *Leviticus 1-16* (AB 3; New York: Doubleday, 1991) 19, 60–61.

was a common ritual unit in the Syro-Palestinian world, and ritual periods of seven days frequently appear in ritual texts.[65] For this reason, the counting off of six days in Daniʾil's initial offering creates an expectation of completion or culmination on the seventh. The formulaic manner of counting off the six days two at a time enhances this expectation.[66] This pattern is found in the offering to the Kotharat (1.17 II 27–40). It is also found in the feasting of the *rpum* (1.22 I 21–26), Kirta's march to Udum as outlined by Il (1.14 III 2–16),[67] and Kothar-wa-Ḫasis's building of Baʿl's palace (1.4 VI 24–32).[68]

The seventh day brings the culmination of the initial feast. On this day "Baʿl drew near in his compassion" (17 I 16). From the larger context, it appears that Baʿl approaches Il, not Daniʾil.[69] Later, when Il blesses Daniʾil, the god formulates the blessing with a third-person reference to Daniʾil (17 I 34–48), and after this Baʿl mediates the blessing in a second-person address to Daniʾil (17 II 1–8; see below), as though Daniʾil had not heard Il speak it. This indicates that Il is not in the same place as Daniʾil. Consequently, the *at,* which occurs in line 16b (see just below) and appears to be a second-person pronoun 'you', may be an error. If *at* is textually correct and taken as a pronoun, the text can be read as containing a brief acknowledgment to Daniʾil of his situation with the address then turning to Il who is in another place.[70] In any case the general sense of the

65. For the consecration of a NIN.DINGIR at Emar, after two or three days of initial ceremonies, a seven-day period is prescribed to conclude the initiation of the priestess (Emar 369: 49, 76, 83; cf. D. Fleming, *The Installation of Baal's High Priestess at Emar: A Window on Ancient Syrian Religion* [HSS 42; Atlanta: Scholars Press, 1992); idem, *Time at Emar: The Cultic Calendar and the Rituals from the Diviner's Archive* (Mesopotamian Civilizations 11; Winona Lake, Ind.: Eisenbrauns, 2000). Biblical ritual shows units of seven days in Lev 8:33–35; 12:2–4; 13:4, 5, 21, 26, 31, 33, 50, 54; 14:38; 15:13–14, 19, 24, 28; 23:3, 6–8, 34–36; Num 19:11–12; Ezek 43:25–26; 2 Chr 7:9. Besides seven-day periods, the number seven appears in ritual contexts in other ways—for example, in the number of items used in a ritual (cf. *CAT* 1.43:7–8, 26; 1.161:27–30; etc.). Cf. C. H. Gordon, "The Seventh Day," *UF* 11 (1979) 299–301; Ashley, *Epic of Aqht*, 12–15.

66. Cf. K. T. Aitken, "Formulaic Patterns for the Passing of Time in Ugaritic Narrative," *UF* 19 (1987) 1–10.

67. In the fulfillment, the pattern is broken up, a fact that has dire consequences for Kirta (1.14 iv 31–48).

68. One can also compare the culmination of mourning for Aqhat in the seventh year (1.19 IV 17–18; cf. 1.6 V 5–10). Compare the progression to seven or a seventh in 1.14 I 15–20; see J. M. Sasson, "The Numeric Progression in Kirta I: 15–20: Yet Another Suggestion," *SEL* 5 (1988) 179–88.

69. Logically, Baʿl goes to Il's abode or approaches him in the council of the gods (cf. Mullen, *Divine Council*, 244–48). See *RTU* 253 n. 15.

70. Margalit (*UPA* 266) suggests that Daniʾil "is made privy to a discussion between Baal and El presumably seated in the 'divine council.'" He notes further (p. 267

passage is clear (1.17 I):[71]

mk . b šbʿ . ymm	Then on the seventh day,
(16) [w]*yqrb . bʿl . b ḥnth*[72]	Baʿl drew near in his compassion.
abyn {at}[73] (17) [d]*nil . mt . rpi .*	"[Da]niʾil, the Rapiʾan, is miserable,
anḫ . ǵzr (18) mt . *hrnmy .*	the hero, the Harnamiyyan, is moaning[74]
	(alternatively, retaining the word *at* as a second-person pronoun:
	You, [Da]niʾil, the Rapiʾan are miserable,
	(You) Hero, the Harnamiyyan, are moaning),
d in . bn . lh (19) *km . aḫh .*	who has no son[75] like his brothers
w . šrš . km . aryh	or scion like his kinspeople.

n. 2) that, since Baʿl needs to recite Il's blessing to Daniʾil, the latter was not privy to all of the proceedings in the divine council.

71. Margalit (*UPA* 169) takes the speech as wholly directed to Il: "Art thou indifferent to Danel the Rapian, to the toil of the hero, devotee of the Rainmaker, for he hasn't a son. . . ." It seems difficult, however, to attribute the terms *abyn* and *anḫ* to the god (semantically and syntactically questionable). De Moor (*ARTU* 227) apparently ignores the term in line 16b and takes the first two lines of the speech as speaking about Daniʾil in the third person: "Is Daniʾilu, the Saviour's man, miserable? Is the hero, the Harnamite man, sighing? Because he has no son . . . !". Del Olmo Lete (*MLC* 368) takes the first two lines as addressed to Daniʾil with the last lines directed to Il.

72. On the form and meaning, see Dijkstra and de Moor, "Passages," 174: the *ḥnt* 'compassion' is that of Baʿl, not Daniʾil. But cf. *GUL* 173: "while he [i.e., Daniʾil] beseeched."

73. This reading follows *CAT.* H. H. P. Dressler's collated reading here is "abynt (?)" (likewise CTA 78; Dressler, "Problems in the Collation of the Aqht-Text, Column One," *UF* 15 [1983] 44, 45). Parker (*UNP* 52) reads a single word, *abynat* (his edition does not distinguish between fully and partly legible characters). This he understands as an abstract noun; he translates lines 16b–18a: 'The longing of Daniel, man of Rapiu! The moan of the hero, man of the Harnemite!' *GUL* 219 reads a second-person pronoun here; so also *DLU* 38 ('¡que pobre estás tu . . . !').

74. On *abyn* and *anḫ*, see Dijkstra and de Moor, "Passages," 174–75; M. Dietrich, O. Loretz, and J. Sanmartín, "Das Nomen *ḥnt* 'Güte, erbarmen' im Ugaritischen," *UF* 8 (1976) 433–34; *MLC* 510, 515. On the lineation and translation above, see M. Dietrich and O. Loretz, "Zur ugaritischen Lexikographie (V)," *UF* 4 (1972) 34. On *abyn* and *anḫ* as a word pair, see the same authors, "Das ugaritisch-hebräische Wortpaar *dl* || (*abyn*)/*ʾbywn* (KTU 1.16 VI 47b–48a)," *UF* 25 (1993) 121. *RTU* 253 reads *abynt* and takes it and *anḫ* as abstracts: 'Baal drew near . . . at the misery of [Da]nel . . . the groaning of the hero . . .'.

75. The translation 'son' (rather than genderless 'child') is chosen because the story is about the birth and death of Aqhat. Pughat, Aqhat's sister, figures in the story but not as a child of equal status to Aqhat. The assumption is thus that a male child is the concern here. For gender issues in the story, see the comments in the appropriate sections below.

(20) *bl . iṯ . bn . lh . k'm aḫh .*	He has no son like his brothers
w šrš (21) *km . aryh.*	or scion like his kinspeople.[76]
uzrm . ilm . ylḥm	Girded-offerings he presented as food to the gods,
(22) *uzrm . yšqy . bn . qdš*	girded-offerings he presented as drink to the holy ones.[77]
(23) *l tbrknn l ṯr . il aby*	Please bless him, O[78] bull, Il, my father!
(24) *tmrnn . l bny . bnwt*	Please benefit him,[79] O creator of creatures!"

Here we find the first spoken words in the portrayal of the rite. The clarification that they provide creates a sense of focus and intensification. This is similar to the function of Il's words in the passage cited above, which describes his mourning after Baʿl's death. Ritual actions—mourning activities—are first described, followed by his exclamation "Baal is dead! What will become of the people! . . ." One significant difference is that, in Daniʾil's ceremony, Baʿl's words are not necessarily to be seen as the first words in the rite. Daniʾil does not seem to have performed his offerings in silence.[80] Baʿl says that Daniʾil is *anḫ* 'moaning'.[81] This may mean that Daniʾil accompanied his offerings with expressed lamentation.

---

76. Del Olmo Lete (*MLC* 368) takes as an interjection: "¡Que pueda tener un hijo como sus hermanos . . . !"

77. B. Margalit (*UPA* 144, 169; "Restorations," 77–79) moves these lines about making offerings up just after the notice about the seventh day because Daniʾil's offering is out of place in the speech to El. This would have Daniʾil making offerings on the seventh day. This would not accord with the pattern in the Kotharat offering, where no offerings are made on the seventh day. Also note that Kirta's march on Udum takes place over six days, but travel ceases on the seventh day (1.14 III 2–16). Note the P creation story in Gen 1:1–2:4, in which creation takes place for six days but ceases on the seventh.

78. The *lamed* may also be taken as a preposition 'to, for' (cf. Gen 14:19; Judg 17:2; 1 Sam 15:13, 23:21; etc.; see D. Pardee, "The Preposition in Ugaritic [II]," *UF* 8 [1976] 221–23; idem, "The Semitic Root *mrr*," *UF* 10 [1978] 251 and n. 9). The vocative seems acceptable, despite the idiom *brk l-*, since the one blessing and the deity to whom the person is recommended are identical.

79. Many have claimed that the root is *mrr* 'strengthen' (← 'bitter'; for example, Gordon, *Ugaritic Textbook,* #1556; M. Dietrich, O. Loretz, and J. Sanmartín, "Die ugaritischen Verben *mrr* I, *mrr* II und *mrr* III," *UF* 5 [197]) 119–22). D. Pardee has convincingly argued against this connection and definition ("The Semitic Root *mrr*"). The meaning 'benefit' here is based solely on the parallelism with *brk* 'bless'. Pardee translates the word 'extol' and takes the verbs in lines 23–24 as 3d-person plurals ("The Preposition in Ugaritic [I],"*UF* 7 [1975] 329–78). *MLC* (583) takes the root *mr*, meaning 'confortar'. Parker (*UNP* 52) translates 'prosper'.

80. On silence in biblical sacrifice, see Knohl, "Between Voice and Silence" (he makes reference to Ugaritic cult, pp. 18–19 n. 3).

81. This is not to be taken as a causative verb, 'I will give rest' (from *nwḫ*; see Merrill, "The Aphel Causative," 46–47; van Zijl, "Discussion," 505–7).

Baˁl's words may in fact summarize what Daniʾil is imagined to have spoken. The words display several basic elements of a classic lament: (a) a complaint, describing Daniʾil's unfortunate state (lines 16b–21a); (b) a rationale for divine aid, that is, Daniʾil gave the gods food offerings (21b–22);[82] and (c) a petition, a call for Il to remedy Daniʾil's hapless condition (23–24).[83] A prayer from Daniʾil would presumably contain the first and third elements, with the second, if not explicitly stated, implied in the offering he was making. If this is right, Baˁl is functioning as an intermediary, carrying Daniʾil's prayer to Il.[84]

The words and actions that follow Baˁl's request for a blessing also continue to define the rite and intensify the description. Baˁl's solicitation of Il actually continues for several more lines, which enumerate the duties that a son is to perform for his father (1.17 I 25–33; see chapter 2 below). These duties are repeated three more times: by Il when he takes up his cup in a gesture of benediction and blesses Daniʾil, by Baˁl when he recites the blessing to Daniʾil, and by Daniʾil when he joyfully responds to the blessing (I 34–48; II 1–9; II 9–23). (For the filial duties and the blessing, see chapters 2 and 3 below.) The blessing and the repetition of filial duties leave no doubt about the purpose of Daniʾil's offering. The repetition of the duties makes them in particular the pinnacle of the offering event.

The intensifying structure discovered in the passage, from the description of the offering to the gods' revelation, continues in the very repetition of the duties. Baˁl's first recitation is part of a request. Since requests require responses, his recitation creates an expectation for an answer. The following recitations of the duties provide the answer, but they do so in stages. Il recites the list, but Daniʾil has not yet apparently heard the list. Baˁl then conveys the blessing to Daniʾil and recites the list. Now Daniʾil has heard. This could provide enough resolution, but the list is repeated one more time, this time by Daniʾil. This recitation contributes to the development because it is recited in joy—a perfect contrast with the state in

82. See the declarations of innocence and the listing of reasons why a psalmist should be blessed found in laments (for example, Ps 26:1–8, 27:6 [sacrifice], 35:13–14, 59:4, 63:6–9; cf. 28:2). The presentation of offerings can be compared to vows to offer sacrifice or praise in other laments (for example, Ps 7:18; 22:26; 35:9, 18; 42:12; 43:3; 51:16–18, 21; 52:11; 54:8 [sacrifice]; 56:13 [sacrifice]; 59:17; 61:9).

83. The complaint and petition portions represent stative and transformative expression, respectively. For a discussion of the dynamic relation of the two, see my "Psalm 109"; "Psalm 58."

84. For the mediation of prayer by one god to another or even by a bird, see my *Disposal of Impurity: Elimination Rites in the Bible and in Hittite and Mesopotamian Literature* (SBLDS 101; Atlanta: Scholars Press, 1987) 82 and n. 27.

which Dani᾿il began his offering—and because of first- rather than third- and second-person pronominal suffixes. The blessing is now completely recognized and personalized.

Dani᾿il's offering, followed by the gods' response and blessing, which is then followed by Dani᾿il's reaction, creates a *Geschehensbogen*, to borrow a concept from Westermann's study of Genesis.[85] Here the *Bogen* is somewhat geographical as well as narrational. The scene begins with Dani᾿il, a human. Action then moves to where Il happens to be, perhaps his dwelling place or the council of the gods. It then moves back to Dani᾿il. Of course, in terms of narration it does not end at exactly the same point it began. Dani᾿il now has the promise. Moreover, the narrative now allows him to speak. In terms of narrative description, his effective silence is a sign of mourning; his speaking is a sign of joy.

Finally, it should be observed that the movement from obscurity to clarity and, with this, the sense of climaxing development are experienced, despite the fact that the missing initial lines of the story may have set out the reason for the offering. Narrative has the power to change presuppositions and perspectives about the world it creates through its varied rhetorical techniques. In our particular case, even though Dani᾿il's motivation may be known at the beginning, the elaborate yet restrained third-person description of the first offering pushes the reader/hearer away from the protagonist, as it were. His mind is hidden, and his activity appears somewhat mysterious. The gods' revelation restores the intimacy we may have had with his situation. In any case, this revelation carries us much further beyond what we might have known about Dani᾿il's situation. It thus furnishes enlightenment and a feeling of ascendance.

The Feast as a Paradigm

The first feast stands as a standard against which all the others in the story are judged and by which they gain significance. It has this capacity, not only because of its placement in the story, but because it is the most elaborate feast in the story, its outcome is successful, and it sets out the basic relationships that operate—or should ideally operate—throughout the story.

Its elaborateness can be judged by comparison with the other six feasts in the story. Table 1 summarizes the essential data. In order to be as specific as possible, I have compared the feasts in seven different features: the length of the feast, the foods present or offered, the place of the

85. C. Westermann, *Genesis 1-11: A Commentary* (Minneapolis: Augsburg, 1984) 190-91 (and editor's comment there).

feast, other notable actions that accompany (auxiliaries), the agents who perform the feast, the recipients, and the number of poetic lines devoted to describing the rite and connected events.[86] The variables enumerated in each category can be ranked to reveal relative degrees of complexity, intensity, or focus. It should be noted that in some of these categories we are dependent on what the text chooses to tell us. Judgments are therefore not always or purely phenomenological but a function of the literary constitution of the text.

Table 1. Comparison of Features of Feasts in Aqhat

Feast	*Length*	*Foods*	*Place*	*Auxiliaries*	*Agents*	*Recipients*	*Lines*
Initial petition	7	food, drink	temple?	alternation of clothing, blessing	Daniʾil	Il, Baʿl, other gods?	107+
Kotharat	6 (+1)	meat, drink	home	—	Daniʾil	Kotharat	19
Kothar-wa-Ḫasis	1	meat, drink	home	—	Daniʾil, Danatay	Kothar-wa-Ḫasis	24
Request for bow	1?	meat, drink	home?	—	Aqhat, family(?)	Anat, other gods?	65+
Aqhat killed	1?	meat	the city Abilum	—	Aqhat, others?	?	48
dbḥ	1	meat	home	incense(?), music, blessing	Daniʾil, Pughat, family	sky/star gods	22
Yaṭupan	1 (twice)	drink	tent	(spell?)	Pughat as Anat	Yaṭupan	21+

Length. Length is a clear sign of complexity. Of all of the feasts, the initial petition offering is the longest. The only competitor in this regard is the offering to the Kotharat. The difference is that the initial feast climaxes on the seventh day, with the revelation to Daniʾil, whereas the feast for the Kotharat simply ends on the seventh day. The Kotharat have no interaction with Daniʾil at this time but depart from his house. For this reason, I have differentiated the initial petition by using a notation of 7, versus 6 (+1) for the offering to the Kotharat.

Foods. The greater the variety of materials offered, the more elaborate the feast. The problem with assessing the first feast in this category is that the content of the *uzr*-offerings is not described. We know, as noted

86. One might also compare the schedule of a feast (that is, whether it is ad hoc or a regular fixed occurrence, and if so, when) and its purpose. These features, however, do not clearly demonstrate elaborateness.

above, that they include solid food and drink. We may presume that the solid food includes animal flesh. Thus the initial offerings would be equal in content to the offerings given to the Kotharat and Kothar-wa-Ḫasis. Note further that the description of making the food and drink offerings in the first rite is more detailed than the description of the other two feasts. The first rite uses separate poetic lines to describe the feeding and drinking; the last feasts combine the feeding and giving of drink in one poetic line. Thus, from a literary point of view, the description of the offerings in the initial feast is more elaborate than the next two.

The initial feast's rival in regard to the food used in offering and in complexity of description is the feast in which Anat requests Aqhat's bow. A variety of feasting activities are recounted there in some detail: cutting the meat with a knife, drinking from cups and flagons, and so forth (see chapter 7). It is difficult to judge which feast is more complex, because the two feasts are quite different, and the description of the feast involving Anat is only partly preserved. It is possible, however, to view the two as essentially equal as far as food and the offering of it are concerned.

Place. The place for Daniʾil's initial offering appears to be a temple.[87] This is not explicitly stated in the extant text, but after the feast he returns to his home (1.17 II 24–25), implying that he is at another location for the offering. This would logically be a sanctuary of some sort. The offerings to the Kotharat and Kothar-wa-Ḫasis, the offering during which Anat requests the bow, and Daniʾil's *dbḥ* 'sacrifice' terminating the mourning for Aqhat are clearly or presumably made at his home. The feast at which Aqhat is killed is located in the city of Abilum, with no further definition given; it is doubtful that it occurs at a temple. The wine service to Yaṭupan is performed at his tents (1.19 IV 50), the equivalent of a home. Since a temple (a sacred place) ranks higher than a home (a profane or common place) from a ritual point of view, the initial petition offering ranks above the others in regard to place of performance.

Auxiliaries. Auxiliary ritual activities are sometimes listed alongside the feasting and are thus a mark of complexity. The other feast that displays a number of auxiliaries is the *dbḥ,* offered after recovery from mourning for Aqhat. It includes an offering of *dǵṯ* (perhaps a type of incense), the playing of music, as well as the blessing of Pughat by Daniʾil. These auxiliaries, however, do not receive the attention that the change of clothing does in the initial feast. Recall that the changing of clothing is

87. So *UPA* 261; *MLC* 334; Mullen, *Divine Council*, 247. It may be Baʿl's temple, since Baʿl is the one who first reacts and must go and get the blessing from Il and then convey it to Daniʾil. Baʿl also plays an important part in Daniʾil's religious world: he calls on him to fell the vultures so that he can look for his son's remains. Additionally, Daniʾil's epithet, Rapiʾan, may be connected with Baʿl (see p. 77 n. 27 on the *rpum*).

indicated explicitly not only in lines at the beginning and end but also in the repetition of *uzr* at the beginning of the lines describing the offering. Moreover, in the first feast, the accompanying blessing comes from a deity, not from a human being, as in the *dbḥ*. The initial feast is thus more elaborate with regard to the criterion of auxiliaries.

Agents. Elaborateness can be gauged by the number of individuals who sponsor the feast or participate as offerers. The feasts for Kothar-wa-Ḫasis, when Anat requests the bow from Aqhat (see the discussion in chapter 7), and the *dbḥ* involve multiple agents. The initial feast is simpler because it involves only Daniʾil as an offerer and human participant.

Recipients. Another criterion of complexity is the number of deities receiving the offerings and their relative rank. In the initial feast, Daniʾil offers to the *ilm* 'gods' in general. The only other rite that explicitly mentions this wide a scope is the *dbḥ*, which is also offered to the *ilm* and in which the *dǵṯ*-incense is offered to *šmym* 'heavenly beings' and *kbkbm* 'astral beings'. The initial rite proves to be of greater complexity because it eventually involves the high gods Baʿl and Il. No other feast in the story explicitly involves these high gods. The feast at which Anat requests the bow may involve several gods, but who they are is not clear. There is reason for doubting that the high gods are present (see chapter 8).

Lines. One purely literary mark of elaborateness is the number of lines devoted to describing a feast. The initial feast has by far the largest number of lines. This is mainly due to the repetition of the list of filial duties.

To summarize, then, the initial rite scores as high as or higher than the other feasts in all of these categories except one, the agents. It is clearly the dominant feast. The detail with which it is described cements in the mind of the hearer or reader what the feasts should entail. It thereby becomes a lens for viewing the other feasts in the story.

As the most elaborate feast, it contains many of the elements that appear independently or in less complex combinations in the feasts that follow. The later feasts can thus be said to participate through synecdoche or metonymy in the initial rite. For example, the feast for the Kotharat contains a six-day course of offerings, as does the first feast. The feasts for the Kotharat and for Kothar-wa-Ḫasis use language for feeding and giving drink to the gods similar to language found in the initial feast. The one-day feasts (for example,the feast for Kothar-wa-Ḫasis, the feast where Anat requests the bow, Daniʾil's *dbḥ*) appear as more or less simple or unmultiplied versions of the initial feast. Even Yaṭupan's wine feast shares with the first rite the motif of served drink, and it specifically uses the verb *šqy*, as did the first feast, to refer to this.[88] By thus sharing materials,

88. Note also the wine service to Baʿl mentioned in Anat's promise to Aqhat, 1.17 VI 30–32.

structure, and language with the first rite, the later feasts call it to mind. This correlates to some extent with Mary Douglas's observation arising from a study of British meals that "the smallest, meanest meal metonymically figures the structure of the grandest, and each unit of the grand meal figures again the whole meal—or the meanest meal."[89] The feasts in the Aqhat story are in this way each part of a conceptual system in which any single instance gains significance in its structural relation to the others.

Another reason why the initial petition feast can serve as a model for those that follow is that its outcome is successful. Daniʾil receives what he desires, and the gods comply with his request without reservation. As a successful performance, nothing about it is objectionable, and readers and hearers do not resist accepting it—*taking it in*—as a standard of what feasts entail. The next two properly operating feasts (to the Kotharat and Kothar-wa-Ḫasis) complement the effect of the petition offering. They secure the impression of what ritual should entail and what it should achieve. The next two feasts after these (those involving Anat) do not proceed smoothly. They undo the consequences flowing from the first three meals and they contradict the pattern set up by the first feast. This places them in sharp relief against the initial felicitous cases. The feasts at the end of the story are also judged in part by the impressions generated by the initial feast. Daniʾil's *dbḥ* is performed without fault. This signals, among other things, that Daniʾil's fortunes are improving, just as they did by means of the first feast. The deception in Pughat's wine service stands in tension with the initial feast and the successful ones that follow. But it does not create an atmosphere of treachery, as did the infelicitous feasts involving Anat. Since readers and hearers are naturally rooting for Pughat, her use of deceit instead arouses the fear that she may not succeed in her plot or that it may result in some other negative consequences.

The initial offering is also paradigmatic because it sets up the basic human-divine relationships that underlie the entire story. It places Daniʾil in subordination to the gods, a position that marks him as a pious individual. It also sets Il over Baʿl, in giving the prerogative of blessing to the the former.[90] By means of the information provided in the list of filial duties, the son is also placed in subordination to the father.

89. M. Douglas, *Implicit Meanings: Essays in Anthropology* (London: Routledge & Kegan Paul, 1975) 257. On analyzing impurity in the priestly legislation in the Bible from this point of view, see my "Spectrum of Priestly Impurity," in *Priesthood and Cult in Ancient Israel* (ed. G. A. Anderson and S. M. Olyan; JSOTSup 125; Sheffield: JSOT Press, 1991) 150–81.

90. On the hierarchical relationship of the high gods, see C. E. L'Heureux, *Rank among the Canaanite Gods: El, Baʿal, and the Rephaʾim* (HSM 21; Missoula, Mont.: Scholars Press, 1979) 3–108; U. Oldenburg, *The Conflict between El and Baʿal in Canaanite Religion* (Supplementa ad Numen, Altera Series, Dissertationes ad Historiam

The text of the first feast never outlines this hierarchy explicitly; the feast is left to portray it indirectly. That it does so as effectively as it does is not because ritual's primary goal is to reflect existing social relationships that have been established in some other setting, to "communicate" symbolically, or to inculcate and teach.[91] Rather, ritual can exhibit hierarchical arrangements because, as Bell has argued, it is actually a means of establishing these sorts of relationships.[92] In other words, ritual does not simply *mean*, it *does*. It is performative and effective.[93] Even though in many cases a rite seems to reflect things as they were before, it is a constitutive act that, if it does not entirely restructure relationships, renews and reestablishes them. This is one of the reasons, by the way, that ritual is often repetitive and periodic. The relationships that ritual creates need constantly to be reaffirmed and adjusted.

This function is as important in narrative as in real life. Story, after all, must create its own self-contained world in which events occur. It does this in part by setting down the presuppositions that readers and hearers are to use in comprehending the text. By these means, story draws readers and hearers into its world and instills a belief in its reality. Ritual is one means of formulating these presuppositions. Readers and hearers participate vicariously with the characters, or at least look over their shoulders, as they negotiate relationships among themselves. The relationships are thereby impressed upon the readers and hearers as if through actual experience.

Establishing the relationships between characters at the beginning of the story through ritual is necessary and significant because the rest of the story will deal with the upheaval of these relations. True, other felicitous rituals will underscore these relations and expand them. For example, the position of Danatay, Dani'il's wife, is demonstrated by the offering to Kothar-wa-Ḫasis. But the feasts in which Anat seeks the bow,

---

Religionum Pertinentes 3; Leiden: Brill, 1969); J. C. de Moor, "The Crisis of Polytheism in Late Bronze Ugarit," *OTS* 24 (1986) 1-20; M. Pope, "The Status of El at Ugarit," *UF* 19 (1987) 219-30; del Olmo Lete, *Canaanite Religion*, 49-55, 324. Walls, *Anat*, 7 n. 7 and pp. 87-88; Gibson, "Theology," 207-8.

91. For these views, see Leach, *Culture*, passim; W. Burkert, "The Problem of Ritual Killing," in *Violent Origins: Walter Burkert, René Girard, and Jonathan Z. Smith on Ritual Killing and Cultural Formation* (ed. R. G. Hamerton-Kelly; Stanford, Calif.: Stanford University Press, 1987) 150-52, 158.

92. Bell, *Ritual Theory*, 182-223 and throughout.

93. R. Girard notes, for example, that the pharmakos ritual does not "merely recall the collective persecution of psychosocial scapegoating: it *is* it" ("Generative Scapegoating," in *Violent Origins: Walter Burkert, René Girard, and Jonathan Z. Smith on Ritual Killing and Cultural Formation* [ed. R. G. Hamerton-Kelly; Stanford, Calif.: Stanford University Press, 1987] 76; cf. Burkert, "Problem," 153).

Anat kills Aqhat, and Pughat offers Yaṭupan wine, as well as Anat's petition before Il, all challenge the hierarchy. The promised boy vaunts himself over Anat, Anat threatens Il's life, and Pughat disguises herself as the goddess and kills the goddess's hireling. The infelicitous rites bring social chaos to the story's world and thus tension and drama.

Concluding Observations

A peripheral observation arising from the study of the complexity of feasts should not go unnoticed. The various feasts can be sorted into three blocks: the initial triad (the initial petition feast, the feast to the Kotharat, and the feast to Kothar-wa-Ḫasis), the following infelicitous pair (the feasts where Anat requests the bow and where she kills Aqhat), and the final pair, which terminates mourning for Aqhat (the *dbḥ* at the end of mourning and the wine service where Yaṭupan is killed). The first feast in each of these blocks is more elaborate than those that follow in the same block (see table 1, p. 42), and the first feasts are contextually determinative for those that follow in their respective blocks. In the first block, the petition feast brings blessing to Daniʾil. The ensuing two feasts complement this. In the second block, the feast at which Anat requests the bow provides the occasion for the goddess's anger, which is responsible for killing Aqhat in the following feast. In the last block, the *dbḥ* brings the family out of mourning and is the context for blessing Pughat so that she can go and kill Yaṭupan while serving him wine.

Finally, one of the reasons for the elaborateness of the initial petition feast is that it seeks to solve the problem around which the story revolves. It needs to overcome the inertia of Daniʾil's sonlessness. Once this has been resolved, the energy spent on offerings to sustain the motion (that is, good relations with the gods) need not be as great. Acceleration in the first feast is gradual. Full speed is not attained until the revelation of the gods. They are, from the context of the story, the real spark if not the fuel behind the ceremony. But if the gods can put on the gas, they can also put on the brakes, as is found in the infelicitous feasts in which Anat is involved. This reveals just how mythologically oriented the texts are, if myth is defined for the moment as story that involves the gods as significant players. While ritual in the story involves humans and cannot occur without them, it also becomes a means for gods to interact with each other and to act according to their sometimes conflicting interests.

Chapter 2
The Filial Duties

Baʿl's request that Il bless Daniʾil with a son includes a list of activities the son is to perform for the father. Several of these pertain to cultic and ritual matters. The list is given four times, with minor and insignificant variations (see the footnotes to the text, below). In addition to Baʿl's first recitation (17 I 25–33), Il repeats the list when he blesses Daniʾil (17 I 42–48, broken off at end), Baʿl repeats it again when, apparently, he delivers word to Daniʾil of the blessing (17 II 1–9, beginning broken; contains second-person prominal suffixes referring to Daniʾil),[1] and Daniʾil repeats it in his joy at hearing the blessing (17 II 14–23; with first-person pronominal suffixes referring to Daniʾil).

The version in Baʿl's request to Il, with its introduction, reads (1.17 I):

(25) *w ykn . bnh.b bt .*	May he have a son in (his) house,
šrš . b qrb (26) *hklh*[2] .	a scion in the midst of his (i.e., the father's[3]) palace,

A

nṣb . skn . ilibh .	who sets up a stela for his ancestral spirit,
b qdš (27) *ztr . ʿmh .*	in the sanctuary, a *ztr*-object(?) for his (deceased) kin;

---

1. About 10 lines are missing at the end of column I, and about 11 lines are missing at the beginning of column II. These missing 21 lines can be accounted for in this way: 4–5 lines (similar to I 29b–33) would come at the end of col. I to complete the blessing; 9 lines (similar to I 36b–44) would come at the beginning of col. II to introduce the blessing; the remaining 7–8 lines would deal with Baʿl's explanation of the situation of blessing (about 5 lines similar to the content of I 23–24, 34–36a) and about 2 or 3 lines explaining Baʿl's movement in blessing Daniʾil, a charge to carry the blessing to Daniʾil, and/or introduction of his speech. Thus there is not much room for anything except the conveyance of the blessing and material supporting it.

2. When Daniʾil recites the list, he uses different words to introduce the list (17 II 14–15).

3. The Ugaritic third-person possessive and object pronouns here and in the duties that follow (A–F), as well as the subject of *šbʿ* in line 31, refer to the son's father, not the son, as can be determined by Baʿl's and Daniʾil's recitations, which have second- or first-person pronouns clearly referring to Daniʾil.

B

l arṣ . mšṣu . qṭrh[4]	who brings forth his incense/smoke from the earth,
(28) lʿ*pr . ḏmr . aṯrh .*	the song of his place from the dust;

C

ṭbq . lḥt (29) *niṣh .*	who covers the evil of him who spurns him,
grš . d . ʿšy . lnh	who expels him that acts against him;

D

(30) *aḫd . ydh . bškrn .*	who takes his hand in drunkenness,
mʿmsh (31) [k] š*bʿ*[5] *yn .*	who carries him [when] he is sated with wine;

E

spu . ksmh . bt . bʿl	who eats his emmer in Baʿl's temple,
(32) [w] m*nth . bt . il*[6] .	[And] his portion in El's temple;

F

ṯḫ . ggh . b ym (33) [ṯi]*ṭ .*	who plasters his roof on a [mud]dy day,
rḥṣ . npṣh . bym . rṯ	who washes his cloak on the day of mire.

The six bicola[7] treat distinct duties, in the briefest manner. Moreover, several of the words and descriptions are not well understood. Commentary on each duty, clarifying these difficulties and explaining their context, is therefore necessary before making conclusions about the structure of the whole and the way it pertains to the matter of ritual in the larger narrative.

Analysis

Duty A: nṣb . skn . ilibh. / b qdš ztr . ʿmh

This duty clearly has a ritual orientation. The most certain element is *nṣb*. It is a verb meaning 'to erect, set up'.[8] It is to be understood as a participle;[9] it heads the list of a number of other participles describing the

4. This poetic line is missing in Daniʾil's recitation (17 II 17–18), presumably a case of homoioarchton.

5. Daniʾil's recitation, which has *šbʿt*, shows that this verb is in the suffixing conjugation.

6. *Spu . ksmh . bt . bʿl . wmnth . bt . il* appears before the *aḫd . ydh . bškrn* line in Baʿl's speech to Daniʾil (1.17 II 4–5).

7. On the stichometry, see p. 58 n. 61, and see the conclusion to this chapter.

8. For this meaning, see *UPA* 268. The lack of a causative form is not a problem.

9. Cf. Dijkstra and de Moor, "Passages," 175 n. 39; *GUL* 143.

activities of the ideal son: *mšṣu*, *ṭbq*, *grš*, *aḫd*, *mʿms*, *spu*, *ṯḫ*, and *rḥṣ*. The participial form is clearly evident in the words with the *m-* affix.

The object of *nṣb* is *skn ilibh*.[10] The term *skn* is disputed. Various interpretations include 'tomb (← storage-place)'[11] and 'steward' (as a participle).[12] It is generally understood to mean 'stela'.[13] This is supported by the appearance of the term on the Dagan stele inscription (*CAT* 6.13): *skn . d šʿlyt ṯryl . l dgn* 'The stele which Ṯariyelli dedicated to Dagan'.[14] The term *skn* appears to describe the object on which the word is inscribed. Emar and Mari texts have the term *sikkānu* 'stele', which appears to be related to Ugaritic *skn*.[15] At Emar, *sikkānus* are symbols for various deities and as such can receive offerings, be anointed with oil, be daubed with blood, and be moved about and set up for cultic functions.[16] At Mari, *sikkānus*, which are four to five cubits in length, can be associated with various gods.[17] In the general geographical-cultural region, stones have been found that represent deities or mark the divine presence: for

10. On participles with direct objects, see Segert, *Grammar*, §64.52. T. J. Lewis (*Cults of the Dead in Ancient Israel and Ugarit* [HSM 39; Atlanta: Scholars Press, 1989] 54) vocalizes the objects as genitive nouns in construct relationship.

11. Margalit, *UPA* 268 and n. 4. He compares the Dolmen structures in the Kinneret and Golan Heights area. Linguistically, he compares (*ʿārê*) *miskĕnôt* from the Bible (Tg. *bty/qrwy ʿoṣrāyyāʾ*). He compares 1.4 I 43 *sknt . kḥwt . yman* 'a closet the size of the plains of YMAN'.

12. E. Lipiński, "*Skn* et *sgn* dans le sémitique occidental du nord," *UF* 5 (1973) 197–99.

13. Huehnergard, *Vocabulary*, 157; Fleming, *Installation*, 76–77; Dijkstra and de Moor, "Passages," 175; K. van der Toorn, *Family Religion in Babylonia, Syria, and Israel: Continuity and Change in the Forms of Religious Life* (SHCANE 7; Leiden: Brill, 1996) 155 n. 9; J. C. de Moor, "Standing Stones and Ancestor Worship," *UF* 27 (1995) 3, 7–10. Cf. M. Dietrich, O. Loretz, and W. Mayer, "*Sikkanum* 'Betyle,'" *UF* 21 (1989) 133–39.

14. So Lewis, *Cults*, 72–79; see the discussion of other options there. I leave the term *pgr*, which follows *dgn*, untranslated; it may be an attempt to define the *skn* as a *pgr*-stele (for the problems with *pgr*, see Lewis's discussion; also D. Neiman, "*Pgr*: A Canaanite Cult-Object in the Old Testament," *JBL* 67 [1948] 55–60; J. F. Healey, "The Underworld Character of the God Dagan," *JNSL* 5 [1977] 43–51; M. Dietrich, O. Loretz, and J. Sanmartín, "*Pgr* im ugaritischen: Zur ugharitischen Lexikographie IX," *UF* 5 [1973] 289–91; Wright, *Disposal*, 122–25).

15. Fleming, *Installation*, 76–77; K. van der Toorn, "Funerary Rituals and Beatific Afterlife in Ugaritic Texts and in the Bible," *BO* 48 (1991) 44. The connection with Akk. *šiknu* is therefore not necessary (cf. W. F. Albright, *Archaeology and the Religion of Israel* [5th ed.; Garden City, N.Y.: Doubleday, 1969] 201; Lewis, *Cults*, 55).

16. See Emar 369:A35–36; 370:41, 43; 373:23, 27, 32, 57–58, 165–66; 375:14, 16; see the gate of the *sikkānus* 373:27, 45, 185–86, 192–93 and the passage of the gods among the *sikkānus* in 373:168, 179, 188, 197, 207–8; See the discussion in Fleming, *Installation*, 76–77; Dietrich, Loretz, and Mayer, "*Sikkanum*."

17. Fleming, *Installation*, 77 n. 27.

example, Hittite *ḫuwasi*-stones, cultic pillars at places like Hazor, and biblical *maṣṣēbôt*.[18] The fact that this last Hebrew term derives from the root *nṣb* and that the verb from this root (though in a causative form, as opposed to the G *nṣb* in the filial duty) is used of setting up these stones (Gen 35:14, 20; 2 Sam 18:18; 2 Kgs 17:10), as well as altars (Gen 33:20), piles of stones (2 Sam 18:17), and other monuments (1 Sam 15:12, 1 Chr 18:3, Jer 31:21),[19] shows that the meaning of 'stela' for *skn* is quite reasonable in this Ugaritic line, which has the same verb. It is not clear, however, if there is only one or if there are several *skn*s here.[20] Perhaps there is one, because *ilib* appears to be singular (see below).

The term *ilib* refers to a supernatural being of some sort.[21] Besides the foregoing evidence in which stelae are associated with deities, this explanation is mainly suggested by the appearance of *ilib* in lists of divinities (1.47:2; 1.118:1) and sacrificial and festival lists (1.41:35; 1.46:2; 1.56:3, 5; 1.74:1; 1.87:38; 1.91:5; 1.109:12, 15, 19, 35; 1.138:2; 1.139:1; 1.148:[1], 10, 23; 1.164:3, 6).[22] The attachment of the pronominal suffix in the duties of the son (*ilibh*, *iliby*; 1.17 I 26; II 16) shows that the term is not a proper noun, at least not in this context.[23] The term is made up of the elements *il* 'god' and *ib* 'father'.[24] The *i*-vowel in *ib* is apparently due to vowel harmonization with the genitive-case vowel at the end of the word

18. Ibid., 76–77.

19. Note Heb *nĕṣîb* meaning 'pillar' Gen 19:26 (of salt); compare *nṣb* as pillar in *KAI* nos. 201:1; 202 A 1, B 14, 18, 19; 214:1, 14, 15; 215:1, 20; 222 C 17.

20. Cf. van der Toorn, "Funerary Rituals," 44.

21. For discussions, see van der Toorn, *Family Religion*, 155–58; idem, "Funerary Rituals," 44–46; idem, "Ilib and 'God of the Father'," *UF* 25 (1993) 379–87; *UPA* 268–70; Lewis, *Cults*, 56–58; J. F. Healey, "The Akkadian 'Pantheon' List from Ugarit," *SEL* 2 (1985) 115–25; Lipiński, "*Skn*," 198–99; B. B. Schmidt, *Israel's Beneficent Dead: Ancestor Cult and Necromancy in Ancient Israelite Religion and Tradition* (Tübingen: Mohr Siebeck, 1994; repr. Winona Lake, Ind.: Eisenbrauns, 1996) 53–59; K. Spronk, *Beatific Afterlife in Ancient Israel and in the Ancient Near East* (AOAT 219; Kevelaer: Butzon & Bercker / Neukirchen-Vluyn: Neukirchener Verlag, 1986) 147–48.

22. For the name attested in 7th-century B.C.E. Philistia and 13th-century B.C.E. Lachish, see Lewis, *Cults*, 56. On *ilib* in the divine lists, see de Tarragon, *Culte*, 154–56; van der Toorn, *Family Religion*, 158–59.

23. Because of the difference of context and form, W. G. Lambert ("Old Akkadian Ilaba = Ugaritic Ilib?" *UF* 13 [1981] 299–301) suggests that *ilib* in the sacrificial lists is not related.

24. On the question of the relationship of Heb. *ʾwb* to Ugar. *ib*, see M. Dietrich, O. Loretz, and J. Sanmartín, "Ugaritisch *ilib* und hebräisch *ʾ(w)b* 'Totengeist'," *UF* 6 (1974) 450–51. Whether the Hebrew term comes from Hittite *api*- or not (see Albright, *Archaeology*, 202 n. 31; Gaster, *Thespis*, 334; H. A. Hoffner, "Second Millennium Antecedents to the Hebrew *ʾōb*," *JBL* 86 [1967] 385–401; M. Vieyra, "Les nom du 'mundus' en hittite et en assyrien et la pythonisse d'Endor," *RHA* 69 [1961] 47–55), it is doubtful that *-ib* is related to Hittite *api* and Heb. *ʾwb*.

/ʾ*ibi*/.[25] This vowel indicates that the terms are in construct relationship /ʾ*ilu* ʾ*ibi*/ (very literally, 'the god of the father'). An Akkadian translation of the Ugaritic term understood it this way, rendering it DINGIR *a-bi*, quite literally, 'god of the father' (RS 20.241:1 = Ug. 5, 44ff.). A Hurrian translation, however, construed the terms in a different relationship. It placed them in apposition: *en atn* /*enni attanni*/ 'god, father' (CTA 166:1).[26] The syntax of the Hurrian and the Ugaritic and Akkadian renderings is consistent, if the term is viewed as referring to a deified father or ancestor, not a more-general deity (such as Baʿl or Il) that the father worships. In the Ugaritic and Akkadian renderings, the genitive should be construed as 'the spirit/ghost of the father' rather than 'the god of (i.e., revered by) the father'.[27] The former translation points to the identity or essential association of the *il* and the *ib* (*ab*). The Hurrian makes the equivalence clearer by appositional identification: 'the spirit/ghost, i.e., the father'.[28]

But who is the "father" in this term: the son's father or the father's father or a more remote ancestor? If the father is dead when the son performs this activity, *ilib* refers to the father's own ghost, since the accompanying possessive suffix refers to the father, as the form with the first-person suffix (*iliby*) shows. Daniʾil uses this form when he joyfully reiterates the blessing; the pronoun has reference to him. If the father is dead, it would not make much sense for the pronoun to refer to an ancestor of the father, since his ancestor would also be the son's ancestor. If this were the case, one would expect the form *ilibh*, in all of these cases, with a third-person pronoun referring to the son.

Similar logic, however, makes it rather clear that the father cannot be dead when the son performs this duty. The term *ʿm* in the next line is parallel to *ilib* and appears to be cognate with Hebrew *ʿam*, meaning 'people, clan', in the context specifically '(deceased) clan/relatives'.[29] This term bears possessive suffixes just as *ilib* does (both *ʿmh* and *ʿmy*, the last in Daniʾil's own recitation of the duties), and they pertain specifically to the

25. So van der Toorn, *Family Religion*, 157; cf. *UPA* 269. Compare Punic *ui* 'my brother' in Plautus's *Poenulus*, whose /u/ vowel may come from harmony with an original nominative case ending (S. Segert, *A Grammar of Phoenician and Punic* [Munich: Beck, 1976] §36.31; cf. Ug. *uḫy*).

26. Cf. van der Toorn, *Family Religion*, 157. For the genitive relation, see *enna attanni-bi-na* 'gods of the father' in E. Laroche, *Glossaire de la langue hourrite* = *RHA* 34–35 (1976–77) 64. *DLU* 25 translates 'dios padre, dios familiar'.

27. Van der Toorn says that the genitive is one of identification, that "*ilib* and *il(i) abi* refer to the father in his capacity as a god" (*Family Religion*, 157). See also idem, "Funerary Rituals," 44.

28. Cf. Lewis, *Cults*, 54, 58–59: 'divine ancestor'. A plural, such as de Moor's 'ancestral gods' (*ARTU* 228) is unlikely.

29. See *UPA* 271.

father. If the father is assumed to be dead, it seems odd to describe the son as making offerings to the *father's* deceased kin, who is also the son's kin. One would expect *ʿmh* 'his kin' in all of the cases, with the suffix referring to the son.

The conclusion must be that the father is alive when the son performs duty A and that the *ilib* is the father's ancestor, though it is not clear how close or remote the ancestor is.[30] That the father is alive in duty A is supported by duty E, which likewise requires viewing the father as alive and the son performing some cultic act for him. It is difficult to imagine that the temple foods in duty E would be termed the father's if the father were dead. This reading is also supported by duties C, D, and F, where the father is clearly alive. Duty B might be thought to be an exception; some have interpreted it as referring to duties performed when the father is dead. But this is not clear. It may in fact refer to actions undertaken during the father's lifetime (see below). If so, the entire list is consistent, involving acts done while the father is alive.

Why the son erects the stela for his father is not clear. It is doubtful that this action implies that the father is uniquely incapacitated.[31] The duties listed are *typical*, the kind that might apply in any father-son relationship. When incapacitation is a factor, it is specifically noted (see duty D). It is perhaps better to assume that erecting a stela reflects a custom of turning some of the father's duties over to the son, either because the responsibilities of the father are demanding or because of a natural decrease of vigor with age.[32]

The words *ztr ʿmh* appear to be parallel to *skn ilibh* because of the common suffix on *ʿm* and *ilib*. Therefore, the second line is probably not a synthetic extension of the first line, with *ztr ʿmh* in apposition to *b qdš* (that is, not to be translated 'Who sets up the stela of his *ilib* / in the *qdš*, (which *qdš* is) the *ztr* of his *ʿm*'.[33]). The meaning of *ztr* is uncertain. It is not to be taken as 'protectors', as a variant of the root *str* 'cover, hide, protect';[34] nor

30. Van der Toorn (*Family Religion*, 160) says that the father is alive while performing this duty. He says, however, that the phrase "to set up the stela of the *ilib*" is only a set expression for performing the cult of the ancestor, which need not be taken literally.

31. So ibid., 154.

32. Compare 2 Sam 19:32–39, in which Chimham undertakes service for his old father, Barzillai.

33. See *UPA* 270–71 for this syntactic option, though Margalit prefers the other rendering.

34. *ANET* 150, 'protectors of his clan'; W. F. Albright, "The 'Natural Force' of Moses in the Light of Ugaritic," *BASOR* 94 (1944) 35 and n. 30. The problems with this interpretation are noted in *UPA* 270. The syllabically written word [z]*u-ut-ta-ru*, attested in a polyglot vocabulary, does not appear to throw light on the meaning of *ztr* (see Huehnergard, *Vocabulary*, 122; he notes that this may be a D infinitive meaning 'to go out[?]').

as 'inscription', connected with Akkadian *šaṭru* 'written';[35] nor as 'marjoram, hyssop, thyme', connected with Arabic *s/ṣ/zaʿtar* 'marjoram, hyssop' and Akkadian *zateru*, a plant name.[36] In view of the first line, we might expect it to refer to a stela or, more generally, some cult object. Matitiahu Tsevat has connected it with Hittite *šittar-* which is defined as 'Sonnenscheibe; Votivscheibe; Scheibe'.[37] This type of object may be made out of gold, silver, or bronze and belongs to or is connected with a deity or divine statue.[38] This would fit nicely with *skn* as an emblem connected with deity. But the connection, despite its attractiveness, is quite speculative.[39]

Finally, *qdš* probably refers to a sanctuary or sacred area.[40] Margalit's 'cemetery' is not acceptable because it is partly dependent on taking *skn* as a tomb.[41] Finding *sikkānus* in Emar texts and *šittars* in Hittite texts used in temples and shrines might lead one to suppose that *qdš* means a sanctuary of some sort.[42] It is not certain if *b qdš* refers to the place where

35. A. van Selms, *Marriage and Family Life in Ugaritic Literature* (Pretoria Oriental Series 1; London: Luzac, 1954) 101 n. 67.

36. Cf. also M. H. Pope, "The Cult of the Dead at Ugarit," in *Ugarit in Retrospect: Fifty Years of Ugarit and Ugaritic* (ed. G. D. Young; Winona Lake, Ind.: Eisenbrauns, 1981) 160 and n. 4; idem, "Notes on the Rephaim Texts from Ugarit," in *Essays on the Ancient Near East in Memory of Jacob Joel Finkelstein* (ed. M. de Jong Ellis; Memoirs of the Connecticut Academy of Arts and Sciences 19; Hamden, Conn.: Archon, 1977) 163–64; J. C. de Moor, "The Ancestral Cult in KTU 1.17:I.26–28," *UF* 17 (1986) 407–9; *ARTU* 228; Spronk, *Beatific Afterlife*, 146. The supposed parallel of *z(ʿ)tr* in 1.43:3 to which de Moor refers is doubtful (see KTU; *CAT*; D. Pardee, "Epigraphic and Philological Notes," *UF* 19 [1987] 199 for the collation). Lewis (*Cults*, 60) notes the difficulty of basing this on parallelism with the following line. Also unlikely is the interpretation of *ztr* as '(votive) cippus' (*RTU* 256).

37. M. Tsevat, "Traces of Hittite at the Beginning of the Ugaritic Epic of Aqht," *UF* 3 (1971) 352. This is accepted by *TO* 1 421 note n; Dijkstra and de Moor, "Problematic Passages," 175; *CML* 104 in n. 4; *MLC* 370, 544–45; de Moor, "Standing Stones," 8. Logographically Hittite *šittar-* (*HW*[1] 194) is written AŠ.ME (= Akk. *šamšatu* "[Sonnen]-Scheibe', AHw 1158b). W. G. E. Watson ("Non-semitic Words in the Ugaritic Lexicon," *UF* 27 [1995] 542) says Tsevat's suggestion "has not been bettered."

38. Cf. KUB 29.4 I 11, 13, 22 (H. Kronasser, *Die Umsiedlung der Schwarzen Gottheit: Das hethitische Ritual KUB XXIX 4 [des Ulippi]* [OAWS 241/3; Graz: Hermann Böhlaus, 1963] 8–9); KUB 17.21 II 14 (*ANET* 399; E. von Schuler, *Die Kaškäer* [Berlin: de Gruyter, 1965] 156–57).

39. Margalit (*UPA* 270 n. 17) notes that Hittite loanwords in Ugaritic literary texts are few: *ḫṯt* 'silver' in 1.14 II 18 (and parallels) and Proto-Hattic *ḫattuš*, presumably meaning 'silver' on the basis of the city name [URU]KÙ.BABBAR 'Ḫattuša' (see, however, H. A. Hoffner, "An English-Hittite Glossary," *RHA* 25 [1967] 80 n. 154); *dǵṯ* (1.19 IV 23–24; see the discussion on pp. 201–2, below) and the stem of Hittite *tuḫḫueššar*.

40. Lewis, *Cults*, 54; van der Toorn, "Funerary Rituals," 44.

41. *UPA* 271.

42. This location of the *ztr* erection makes it unlikely that the duty is associated with burial of family members in the house, as found at Ugarit (M. Yon, "Ugarit: The Urban Habitat–The Present State of the Archaeological Picture," *BASOR* 286 [1992] 29).

the *skn* would be set up or only to the place where the *ztr* is.

In sum, the bicolon appears to refer to the son setting up a stela on behalf of his living father for his father's ancestral god and deceased kin in a sanctuary or otherwise holy area. The actions are not necessarily connected with interment; they may be ways of honoring deceased kin apart from a funerary context. Perhaps they had to do with perpetuating the memory of the ancestors. Absalom is said to have set up a *maṣṣēbâ*, since he had no children to keep his name alive (2 Sam 18:18).

Duty B: l arṣ . mšṣu . qṭrh / lʿpr . d̲mr . at̲rh

Though the basic meanings of the words, except for *d̲mr*, are clear, duty B is the most difficult of all of the duties to interpret. The primary difficulty is the term *qṭrh*.[43] Several have taken it to be a metaphor referring to the ghost of the father. This is based not only on an argument about semantic logic[44] but also on the description of Aqhat's death, which includes the simile *tṣi . km . rḥ . npšh . km . it̲l brlth. km . qṭr . b aph* 'Let his breath exit like wind, / like an *it̲l*-plant, his spirit, / like smoke from his nose' (1.18 IV 24–26; see 36–37).[45] This passage makes it look as though *qṭr* could refer to a person's ghost after death.[46] More specifically, duty B could be referring to a ritual of raising the dead performed by the son. The term *d̲mr* in the b-line could be understood as being parallel to *qṭr* and referring to a protective deity/spirit (or deities/spirits).[47]

43. On the root, see K. Aartun, "Neue Beiträge zum ugaritischen Lexikon (II)," *UF* 17 (1986) 20.

44. See Albright, "Natural Force," 35 n. 31, where he justifies his translation of *qṭr* 'spirit' by noting that *quṭru* means 'vapor, steam, smoke' [= Germ. 'Rauch'] and that the "semantic development to 'spirit' is very easy and has many parallels." He translates the lines 'Who frees his spirit from the underworld, from the dust (death) keeps his footsteps'.

45. Lewis, *Cults*, 61; *TO* 1 422 note q; de Moor, "Ancestral Cult," 409; Spronk, *Beatific Afterlife*, 149; M. J. Boda, "Ideal Sonship in Ugarit," *UF* 25 (1993) 15. Tropper (*Nekromantie*, 132–33) does not take it as a metaphor for the dead but as a description of the dead soul. He translates the bicolon '(Ein Sohn), der aus der "Erde" seine (scil. Daniels) "dunklen (Geister)" herauskommen läßt, aus dem "Staub" die Beschützer seines Platzes'. J.-M. Husser ("Culte des ancêtres ou rite funéraires? A propos du 'Catalogue' des devoirs du fils [KTU 1.17:I–II]," *UF* 27 [1995] 115–27) has recently argued that *qṭr* refers to the ghost of the father and that this duty refers to a rite in which the father's ghost is brought to its post mortem abode in the underworld. Husser translates the duty 'qui fait sortir son "souffle" vers la terre, protège sa marche vers la poussière'.

46. Cf. *CML* 104: 'one to free his spirit from the earth, to protect his tomb from the dust'.

47. Cf. *ARTU* 228: 'someone to make his smoke come out from the earth, from the dust the Protectors of his place'; *UPA* 145 (cf. 272–73): 'To draw out his (father's) "smoke" from the ground, the protector of his "place" (as spirit) from the earth'. Compare *RTU* 256–57: 'into the earth sending forth his dying breath, into the dust, protecting his progress'.

All of these spirits are raised from the underworld. The rite would be similar to evocation of dead royalty in CAT 1.161[48] and the raising of Samuel in 1 Samuel 28.[49]

Two considerations throw this into question. First of all, even though conjecturing a development from "smoke" to "spirit" seems logical, the latter meaning for the word is not attested in Ugaritic or in other Semitic languages. Specifically, the passage describing the death of Aqhat does not provide the support for this interpretation that some contend, since *qṭr* there describes the *movement* or *disposition* of the 'spirit' (*npš* and *brlt*); it is not a word for 'spirit' itself.[50] The use of *qṭr* in this way in a simile and with the verb *yṣʿ* is also found in incantation 1.169: 2–3: *wtṣu . lpn . ql ṯʿy k qṭr urbtm* 'You shall depart at the voice of the *ṯʿy*-priest, like smoke through a hatchhole'.[51] Second, if my interpretation of duty A is correct, all of the other duties deal with situations in which the father is still alive. This may be the case here in B as well.[52] If so, *qṭrh* meaning 'his (i.e., the father's) ghost/spirit' does not make sense. These objections force us to a more literal rendition of the term, as 'smoke' or 'incense'.[53]

---

48. *CAT* 1.161 is a *dbḥ ẓlm* 'feast of the shades (?)'. For a partial discussion of the contents, see pp. 77–78 below. I would not go so far as to say that this evocation of royalty is connected with the institution of the *mrzḥ* (see *UPA* 267, 273, which makes the connection). Though 1.161 is called a *dbḥ* like 1.114:1, this is only a general term for sacrificial feast (see Daniʾil's *dbḥ*, pp. 200–203 below). On the connection of the *marzeaḥ* with the dead, see the discussion on duty D.

49. Margalit (*UPA* 272) also compares the case of Ulysses in the Odyssey XI. Dijkstra and de Moor ("Problematic Passages," 171–72) compare this with the *rpum* text 1.22. Compare soliciting the dead in Isa 8:19.

50. This is observed by van der Toorn, "Funerary Rituals," 45.

51. See D. Fleming, "The Voice of the Ugaritic Incantation Priest (RIH 78/20)," *UF* 23 (1991) 141–54; J. C. de Moor, "An Incantation against Evil Spirits," *UF* 12 (1980) 427–32; idem, "Ugaritic Lexcographical Notes I," *UF* 18 (1986) 255–56; Y. Avishur, "The Ghost-Expelling Incantation from Ugarit (Ras Ibn Hani 78/20)," *UF* 13 (1981) 14; H. Caquot, "Une nouvelle interprétation de la tablette ougaritique de Ras Ibn Hani 78/20," *Or* 53 (1984) 166; Wright, "Psalm 109," 390.

52. Some take *qṭr* as referring to the 'life' of the father: *TO* 1 422 (and note p): 'qui déliverera de la terre son âme, (et) de la poussière gardera ses pas'; Lewis, *Cults*, 54, 60–65: 'One who delivers his life from the Underworld, one who guards his footsteps from the Dust'. This requires an extension of the meaning of *qṭr* as 'spirit' to refer to the living father as a whole, as opposed to referring to his breath/spirit (*npš*, *brlt*), and thus it is questionable. Furthermore, the passages that these researchers cite from the Bible about a person's being saved from the underworld involve the deity as agent (Ps 25:15; 30:4; 31:5; 40:3; 107:14, 28; 142:8). Biblical salvation is miraculous and hard to consider to be the normal duty of a son.

53. Akk. *qutru* 'Rauch' (AHw 931a); Heb. *qĕṭōret* 'smoke, incense'. It is not clear if 'smoke' in Parker's translation ('To rescue his smoke from the Underworld, / To protect his steps from the Dust'; *UNP* 53) is to be taken as literal smoke or if it refers to the father's ghost.

The term may be taken in a rather mundane sense. For example, van der Toorn renders the lines '[who] on earth, makes his smoke go up; on the dust, keeps up/protects his place'.[54] Here, "the image of the ascending smoke [*mṣṣu qṭrh*] refers to the domestic hearth, which is a symbol of the family. An uninterruptedly burning hearth symbolizes the lasting vitality of the family." He buttresses his argument by reference to the Babylonian idiom in which a man without male descendants is one 'whose brazier is extinguished (*ša kinūnšu belû*)',[55] as well as to 2 Sam 14:7, which says, "Thus they would quench my coal which is left, and leave to my husband neither name nor remnant upon the face of the earth." This interpretation is not without difficulty. The Babylonian and biblical idioms are only metaphors for the existence of children to carry on the family line; they do not refer to customs of keeping the hearth burning to symbolize the vitality of the family. Moreover, the notion that the hearth has to be uninterruptedly burning is questionable; van der Toorn does not give support for this as a symbolic practice. Furthermore, the preposition *l-* with the verb *mṣṣu* seems better construed as separative rather than locative, despite 2 Sam 14:7, which has the phrase "upon the face of the earth,"[56] and despite the fact that elsewhere in Aqhat the use of the verb *yṣʾ* to mark separation is accompanied by the preposition *b-*.[57] Finally, the words *arṣ* and *ʿpr*, paired as they are here, are easily taken as terms for the underworld.[58] The interpretation of these as 'on earth . . . on the dust' seems to lack significance; the words thus appear to be superfluous.[59]

It is possible to take *qṭr* literally but in a ritual or cultic sense.[60] Several

54. Van der Toorn, "Ilib," 383; "Funerary Rituals," 45–46; *Family Religion*, 165–67. The citation of his translation conflates his slightly varied renderings.

55. See M. Bayliss, "The Cult of Dead Kin in Assyria and Babylonia," *Iraq* 35 (1973) 120.

56. The phrase in this verse has a different semantic relationship to its context than *l arṣ* and *l ʿpr* in the Aqhat text.

57. Noted by Husser, "Culte," 123–24. The verb *mṣṣu* demands an adverbial of separation. Husser's translation ('quit fait sortir son "souffle" vers la terre') leaves a question about whence the ghost comes.

58. Cf. 1.114:22; 1.161:21–22 (the term *aṯr* that appears in this last passage seems to provide no parallel to *aṯr* in 1.17 I 28, contra *UPA* 272). Van der Toorn's interpretation is not dissimilar from Gaster's (*Thespis*, 335–36 n. 2). He works from the second line backward. This line refers to guarding the father's place on the earth. The first phrase means something similar to our modern "keep the home fires burning." Gaster translates (pp. 333–34): 'Who may make his smoke to go forth from the ground, who may guard his place upon earth'. One problem with this is that *l-* prepositions that come before paired words are translated differently.

59. See also the objections of M. Dietrich and O. Loretz, "Zur Debatte über 'Funerary Ritual and Beatific Afterlife in Ugaritic Texts and in the Bible,'" *UF* 23 (1991) 86.

60. Other cultic interpretations include: M. H. Pope ("Notes on the Rephaim Texts from Ugarit," in *Essays on the Ancient Near East in Memory of Jacob Joel Finkelstein* [ed.

have attempted to do this. Some interpretations are given a funerary context. For example, Julian Obermann translates 'to make his incense go forth from the ground [ʿpr]. To guard his path'.[61] He dissociates the second line from the first and takes the first as referring to the incense burned at the grave on behalf of the dead. A. van Selms translates: 'who sends out to the earth his incense, to the dust wine after him'.[62] These acts belong together and are performed at the grave of the dead. J. F. Healey renders: 'From the earth to make go forth his incense, from the dust someone to protect his chapel'.[63] He connects this with the cult of the ancestors. Brian Schmidt's rendition is similar to Healey's. He says that this may be part of a funerary rite in which incense is placed at the tomb.[64] Manfried Dietrich and Oswald Loretz translate 'Der aufgehen läßt von der Erde seinen [= *ilib*] Weihrauch, vom Staub den Gesang seines/r Ortes/Kultstätte'.[65] They point out that the cult that the father undertook would be continued by the son. D. Pardee does not connect the lines with funerary activities yet sees them as general cultic acts performed after the father is dead. He renders the lines 'who sends forth his incense for the country, song for the land after him'.[66] Yitzhak Avishur is not clear about how he understands the context of the lines. He translates 'He brings up

M. de Jong Ellis; Memoirs of the Connecticut Academy of Arts and Sciences 19; Hamden, Conn.: Archon, 1977] 164; "Cult of the Dead," 160 and n. 5), who takes *qṭr* as a spice, conceptually similar to *ztr* in the previous line, which he translates 'thyme' (these spices are "trickled down into the grave"); Gray (*Legacy*, 109 n. 4; "Social Aspects," 173 and n. 4), who takes it as a "liquid-offering" based on Arab. *qṭr* 'dripping of water'.

61. Obermann, *Daniel*, 6, 16. He takes the phrase *l arṣ* with the line before it, which is doubtful in view of the stichometry, clearly set out by Y. Avishur, "The 'Duties of the Son' in the 'Story of Aqhat' and Ezekiel's Prophecy on Idolatry (Ch. 8)," *UF* 17 (1986) 49–50. U. Cassuto (*Biblical and Oriental Studies* [vol. 2; Jerusalem: Magnes, 1975] 200) and Gordon (*Ugaritic Literature*, 86; "Poetic Legends," 10) divide the lines in a way similar to Obermann.

62. Van Selms, *Marriage*, 100.

63. Healey, "The *Pietas* of an Ideal Son in Ugarit," *UF* 11 (1979) 356.

64. Schmidt, *Israel's Beneficent Dead*, 59–62.

65. M. Dietrich and O. Loretz, "Ugaritisch *ʾṯr, aṯr, aṯryt* und *aṯrt*," *UF* 16 (1984) 60 (though not accepted in their "Debatte über 'Funerary Ritual'," 86, where *qṭr* is taken as referring to the ghost of the dead by reference to Akk. *zīqīqu* 'Wind; Totengeister'). In "Bermerkungen zum Aqhat-Text," 68, Dietrich and Loretz translate 'zur Erde hin darbringt seinen Weihrauch, zum Staube hin den Gesang seines Heiligtums'.

66. D. Pardee, "The Ugaritic Text 147(90)," *UF* 6 (1974) 276 n. 6 (see his "Preposition in Ugaritic [I]," *UF* 7 [1975] 349; and discussion in his "Preposition in Ugaritic [II]," 336–38). See also his paper, "*Marziḫu, Kispu*, and the Ugaritic Funerary Cult: A Minimalist View," in *Ugarit, Religion and Culture: Proceedings of the International Colloquium on Ugarit, Religion and Culture–Edinburgh, July 1994* (ed. N. Wyatt, W. G. E. Watson, and J. B. Lloyd; Ugaritische-Biblische Literature 12; Münster: Ugarit-Verlag, 1996) 280.

from the soil his incense, from the dust the perfume of his place'.[67] He explains that the "role of the son is to offer incense and perfume and the clouds of incense smoke and perfume are seen as rising up from the earth and from the soil." This may or may not have a funerary context.

None of these renderings and interpretations is completely satisfactory. As noted above, the preposition *l*- makes best sense as marking separation, and the terms *arṣ* and *ʿpr* should probably be construed as references to the underworld, not simply the ground or the land or country. It is possible, however, that as terms for the underworld they refer to the grave. Only the interpretations of Obermann (the a-line only), Healey (and Schmidt), and Dietrich and Loretz are acceptable in regard to these matters. The other difficulty in many of these renderings is the word *ḏmr*. The term appears to be parallel to *qṭr* in the previous line;[68] therefore, interpretations like Obermann's and Healey's (and Schmidt's) are doubtful. Van Selms's connection of the word with Hebrew *šemer* 'wine' (Isa 25:6)[69] is questionable because it is not clear how wine would come forth from the earth in a way parallel to smoke. Avishur's connection of *ḏmr* with Hebrew *zimrat hāʾāreṣ* (Gen 43:11) and *zĕmôrâ* (Ezek 8:17), understood to refer to fragrances or aromatics, is also doubtful. In the Genesis passage, the term seems to refer to the wide range of materials that are later enumerated in the verse, which include more than aromatics.[70] In the Ezekiel passage, the meaning of *zĕmôrâ* is not clear and may be connected with social, not cultic, wrongdoing, as indicated by the context of the verse.[71]

A more suitable parallel to *qṭr* as incense (or cultic smoke more broadly) is provided when one translates *ḏmr* 'song', as Pardee and Dietrich and Loretz do.[72] Two pieces of evidence support this. The first is the appearance of the root *ḏmr* meaning 'sing' in *CAT* 1.108:3: *d yšr . w yḏmr* 'who sings and who chants'.[73] This is comparable to *ʾašîrâ waʾăzammĕrâ*

67. Avishur, "Duties," 52–53, 57. He translates the second line 'From the dust the perfume of his place'.

68. So Dietrich and Loretz, "Ugaritisch *ʾṯr*."

69. Accepted by Gray, "Social Aspects," 173–74 n. 5.

70. Cf. Y. Feliks, "The Incense of the Tabernacle," in *Pomegranates and Golden Bells: Studies in Biblical, Jewish, and Near Eastern Ritual, Law, and Literature in Honor of Jacob Milgrom* (ed. D. P. Wright, D. N. Freedman, and A. Hurvitz; Winona Lake, Ind.: Eisenbrauns, 1995) 127.

71. Cf. M. Greenberg, *Ezekiel 1–20* (AB 22; Garden City, N.Y.: Doubleday, 1983) 172–73.

72. Compare also Pope ("Notes on the Rephaim Texts," 163–64; "Cult of the Dead," 160): 'To Earth sends forth his spice, to the Dust sings toward him' (I substitute third-person pronouns for consistency with the analysis here).

73. Cf. D. M. Clemens, "KTU 1.108.3–5 (RS 24.252): *dyšr.wyḏmr . . . ,*" *UF* 25 (1993) 63–74; A. J. Ferrara and S. B. Parker, "Seating Arrangements at Divine Banquets," *UF* 4

in Ps 27:6. The difficulty with this is that, etymologically, one would expect to find the root *zmr* for the noun and verb. Therefore, it has been suggested that *yḏmr* in 1.108:3 is a mistake and that *ḏmr* in the Aqhat passage has nothing to do with song.[74] But 1.69:4 and 1.70:3-4 (see 1.67:20: *aḏ*[mr]), Akkadian religious texts written in cuneiform alphabetic script (and a scribal exercise), have *azammar* 'I sing' written as *aḏmr*.[75] This may indicate that the writing in 1.108:3 is not a mistake, just a variant writing.

Taking *ḏmr* as 'song' in duty B is also supported by the context of the *dbḥ* that Daniʾil offers when the mourning for Aqhat is complete (1.19 IV 17-26; see pp. 200-201). As part of this, he offers *dǵt*, which is apparently some sort of incense (see the discussion on the word below, pp. 201-2). This is described by the verb *yšʿly* 'he made rise', which reminds one somewhat of *mšṣu* in filial duty B. The *dbḥ* also includes music. The text says, l hklh xxx mṣ*ltm* . *mrqdm* . *d* šn . l bt[h] 'To his palace cymbals (were brought??), dance-instruments of ivory to [his] house'. Incense and music are paired in this passage. This means that a pairing of these phenomena is also reasonable in duty B.

A datum that should not be overlooked in examining these pieces of evidence is that the musical instruments that are listed in Daniʾil's *dbḥ* are also listed in 1.108 as defining the context of the singing and chanting. The fuller text reads (lines 3-5): *d yšr . w yḏmr b knr . w ṯlb . b tp . w mṣltm . b mrqdm . d šn* 'who sings and chants with the lyre, the shawm, the frame-drum, cymbals, and dance-instruments (clappers?) of ivory'. This text connects the action indicated by *ḏmr* with the instruments in Aqhat and makes the parallel between duty B and the *dbḥ* more cogent.

Given the foregoing interpretation of *ḏmr*, the larger phrase *ḏmr aṯrh* means 'the song of his place'. 'Place' here may refer specifically to a cult place.[76]

(1972) 37-39; J. C. de Moor, "Studies in the New Alphabetic Texts from Ras Shamra I," *UF* 1 (1969) 175.

74. J. Blau and J. C. Greenfield, "Ugaritic Glosses," *BASOR* 200 (1970) 11-12; Lewis, *Cults*, 62.

75. Noted by Blau and Greenfield, "Ugaritic Glosses," 12 n. 3. See S. Segert, "Die Orthographie der alphabetischen Keilschrifttafeln in akkadischer Sprache aus Ugarit," *SEL* 5 (Loretz Fs.; 1988) 190-91, where he notes the /*z*/ of the root *z-m-r* 'preisen' is written with *ḏ*. Compare also the word *ḏmrk* in 1.69:3, 4.

76. *SP* 194; Dijkstra and de Moor, "Problematic Passages," 176; Dietrich and Loretz, "Ugaritisch *ʿṯr*," 59-60. Some translate *aṯrh/aṯrk* in 1.20 II [1], 2; 1.21 II 3, [4], 11, [12]; 1.22 I 3; II 5, 10, 11, [20], 21 as 'holy place' (cf. de Moor, *Anthology*, 266-73; the *-h* suffix is sometimes taken as an adverbial marker of direction). *Aṯr* there, however, may be a preposition (see *MLC* 519). Gordon (*Ugaritic Textbook*, §424) notes that it refers to a Baʿl shrine in 1.6 I 7 (cf. 1.5 VI 24). The problems discerned by Lewis (*Cults* 64-65) with taking the term as 'holy place' are not real if *ḏmr aṯrh* is taken as an

Of the cultic interpretations that take *qṭr* literally and that have been listed above, Dietrich and Loretz's interpretation is the closest to what I believe is correct. The difficulty with their rendering is taking the referent of the possessive suffix to be the *ilib*. The son's father should be viewed as the referent of the pronoun, as is the case for the pronoun throughout the duties. Thus the ritual action performed has a chthonic or funerary character. The image is not entirely clear, but at minimum one can say that the son burns incense with accompanying song. The incense and song arise symbolically either from the underworld or from a tomb. The activity may be connected with the ancestral cult as is the activity in duty A, though this is not certain, especially since each of the other duties is not necessarily related phenomenologically to those that precede or follow. There is nothing to indicate that the father is dead when the son performs this duty. In fact, if this is to be connected with duty A, then we may assume that, since there the father is alive, here he is also alive.

Duty C: ṭbq. lḥt niṣh. / grš. d. ʿšy. lnh

The meanings of *niṣ* and *grš* are basically clear. The former means 'spurn, show contempt' (so Hebrew *nʾṣ*) and the latter 'drive away, expel'. The word *ṭbq* can be defined by reference to Arabic *ṭbq* 'cover (up)'.[77] The meaning of *lḥt* is less clear. The word has been connected with Hebrew *luḥôt* to mean 'boards, tablets, plates';[78] with the Hebrew root *lḥḥ* 'moistness' to mean 'life force';[79] with Semitic *lḥy* to mean 'jaws';[80] and with the Arabic verb *laḥâ* 'abuse, insult'[81] and the Aramaic root *lḥy* 'evil' to mean 'abuse, slander, evil'.[82] The last option fits the context best; the line refers to stopping the abuse of a person who has contempt for the father. In the b-line of duty C, the term *lnh* can be understood as a preposition with

object of *mšṣu*. Other interpretations include: 'footsteps' (Albright, "Natural Force," 35; *ANET* 150; *TO* 1 422; Coogan, *Stories*, 33); 'tomb' (*CML* 104 and n. 6; Lewis, *Cults*, 64); the father's physical remains (*UPA* 273: "what the deceased 'leaves behind' "); a preposition, for example, 'after' (cf. Pope, "Notes on the Rephaim Texts," 163; "Cult of the Dead," 161). Some merely render it 'place', without definition (Gaster, *Thespis*, 334; *ARTU* 228; van der Toorn, *Family Religion*, 154).

77. *DMWA* 552; cf. Lewis, *Cults*, 66; *UPA* 274.

78. Cassuto, *Biblical and Oriental Studies II*, 200, 202; Gordon, *Ugaritic Literature*, 86; van Selms, *Marriage*, 100, 102.

79. Albright, "Natural Force," 35; *ANET* 150.

80. Cf. *lḥm* 'jaws, cheeks' 1.5 VI 19; Dijkstra and de Moor, "Problematical Passages," 176; *TO* 1 422; *CML* 104.

81. *DMWA* 862.

82. *UPA* 274; Lewis, *Cults*, 66; Dijkstra and de Moor, "Problematical Passages," 176; K. Koch, "Sohnesverheissung an den ugaritischen Daniel," *ZA* 58 (1967) 214; Gaster, *Thespis*, 334.

suffixed *-n-* before a pronominal suffix.[83] This is simpler than the option 'body' or 'form'.[84] The word *ʿšy* is the only serious problem. Phonologically, the best option is to correlate it with Hebrew *ʿśh* 'do, make, act'.[85] Hence, the b-line parallels the a-line and describes the expulsion of one who acts against the father.

If the foregoing basic meaning of the words is accepted, the son is protecting the father from at least verbal, if not also physical, assault. The specific context of this protection, however, is not clear. It may refer to the ritual repelling of slander or evil. Compare *CAT* 1.169:9, where an accusing sorcerer is expelled (*kšpm . dbbm . ygrš* 'he expels the sorcerer who accuses').[86] An evil word or slander is a not infrequent object of anti-sorcery/witchcraft ritual in other Near Eastern texts, including the Psalms.[87] But nothing in the bicolon requires a ritual interpretation, and elsewhere in the list mundane activities occur (duty F).[88]

Duty D: aḫd .ydh .bškrn. / mʿmsh [k] šbʿyn

This is the easiest of the six bicola to decipher; the meaning of no word is in dispute. The son is the father's "designated driver," supporting and carrying him, presumably homeward, when he is inebriated.[89] Clearly the father is alive. The question is whether this is a ritual or mundane activity.

This duty has been compared to *CAT* 1.114, which describes a *mrzḥ*-feast of Il.[90] The god is sacrificing (*dbḥ*) and holding a banquet (*mṣd ṣd*)

83. *UPA* 276.

84. So *TO* 1 422. It is also unlikely that it derives from the root *lw/yn* 'spend the night', meaning something like 'dwelling' or 'those that dwell' (noted by Lewis, *Cults*, 67).

85. Dijkstra and de Moor, "Problematic Passages," 176–77 (on the correspondence of Ugaritic *š* with Hebrew *ś*, see Segert, *Basic Grammar*, 34). Heb. *ʿśh* II 'press, squeeze' is probably cognate with Arabic *ǵašiya* 'to do a forbidden act' (accepted with qualification by *TO* 1 422) and so does not fit here (Lewis, *Cults*, 67). Aistleitner (*Wörterbuch*, 243–44) compares Akk. *ešû* 'trouble, confuse'. Margalit's argument (*UPA* 150) that *ʿšy* means 'spleen' (the wine Anat drinks "[verily swelled] *the spleen in* [her] *girdle*") is based on a broken and problematic passage (1.17 VI 8; cf. 1.5 IV 20) .

86. See Fleming, "Voice," 151.

87. See Wright, *Disposal*, 36, 43, 58, 66, 84, 262, 266.

88. Boda ("Ideal Sonship," 16–17) suggests a connection with the *marzeaḥ* context of the next duty.

89. For *ʿms* in another case of incapacitation, note Shapsh's loading (*ʿms*) of Baʿl's corpse on Anat (1.6 I 12).

90. For general discussions of the *mrzḥ* and/or this text, see J. McLaughlin, "The *marzeaḥ* at Ugarit: A Textual and Contextual Study," *UF* 23 (1991) 266–81; Pardee, "*Marziḥu*," 277–81; Lewis, *Cults*, 80–94; Schmidt, *Israel's Beneficent Dead*, 62–66; Y. Breslavi, "'Al Tavo' Bet Marzeaḥ' (Jer 16:5); 'weSar Marzeaḥ Seruḥim' (Amos 6:7)," *Beth Mikra* 48/1 (1971) 5–16. More specifically see N. Avigad and J. C. Greenfield, "A

at his residence. He calls (*ṣḥ*) the gods to eat and drink: *tlḥmn ilm . w tštn . tštn y*⟨n⟩ *ʿd šbʿ trṯ* . ʿd . škr 'Eat, gods, and drink, drink wine to the full, new wine to inebriation' (lines 3–4). After an episode in which Yariḫ is fed and beaten under the table by gods who either do recognize him or do not, and after ʿAthtart and Anat are rebuked for feeding him, Il himself is rebuked, apparently with words that recapitulate his own call to the gods: *yṯb*. il. kr ašk[xxx] *il. yṯb. b mrzḥh* yšt. [y]n. *ʿd šbʿ. trṯ. ʿd škr* 'Il sits . . .[. . .]; Il sits at his *marzeaḥ*-feast; he drinks wine to the full, new wine to inebriation' (lines 15–16).[91] The rebuke appears to point to Il's inability to control his guests. Il goes home (or to his room[92]) with the help of two, maybe three, individuals. This is described in language similar to duty D: *yʿmsn.nn . ṯkmn w šnm . w ngšn.nn . ḥby* 'Ṯkmn-and-Šnm carried him and brought him to Ḥby (or: Ḥby brought him)' (lines 18–19).[93] His drunkenness (as well as helplessness) is emphasized by the description *b ḫrih . w ṯnth . ql . il . k*m mt *il . k yrdm . arṣ* 'He had fallen in his excrement and urine, Il was like a dead person, Il was like those that descend to the underworld' (lines 21–22).[94]

Bronze *phialē* with a Phoenician Dedicatory Inscription," *IEJ* 32 (1982) 118–28; R. D. Barnett, "Assurbanipal's Feast," *ErIsr* 18 (1985) 1*–6*; K. J. Cathcart and W. G. E. Watson, "Weathering a Wake: A Cure for a Carousal," *Irish Biblical Association Proceedings* 4 (1980) 35–58; M. Dietrich and O. Loretz, "Sprachliche und syntaktische Probleme im *mrzḥ*-Text KTU 3.9," *UF* 10 (1978) 421–22; "Der Vertrag eines *mrzḥ*-Klubs in Ugarit: Zum Verständnis von KTU 3.9," *UF* 14 (1982) 71–76; T. L. Fenton, "The Claremont 'Mrzḥ' Tablet," *UF* 9 (1977) 71–75; R. E. Friedman, "The *Mrzḥ* Tablet from Ugarit," *Maarav* 2/2 (1979–80) 187–206; P. J. King, "The Marzeah Amos Denounces," *BARev* 15 (1988) 34–44; L'Heureux, *Rank*, 206–23; de Moor, "Studies . . . I," 167–75; Pope, "A Divine Banquet at Ugarit," in *The Use of the Old Testament in the New and Other Essays: Studies in Honor of W. F. Stinespring* (ed. J. M. Efird; Durham, N.C.: Duke University Press, 1972) 170–203.

91. De Moor (*ARTU* 136) takes this as a citation, which makes sense after the verb *ǵʿr* (as in the case of its use a few lines earlier). Caquot and Tarragon (*Textes Ougaritiques II*, 76) and Cathcart and Watson ("Weathering a Wake," 38) take it as a simple description of what Il is doing.

92. McLaughlin ("*Marzeaḥ*," 270–73) notes that the feast may have occurred in his own house compound and he is merely going to his room.

93. For *ḥby* as 'steward', see de Moor and Spronk, *Cuneiform Anthology*, 137. For other possibilities, see Caquot, *Textes Ougaritiques II*, 76–77, n. 240; Caquot and Cathcart and Watson ("Weathering a Wake," 38) take this as a proper noun. The second line may actually be separate; see Caquot's 'Habay s'approche de lui'. De Moor and Spronk (*CARTU* 154) take the verb as a D-stem 'bring near'.

94. The stichometry of the passage is not clear. I tend to agree with de Moor (*ARTU* 136) that the verbs *yʿmsn.nn* and *ngšnn* are parallel, that *bʿl . qrnm . w ḏnb . ylšn* is a distinct line, and that the root of the verb *ylšn* is *lšn* and means 'speak' or specifically 'scold'. A new line starts with *b ḫrih*. . . .

It is clear from this little myth that, though food was served, drink was a preeminent feature of the *mrzḥ*.[95] An Akkadian economic text documenting the acquisition of a vineyard for a *mrzḥ* group also shows that wine was a key element in the groups' activities.[96] Further, while the nature of the *mrzḥ* institution in and around Ugarit is not fully known (and one must be cautious about connecting it with the dead[97]), we can say that the various associations had buildings and/or rooms dedicated to them[98] and that they were supported by the city and state officials;[99] thus, gatherings may have been frequent, if not regular. A well-to-do citizen might well have been a member of such an organization and, on many occasions, needed someone to lead him home. Thus, it is not impossible to connect duty D with a *mrzḥ* situation in particular.[100]

With this said, however, we probably should not assume that all opportunities for drunkenness involved the *mrzḥ*. There were other feasts where drink was present in abundance. For example, later on in the Aqhat story, when Anat covets Aqhat's bow, there is drinking (as well as eating), but this cannot be said to be a *mrzḥ* gathering. Likewise, various other feasts and sacrifices in the story involve drinking and the use of wine but are not connected with the *mrzḥ*.[101] Since this filial duty is not

95. One must be careful, however, to realize that this story is being told for a particular purpose, apparently as a prelude to prescribing a cure from drinking (on the purpose, see McLaughlin, "*Marzeaḥ*," 270–74).

96. RS 18.01 = PRU 4, 230, pl. 77. Compare *CAT* 4.642:3, where a vineyard (*šd kr*[m]) is mentioned in connection with a *mrzḥ* ʿ*n*[t] '*marzeaḥ* of Anat'.

97. Advocates include Pope, "Cult of the Dead," 176; see the cautions of Lewis, *Cults*, 84–94. The main evidence for connecting it with the dead is 1.21 II 1, 5 (with the variant spelling *mrz*ʿ); here the *rpum* are invited to the *marzeaḥ*.

98. See *CAT* 3.9, which exhibits some of the economic concerns and troubles that might afflict a *marzeaḥ* association (Dietrich and Loretz, "Vertrag," 71–76; Dietrich and Loretz, "Sprachliche und syntaktische Probleme"). The Akkadian legal texts RS 15.70 (PRU 3, 130, pl. 17, a contract) and 15.88 (PRU 3, 88, pl. 20, a royal grant) deal with the exchange or acquisition of houses by the men of the *marzeaḥ*. A more obscure contract in Akkadian from Ugarit mentioning the *marzeaḥ* is RS 14.16 (C. Virolleaud, "Six textes de Ras Shamra provenant de la XIV[e] campagne [1950]," *Syria* 28 [1951] 173–79).

99. Legal texts RS 15.70, 15.88, and 18.01 bear royal seals.

100. The *marzeaḥ* is geographically and chronologically more widely attested than just at Ugarit. See Amos 6:7; Jer 16:5; Phoenician texts (*KAI* nos. 69:16; 60:1; and Avigad and Greenfield, "A Bronze *phialē*"); an Elephantine ostracon (B. Porten, *Archives from Elephantine: The Life of an Ancient Jewish Military Colony* [Berkeley: University of California Press, 1968] 184); Nabatean inscriptions (see Lewis, *Cults*, 90–91); Palmyrene inscriptions (cf. ibid., 91 n. 49). Also mentioned in *Tg. Ps.-J. Num.* 25:2; *Sipre Num.* 131 (on Numbers 25) (ibid., 92); and in the Madeba map (ibid., 92–93).

101. For example, 1.3 I 2–17; 1.4 III 40–44; IV 35–38; V 45–48; VI 40–59; 1.5 IV 10–21; 1.15 IV 4–28, V 10, VI 4; 1.23:6; 1.41:22–23; 1.108:1–6, 13. See also de Tarragon, *Culte*, 43.

connected with a specific occasion for drunkenness, we should not limit it to the *mrzḥ*.

In any case, whether it be the *mrzḥ* or other feasting occasions, the drinking in these lines occurs during a ritualized event of some sort. However, note that the filial duty is not an immediate part of this event; caring for the father comes in the aftermath of a feast. Thus, this duty bridges the gap between ritual time and mundane time. In this case, there is no delegation of ritual performance to the son. The father, though incapacitated as a result of the feast, is not incapacitated by age or health to the point of being unable to attend the feast in the first place.[102] Perhaps the son attends with the father and thus is available to lead him home.

Duty E: spu . ksmh . bt . bʿl / [w] m*nth . bt . il*

What the performance of duty E involves is not clear, but it is clearly cultic in some way. First, the meaning of the verb *spu* must be clarified. It has been argued that the Ugaritic G-stem means 'to give to eat' rather than 'to eat', on the basis of the Jewish Aramaic cognate *sĕpê/sĕpāʾ* (G-stem), which means 'give to eat'.[103] This argument assigns the meaning 'to eat' to the N-stem (literally, 'to feed oneself'), which is said to exist in verbal forms that have an *-i* vowel marked after the root letter *-p-*: *ispi* (1.5 I 5); *yspi* (1.20 II 10). But these forms may be understood as G jussives in which the *-i* marks only final *ʾalep*, without necessarily indicating the preceding (or following?) vowel (hence /*ʾispaʾ*/[104] and /*yispaʾ*/).[105] The jussive is written once with the expected final *a*: *ispa* /*ʾispaʾ*/ (1.6 V 20). What assures the meaning 'to eat' for the G-stem is the apparent G infinitive plus suffix: *spuy* (1.6 VI 11, 15). This is parallel to the D infinitive plus suffix *klyy*. The suffix on the latter is a subjective genitive, 'my consuming'; thus one expects the pronoun on the former to be a subjective genitive as well. Hence *spuy* should be 'my eating', not 'my feeding' (conceptually 'feeding me'). The indicative form with *direct object* of what is consumed in a *šumma izbu* text (*ibn . yspu ḥwt* 'our enemy will consume the land'; 1.103:51)[106] also must be a G-stem with the meaning 'to eat'.

---

102. As a customary activity, drinking to the point of drunkenness should also not be considered a moral or social failing. As Margalit notes (*UPA* 277), "Danʾel is no drunken sot!"

103. *SP* 233; Dijkstra and de Moor, "Problematic Passages," 177; *CARTU* 157. This is also the interpretation in *CML* 153. *Sph* in Postbiblical Hebrew has the same meaning, but it can also mean 'have a share in a meal' (M. Jastrow, *A Dictionary of the Targumim, the Talmud Babli and Yerushalmi, and the Midrashic Literature* [New York: Judaica, 1971] 1013).

104. So Segert, *Grammar*, 63.

105. Ibid., §21.4.

106. M. Dietrich, O. Loretz, and J. Sanmartín, "Der keilalphabetische *šumma izbu*-Text RS 24.247+265+ 268+328," *UF* 7 (1975) 135, 139.

Therefore, to perform this duty, the son is to eat his father's *ksm* in the Baʿl temple and his father's portion (*mnt*) in the Il temple.[107] The word *ksm* (sometimes spelled *kšm*) is a type of grain, perhaps emmer.[108] It is used in the cult (1.39:9; 1.41:19), listed in records alongside *ḥṭm* 'wheat' and *šʿrm* 'barley' (*CAT* 4.269:20, 30; 4.345:2, 4, 9; see also 1.16 III 9–10), and is cognate with Hebrew *kussemet*. While *ksm* specifies a particular substance, *mnt* 'portion' does not appear to do so.[109]

It is not clear whether the father is alive or dead. If the father is dead, it is doubtful that this duty is a symbolic (and/or cannibalistic) consumption of the dead, as Pope suggests.[110] More likely, it would be connected with the funerary rites, during which offerings made to the father are consumed by the son, as his prebend, or the son symbolically consumes the offerings for the father. The rites in duty E, however, involve the gods Baʿl and Il and consequently appear to be part of the high cult devoted to those gods[111] rather than worship involving the father's ghost. Therefore, we should probably infer that the father is alive, in which case, as some have argued, perhaps the son is consuming the offering portions as a representative or substitute for his father. The father bestows the rights of representation on his son as a ritual privilege or delegates his participation in the ceremony.[112]

Duty F: *ṭḫ . ggh . b ym* [ṯi]ṭ . / *rḥṣ . npṣh . bym . rṯ*

The activities in duty F are custodial duties performed for the father. In the first line, *ṭḥ* refers to coating or plastering (compare the Hebrew word) and *ṯiṭ* to 'mud' (compare Arabic *ṯaʾṭat-*).[113] It is not clear whether the line means that the mud is used to recoat the roof. A technique used for constructing roofs in the ancient Near East and in Ugarit was packing earth down on reeds that had been placed on ceiling beams. When it rained, a roof-roller was used to compact the earth.[114] In the second line, the son washes the father's clothing on a day of *rṯ*. This word may be

---

107. On the possibility of the Il temple's being identical to the Dagan temple in the acropolis of Ugarit, see H. Niehr, "Überlegungen zum El-Tempel in Ugarit," *UF* 26 (1994) 419–26.

108. M. Dietrich, O. Loretz, and J. Sanmartín, "Zur ugaritischen Lexikographie (VII)," *UF* 5 (1973) 90–91; Dijkstra and de Moor, "Problematical Passages," 177.

109. It is doubtful that it is to be read *mtntk*, which Dijkstra and de Moor suggested could be understood as a 'grain offering' (ibid.).

110. Pope, "Cult of Dead" 162.

111. Cf. *UPA* 267.

112. Ibid., 267, 278. Margalit compares this delegating of authority to the rite of making sons priests in the Bible (Judg 17:5, 1 Sam 7:1, 2 Sam 8:18) and to institutionalized hereditary priesthood. Cf. Lewis, *Cults*, 67.

113. Ibid., 68.

114. Yon, "Urban Habitat," 32.

defined on the basis of Arabic *ratta* 'be old and dirty (of clothing)' or from Akkadian *rūšu*, *ruššu* 'Schmutz'.[115]

Though there are two distinct duties in these lines, they cohere as a unit. Of all of the duties, duty F is the one that is most clearly mundane.[116] To be sure, one might argue that the building and clothing are connected with cultic acts.[117] The fact that the son, rather than a female member of the family, washes might be taken as a sign that this washing is unique and therefore ritual in nature. But this conclusion is not certain. Mud is the object being washed, not blood, impurity, or abstract evil; this fact indicates that the cleansing is of a profane nature. Moreover, since duty C probably involves nonritual activities, it is possible that other duties in the list may also contain nonritual activities. In view of all this, it is best not to impose a ritual context on duty F.

Finally, we know that in this duty the father is alive because it is his dwelling and his clothes that are being repaired and cleaned.

Conclusion

The foregoing survey shows that we cannot be absolute in making conclusions about ritual in the filial duties. Nonetheless, some general observations are possible. In regard to structure, the passage contains six bicola, each of which is a conceptual unit. This is true for the three bicola that have two verbs rather than one (C, D, F), a circumstance that may cause the reader to think that they speak of more than one duty. Both lines in duty C deal with the single idea of defending the father's reputation, both lines in D deal with the single act of helping the father when drunk, and both lines in F deal with the single issue of maintenance. Each bicolon is a self-contained and thematically coherent unit yet at the same time quite unrelated to the other bicola. Thus, it appears best to view the list as containing six basic duties, rather than twelve (a "dodecalogical" structure),[118] nine, or eight (based on the number of verbs that actually occur or are thought to occur).[119] The fact that more than six

115. Lewis, *Cults*, 68.

116. Margalit (*UPA* 279–80) surmises that the washing of the *npṣ* by the son has to do with "holy" war clothing (*npṣ ǵzr*; cf. 1.19 IV 44), which could not be used or washed by women. This would place the activity within the ritual realm. This explanation, however, seems unlikely.

117. See Boda ("Ideal Sonship," 21–22) for a cultic interpretation of this duty.

118. O. Eissfeldt, "Sohnespflichten im Alten Orient," *Syria* 43 (1966) 42–44 (he sees twelve verbs: *nṣb, ẓtr, mššu, d̲mr, ṭbq, grš, aḫd, mʿms, spu* [bis], *ṭḫ, rḥṣ*); Koch "Sohnesverheissung," 211–21.

119. Margalit (*UPA* 267–80) counts eight duties (based on the participles or verbs that appear; *mʿmsh* does not count as a separate duty). He notes (p. 267 n. 2) that eight

verbs are used may be due to poetic constraints: instead of writing a b-line with the verb elided and implied from the a-line, the poet chose to compose two lines, each with its own participle.[120]

In terms of content, ritual matters appear in four of the six bicola. They display a pattern. The list divides into two halves, with the first two duties of each half dealing with ritual matters, and the last dealing with mundane matters:

A	ritual (setting up stela)	D	ritual (drinking feast)
B	ritual (incense, song)	E	ritual (consumption of offerings)
C	mundane (renouncing detractors)	F	mundane (patching roof, cleaning clothes)

This pattern helps explain the rather odd and very mundane duties in F, which seem somewhat out of place. The pattern, if part of the composer's craft, required the inclusion of a duty at the end of each half that was unlike the duties immediately before it and unlike the majority (A, B, D, E) in the list. The division of the list into two halves is supported by a structural feature. The lines of the first half regularly end in pronouns; those of the second half do not.[121]

The movement in and out of ritual and mundane matters and the distinctiveness of the six duties give the impression that a son's responsibilities toward the father have been rather completely delineated. It is a synecdochic charting of the whole by means of the part. Completeness is also conveyed by the rather wide range of duties. The list runs the gamut from solemn (A, B, E) to perhaps more light-hearted (D) ritual duties, from verbal accusations and assaults (C), which perhaps involve the legal, economic, and political spheres, to everyday and human experiences (F; compare D). The lack of logical flow from one to the next also conveys the impression that the duties deal with a broad range of activities.

---

fits well with the seven + one pattern, though he says elsewhere (p. 281) that, in view of the desire to use typological numbers (three, seven, ten), the list may have one commandment too many, specifically, the one that I have labeled E, which he counts as a single duty.

120. Note that the six bicola are similar in structure. Duties A–D have three words in each line (counting prepositions as part of the following words). E–F have a slightly different weight. The first line of E and both lines of F have four words. If, however, the last two words in each of these longer lines are counted as a single word unit because they are in construct relationship, then they align themselves with the lines in A–D.

121. Observed by Husser, "Culte," 116–17 (cf. Husser, "Birth of a Hero," 96). The pronouns in the second half occur within the lines. The syntax of the second half has more regularity (five times the order is verb, object, adverb) than the more varied syntax of the first half. *RTU* 258 n. 37 observes the pattern a:a:b:b:a:b in the duties, dependent on whether the father is dead (a) or alive (b) when the duty is performed.

In terms of the larger issue of ritual in narrative, the description of the son's duties stands apart from the other descriptions of ritual in the immediate environment, even though the list is enumerated four times. The duties deal with ritual matters beyond feasts, which is the major ritual concern in the first part of the story. The duties appear to stand apart from the narrative as well, because they do not describe what is actually occurring in the course of the narrative but instead portray ideal behavior. Nonetheless, the duties have connections to the theme of feasts. Duty B features elements that may be associated with feasts, such as are found in the *dbḥ* at the end of the text. The drinking lying behind duty D and the consumption of portions in the high gods' temples in E are feast situations. The former reminds us of the drinking that plays an important part in the feast in which Anat asks Aqhat for his bow. The latter reminds us of Daniʾil's feasting of the gods, presumably in a temple (see chapter 1). A structural echo of Daniʾil's initial feast is found in the larger list: the list contains six duties and Daniʾil's feast lasts six days. It is almost as though the promised son is going to provide Daniʾil with one act of service for each offering he presented.

The duties also have a larger function in the context of the story. As noted, they show where Aqhat fits into the hierarchical scheme of things and how he is expected to behave. He is subordinate to his father, which means the son is subordinate to the gods, to whom Daniʾil is subordinate. If he follows through with his responsibilities as outlined in the list, he should be as pious and blessed as his father. It turns out, however, that he fails to attain this ideal, specifically and surprisingly with regard to ritual matters. In the coming feast with Anat, he fails to please the goddess and even rebels against her. Instead of being obedient, a trait that may even be reflected in his name,[122] Aqhat is recalcitrant and unreconciling. Because of the list's important thematic role in the story, it is no wonder that it is presented four times. This is a way of anchoring the list's ideals firmly in the reader's mind.[123] Thus, the initial petition offering provides, by its elaborateness, a paradigm for how feasts should operate, and the duties provide a paradigm for how the son should behave. Both of these paradigms are upset, in a single instant.

---

122. Margalit argues that his name means 'most-obedient' (*UPA* 280 n. 49).

123. Pace Margalit (ibid., 280), who argues that the "lengthy repetitions of the list . . . appear to lack any literary justification and indeed tend to disturb the tight internal unity of the poem and to mar its structural compactness." This, by the way, is one reason Margalit views the passage as secondary. The uniqueness of its vocabulary is perhaps also another hint of its secondariness. Boda ("Ideal Sonship," 11) recognizes the uniqueness of the passage but says it still may not be secondary; it may be a preexisting passage or tradition used in the original composition.

Chapter 3

The Blessing of Daniʾil

Just as humans use ritual to make contact with the gods, so the gods use ritual to communicate with humans. As soon as Baʿl makes his request, Il complies and grants a blessing to Daniʾil. His blessing, the high point of the initial petition offering complex, involves a ritual gesture, an oath, and a descriptive blessing (1.17 I):

(34) [ks .]*yiḫd . il* . ⟨bdh	Il took [the cup] ⟨in his hand,
krpn . bm . ymn	the flagon in (his) right hand.
brkm . ybrk .⟩ *ʿbdh* .	He blessed his⟩ servant,
ybrk (35) [dni]*l . mt . rpi* .	he blessed [Daniʾi]l, the Rapiʾan,
ymr . ǵzr (36) [mt . h]*rnmy* .	he benefited[1] the hero, the Harnamiyyan.
npš . yḥ . dnil (37) [mt . rp]i .	"By my life, may Daniʾil, [the Rapiʾ]an, live,
brlt . ǵzr . mt hrnmy	by my soul,[2] the hero, the Harnamiyyan,
(38) [w? (.) r]ḥ? . *hw . mḫ* .[3]	[and(?) by] my(?) [bre]ath, (that) is my(?) vitality!
l ʿršh . yʿl (39) [w yšk]b .	He shall mount his bed [and lie do]wn,
bm . nšq . aṯth (40) [w hr].[4]	by kissing his wife [there will be conception],
b ḥbqh . ḥmḥmt	by embracing her there will be pregnancy,
(41) [xxxx]xt*n . ylt* .	[. . .] . . . the pregnant woman,
ḥmḥmt (42) [l mt . r]pi .	pregnancy [for the Ra]piʾan.
w ykn . bnh (43) [b bt]	Let there be a son [in (his) house],
[šrš] . *b qrb . hklh*	a scion in the midst of his palace."

(Il continues with the filial duties; see the discussion in chapter 2.)

1. See p. 39 n. 79, above, on the verb *mr(r)*.

2. On *brlt*, see B. Cutler and J. Macdonald, "An Akkadian Cognate to Ugaritic *brlt*," *UF* 5 (1973) 67–70.

3. See the discussion below for this difficult line.

4. Restoration based on 1.23:51 (followed by *CARTU* 103; cf. *UPA* 119).

The Cup

The text at the beginning is clearly defective. Homoioteleuton has occurred where the copyist's eyes skipped from *bdh* 'in his hand' to *ʿbdh* 'his servant'.[5] What was left out can be gathered from a similar blessing that Il gives Kirta: *ks . yiḫd .* [il . b] *yd . krpn . bm* [ym]n . *brkm . ybrk* [ʿbdh] . *ybrk . il . krt* [ṯʿ . ym]*rm . nʿm*[n .] *ǵlm . il* '[Il] took (his) cup [in] (his) hand, (his) flagon in (his) [right] hand. He blessed [his servant], Il blessed Kirta, [the magnificent, he bene]fited the grac[ious one], the lad of Il' (1.15 II 16–20). That the substance of this passage should be restored is supported by the larger context of Kirta's blessing, which is similar to the blessing of the Aqhat text. There, as in the Aqhat story, Baʿl asks Il to bless Kirta and his wife Hariy. Moreover, Kirta's blessing, which is quite long (1.15 II 21–III 16), also includes the prediction that Hariy will bear several children, which reminds the reader of Daniʾil's blessing, according to which he and his wife will conceive and bear a child.[6]

A few sculptures and drawings from the region of Ugarit may give an indication of what the blessing gesture involved. They show an individual, apparently Il, holding what seems to be a cup in one hand and holding up the other hand, apparently in blessing.[7] In a relief on a stele, the god holds a vessel[8] in the right hand and raises the left, with palm

5. D. Pardee argues for the full emendation ("An Emendation in the Ugaritic Aqht Text," *JNES* 36 [1977] 53–56); cf. Margalit, "Restorations," 82–84; *UPA* 281; *RTU* 260. Several suggest a more limited emendation of *ʿbdh* to . *bdh* (cf. Dijkstra and de Moor, "Problematical Passages," 177; J. J. Jackson and H. H. P. Dressler ("El and the Cup of Blessing," *JAOS* 95 [1975] 99–101); S. Loewenstamm, "The Wording of KTU 1.17 I 34," *UF* 12 [1980] 416; S. Parker, "Some Methodological Principles in Ugaritic Philology," *Maarav* 2 [1979] 19–22; *UNP* 53). A limited emendation is rejected by Dietrich and Loretz, "Bemerkungen," 70–71.

6. The gesture may also be restorable in 1.16 V 40–41: *ks* .[yiḫd . il . b yd] *kr*[pn . bm . ymn] (restoration followed by *CML* 100). This immediately precedes the commissioning of the healing genie Shaʿtaqat.

7. A. Caquot and M. Sznycer, *Ugaritic Religion* (Iconography of Religions 15/8; Leiden: Brill, 1980) plates 7 (= *ANEP* 493), 8 (= *ANEP* 826), 22. Cf. Dijkstra and de Moor, "Problematical Passages," 178 and n. 66; *ARTU* 205 n. 49. Cf. F. M. Cross, *Canaanite Myth and Hebrew Epic* (Cambridge: Harvard University Press, 1973) 35.

8. It is not clear if this is a cup or bowl. Others have interpreted it as a censer, scepter, offering gift, or flower. H. Niehr ("Ein umstrittenes Detail der El-Stele aus Ugarit," *UF* 24 [1992] 293–300) sees it as the Anatolian–North Syrian, W-shaped name symbol of the weather god, often found in seals in the hand of the god. The W-shape of the vessel in this stele, however, is quite different from the weather-god symbol. Moreover, the seals that Niehr adduces for comparison do not have the other hand of the deity held up, as found in the stele.

to the front and elbow against the body as "a gesture of welcome."[9] An approaching figure is making an offering.[10] A statuette of an old man (Il?), which may have had horns, holds a cup in the left hand, the right hand raised with the palm to the front, similar to the previously mentioned relief. A painting on a mug has what appears to be a banquet scene with Il, who holds a cup in his raised right hand (the disposition of the left hand is not clear). If these are connected with the gesture described in the Aqhat and Kirta texts, then the texts describe only part of the gesture. We have to imagine that the other hand is raised in blessing.[11]

Exactly what the raised cup signifies is not clear. It is not certain that it is to be connected with giving or receiving libations or with the presentation of wine, as might be suggested by Pughat's service of wine to Yaṭupan (1.19 IV 53-61). What the cup contains, how it got there, and what Il does with it are nowhere explained, nor does the parallel from the Kirta text help. However, the later feast, at which Anat covets Aqhat's bow, may contain a hint of the meaning of the cup raising (1.17 VI 15-16; see chapter 8 for discussion). When Anat's mind turns away from the feast and becomes set on acquiring the bow, she throws down her cup. This marks the point when that feast begins to sour. Hence, when the cup is raised in the blessing gesture, it may, by contrast, mean that the feast is agreeable to the god and that the human host is worthy of the god's good wishes. In other words, it is a kind of toast or salute, a symbolic nod denoting acceptance.

The Blessing

The description of what Il does after raising the cup follows Baʿl's request in 1.17 I 23-24 (see the text, above), just as Il follows Baʿl's request in the Kirta text (1.15 II 14-20): he 'blesses' (*brk*) and 'benefits' (*mrr*) the man. The introduction to the blessing is similar to the introduction to Pughat's blessing at the end of the story, in which Dani'il fortifies his daughter as she is about to exact vengeance for her brother's death. It is therefore language that humans as well as gods can use (1.19 IV):

9. Caquot and Sznycer, *Ugaritic Religion*, 23.

10. N. Wyatt ("The Stela of the Seated God from Ugarit," *UF* 15 [1983] 271-77) identifies the god as El and the approaching figure as the king. He argues that artistic convention forced the inscriber to have the god raise the left hand rather than the right. He compares the gesture to an identical one in Hindu iconography that means something like "Fear not!"

11. Margalit (*UPA* 281-82) apparently suggests that the rite involves a libation, the god standing and pouring it out while pronouncing a blessing. This cannot be verified for our text.

w yʿn . dn(36)*il* . *mt* . *rpi* .	Daniʾil, the Rapiʾan, answered:
npš . tḥ [.] pǵ[t] (37) ṯkmt . *mym* .	"By my life, may Pughat, who shoulders water, live,
ḥspt . *l šʿr* (38) ṭl .	who extracts dew from the fleece,
ydʿt [.] *hlk* . *kbkbm*[12]	who knows the course of the stars!
[w(?) (.)] (39) *npš* . *hy* . *mḫ* .	[And(?)] by my(?) life, (that) is my(?) vitality!

Both introductions begin with the oath formula: *npš* '(by) my life'.[13] This is followed by calling the person by name and wishing him or her life. The person's name is accompanied by epithets. By using the "full name" of the recipient, the poet clearly identifies him or her. In naming Daniʾil, Il adds another oath formula: *brlt* '(by) my soul'. This is lacking in the blessing of Pughat, probably because her epithet is more complex and therefore takes the second oath formula's place. After the naming of the individual to be blessed, a line follows that appears to be similarly formulated in both introductions (line 38 in Daniʾil's blessing; 38b–39 in Pughat's blessing). Since its meaning is not clear, some discussion is here required.

In this line the term *mḫ* appears with a preceding pronoun. The position of the line and the similarity of elements suggest that *mḫ* and *npš* are roughly synonymous.[14] Since in the blessing of Pughat the noun *npš* appears before the pronoun (*hy*), one expects the same term or at least a synonymous term to appear in the blessing of Daniʾil before the pronoun (*hw*). *CAT* reads a *-ḥ* or *-ṭ* before the pronoun in the latter case. It is possible that *-ḥ* should be read and taken as the last letter of *rḥ* 'wind'. This term appears in association with *npš* and *brlt* in the passage referring to Aqhat's death, 1.18 IV 24–25, 36–37; 1.19 II 38–39. In this case, the terms [r]ḥ and *npš* in the two blessings could figuratively refer to the person giving the blessing. The term *mḫ* 'marrow' could be taken in the extended sense of 'vitality' and also, in some way, refer to the being of the blesser. The difference in the gender of the pronouns (*hw, hy*) may be due, not to their referring to the different persons being blessed, but to their referring to the different nouns that precede them. *Npš* is clearly attested as feminine in the passages about the expiration of Aqhat, noted above. The gender of *rḥ* is not clear from Ugaritic texts. In Hebrew, *rûaḥ* is generally feminine but is attested as a masculine word. The cognate *rûḥ-* is found as both masculine and feminine in Arabic.[15]

12. So KTU, CTA. *CAT* has *kbkm*.

13. Dijkstra and de Moor, "Problematical Passages," 178.

14. Margalit's restorations, translations, and lineation of the two passages cannot be entirely accepted because the two passages are different from one another (*UPA* 118–19, 140, 145, 165).

15. *DMWA* 365.

With regard to what precedes [r]ḥ and *npš* in the two texts, there is room for one or two signs, according to *CAT.* It is likely that a preposition or conjunction should be read in this position and perhaps a post-conjunction word divider, especially in Dani'il's blessing. Restoring a conjunction allows the terms to be seen as bearing an unmarked first-person pronoun and thus recapitulating the *npš* = /*napšī*/ '(by) my life' that begins both blessings and recapitulating the *brlt* '(by) my soul' that appears in the blessing of Dani'il. Furthermore, the following *hw/hy mḫ* may serve to define the [r]ḥ and *npš* that precede in each case, '(By) my spirit/life, i.e., my vitality (*muḫḫī*)'.[16]

Taking an oath by one's *npš* raises the question whether a ritual gesture is involved. For example, some scholars have suggested that Yahweh's oath by his *nepeš* in Jer 51:14 and Amos 6:8 may be related to the Mari treaty gesture of *napištam lapātum* 'touching the throat'.[17] This gesture demonstrates the penalty that one is to suffer upon breaking the treaty. In this case, the word may best be translated 'throat', a meaning found for Hebrew *nepeš* (Judg 12:3; 1 Sam 28:21; Jonah 2:6; Pss 69:2, 124:4–5). Ugaritic *brlt* and *npš* both have the meaning 'appetite', which we will see in the feast given to Kothar-wa-Ḫasis (1.17 V 17–18, 23–24), and may refer more concretely to the esophageal-tracheal tract. The word [r]ḥ in line 38 of Il's blessing of Dani'il, if the restoration is correct, would be consistent with this, referring to one's breath. But while this understanding of *npš* in Ugaritic or Hebrew or *brlt* in Ugaritic is possible in oath contexts, it is not necessary. Oaths may be taken by the life of a god (compare Hebrew *ḥay yhwh* 'As Yahweh lives' in Judg 8:19; 1 Sam 14:39, 45; 19:6; 20:21; 25:34; 26:10, 16; 28:10) or by the life of the person to whom the oath is made (1 Sam 20:3; 25:26; 2 Sam 11:11), and thus *npš* in the Hebrew and Ugaritic oaths and *brlt* in the Ugaritic oath may simply refer to the life of the individual, without an accompanying gesture. The words are elliptical for a fuller expression indicating that the life is forfeit if the oath is not kept.[18]

16. Dijkstra and de Moor ("Problematical Passages," 178–79) read *arḥ hw/hy mḫ* 'May his/her way be successful', with *arḥ* as an inf. abs. and *mḫ* an adjective used as an adverb.

17. H. W. Wolff, *Joel and Amos* (Hermeneia; Philadelphia: Fortress, 1977) 281 and n. 8; S. Paul, *Amos* (Hermeneia; Minneapolis: Fortress, 1991) 213 n. 1. See CAD L 84–85, 201; A. Kilmer, "Symbolic Gestures in Akkadian Contracts from Alalakh and Ugarit," *JAOS* 94 (1974) 183.

18. Cf. *UPA* 282 n. 3. Note biblical expressions in which persons say they will suffer (1 Sam 3:17, 14:44, 20:13, 25:22; 2 Sam 3:9, 35; 1 Kgs 2:23, 19:2, 20:10; Ruth 1:17). It is doubtful if the terms *npš* and so forth should be understood simply as intensive reflexive pronouns referring to oneself and not one's life. The Israelite god swears by himself in Ezek 17:16, Zeph 2:9; note *bî nišbaʿtî*: Gen 22:16; Isa 45:23; Jer 22:5, 49:13; *nišbaʿtî bišmî haggādôl*: Jer 44:26.

The oath with its accompanying blessing is a promissory oath. This is a type of oath in which one takes on an obligation that must be fulfilled.[19] It is therefore to be distinguished from an assertatory oath, in which a person makes a declaration about a state of affairs, often in contexts of exculpation. A promissory oath is also distinguished from a vow. The latter is a *conditional* promissory oath, which depends upon the fulfillment of circumstances that are expressed at the time of making the oath.

A prime example of a vow in Ugaritic literature is Kirta's promise to give Athirat gifts *if* she helps him succeed in obtaining Hariy as a wife (1.14 IV):

ym[*ǵy* .] l *qdš* (35) *aṯ*rt [.] *ṣrm* .	He arr[ived] at the sanctuary of Athirat of Tyre,
w l ilt (36) *ṣdynm* .	and the goddess of Sidon.
ṯm (37) *ydr* [.] *krt* . *ṯʿ* (38) {*i*}*iṯṯ*[20] .	There Kirta the noble vowed a gift(?):
aṯrt . *ṣrm*	"O, Athirat of Tyre,
(39) *w ilt* . *ṣdynm*	and goddess of the Sidon,
(40) *hm*[21] . *ḫry* . *bty* (41) *iqḥ* .	if I take Hariy into my house,
ašʿrb . *ǵlmt* (42) *ḥẓry*	bring the maiden into my court,
ṯnh . *k'spm* (43) *atn* .	(then) I will give twice her (weight?) in silver,
w . *ṯlṯth* . *ḫrṣm*	and thrice her (weight?) in gold."

19. See J. Milgrom, *Numbers [Ba-midbar]: The Traditional Hebrew Text with the New JPS Translation, Commentary by Jacob Milgrom* (JPS Torah Commentary; Philadelphia: Jewish Publication Society, 1990) 488–90 on oaths and vows.

20. Here the first *i* is seen as resulting from dittography (so L. R. Fisher, "Literary Genres in the Ugaritic Texts," *Ras Shamra Parallels: The Texts from Ugarit and the Hebrew Bible, Vol. II* [ed. D. E. Smith and S. Rummel; AnOr 50; Rome: Pontifical Biblical Institute, 1975] 147; "Two Projects at Claremont," *UF* 3 [1971] 27; Parker, "The Vow in Ugaritic and Israelite Narrative Literature," *UF* 11 [1979] 694–95 n. 8; T. W. Cartledge, *Vows in the Hebrew Bible and the Ancient Near East* [JSOTSup 147; Sheffield: JSOT Press, 1992] 109–10 n. 3). Some have read *iṯṯ* as an inflected particle of existence, with the {*i*} before it as a particle of emphasis: "As surely as Athirat of Tyre exists, yes, the goddess of Sidon" (so M. Dietrich and O. Loretz,"Ugaritisch *iṯ, ṯyndr* und hebräisch *ʾšh, šy* [KTU 1.14 IV 38; 2.13:14–15; 2.30:12–14a]," *UF* 26 [1994] 63–72; *ARTU* 200; cf. J. C. de Moor, "Frustula ugaritica," *JNES* 24 [1965] 357–58; see Cartledge, *Vows*, 109 n. 3 for others who interpret similarly). If this is correct, the human is effectively making the vow by the life of the god. The word *iṯṯ* meaning 'gift' (G. R. Driver, "Ugaritic and Hebrew Words," Ug. 6 181–84; J. Hoftijzer, "Das sogenannte Feueropfer," *Hebräische Wortforschung: Festschrift zum 80. Geburtstag von Walter Baumgartner* [VTSup 16; Leiden: Brill, 1967] 132–34; to which biblical *ʾiššeh* is presumably cognate) may appear in 2.13:14–15 and 2.30:13–14 in proximity to the term *ndr* (cf. Pardee, "The Preposition in Ugaritic [II]," 256; but contrast *TO* 1 323).

21. For this particle in oaths, see 1.22 II 16 *ydr* . *hm* 'He vowed: "If . . ." '.

The form of this vow is similar to biblical vows, especially Hannah's in 1 Sam 1:11, "she made a vow and said: '[*invocation*:] Yahweh of hosts, [*protasis*:] if you will be cognizant of the affliction of your maid-servant and remember me, not forgetting your maid-servant, and give to your maid-servant a male child, [*apodosis*:] then I will give him to Yahweh all the days of his life, and a razor shall not come upon his head.'"[22]

The content of Kirta's vow also correlates with the content of Hannah's: both are interested in securing or building up a family. According to Simon Parker's study of vows in the Bible and Ugaritic texts, this is one of the three main reasons that vows are taken, the other two being to secure military victory and to ensure a safe return from abroad.[23] Since vows are a means of invoking blessing, it is not unusual that Il's oath-blessing of Dani'il and his blessing of Kirta, as noted above, are also concerned with building families. Even Dani'il's oath-blessing of Pughat may be seen as reflecting the same general concern by its seeking to aid in avenging the loss of a family member.

Vows and Dani'il's Initial Offering and Blessing

While we are inspecting vows, it is worth looking at an example in an actual ritual text that casts some light on the nature of Dani'il's initial offering. The vow pertains to the category of military victory. It specifically defends against enemy attack of Ugarit (1.119):[24]

(26) *k gr ʿz* . *ṯǵrkm* .	When a strong (enemy) attacks your gates,
q*rd* (27) *ḥmytkm* .	a warrior, your walls,
ʿn*km* . *l* . bʿ*l tšun*	lift your eyes to Baʿl (and say):
(28) *y b*ʿl*m* . [a]l [.] t*dy* ʿ*z l ṯǵrn*	"O Baʿl, dispel the strong (enemy) from our gates,
(29) *y* . *qrd* [l] ḥ*mytny* .	the warrior [from] our walls.
ibr y (30) *b*ʿ*l* . *nš*q*dš* .	We will consecrate a bull, O Baʿl,
*m*ḏ*r*[25] *b*ʿ*l* (31) *nmlu* .	we shall fulfill a vow(?) to Baʿl.
d*kr b*ʿl . *n*š[q]dš	We shall con[se]crate a male to Baʿl,
(32) *ḥ*tp *b*ʿl [.] n*mlu* .	we shall fulfill a *ḥtp*-offering to Baʿl,

22. Fisher, "Literary Genres," 151; Parker, "Vow," 693–94.

23. Ibid., 699 (cf. p. 695).

24. Cf. *ARTU* 171–74; Xella, *I Testi rituali*, 25–34; P. D. Miller, "Prayer and Sacrifice in Ugarit and Israel," in *Text and Context: Old Testament and Semitic Studies for F. C. Fensham* (ed. W. Classen; JSOTSup 48; Sheffield: JSOT Press, 1988) 139–55.

25. On the phonological problems with this word, see Cartledge, *Vows*, 118–19 n. 3. If the word does not mean 'vow', the context of the prayer still shows that, conceptually, a vow is being made.

ʿšrt . bʿl . n[ʿ](33)šr .	we shall p[a]y a tenth (or: hold a feast) to Baʿl.
qdš bʿl . nʿl .	We shall ascend Baʿl's sanctuary,
*ntbt b*t [. bʿl] (34) *ntlk .*	we shall walk in the paths of [Baʿl's] temple."
*w šm*ʿ [. b]ʿl . *l .* ṣlt[km]	[Ba]ʿl will hear [your] prayer;
(35) *ydy . ʿz . l ṯǵrk*m [.]	he will expel the strong (enemy) from your gates,
[qrd] (36) *l ḥmytk*m [ ]	[the warrior] from your walls.

This vow promises the performance of *seven* cultic activities, five pertaining to offerings and two pertaining to visitation of Baʿl's temple (lines 29b–34a). This reminds the reader of the offerings in the *dbḥ ẓlm* 'sacrifice for the shades' in 1.161.[26] This text presents a list of seven deceased kings (*ulkn, trmn, sdn, rdn, ṯr ʿllmn, ʿmṯtmr, nqmd*), the first five of whom appear to be included in the term *rpum qdmym* 'the ancient *rpum*', and all of whom appear to be included in the term *rpi arṣ* 'the underworld *rpum*' and *qbṣ ddn* 'the assembly of Ditan'.[27] The ritual in the text may be

26. Cf. P. Bordreuil and D. Pardee, "Le rituel funéraire ougaritique RS. 34.129 [= KTU 1.161]," *Syria* 59 (1982) 121–28; Pardee, "*Marziḥu*," 274–75; J. F. Healey, "Ritual Text KTU 1.161: Translation and Notes," *UF* 10 (1978) 83–88; J. W. Wesselius, "Three Difficult Passages in Ugaritic Literary Texts," *UF* 15 (1983) 312–14; Schmidt, *Israel's Beneficent Dead*, 100–122; W. Pitard, "The Ugaritic Funerary Text RS 34.126," *BASOR* 232 (1978) 65–75.

27. In Ugaritic texts, *rpum* is generally a term for the dead and perhaps specifically for deceased royalty. The same terms that we find for the seven deceased kings in 1.161 appear in Kirta's blessing of paternity: *mid* . rm . [krt] *b tk . rpi .* ar[ṣ] *b pḫr . qbṣ . d*tn 'Kirta shall be greatly exalted among the *rpum* of the underworld, among the council of the Ditan's assembly' (1.15 III 13–15; restorations from 2–4). Being a king, for whom there are expectations of continuing life (see 1.16 II), he will be exalted among the royal dead. According to one (broken and difficult) hymn/incantation (1.108:20–27), a *king* derives strength, protection, power, authority, and splendor from the *rpu mlk ʿlm* (referring to a single god) and the *rpu arṣ* (apparently a supernatural plurality). In 1.6 VI 45–49 we read: *špš rpim . tḥtk špš . tḥtk ilnym ʿdk . ilm . hn . mtm ʿdk* 'Shapash, the *rpum* are under you, / Shapash, the *ilnym*-beings are under you, / toward you (come?) the supernatural ones, / yes, the dead (?) toward you'. Here the *rpum* are in a context with the deceased. The theme of kingship is not immediately present, but Mot does appear a few lines earlier to say: *bʿl* [.] yṯṯbn [. l ksi] *mlkh .* ln[ḫt . lkḫṯ] drkth 'Let Baʿl sit on his royal throne, on the cushion of the seat of his dominion' (lines 33–35). The so-called *rpum*-texts (1.20–22) may suggest that the individuals are alive, since they travel on chariots, apparently horizontally rather than vertically, something one might not expect from the dead (1.20 II 1–6; 22 II 22–24; cf. 21 II 3–5, 11–12; for the general difficulties of these texts, see W. Pitard, "A New Edition of the 'Rāpiʾûma' Texts: KTU 1.20–22," *BASOR* 285 [1992] 33–77). At the same time, they are defined by the parallel term *ilnym* 'divine/supernatural beings', once perhaps by the term *qd*[*mym*] 'the ancients' (1.20 II 10; cf. *rpim qdmym* in 1.161:8), and the protagonist (Daniʾil?) may even make a vow to them (1.22 II 16–20). These points indicate that they are supernatural

connected with the recent death of *nqmd*. At the end of the text, seven offerings are made, perhaps to the seven former kings (lines 27–30). These offerings have a goal similar to the vow in 1.119: the goal of the vow is the *šlm* 'well-being' of the (new) king Ammurapi, the queen, the royal family, and Ugarit, similar to the concept of this offering, though *šlm* is not mentioned.

The sevenfold offerings or cultic actions in these two rituals that bring well-being recall the six-plus-one-day offering performed by Dani'il. They are apparently performed to solve relatively serious and pressing problems. They thus provide a gauge against which the gravity of Dani'il's offering can be measured. (See the discussion on the initial offering, in chapter 1.)

---

beings. A royal context may be involved here too since, in the passage that appears to involve a vow, royal themes may be present (ym[ ] may be restored ym[lk] in 1.22 II 16; more clearly, *nḫ!t kḥṯ* dr[kt] in line 18 suggests royalty). Concern about supernatural deceased royalty is found in the list (a ritual?) 1.113 rev. (though here they are not called *rpum*). The Bible reflects the tradition of the term's being applied to the royal dead in Isa 14:9, though the term seems democratized to refer to the ghosts of all (Isa 26:14, 19; Ps 88:11; Prov 2:18; 9:18; 21:16; so also Phoenician and Late Punic texts *KAI* nos. 13, 14, and 117). The term *rpu*, in Dani'il's epithet *mt rpi*, in the divine epithet *rpu mlk ʿlm* (see above), and perhaps also in 1.166:13, *rpi . yqr* [ ], may be a divine name and not directly connected to the terms *rpum* and *rpu arṣ* (for example, it is not clear if this singular entity is the head of the *rpum*), though it is not clear if this is a high god (for example, Baʿl or Il) or a lesser deity. The patronage of Baʿl otherwise in the Aqhat story may suggest that it is Baʿl. The biblical *rĕpā'îm*, referring to the inhabitants of East Jordan and to giants, may also go back to the divine name *rp'*. For arguments along this line, see J. N. Ford, "The 'Living Rephaim' of Ugarit: Quick or Defunct?" *UF* 24 (1992) 73–101; *UPA* 251–60; G. C. Heider, *The Cult of Molek: A Reassessment* (JSOTSup 43; Sheffield: JSOT Press, 1985) 113–49; van der Toorn, *Family Religion*, 160, 170–71. See also A. Caquot, "Les Rephaim ougartiques," *Syria* 36 (1959) 90–101; A. Cooper, "*mlk ʿlm*: 'Eternal King' or 'King of Eternity'?" in *Love and Death in the Ancient Near East: Essays in Honor of Marvin H. Pope* (ed. J. H. Marks and R. M. Good; Guildord, Conn.: Four Quarters, 1987) 1–7; M. Dietrich and O. Loretz, "Rāpi'u und Milku aus Ugarit: Neuere historisch-geographische Thesen zu *rpu mlk ʿlm* (KTU 1.108: 1) und *mt rpi* (KTU 1.17 i 1)," *UF* 21 (1989) 123–31; idem, "Baal *rpu* in KTU 1.108; 1.113 und nach 1.17 VI 25–33," *UF* 12 (1980) 171–82; M. Dietrich, O. Loretz and J. Sanmartín, "Die ugartisichen Totengeister *RPU(M)* und die biblischen Rephaim," *UF* 8 (1976) 45–52; Dijkstra, "Legend of Danel," 35–52; Dijkstra and de Moor, "Problematical Passages," 172; Healey, "The Ugaritic Dead: Some Live Issues," *UF* 18 (1986) 27–32; W. J. Horwitz, "The Significance of the Rephaim," *JNSL* 7 (1979) 37–43; A. S. Kapelrud, "The Ugaritic Text RS 24.252 and King David," *JNSL* 3 (1974) 35–39; C. E. L'Heureux, "The *yᵉlîdê hārāpā'*: A Cultic Association of Warriors," *BASOR* 221 (1976) 83–85; idem, *Rank among the Canaanite Gods: El, Baʿal, and the Repha'im* (HSM 21; Missoula, Mont.: Scholars Press, 1979) 111–223; del Olmo Lete, *Canaanite Religion*, 166–212; S. B. Parker, "The Ugaritic Deity Rāpiu," *UF* 2 (1972) 97–104; idem, "Feast of Rapiu"; W. Pitard in *HUS* 263–69; Pope, "Notes on the Rephaim Texts"; Schmidt, *Israel's Beneficent Dead*, 71–100.

Dani'il's offering gains further significance by its contrasts with the foregoing Ugaritic vows. Given the fact that vows can be made for securing blessings pertaining to family, Dani'il could easily have made a vow. This might have been the easier route because, if the gods did not grant his request, he would not have expended his means in vain. (Of course he might have created more trouble for himself, as Kirta did, by not fulfilling the vow after he received the blessing!) Dani'il presented his offering first, however, thus laying himself open to loss through the gods' rejection. In this way, Dani'il's performance appears more devout. It is a sign of his trust as well as his need. Il responds with equal determination by formulating the blessing in the context of an oath, which assures the promise. This oath with attending blessing, then, can be viewed as the specific high point of the initial offering.

The Narrative Context

Besides forming the climax of the initial offering, and besides providing the promise that will be fulfilled but then fails because of what follows, the oath-blessing relates to the larger context of the story in other ways. For example, Il might have simply pronounced the blessing found in lines 42b–43b: "Let there be a son [in (his) house], a scion in the midst of his palace." However, he provides a "prophetic" narrative leading up to this, giving the cause for the effect. He says that Dani'il will mount the bed and lie down, euphemistic metonyms for sexual intercourse.[28] He describes the sexual act further by mentioning Dani'il's and his wife's kissing and embracing. He notes that *ḥmḥmt* will take place, perhaps referring to pregnancy or perhaps more specifically referring to the "heat" of orgasm.[29]

This description provides information that the narrative does not give later on. When Dani'il goes home after his successful entreaty of the gods, the story does not tell how Aqhat is conceived. The Kotharat, birth and conception goddesses, visit Dani'il and receive a six-day feast from him. Then, immediately after their departure, Danatay's months of pregnancy are counted off (1.17 II 43–47). Nothing is said about Dani'il's and

28. Cf. Dijkstra and de Moor, "Problematical Passages," 179. On such euphemistic metonyms, see my "David autem Remansit in Hierusalem: Felix Coniunctio!" in *Pomegranates and Golden Bells: Studies in Biblical, Jewish, and Near Eastern Ritual, Law, and Literature in Honor of Jacob Milgrom* (ed. D. P. Wright, D. N. Freedman, and A. Hurvitz; Winona Lake, Ind.: Eisenbrauns, 1995) 221–22 n. 22.

29. So Dijkstra and de Moor, "Passages," 179; *ARTU* 229 n. 41. Margalit (*UPA* 282) says that Il includes this information because he enjoys the erotic (see 1.4 IV 38–39; 1.23:32–35). For the word as a noun, see *DLU* 177. *GUL* 176 takes *ḥmḥmt* as a verb 'she became sexually aroused'.

Danatay's coming together. Il's blessing therefore provides the conception scene in advance, which is to be understood as occurring around the time of the Kotharat's visit.

The blessing also anticipates a small but significant element in the feast during which Anat seeks possession of Aqhat's bow. As indicated above, the main part of the blessing follows the introductory oath. Nevertheless, the oath itself contains a brief and general statement of blessing. This is the wish that Daniʾil live (*yḥ* 'may he live'; 1.17 I 36). This probably does not have specific reference to having children,[30] since Pughat's blessing contains the same element in the same point in its oath structure (*tḥ* 'may she live'; 1.19 IV 36). This must instead be seen as an expression of a hope of general well-being and prosperity for the individual. Anat offers Aqhat a blessing of well-being of the highest order—eternal life (1.17 VI 25-33). Aqhat, being smart or foolish—it is hard to tell—rejects it as an unfulfillable offer. Aqhat thus, symbolically speaking, rejects the very promise that Il makes to Daniʾil. Moreover, the life promised to Daniʾil would have been fulfilled through the life of the son. Aqhat's death, however, annuls this promise to Daniʾil.

30. Contrast *UPA* 282.

Chapter 4
The Offering to the Kotharat

As soon as Daniʾil recites the duties that the promised son will perform, he goes home (1.17 II 24–25). Immediately after he arrives, the Kotharat come. Daniʾil gives them a meal that is in many respects similar to the meal he gave the gods during his petition offering. By means of this similarity, the second feast emphasizes many of the characteristics of the initial offering. However, the meal presented to the Kotharat also exhibits notable differences. These provide nuances to the development and flavor of the story.

Comparison to the Initial Offering

The passage is relatively straightforward, with few problems (1.17 II):

(26) *ʿrb . b bth . kṯrt .*	The Kotharat[1] entered his house,
bnt (27) *hll . snnt .*	the daughters of the Moon Crescent,[2] the Swallows.[3]
apnk . dnil (28) *mt . rpi .*	So Daniʾil, the Rapiʾan,
ap{.}*hn . ǵzr . mt* (29) *hrnmy .*	then, the hero, the Harnamiyyan,
alp . yṭbḫ . lkṯ(30)*rt .*	slaughtered an ox for the Kotharat.
yšlḥm . kṯrt . w y(31)*ššq .*	He fed the Kotharat and gave drink,
bnt . hll *. snnt*	to the daughters of the Moon Crescent, the Swallows.
(32) *hn . ym . wṯn*	Yes, for one day and a second (day),
yšlḥm (33) *kṯrt . w . yššq .*	he fed the Kotharat and gave drink,
bnt . hl[l] (34) *snnt .*	to the daughters of the Moon Crescent, the Swallows.

1. On the questionable vocalization of the name, see Huehnergard, *Vocabulary*, 141.

2. Arab. *hilāl* 'new moon, crescent' (compare Heb. *hêlel*, Isa 14:12). He is *bʿl gml* (1.24:42), the latter term possibly referring to a star or constellation (CAD G 35b) or to "curvature" (see *UPA* 286 n. 4). Some have unconvincingly connected *hll* with terms dealing with praise (compare Heb. *hillēl* and see Gordon, *Ugaritic Textbook*, #769).

3. Compare Akk. *sinuntu*; Rabbinic Heb. *sĕnûnît*; Arab. *sunūnū*; Margalit (*UPA* 286 n. 5) connects *snnt* with Arab. *sny* 'shine, gleam' and Jewish Aram. *snn* 'refine (metal); glitter' and translates 'radiant ones'.

t̲lt̲ . rb*ʿ ym* .	For a third, a fourth day,
yšl(35)*ḥm* . *kt̲rt* . w yššq	he fed the Kotharat and gave drink,
(36) *bnt* . *hll* . sn*nt*.	to the daughters of the Moon Crescent, the Swallows.
ḫmš (37) *t̲dt̲* . ym.	For a fifth, a sixth day,
yšlḥm . kt̲*rt* (38) *w yš*šq .	he fed the Kotharat and gave drink,
b*nt* . *hll* . snnt	to the daughters of the Moon Crescent, the Swallows.
(39) *mk* . b šbʿ . *ymm* .	Then on the seventh day,
tbʿ . *b bth* (40′) *kt̲*rt .	the Kotharat departed from his house,
b*nt* . hl*l* . *snnt*	the daughters of the Moon Crescent, the Swallows,
(41) m*ddt* . nʿ*my* .ʿ*r*š . hrt	the beloved ones[4] of conception bed pleasure(?),
(42) y*smsmt* .ʿrš . ḫllt[5]	the graceful ones[6] of the labor(?) bed.

The similarities between this feast and the first feast involve various structural and contextual matters. (1) The descriptions of the offerings themselves begin with *aphnk* and *aphn* clauses, introducing Daniʾil with his epithets (I 1–2, partially restored; II 27–29). (2) Both have a general statement about making offerings to the gods (I 2b–3a; II 29b–31), followed by a six-day itemization (I 5b–13a; II 32–38). (3) The six-day itemization is broken down into pairs of days, with statements about feeding and giving drink to the gods. (4) Both end in an event other than an offering occurring on the seventh day (I 15b–16; II 39–42). (5) Daniʾil performs both rites.

While there are differences between the two, mainly in the second feast's being less elaborate and not having further engagement with the gods on the seventh day (see also below), the second can be seen as an echo or reflection of the first. It therefore has the effect of carrying forward some of the impressions gained by the reader about Daniʾil from the description of the first offering. It confirms Daniʾil's piety and devotion. It shows that he is fully knowledgeable in the etiquette of approaching and interacting with divine beings. It also affirms his subordination to the gods by his giving them offerings, especially since this is a group of gods different from those explicitly mentioned in the first offering. He

4. Arab. *wadda* 'love, like'; Heb. *yādîd* 'beloved' and compare PN *mêdad* (see *UPA* 147; *MLC* 373, 'amigas'). De Moor differs, rendering 'those who measure' (*ARTU* 232; root *mdd*).

5. De Moor and Spronk (*CARTU* 104) and Gibson (*CML* 106) read ḫlln but take it to mean 'childbirth'. Margalit (*UPA* 121) reads ḫ*ld*(?)n and divides the line differently.

6. Compare Arab. *wasīm* 'graceful, pretty'; *wasāmat* 'grace, beauty'.

fears not only the high gods but also lesser deities. The second feast, furthermore, recapitulates the paradigm for making proper offerings set down in the first.

While this offering is independent of the first, both appear to bracket the revelation of Baˁl and Il and the accompanying promise of a son. This structure sets the revelation and promise off in relief and highlights them.

The Purpose of the Offering

The second offering is similar to the initial offering, but it also proceeds in new directions. A major difference is mood. The first feast is marked by introspection, loneliness, melancholy, deficiency, and uncertainty. Only after the offering is performed, when Il decides to bless Daniʾil and Daniʾil receives word, does the spirit change to one of hope, prosperity, and confidence. Daniʾil's joy is explicit, if somewhat formulaic (see 1.6 III 14–16), in the description after the revelation: *b* d!*ni*l *pnm . tšmḫ . w ˁl . yṣhl* pit *yprq . lṣb . w yṣḥq* 'Daniʾil's face showed joy, (his) brow above glowed, he parted his mouth and laughed' (1.17 II 8–10). The feast for the Kotharat presupposes and builds on these later attitudes. Thus, though this rite echoes the first rite structurally, it does so in a major rather than a minor or diminished key.

Though the rite has a positive mood, its specific meaning is not clear. In the flow of the context, one imagines that it is in part a means of thanking the high gods for their blessing. That is to say, any offering given in a positive spirit coming after the gods' generous blessing would be felt to be a display of gratitude. The fact that this feast involves deities other than Il and Baˁl, however, is evidence that the gratitude shown must be a background feature.

More evident is the motive of hospitality. Daniʾil is at home and the Kotharat are visitors. As soon as they come, Daniʾil prepares the ox. In this respect the offering is similar to the feast given to Kothar-wa-Ḫasis and is somewhat similar to biblical hospitality meals, such as the one in Genesis 18 (for a discussion of these occasions, see chapter 5).

The primary meaning of the feast becomes clear when the character and function of the Kotharat are understood. The Aqhat text here, as well as the myth-hymn 1.24 (Yariḫ's marriage to Nikkal-wa-ʾIb), provide the primary information about these beings. They are called goddesses (*ilht*; 1.24:11, 40). Genealogically speaking, they are the daughters of *hll*, the moon crescent.[7] They are expressly connected with conception and

7. 1.17 II 26–27, 31, 33, 36, 38, 40; 1.24:6, 15, 40–41.

childbirth.[8] At the end of the Aqhat passage they are called 'the beloved ones of conception bed pleasure' (m*d*d*t* . nʿ*my* . ʿ*rš* . hrt, line 41) and, if the reading and interpretation is correct, the 'graceful ones of the labor bed' (*ysmsmt* . ʿrš . ḫllt, line 42). In 1.24 they are associated with Yariḫ's love-making to Nikkal-wa-ʾIb and her giving birth (lines 4–7, 11, 15). This appears to be the talent that is indicated by their name *kōṯarāt*, which means something like 'skilled-ones'.[9] A hymn to the Kotharat at the end of the text may even list their names, seven in total (1.24:47–50).[10] This may be seen as corresponding poetically with the seven-day regimen of offerings in the Aqhat text. The foregoing evidence regarding the function of the Kotharat indicates that the primary purpose of the feast is to secure the blessing of these goddesses in the conception, gestation, and birth of the promised son. This provides extra insurance for the divine promise that Daniʾil had already received.[11]

This purpose is confirmed by the context. Immediately after the Kotharat leave, pregnancy begins and, in terms of literary space, is quickly brought to term (1.17 II):

(43) *yṯb* . d*n*il . [ys]p*r* . yrḫh	Daniʾil sat down, he counted her months:
(44) *yr*ḫ . *yr*ḫ . ṯn [.] yṣi	One month, a second month passed(?),
(45) *ṯl*ṯ . rbʿ[. y]r[ḫ . ʿš]r	a third, a fourth [month. The ten]th[12]

8. Margalit (*UPA* 285) notes that a multilingual text (he gives no reference) defines them as *šassūru* 'midwife'. He is certainly correct in seeing this as an approximation, because, as he says, they "are involved not only in the delivery stage but also—perhaps even primarily—in the earliest phases of the reproductive process." He also notes (p. 286) that the lunar connection may link them with the menstrual cycle. On the Kotharat, see J. F. Healey, "The 'Pantheon' of Ugarit: Further Notes," *SEL* 5 (1988) 103–11, 107–8; B. Margalit, "The *Kôšārôt/kṯrt*: Patroness-Saints of Women," *JANES* 4 (1972) 53–61; idem, "Of Brides and Birds: A Reply to M. Lichtenstein," *JANES* 4 (1972) 113–17; M. H. Lichtenstein, "Psalm 68:7 Revisited," *JANES* 4 (1972) 97–111; A. van Selms, "The Root *k-ṯ-r* and Its Derivatives in Ugaritic Literature," *UF* 11 (1979) 743–44.

9. *UPA* 286. Also possible is connecting their name with Arab. *kaṯa/ura* 'to exceed in number; be numerous', perhaps referring to their reproductive role. For another derivation, see van Selms, "The Root *k-ṯ-r*."

10. See *ARTU* 145 and *MLC* 461. Margalit (*UPA* 285 n. 2) reads only five names, taking *ṯlḫh* . *wmlghy* (!) as *ṯlḫh*⟨n⟩ . *wmlgh*⟨n⟩. 'bridal gifts and trousseau'. Gibson (*CML* 129) does not take the terms to be names.

11. The term *kôšārôt* in Ps 68:7, which cannot be said to refer to these deities, nevertheless may have the meaning 'fruitfulness' in contrast to *ṣĕḥîḥâ* 'barrenness' in the next line (so H.-J. Kraus, *Psalms 60–150* [Continental; Minneapolis: Augsburg, 1989] 46 note j).

12. Compare this counting of months of pregnancy with culmination in the tenth month in Atrahasis I 278–80 and the Appu tale (Siegelová, *Appu-Märchen*, 10–11). (See also the texts noted by D. T. Tsumura, "A Problem of Myth and Ritual Relationship: CTA 23 (UT 52):56–57 Reconsidered," *UF* 10 [1978] 392, though it is doubtful KTU

(46) *yrḫm* . ymǵy[xxxx]	month arrived [. . .]
(47) rḥm . . .	womb . . .

As noted above in the discussion of the blessing by Il (chapter 3), the text does not mention the conception of Aqhat in the narrative. This is only anticipated in Il's blessing. The visit of the Kotharat can be seen as a metonymical means of signaling that conception occurs at approximately this point in the narrative. The ritual description thus signifies more than simply recounting that a meal took place.

Though from the beginning of the pericope it would have been clear to a native audience who the Kotharat were and why they were present, the text delays revealing their epithets as the "beloved ones of conception bed pleasure, the graceful ones of the labor bed" until the end of the scene.[13] Detailing this information at the end thus creates a small climax, similar to the more elaborate intensifying structure in the initial feast. One of the reasons that this climax is not as impressive is that none of the characters speaks, as Baʿl did in response to Daniʾil's petition offering. Furthermore, the Kotharat depart on the seventh day; they do not have any interaction with Daniʾil or his wife. Keeping the feast's development to a minimum allows Danatay's pregnancy and the birth of Aqhat (which is missing but surely must have been told) to appear more prominent, as the culmination of the chain of events of which the feast is part.

The mood of this feast is different, an indication that, while Daniʾil is still subordinate to the gods, his relationship to them has changed. A physical sign of this change in the relationship is the place of the feast. It takes place not in a temple but in Daniʾil's home. Moreover, Daniʾil is not the initiator of the situation.[14] He does not go to the gods as he did before; the gods come to him. The causal relationship of the feasts to the gods is different as well: in the first example, the offering leads to the gods' action; in the second, the gods' action leads to the offering. This

1.23:56–57 should be read as he suggests [see p. 387 and contrast the reading of *CAT*].) On counting months for pregnancy, see Job 39:2. The ten-month formula and the context make it unlikely that Aqhat has already been born at this point of the story, despite the argument of Husser, "Birth of a Hero," 89–93 (cf. *RTU* 266 n. 69).

13. Margalit (*UPA* 285) notes that "even the ancient reader, no doubt better informed than we, is kept in the dark with respect to the manner of their activity during their week-long visit." See W. G. E. Watson, "Delaying Devices in Ugaritic Verse" (*SEL* 5 [1988] 207–18) for other cases in which the narrative holds back information until the end of a passage.

14. There is no reason to think that the lines missing between the end of column I and the beginning of column II contained any information about the visit of the Kotharat. See above.

marks how Daniʾil's position has changed. To use a "container" metaphor, in the first feast Daniʾil is on the *outside*: away from home and searching. In the second feast he is on the *inside*: at home and nearly fulfilled. The play between inside and outside will be of importance later in examining the rites Daniʾil undertakes in response to Aqhat's death. Those rites display an alternation between performances at home and performances abroad. The rites performed abroad show intensity while the ones at home tend to exhibit, from a relative point of view, more calm.

In sum, though the feast of the Kotharat has certain thematic and structural ties with the first feast and reinforces the effect of the first feast, it consolidates what has been achieved and puts the story on a new footing. Expectations that Daniʾil will have a fruitful family life are raised beyond those created by the first feast. That the Kotharat come to his home and that their feast is partially the result of hospitality indicate that Daniʾil's household is indeed prospering.[15]

15. If the Kotharat's epithet *snnt* means 'swallows', they may be contrasted with the *nšrm* 'vultures' that appear later in the story and are involved in Aqhat's death.

Chapter 5

The Meal for Kothar-wa-Ḫasis

After a break of 150 to 160 lines, including the total absence of columns III and IV, the text picks up again with the gift to Daniʾil of a bow and arrows,[1] apparently made by the Ugaritic Hephaistus, Kothar-wa-Ḫasis.[2] What happens in the break between Daniʾil's counting the months of his wife's pregnancy and the appearance of Kothar-wa-Ḫasis can only be surmised. The beginning of the break surely contained the conclusion of the description of the pregnancy and a description of the birth of Aqhat. The end of the break must have included a description of the construction of the bow, perhaps in some detail, similar to Aqhat's instructions to Anat about how to make a bow and arrows (1.17 VI 20–25). In addition to these items of relative certainty, the break may have also contained some words about the childhood and early youth of Aqhat. Columns V and VI already present him as a youth who seems capable of hunting and who is certainly capable of putting up a defense before a deity. The break may have also established a rationale for making the bow and arrows.

In addition to these rather mundane matters, the missing text may also have told of certain ritual activities–for instance, rites accompanying childbirth. Moreover, the gift of the bow may have been due to an obligation placed on the gods, created perhaps through a ritual performance described in the lost portion. In addition to these possibilities, ritual activity may have appeared just before the text picks up again in column V. The text has someone, apparently Kothar-wa-Ḫasis, say, a*bl* . *qš*t [.] xmn[x] *ašrbʿ* . *qṣʿt* 'I will transport the eight-part bow, I will bring[3]

1. For the arrows, see n. 4 (p. 88) below.

2. On Kothar-wa-Ḫasis's construction activities, see W. F. Albright, "The Furniture of El in Canaanite Mythology," *BASOR* 91 (1943) 39–44; T. H. Gaster, "The Furniture of El in Canaanite Mythology," *BASOR* 93 (1944) 20–23; M. Dietrich and O. Loretz, "Die sieben Kunstwerke des Schmiedegottes in KTU 1.4 I 23–43," *UF* 10 (1978) 57–63; E. Lipiński, "Ea, Kothar et El," *UF* 20 (1988) 137–43; Ashley, *Epic*, 319–24. As a maker of clubs for Baʿl, see 1.2 IV 11.

3. Margalit (*UPA* 290) suggests that *ašrbʿ* is cognate with Heb. *hirbîaʿ* 'to make lie down' and refers to the construction of the composite bow, made by imposing one layer on another. This interpretation requires him to take *abl* as 'I shall fashion'. In the context, a statement that the bow is being fashioned seems too late. Furthermore, *qṣʿt*,

four arrows' (17 V 2–3).[4] After this, on the seventh day, the god brings the bow (see the text below). There must have been a six-day description prior to this, which may have involved some ritual activity.[5]

---

the object of *ašrbʿ*, seems to refer to arrows, not a bow (see n. 4 below). Therefore, I construe *ašrbʿ* according to the generally accepted sense of the parallel term *abl* 'I shall bring' (see Gordon, *Ugaritic Textbook*, #2303). It is doubtful that *ašrbʿ* has a numerical sense, such as 'I will take/have four arrows' (*MLC* 622; *ARTU* 234).

4. The meaning of *qṣʿt* is disputed: some see it as a term for the bow or a part thereof; others take it as meaning 'arrows' (see Ashley, *Epic*, 62–64). Margalit (*UPA* 304; cf. his "Lexicographical Notes on the Aqht Epic [Part I: KTU 1.17–18]," *UF* 15 [1983] 78–79) observes that arrows do not seem to require the special craftsmanship of Kothar-wa-Ḫasis. Thus *qṣʿt* may be another word for bow. Gordon, too, says that 'arrows' as a b-word in a word pair is somewhat anticlimactic; thus a word for 'bow' fits better (*Ugaritic Textbook*, #2258). Nevertheless, one expects a gift of a bow to be accompanied by arrows (1.17 V 13). Furthermore, in 1.10 II 6–7, Baʿl/Hadd is described as being on the road with archer's equipment: *qšthn . aḫd . b ydh w qṣʿth . bm . ymnh* 'He has taken his bow in his hand, / and his *qṣʿt* in his right hand'. (Y. Sukenik, "The Composite Bow of the Canaanite Goddess Anath," *BASOR* 107 [1947] 15, notes Ezek 39:3, "And I will strike your bow out of your left hand and make your arrows fall from your right hand.") Though *ymn* is a normal parallelistic match for *yd*, its literal significance should not be ignored. Most humans are right handed and would therefore hold a bow in the left hand and draw the string with the right. They would probably have held the bow the same way while traveling, in order to be ready to shoot: the bow would be in the left hand and the arrows in the right. This posture is attested in picture and models throughout the ancient Near East. When carried and not strung over the back, bows are carried or held in the left hand in the vast majority of cases in *ANEP*: 3, 12, 25, 172, 183 (from Ras Shamra), 190, 309, 318, 321, 327, 344 (note the position of the hands, which indicates that they are left hands [note the forefinger steadying the arrow], despite the bow string that seems to go across the front figure), 358, 368 (despite the fact that the string goes across the body, the finger position of both hands, the lack of the top half of the string across the head, and the arrow "under" the beard indicate that the bow is in the left hand), 369, 372, 373, 390, 519, 536, 626, 821. There is only one clear case of a bow in the right hand, in *ANEP* 12. *ANEP* 362 and 365 have a number of bowmen shooting in opposite directions. Men shooting toward the right, especially in 362, appear to have the bow in the left hand (note the fingers on the bow and the drawing hand over the front of the body). Men shooting toward the left may be interpreted as holding the bow in the right hand (esp. 365 and the lightly incised figure in the city/tower in 362). Perhaps this is only an artistic attempt to be symmetrical. Otherwise, the people with the bow in the right hand may be explained according to the unusual perspective found in 368. Note that 821 is consistent in placing the bow in the left hand, even when individuals face in opposite directions. There are a few especially notable cases in which the bow is found in the left *and arrows in the right* (12 [?], 184, 185, 351, 371). *ANEP* 791 and 179 fit the possible image given in *CAT* 1.10 II 6–7: people are on the march or hunt with bows in the left hand and arrows in the right. Parker (*UNP* 58 and 183) takes *qṣʿt* in both the Aqhat text and 1.10 as 'arrows'. On the *qšt* // *qṣʿt* association in hunting contexts, see Aitken, "Word Pairs," 29.

5. It is not clear whether this supposed ritual activity is connected with Daniʾil's feast. De Moor ("Seasonal Pattern in the Legend of Aqhatu," 63–64) appears to make the connection, specifically calling it a new year rite.

This is all very speculative and remains outside of the analysis undertaken here. The point is simply to note that ritual situations probably appeared in this break. Our assessment about the concatenation of ritual elements would probably require modification were this missing section available. In any case, the meal given to Kothar-wa-Ḫasis complements the first two offerings in the story. This triad of felicitous feasts constitutes the broad ritual introduction to the story.

The Scope of the Rite

Kothar-wa-Ḫasis apparently arrives unexpectedly. Daniʾil responds by hurriedly having a meal prepared (1.17 V):

(3b) *w hn*.šb[ʿ] (4) *b ymm* .	On the seven[th] day,[6]
apnk . dnil . *mt* (5) *rpi* .	Daniʾil, the Rapiʾan,
a⟨p⟩*hn* . *ġzr* . *mt* . *hrnm*[y]	then, the hero, the Harnamiyyan,
(6) *ytšu* . *yṯb* . *b ap* . *ṯġr* .	got up,[7] sat in front of the gate,
tḥt (7) *adrm* . *d b grn* .	before the distinguished ones on the threshing floor.
ydn (8) *dn* . *almnt* .	He judged the widow's cause,
yṯpṭ . *ṯpṭ* . ytm	he decided the case of the fatherless.
(9) *b nši* . *ʿnh* . *w yphn* .	When he lifted his eyes, he saw,
b alp (10) *šd* .	from a thousand *šd*-measures,
rbt . *kmn* .	from ten thousand *kmn*-measures—
hlk . *kṯr* (11) *k yʿn* .	he observed the approach of Kothar,
w yʿn . *tdrq* . *ḫss*	he observed the advance[8] of Ḫasis.
(12) *hlk* . *qšt* . *ybln* .	He carried the bow,
hl . *yš*(13)*rbʿ* . *qṣʿt* .	he brought the arrows.[9]
apnk . *dnil* (14) *mt* . *rpi* .	So Daniʾil, the Rapiʾan,
aphn . *ġzr* . *mt* (15) *hrnmy* .	then, the hero, the Harnamiyyan,
gm . *l aṯth* . *k yṣḥ*	called aloud to his wife:
(16) *šmʿ* . *mṯt* . *dnty* .	"Hear, lady Danatay,
ʿdb (17) *imr* . *b pḫd* .	prepare a lamb[10] from the flock,

6. Margalit (*UPA* 291) speculates that this is a "sabbath" rather than part of a preceding six-day progression culminating in the seventh.

7. Margalit (*UPA* 148) interprets this as Daniʾil's moving to a raised seat. Otherwise, it may simply indicate preparing to undertake an action (see Dijkstra and de Moor, "Problematical Passages," 181).

8. For the interpretation 'pack' (i.e., a piece of baggage) from Akk. *darāku* 'pack', see *UPA* 293–94 n. 13.

9. On the terms in this line, see nn. 3–4 above.

10. On *imr* in the context of *lḥm/šty*, see M. Dietrich and O. Loretz, "Das ugaritische Hapaxlegomenon *pḫd* und das Wortpaar *lḥm* || *šqy*: Bemerkungen zu ugaritisch *pḫd*, *pḫr* und hebräisch *pḥd* I, **pḥr*?" *UF* 23 (1991) 75–78.

l npš . kṯr (18) *w ḫss .*	for the appetite of Kothar-wa-Ḫasis,
l brlt . hyn d (19) *ḥrš yd .*	for the craving of Hyn,[11] the craftsman.
šlḥm . ššqy (20) *ilm .*	Feed, give drink to the god,
sad . kbd . hmt .	reverence, honor him,
bʿl (21) *ḥkpt . il . klh .*	the lord of Memphis,[12] the god of it all(?)."
tšmʿ (22) *mṯt . dnty .*	Lady Danatay complied.
tʿdb . imr (23) *b pḫd .*	She prepared a lamb from the flock,[13]
l npš . kṯr . w ḫss	for the appetite of Kothar-wa-Ḫasis,
(24) *l brlt . hyn . d ḥrš* (25) *ydm .*	for the craving of Hyn, the craftsman.
aḫr . ymġy . kṯr (26) *w ḫss .*	After this, Kothar-wa-Ḫasis arrived.
bd . dnil . ytnn (27) *qšt .*	He placed the bow in the hand of Daniʾil,
l brkh . yʿdb[14] (28) *qṣʿt .*	he set the arrows on his knees.
apnk . mṯt . dnty (29)	Then lady Danatay
tšlḥm . tššqy ilm	fed, gave drink to the god,
(30) *tsad . tkbd . hmt .*	she reverenced, honored him,
bʿl [[ḥ]] (31) *ḥkpt il . klh .*	the lord of Egypt, god of it all(?).
tbʿ . kṯr (32) *l ahlh .*	Kothar departed to his tents,
hyn . tbʿ . l mš(33)*knth*	Hyn departed to his dwelling places.

This feast is similar to the first two feasts in propriety and in demonstrating Daniʾil's piety and subordination to the gods. It differs, however, in form and function. It is a short feast, lasting only one day rather than seven days. The animal it uses is less expensive–a lamb (*imr*) not an ox (*alp*), as in the Kotharat feast (what animals, if any, are used in the initial petition are not known; see pp. 42–43).[15] These facts indicate that, while still important, this feast is less central than the others, which is significant from a narrative point of view. The first feast was the most elaborate because it addressed the chief problem in the first part of the text,

11. This may be an epithet meaning 'skilled'; compare Syriac *hawwīnā* (cf. Segert, *Basic Grammar*, 184; *CARTU* 136).

12. On *ḥkpt* as Memphis (Amarna Akk. [uru]*Ḫi-ku-up-ta-aḫ* 'city of Ptaḫ'; *CML* 55 n. 1) and Kothar-wa-Ḫasis's dwelling place, note the geographical journey from Syria to Egypt in 1.3 VI 4–23 (cf. *SP* 51 n. 52). Margalit (*UPA* 293) discusses the connection of Kothar-wa-Ḫasis to Ptaḥ and Greek Hephaistos.

13. Akk. *puḫādu* 'Lamm' (AHw 875). Dietrich and Loretz ("Das ugaritische Hapax-legomenon") argue that *pḫd* should not be taken as 'meal, grain' (for this option, see P. Xella, "L'episode de Dnil et Kothar [KTU 1.17 (= CTA 17) V 1–31] et Gen. XVIII 1–16," *VT* 28 [1978] 483–88). Dijkstra and de Moor ("Passages," 182–83) say that *imr b pḫd* literally means 'lamb from the rams' (see Num 15:11).

14. On the verb, see M. Dietrich and O. Loretz, "Zur Debatte über die Lautentwicklung *z* → *d* im Ugaritischen (*zrʿ* / *drʿ* 'säen', *ʿḏb* / *ʿdb* 'legen, setzen')," *UF* 25 (1993) 127–28.

15. On the relative worth and importance of animals in these rites, see *UPA* 287.

Daniʾil's sonlessness. As noted above, the narrative needed to overcome the inertia of his adversity. After the gods promise a son, the feasting of the Kotharat does not need to be as elaborate. In the third feast, with the son having been born, feasting need not be developed at all. The complexity or simplicity of feasting is therefore a function of the state of Daniʾil's family situation.

The Purpose of the Offering

The object of Kothar-wa-Ḫasis's feast is different from the preceding seven-day feasts. The earlier events seek mainly to obtain blessing from the deities: the first to obtain the promise of a son, the second to obtain the good graces of the Kotharat to insure successful conception and birth. In the case of Kothar-wa-Ḫasis, the meal is more clearly for hospitality and thanksgiving. One indication that hospitality is involved is that Daniʾil has the meal prepared as soon as he sees the god approaching. He seems anxious to please and fulfill the needs of his guest. While the meal effects the smooth transfer of the bow, it does not seem to have been offered with the specific intent of obtaining the bow. The god(s) had already apparently determined to give the bow to Daniʾil. The rite thus signals that Daniʾil's seeking has come to an end; his needs are satisfied.

This meal can be compared to similar meals in the Bible. Three men visit Abraham at Mamre (Gen 18:1–15). He has a meal prepared for them, it appears, simply for the sake of hospitality, before they continue on their way. It includes meat, breads, and dairy products. He also allows them to rest and wash their feet. There is no expectation of receiving a gift, but the visitors, who apparently are supernatural, promise Abraham a child. The motivation for the meal is much the same as the case of Kothar-wa-Ḫasis. Interestingly, what is given to Abraham is what Daniʾil sought in his first offering to the gods.

The food gift that Manoah and his wife give to their divine visitor can also be adduced in comparison (Judg 13:2–25). When the visitor returns to confirm his promise, Manoah wants to prepare a kid as a meal for the angel. The angel instructs him to make it a burnt offering. This meal or offering appears to be more for thanksgiving than hospitality, but the latter element is still present.

A similar meal, though not involving childlessness, is Gideon's presentation of a kid, broth, and breads to an angel who calls him to rescue Israel (Judg 6:11–24). The meal is a gift (*minḥâ*) to the angel (v. 18). It appears to be offered for hospitality, thanks, and even appeasement. Like Manoah's angel, this angel does not eat the food, but has Gideon present it as an offering, which then becomes an opportunity for proving the verity of the angel's word.

These examples share with the meal to Kothar-wa-Ḫasis the motifs of a visit from a divine being, receiving a gift from the visitor that in two cases involves the promise of a son, and a gift to the visitors mainly for reasons of hospitality but also for thanks.[16] The Bible stories, however, have transformed this folkloric motif to suit their theology. The narrator of the examples from Judges does not allow the divine being to eat the food gifts. This correlates with the attempt to deny that offerings are literally food for deity in Psalm 50. They are turned into offerings to the high god.[17]

The Culmination of the Three Felicitous Offerings

The meal that Abraham gives is similar to Daniʾil's in the role that the wife plays in the preparations. Abraham, though he has a servant prepare the bovine (Gen 18:7), has Sarah prepare the bread. Daniʾil has Danatay prepare the meal—apparently in its entirety. A wife's involvement is found also in meals in the Kirta story, though it should be noted that Kirta is ill and weak on these occasions and cannot perform any of the work himself (1.15 IV 2–28; 1.16 VI 16–21; his sickness is apparently the reason for holding these meals in the first place).

The involvement of Danatay as caterer in feasting Kothar-wa-Ḫasis has significance for the hierarchical scheme set up by the various ritual scenes in the story to this point. It puts her in symbolic subordination to Daniʾil. Thus, by the end of this third feast, we have a very full picture of the social cosmos: the gods are at the head, with Il apparently being superior. The lesser gods, the Kotharat and Kothar-wa-Ḫasis, because they supplement the initial and primary promise of Il, are subordinate to the high gods Il and Baʿl. Humans are subordinate to all of the gods. In the family, the father is chief over wife and son.

But the appearance of Danatay symbolizes more than this. She could have easily been included in the feasting of the Kotharat. There, however, only Daniʾil is described as preparing the ox (1.17 II 29–30) and feeding the goddesses (see above). The present feast involves the express participation of the couple together. This can be taken as a sign of social integrity and fulfillment. These features can be found elsewhere in the context of the rite. The gift of the bow involves Aqhat in some way: he ultimately

16. For a discussion of other biblical stories and the genre, see Parker, "Death and Devotion," 74–75; Xella, "L'episode."

17. See the discussion in chapter 1 on offerings as meals for deity.

receives it as his own (see the next chapter), quite soon after Kothar-wa-Ḫasis leaves. Therefore, the son is implicitly involved in the larger context of the feast. Additionally, when Daniʾil spies Kothar-wa-Ḫasis approaching, he is sitting among the 'distinguished ones' (*adrm*)[18] at the threshing floor and is adjudicating the cause of the widow and fatherless–an ethical act that, by the way, conveys something further about Daniʾil's character and shows his involvement with the larger community.[19] The description therefore brings almost the whole of society into play, and all of its members are in their appropriate social places. The situation is far different from the situation at the beginning of the story, where Daniʾil was alone, lamenting, and without promise.

---

18. Cf. Dijkstra and de Moor, "Passages," 181; *UPA* 292. This does not refer to trees, because they do not fit the context of the threshing floor.

19. See F. C. Fensham, "Widow, Orphan, and the Poor in Ancient Near Eastern Legal and Wisdom Literature," *JNES* 21 (1962) 134 (cf. *UPA* 361 n. 15). Kirta does not do this (1.6 VI 44–50). On the sense of the root *ṯpṭ*, see H. Cazelles, "'*mṯpṭ*' à Ugarit," *Or* 53 (1984) 177–82; F. C. Fensham, "The Ugaritic Root *ṯpṭ*," *JNSL* 12 (1984) 63–69.

Chapter 6
The Blessing of Aqhat

Daniʾil now speaks to his son about the bow and the firstfruits of his hunt. There is too much damage to the tablet, however, to permit full comprehension of this passage. It nevertheless seems that Daniʾil hands the bow over to Aqhat and gives him a blessing. This blessing provides the conclusion to the series of felicitous rites at the beginning of the story.

The text continues immediately after the departure of Kothar-wa-Ḫasis, as follows (1.17 V):[1]

(33) *apnk* . *dnil* . m[t] (34) *rpi* .	Then Daniʾil, the R[a]piʾan,
aphn . *ǵzr* . mt (35) *hrnmy* .	so the hero, the Harnamiyyan,
qšt . *yqb* . [yb](36)*rk* .	designated the bow (and) [offered a ble]ssing,
ʿ*l* . *aq*ht . *k yq*[bh]	for Aqhat he did desi[gnate it]:
(37) *pr*ʿ*m* . *ṣdk* . *y* bn[.]	"The firstfruits[2] of your hunt, O my son,
[bln][3] (38) *pr*ʿ*m* . *ṣdk* .	[bring me] the firstfruits of your hunt,
hn p[rʿm][4] (39) *ṣd* . *b hk*ly	yes, the fir[stfruits] of the hunt into my palace. . . ."

(The rest is broken.)

The chief problem in regard to our interests is what comes before the *rk* at the beginning of line 36. It is doubtful that *rk* is a word in and of itself; therefore, the end of line 35 must have contained its initial letters. The restoration of [yb]*rk* seems to be the best solution since this restoration serves as an introduction to 37–39, which must be direct speech by Daniʾil to Aqhat.[5]

1. The text here follows *CAT* and *CARTU* 106; cf. Dijkstra and de Moor, "Passages," 182.

2. Heb. *pera*ʿ 'leader'; Arab. *fara*ʿ*a* 'surpass, excel' (cf. *SP* 172). See p. 143 n. 34 below on the term in Anat's lament.

3. On the restoration, see Dijkstra and de Moor, "Passages," 183.

4. De Moor and Spronk (*CARTU* 106) read only p[rʿ].

5. Margalit (*UPA* 123) restores [wyš]*rk*, apparently based on his understanding of *yqb* as 'bend', referring to the bow. He translates *qšt yqb* [wyš]*rk* '(He) did bend the bow and did brace (it)' (see pp. 123, 149; cf. p. 291). Parker (*UNP* 59) restores [yd]*rk*,

The term *yqb*, which appears in line 35, is also difficult. The root can be seen as *nqb*, which in Hebrew means 'pierce' but also 'ascertain, designate'.[6] Thus, rather than referring to *naming* the bow as Dijkstra and de Moor have suggested,[7] it may refer to *designating* it *for* Aqhat. This solves the question how the bow, which is given to Daniʾil (see the previous section), comes to be in the possession of Aqhat, who would be able to give it to Anat, were he willing. In line with this, it makes sense to restore *k yq*[bh] in line 36 rather than *k yq*[m] 'he did arise'.[8]

According to this understanding, the noun *qšt* 'bow' in line 35 is the object of the verb *yqb*. It may also be the object of the verb [yb]*rk*.[9] But I doubt that this is the case because, according to the context of lines 37–39, it is Aqhat who is actually blessed, not the bow. Perhaps *qšt yqb* should be taken as a unit, 'he designated the bow', and the following [yb]*rk* is to be taken separately, paralleling the entirety of *qšt yqb* and not including *qšt* as an object. That is, the designation of the bow and the blessing are two actions that Daniʾil will perform for the benefit of Aqhat.

If this interpretation is correct, here we have the narrative's first example of Daniʾil's giving a blessing. Later on in the story (1.19 IV 36–40), he blesses his daughter, Pughat, as she goes off to avenge Aqhat's death, which I noted in the discussion of Il's blessing of Daniʾil (see chapter 3). The blessing accompanying the transfer of the bow differs from the other two blessings in that it does not have an oath formula introducing it. Daniʾil goes directly to the point and, if the restoration [bln] in line 37b is correct, expresses the hope, reminiscent of the Bible's Isaac, that Aqhat bring him the first animal(s) that he kills.

One wonders if giving the bow to Aqhat is a failing on Daniʾil's part that sets in motion the catastrophe that soon follows.[10] If the bow was really for Aqhat, why did Kothar-wa-Ḫasis give it to Daniʾil rather than his son? The text before and after the bestowal of the bow is too broken to make a certain conclusion but, since Daniʾil is generally portrayed as

---

which is a verb used, for example, in Hebrew of bending a bow preparatory to shooting (Ps 7:13, Lam 2:4, etc.). His whole reading and translation is: *qšt.yqb* [*gm*(?) *yd*(?)]/*rk* *ʿl.aqht. kyq*[*rb*(?)] '[Daniel] Strings(?) [and bends(?)] the bow, / [Draws(?)] near to Aqhat'.

6. Cf. *HALAT*³ 678–79.

7. Cf. Dijkstra and de Moor, "Passages," 182; *ARTU* 235 and n. 74. The latter refers to 1.2 IV 11, 18 for the naming of weapons, but the formula there is different (*ypʿr šmthm*).

8. For the latter, see *UPA* 123. See also Parker's restoration in n. 5, above. *RTU* (271–72 and n. 84 there) takes *yqb* as 'he bent (the bow)'.

9. So *ARTU* 235, '(he) named (and) blessed the bow'.

10. Some argue that the bow was for Daniʾil (noted by *UPA* 289, but no references are given).

upright, the transfer of the bow should probably not be viewed as an error.[11] The bow may have been given to Daniʾil only to be presented to his son. The specific reason for proceeding in such a manner may have been to bestow a gift on the son upon his reaching manhood.[12] If so, this can be seen as the true culmination of the gods' blessing to Daniʾil.[13] He has not only been given a son, but the son has grown, to the point that he might now begin to fulfill the filial duties outlined in the blessing. Daniʾil's blessing, in fact, adds another duty the son can perform for his father: bringing him food from the hunt.

Though this transfer of the bow can be deemed an acceptable act, it nevertheless creates problems when Anat later covets it. Many gifts and endowments are the cause of jealousy, and jealousy can have tragic consequences.[14]

---

11. One thinks of the otherwise upright Kirta, however, who fails by not paying his vow.

12. Here I basically agree with *UPA* 289.

13. Margalit (*UPA* 299–300) calls it a "second birth."

14. Contrast this occasion with the story of Kirta, in which a (promised) gift from a *human* to a god creates strife.

Chapter 7
Conclusion to Part 1

Up to this point in the story, all of the ritual has been positive. It has achieved the goals of the various agents involved, and no conflicts have appeared. The primary cases are the three feasts: to the high gods, to the Kotharat, and to Kothar-wa-Ḫasis. These, despite some differences in purpose, form, and context, have worked in a complementary fashion to provide Daniʾil with a son. Other cases of properly working ritual are Il's blessing of Daniʾil and Daniʾil's blessing of Aqhat. Also to be included are the ritual activities listed in the filial duties; because they deal with ideal situations, they contribute to the spirit of ritual appropriateness.

All of these occasions are *contextually* set off from the instances that immediately follow because the coming rituals have the opposite ethical character, as we will see. The blessing of Aqhat also provides a *structural* delimitation for the series of felicitous rituals. The story began with a feast, the high point of which was a blessing by the god Il. A roughly similar pattern is found at the end of the block. A meal is given to Kothar-wa-Ḫasis; this is followed by a blessing. To be truly similar to the first complex, Kothar-wa-Ḫasis should be blessing Aqhat instead of Daniʾil and using a blessing with a form similar to the first. But blesser and blessing need not be as elaborate for Daniʾil as for Il, now that the promises made to Daniʾil have been fulfilled. He is now, through his son, pursuing desires—luxuries—rather than needs.

There is a logic in the two blessing situations that further answers the question of why a god does not bless Aqhat. The blessings follow the logical, hierarchical pattern manifested in the various feasts and in the filial duties: Daniʾil and Aqhat are blessed by the being more or less immediately superior to them. Daniʾil is a chieftain or noble, if not a king (see pp. 183–85), and consequently is in a preeminent social position. Since blessings should come from superiors, he is blessed by the gods, specifically Il. It is true that in the story Il is the highest god; one might therefore expect Daniʾil to be blessed by lower gods. But later he is visited and benefited by the Kotharat and Kothar-wa-Ḫasis. Moreover, the blessing is not given to him directly but is mediated through Baʿl, Il's executive secretary. Thus, the hierarchical principle does seem to be operative. Aqhat's father is immediately superior to him and therefore provides his blessing. The principle also holds in the case of Pughat, whose blessing is formally similar to the one that Il gives Dani'il (see above). Pughat's immediate superior, her father, blesses her, as well.

Thus the blessing that Dani'il gives can be viewed as contextually similar, to a degree, to the blessing that Il gives. The second blessing and the first form an envelope around the felicitous feasts at the beginning of the story. The second blessing thus marks the close of this portion of the narrative.

Part 2

Infelicitous Feasts and Offerings

The feasting, both as performed within the narrative of the story and as connected thematically in the list of ideal filial duties, has been positive up through the feasting of Kothar-wa-Ḫasis. The next two feasts, both mainly involving Aqhat and Anat, have the opposite quality and thus stand out against the first feasts. In the first of these two, Anat turns against Aqhat because he will not surrender his bow to her. In the second, Anat kills Aqhat, apparently to gain possession of his bow as well as to punish him for his insolence. In between the two unfavorable feasts, Anat bears her complaint against Aqhat to Il. Even then, the ritual activity that regulates the relationship of the lesser gods is colored adversely by Anat's rage. This chain of ritual misfires shifts the tenor and course of the narrative decisively. The happy and positive atmosphere is destroyed, and the blessings and promises are effectively annulled. So much is lost that feasting and offerings are not, indeed cannot be, resumed without the performance of a complex series of mourning and retaliatory rites (for these, see parts 3 and 4).

Chapter 8

The Feast with Anat

The feast at which Anat contends with Aqhat for possession of the bow is not wholly discordant. It begins harmoniously. Only in the middle does mischief appear, causing the occasion to end in failure. The harmony between the divine and human worlds is disrupted, and the life of the promised child, Aqhat, is endangered.

The Outline and Nature of the Feast

About 20 lines are missing between the end of column V, concluding with the blessing of Aqhat, and the beginning of column VI, in which the description of the feast with Anat is already in progress. The description is very broken (1.17 VI).

(2) [. . . lḥm . b l]*ḥm*[. ay(?) . xx?]	[. . . Eat of whatever f]ood(?) [. . .]
(3) [xx? w šty . b ḫmr .(?) y]n . *ay* .	[. . .and] [drink of] whatever [fermenting wi]ne!(?)
š(?)[pq .] (4)[mrǵtm . ṯd .(?)]	They were(?) f[urnished with a suckling,]
[b ḥ]r*b* . *mlḥ*[t . q]ṣ (5) [mri .]	[with a] salted [kn]ife [they slic]ed [a fatling].
[tšty . krpnm] . *yn* .	[They drank] wine [(from?) flagons],
b ks . ḫrṣ (6) [dm . ʿṣm .]	From gold cups, [the blood of the vine-stock(?).]
[ymlu]*n* . *krpn* . *ʿl* . k*rpn*	[They fill]ed flagon after flagon.
(7) [w xx? ṯṯnyn. š]q*ym* .	[The cu]pbearers [came again](??),
w tʿl . tr*ṯ* (8) [xxxx]	they brought up new-wine [to . . .](??),
[xxxx li]n . *yn* . *ʿšy* .	[to . . . until n]o prepared wine was left(??).
l ḥbš (9) [xxxxxx][1]	For (a?) *ḥbš* [. . .].

Compared with other feasts in the story, the overall description of this feast is unique. However, it contains elements and motifs found in feasts

1. According to the photo, there seems to be room for about six signs before the restoration [w aqht . y]nḥ*tn* . . . in line 9 (see the text, p. 108, below). These six signs would contain the completion of the poetic line beginning with *l ḥbš*.

in other Ugaritic texts. They provide a basis for restoring this text, or at least for forming an idea of the occasion's basic outline and tenor.

The indefinite pronoun *ay* in line 3 and the preceding [ ]*ḥm*[ ] bring to mind the ritual invitation in 1.23:6:

lḥm . b lḥm . ay	Eat of whatever food,
w šty *. b ḥmr yn ay*	and drink of whatever fermenting wine![2]

This invitation appears to have been directed toward the *ilm nʿmm* 'two kindly deities' that were invoked (line 1), perhaps also human participants, including the *ʿrbm* (lines 7, 12), and perhaps the king, queen, and the *ṯnnm* (line 7), if not others.

This similar text may indicate what should be restored in lines 2–3 of the Aqhat text.[3] Caution must be observed, however, because the space available here (according to *CAT*) is greater than the space taken up by the ritual invitation in 1.23. Moreover, 1.23 is of a genre different from the Aqhat text; it is a ritual text, including hymns and incantations, plus an accompanying myth.

Reconstruction of the following lines is a little more secure. The phrase *bḥrb mlḥt qṣ mri* and/or the term *ks ḫrṣ* are found in five feast scenes in the Baʿl cycle. These are important, not only for restoration of the text, but for their feasting contexts, which can elucidate the events in the Aqhat scene.

(a) 1.3 I 2–17

In the first scene, Baʿl is being served, apparently alone, by a divine attendant. The feast's motivating factors and purposes are not clear because of breakage before the description and then later in the column:[4]

(2) *p rdmn . ʿbd . ali*[yn] (3)*bʿl .*	So Rdmn (?) attended to Mighty Baʿl,
sid . zbl . bʿl (4) *arṣ .*	he reverenced[5] the Prince, Lord of earth.
qm . yṯʿr (5) *w . yšlḥmnh*	Having arisen, he made preparations[6] and gave him food.

2. Cf. O. Loretz, "Ugaritisch-hebräisch *ḫmr/ḥmr* und *msk(/mzg)*: Neu- und Mischwein in der Ägäis und in Syrien-Palästina," *UF* 25 (1993) 247–58, on *ḫmr yn*.

3. Similarly de Moor (*ARTU* 236) and Margalit (*UPA* 123); Margalit's estimate of the space does not appear to be correct.

4. On the passage, see E. Lipiński, "Banquet en l'honneur de Baal: CTA 3 (V AB), A, 4–22," *UF* 2 (1970) 75–88.

5. See 1.17 V 20, parallel to *kbd*. It is not clear if *sid* is a participle or a suffixing form vis-à-vis an infinitive *sad* in 1.17 V 20.

6. See *SP* 69 (parallel in CTA 24:34–35 to *št* 'place'). In 1.3 II 20–21, 36, its objects are *ksat* and *ṯlḥnt*.

(6) *ybrd . ṯd . l pnwh*	He divided(?) a "teat"[7] before him,
(7) *b ḥrb . mlḥt* (8) *qṣ . mri .*	with a salted(?) knife he sliced a fatling.
ndd (9) *yʿšr . w yšqynh*	Having stood,[8] he made ready[9] and gave him drink.[10]
(10) *ytn . ks . bdh*	He put a cup in his hand,
(11) *krp*[[m]]*nm . b klat . ydh*	flagons in both of his hands,[11]
(12) *bk rb . ʿẓm . ri*	a great and noteworthy beaker(?),
dn (13) *mt . šmm .*	a *dn*-vessel(?)[12] of the men of heaven,
ks . qdš (14) *l tphnh . aṯt .*	a holy cup that a woman must not see,
krpn (15) *l tʿn . aṯrt .*	a flagon that (even) Athirat must not view.
alp (16) *kd . yqḥ . b ḫmr*	He took one thousand pitchers from fermenting-wine,
(17) *rbt . ymsk . b mskh*	He mixed ten thousand (pitchers) from spiced-wine.[13]

7. De Moor (*SP* 70) notes that, in view of the parallels (in 1.4 III 41-43; VI 56-57; 1.5 IV 13-14) where *mrǵṯm ṯd* comes before the *ḥrb mlḥt* phrase and where *ṯd* means 'teat', the word must have a similar meaning here, not 'breast' or the like. He also doubts that *ybrd* is related to *prd* 'be separated, divided'. It is possible that *mrǵṯm* has accidentally been omitted. Perhaps *ṯd* stands metonymically for *mrǵṯm ṯd* (see n. 14 below). De Moor proposes redividing the phrase *ybr dṯd*. In this case, he connects the resulting verb *ybr* with *bry* 'to cut' (with Arab. and Aram. cognates; see there) and translates 'he carved a suckling before him' (p. 67). I tentatively accept the *brd/prd* connection (noted by others, cited by de Moor), though this is not wholly acceptable.

8. On the verb *ndd*, see *SP* 71 and especially J. Tropper and E. Vereet, "Ugaritisch *ndy, ydy, hdy, ndd* und *d(w)d*," *UF* 20 (1988) 346-47. The verb is an N-stem of the root *d(w)d* 'sich hinstellen, hintreten'. Note the extended parallelism with *qm* in line 4b (also in 1.4 III 12) and the use alongside *qm* in 1.10 II 17-18 (with antonyms *krʿ* and *ql*).

9. On the verb *ʿšr*, see *SP* 71-72: 'to prepare/make the necessary arrangements for a banquet (or, more specifically, a drinking bout)'. The word *ʿšr* appears before *yššqy* in 1.17 VI 30 (Anat's promise to Aqhat); *dbḥ dbḥ* is parallel to the phrase *ʿšr ʿšrt* in 1.16 I 39-40.

10. On the verb *šqy* as a G-stem, see the discussion in chapter 1 (and cf. *SP* 72).

11. On the meaning of *klat ydh*, see *SP* 72.

12. Lines 12-13a are difficult. In the larger context, one expects vessels to be described. The word *bk* can be connected with Heb. *pak* 'phial, flask' (BDB 810). The terms *rb* and *ʿẓm* can be taken as adjectives to *bk*. The sequence *ridn*(13)*mt* is most difficult. It appears best to take *dn* also as a type of vessel (Arab. *dann-* 'earthen wine jug' [*DMWA* 293]; Akk. *dannu* 'vat [used mostly for storing beer, wine, etc.]' [CAD D 98b]). This allows *ri* to be taken as an infinitive following *ʿẓm* = 'noteworthy, remarkable' (literally, 'great of appearance/seeing'). The phrase *mt šmm* can be taken as 'men of heaven' which, in its masculinity and divinity, finds contrast in 13b-15. For this translation, see *ARTU* 2-3 (similarly, *CML* 47; *MLC* 179-80). For arguments and alternatives, see *SP* 72-74.

13. On the meaning of *msk* (in addition to *ḫmr*), see Loretz, "Ugaritisch-hebräisch *ḫmr/ḥmr*," 247-58 (cf. Dietrich and Loretz, "Zur ugaritischen Lexikographie [V]," 28-29).

(b) 1.4 III 40–44

This is the feast that Athirat prepares for Baʿl and Anat after they give presents to Athirat to solicit her help in establishing a palace for Baʿl. At least these three gods participate:

(40) [xxx tl]*ḥm* . *tšty* (41) [ilm .]	[. . .t]hey ate, the [gods] (41) drank,
[w tp]q . *mrǵṯm*[14] (42) [ṯd .]	[and] they were fu[rnished with] a suck[ling].
[b ḥrb . m]l*ḥt* . *qṣ* (43) [mri .]	[With a] sal[ted(?)[15] knife] they sliced up[16] [a fatling].
tšty .] k*rpnm yn*	[They drank] flagons[17] of wine,
(44) [w b ks . ḫrṣ . d]m . *ʿṣm*	[and with gold cups,[18] the bl]ood of vines(?).
(The rest is too broken.)	

(c) 1.4 IV 33–38

When Athirat goes to Il to request a palace for Baʿl, Il asks her why she came and then offers hospitality:

(33) *rǵb . rǵbt . w* tǵt[r]	Are you hungry? Just make a request![19]
(34) *hm . ǵmu . ǵmit . w* ʿs[t]	Or are you thirsty? Drink!
(35) *lḥm . hm . štym .*	Eat and drink!
lḥ[m] (36) *b ṯlḥnt . lḥm*	Eat food from the tables,
št (37) *b krpnm . yn .*	drink wine from flagons,
bk⟨s⟩ . *ḫrṣ* (38) *dm . ʿṣm .*	from gold cups, the blood of vine-stocks(?)!

(d) 1.4 VI 40–59

This passage describes the feast held after Baʿl's palace is completed. This is an elaborate ceremony, with numerous deities present:

---

14. Compare Arab. *raǵaṯa* 'to suck' (*DMWA* 347); hence, *mrǵṯm ṯd* is 'breast sucker' (construct with enclitic *-m*). Probably a singular in parallel with [mri] in line 43. A singular also probably appears in 1.4 VI 56, even though there is a large number of attendees.

15. 'Salted' is only a possibility for *mlḥt*; see *SP* 70–71 and *MLC* 578, for other possibilities.

16. Syntactically, *qṣ* should probably be a verb, since it is difficult to see the preceding verb [tp]q doing double duty. The only problem may be the case of [mri] (apparently genitive), but *SP* 71 notes an instance where *mri ilm* (1.22 I 13) appears for *mra ilm*. The *-i ʾalep* marks the preceding not the following vowel.

17. Probably k*rpnm* is an absolute plural with *yn* being an accusative of content (*CML* 58 and *ARTU* 51 take it as a plural; *MLC* 199 takes it as a singular). This syntax of *yn* would parallel that of the next sentence. For the type of vessel (a drinking vessel), see *SP* 72.

18. Plural in *ARTU* 51; *CML* 58; singular in *MLC* 199.

19. Compare *ǵtr* to Heb. *ʿtr* 'pray, supplicate'. The root has a wider sense, 'töten, schlachten, opfern, bitten', according to Dietrich, Loretz, and Sanmartín, "*šumma izbu*," 138. In 1.24:28 the verb appears to mean 'intercede' or the like.

(40) . . . *ṭbḫ* . *alp*m [. ap] (41) *ṣin* .	. . . He (Baʕl) slaughtered oxen [as well as] flock animals,
šql . *ṯrm* [. w]m(42)*ria* . *il*⟨m⟩[20].	he slew bulls [and] ram fatlings,
ʕglm . *d*[t] (43) *šnt* .	calves [a] year old,
imr . *qmṣ* . l[l]*im*	lambs, an abundance of young flock animals.[21]
(44) *ṣḥ* . *aḫh* . *b bhth* .	He called his brothers into his residence,
aryh (45) *b qrb hklh* . *ṣḥ*	his relatives into his palace,
(46) *šbʕm* . *bn* . *aṯrt*	he called the seventy sons of Athirat.
(47) *špq ilm* . *krm* . *yn*	He furnished the gods with rams[22]–and wine.
(48) *špq* . *ilht* . *ḫprt* [. yn]	He furnished the goddesses with ewes[23]–and wine.
(49) *špq* . *ilm* . *alpm* . y[n]	He furnished the gods with oxen–and wine.
(50) *špq* . *ilht* . *arḫt* [. yn]	He furnished the goddesses with cows–and wine.
(51) *špq* . *ilm* . *kḥṯm* . *yn*	He furnished the gods with seats–and wine.
(52) *špq* . *ilht* . *ksat* [. yn]	He furnished the goddesses with thrones–and wine.
(53) *špq* . *ilm* . *rḥbt* yn	He furnished the gods with jars[24]–and wine
(54) *špq* . *ilht* . *dkr*⟨t yn⟩	He furnished the goddesses with jugs[25]–and wine.
(55) *ʕd* . *lḥm* . *šty* . *ilm*	While the gods ate (and) drank,
(56) *w pq* . *mrǵṯm* . *ṯd*	they were furnished with a suckling.[26]
(57) *b ḥrb* . *mlḥt* . *qṣ* [. m]r(58)*i* .	With a salted (?) knife they sliced up a [fat]ling.
tšty . *krp*[nm . y]n	They drank fla[gons of wi]ne,
(59) [b]ks . ḫrṣ . d[m . ʕṣm]	[with] gold cups, the bl[ood of the vine-stock(?)].

(Lines 60-64 are fragmentary.)

(e) 1.5 IV 10-21

This is a feast from which Baʕl is absent; because he is absent, he is sought out. The feast apparently takes places at Il's house:

20. Compare *mri ilm* in 1.22 I 13.

21. For *qmṣ* and *llu*, see *SP* 122.

22. Heb. attests *kar* 'he-lamb'.

23. Del Olmo Lete (*MLC* 553) notes that metathesis may have occurred and compares Arab. *ḫarūf* 'young sheep, lamb, yearling' (*DMWA* 235) and Akk. *ḫarāptu* (not in CAD).

24. For *rḥbt* as large containers, see *SP* 204.

25. *SP* 204 compares this to Akk. *diqāru* 'bowl, pot' (CAD D 157: 'a bowl with a round bottom, for serving and heating').

26. A singular because of the following singular *mri*.

(10) *yqrb* . x[ ]	He (Baʿl) drew near [ ]
(11) lḥm . mṣ[dy]	the food of [my ban]quet [ ]
(12) *ʿd* . *lḥm*[. šty . ilm]	While [the gods] ate [(and) drank],
(13) *w pq* . *mr*[ǵṯm . ṯd]	they were furnished with a suc[kling],
(14) b *ḥrb* . [mlḥt . qṣ . mri]	with a [salted(?)] knife [they sliced a fatling].
(15) *šty* . *kr*[pnm . yn]	They drank fla[gons of wine],
(16) b *ks* . *ḫr*[ṣ . dm . ʿṣm]	from gol[d] cups, [the blood of the vine-stock(?)].
(17) *ks* . *ksp*[. ymlun]	[they filled] silver cups,
(18) *krpn* . [ʿl . krpn]	flagon [upon flagon].
(19) *w ṯṯny*[n . šqym]	[Cupbearers c]ame again,
(20) *tʿl* . *trṯ*[. bt . bʿl]	they brought up new-wine [to Baʿl's temple,]
(21) *bt* . *il* . *li*[n . yn . ʿšy][27]	to Il's temple until n[o prepared wine was left].

The phrase *b ḥrb mlḥt qṣ mri* appears whole or partly restored in examples (a), (b), (d), and (e). In all of these cases it is parallel to a preceding *w (t)pq mrǵtm ṯd* (b, d, e) or the related *ybrd ṯd l pnwh* (a). There seems to be enough room in the Aqhat passage for the first version, but either an *ʿayin* or a *šin* must be read in line 3 after *ay.*[28] The Š-stem of the root *pyq*, used in the sense of providing an offering, is found repeated in example (d) (lines 47–54). This may be read in the Aqhat text.[29]

The term *ks ḫrṣ* is found in examples (c), (d), and (e) and restored in (b) (line 44). In example (c) and apparently in (d), its contents are described as *dm ʿṣm* 'blood of the vine-stock(?)'. The connection of this container and liquid leads to the restoration of one or the other in examples (b) and (e) and it makes a restoration of *dm ʿṣm* a likelihood in the Aqhat text (line 6). On the basis of examples (b), (c), (d), and (e), one expects a preceding parallel line of *tšty/št (b) krpnm yn* (line 5b of the Aqhat text).[30]

The word before the break, to which the *-n* in line 6b belongs in the Aqhat text, is perhaps [ymlu]*n*, following *CAT* and de Moor.[31] If the same

27. See below for the restorations here.

28. Cf. *CAT*; *UPA* 123, 178.

29. Contra Margalit (*UPA* 123, 178 n. 40), whose judgment regarding the amount of space does not accord with the photograph. Lines 16, 26, and 27 show that short lines may be written.

30. De Moor and Spronk (*CARTU* 106) restore: [šty . krpnm] . *yn* . *b ks* . ḥr[ṣ . dm] (6) [ʿṣm . ks . ksp . ymlu]*n* , with the translation (*ARTU* 236): '[They drank beakers of] wine, from golden cups [the blood of trees]. [They fille]d [the cups of silver]'. All of this is acceptable except the restoration of [ks . ksp], for which there does not seem to be room. *CAT*'s restoration [. . . tšty b ks ksp] in line 5 does not seem correct according to the other texts we have examined.

31. Margalit's reconstruction [drkt y]n (*UPA* 123, 178) is not attractive. The Aqhat text in this area is closer to example (e) than (d) whence the restoration comes (line 54).

verb is to be restored in example (e) (line 17), one might expect *ks* . *ksp* of (e) to come before the verb and after *dm* . *ʿṣm* in the Aqhat text. There may not be enough room for this, however. If it did appear there, the line would have to be written in a very cramped manner. One of the problems arising from the reconstruction without *ks* . *ksp* of the Aqhat passage is that, given the correctness of the restorations of lines 16–18 in example (e), the Aqhat text has a different poetic lineation. Are we to imagine that the broken part of line 6 of the Aqhat text contained a textual error?[32]

The reconstruction of the beginnings of lines 7 and 8 is more speculative but can partially follow the recommendation of Dijkstra and de Moor that we use example (e), lines 19–21.[33] There are two parallels between the two texts in these lines: *wtʿl trṯ* || *tʿl trṯ* and *l ḥbš* || *ʿl ḥbš*. Dijkstra and de Moor simply shuffle the two passages together to flesh out each of them. The following readings are from the text in *CARTU*,[34] which slightly modifies the reading that Dijkstra and de Moor originally offered to fit the available space better:

1.5 IV (example [e])	1.17 VI (Aqhat)
(19) *w tṯtny*[n . šqym]	(7) [w hn . tṯtnyn . š]q*ym*
(20) *tʿl* . *trṯ* [b bt . bʿl]	*w tʿl trṯ* (8) [bt . bʿl .]
(21) *bt* . *il* . *l* i[n . yn ʿšy]	[bt il . l̄ i]n . *yn* . ʿšy .
(22) *ʿl* . *ḥbš* . p[ ]	*l ḥbš* (9) [ ]

The main problem with this reconstruction is that, while the cultic locales suit the context of example (e)—that is, the *bt bʿl* /*il* 'house (temple) of Baʿl/Il'—they do not fit the context of the Aqhat story. This is true even though the gods Baʿl and Il are prominent in the initial feast of the Aqhat story, Baʿl plays a part later in the text (1.19 I 42–46; III 2, 12, etc.; IV 5), *bt bʿl* 'Baʿl's temple' and *bt il* 'Il's temple' appear in the filial duties (1.17 I 31–32), and *bt il* is mentioned in a curse (1.19 III 47). It appears, rather, that the feast is conducted at Daniʾil's house.

One reason for this conclusion is that the feast is allied with the blessing of Aqhat that took place at Daniʾil's house, judging from the context of the feast for Kothar-wa-Ḫasis that immediately precedes and takes place, by all appearances, at Daniʾil's residence. The connection between the blessing and the feast is evident in how close, textually speaking, the feast is to the blessing. Recall that the blessing occurs right at the end of column V, and the description breaks off in the middle. A number of other

32. That is, haplography due to the similarity of *ks ksp* to the preceding *ks*.

33. Dijkstra and de Moor, "Passages," 184. Margalit restores *ad sensum* (*UPA* 123, 179): [lšty . ʿnt . lš]q*ym wtʿl* . *trṯ* (.) [lrišh . lyḥbl]. *yn*. . . .

34. *CARTU* 106.

lines are necessary to complete it. At the same time, the feast is already under way at the extant beginning of column VI. A number of preceding lines are necessary before this to introduce the scene. Consequently, a significant portion of the 20 lines missing between the columns must be devoted to the blessing and the feast. This does not leave much room for setting up a new context for the feast. It is likely, then, that the feast is a continuation of the context in which Aqhat is blessed.

The prominence of the bow in the feast also seems to indicate that there is a connection between the blessing and the feast (for this, see the text that continues the feast scene, below). The bow is described in some detail. It may be that it catches Anat's attention as it is being shot. It is reasonable to assume that it plays a prominent role, because the feast continues the circumstances in which the bow was given to Aqhat.[35]

There is an additional reason to believe that the feast cannot take place at the temples of Il and Baʿl. Were these the locations of the feast, these high gods would be in attendance. But they appear to be absent. Not only are they not mentioned in the context, Il is at his distant home at the source of the rivers, the place to which Anat heads immediately after negotiations for the bow break off with Aqhat (1.17 VI 47–50). Moreover, Il apparently has no knowledge of how Aqhat has offended Anat.[36] Therefore, he could not have been at the feast. Baʿl appears to be absent, because Anat seems to be perfectly free to make Aqhat the radical offer of eternal life and accompanying honors—things that Baʿl has. One would expect this offer to make Baʿl jealous or at least to make him concerned, if he were in attendance.[37]

For all of these reasons, it is probably best to imagine that the feast occurs in Daniʾil's home. It may be that instead of *bt il* and *bt bʿl*, as in example (e), other place names appeared in the Aqhat text, such as *bt dnil*.

35. An alternative explanation for the presence of and focus on the bow is that the feast celebrates the firstfruits of the hunt, which are mentioned in the blessing. But this interpretation is doubtful because there is probably not enough room in the 20 missing lines to describe a hunting scene. Also, later on in 1.18 I 29, Anat may be offering to teach Aqhat how to hunt (*almdk* . ṣ[d] 'I will teach you to hu[nt]'), meaning that he had not yet been successful. It is better to assume that the feast continues the celebration of Aqhat's coming of age, begun presumably by his being blessed and receiving the bow.

36. The assumption is that the argument is not a private affair. Margalit (*UPA* 299, 300) thinks that the others see and hear the dispute.

37. Margalit's arguments (*UPA* 299). H. F. van Rooy argues that the passage shows competition between Anat and Baʿl; that is, Anat does not seem to be saying something that is wholly pleasing to Baʿl ("The Relation between Anat and Baal in the Ugaritic Texts," *JNSL* 7 [1979] 85–95).

Infelicity

The banquet proceeds well at first but then disintegrates when Anat sees Aqhat's bow (1.17 VI):

[w aqht y]nḫ*tn* . *qn* .	[Aqhat lo]aded an arrow(?),[38]
yṣbt (10) [qšt . bnt . kṯ]r[39] .	the [bow made by Kotha]r was drawn(?).
b nši ʿnh [.] w t*phn*	As she lifted her eyes, she saw it.
(11) [xxxxxxxxxx]x*l* . *kslh* .*k* br*q*	[. . .] . . . its back, like lightning
(12) [xxxxxxxxxx]k . *yǵḏ* . *thmt* . *brq*	[. . .] as(??) lightning shakes[40] the ocean(??),
(13) [xxxxxxx .]qnh .	[. . .] . . . its/his arrow.[41]
tṣb . *qšt* . *bnt* *k*(14)[ṯr . w ḫss .]	She would draw the bow[42] made by Ko[thar-wa-Ḫasis],
[d qr]*nh* . *km* . *bṯn* . *yqr*	[who]se [en]ds curl[43] like a serpent's
(15) [krpnh . tdy .] l *arṣ* .	[She cast her cup] to the ground,
ksh . *tšpkm* (16) [l ʿpr .]	she poured out her cup [on the dust].
[tšu . gh .]w *tṣḥ* .	[She raised her voice] and cried:
šmʿ . *mʿ* (17) [l aqht . ǵzr .]	"Hear now, [O Aqhat, hero]!
[i]rš . *ksp* . *w atnk*	[As]k for silver, and I will give (it) to you,

38. So Dijkstra and de Moor, "Passages," 185. It is not clear if *qn* means 'arrow', especially since *qṣʿt* appears to have this meaning (see p. 88 n. 4, above, and p. 109 n. 47, below). The word *qnm*, apparently literally 'reeds', appears in the list of materials for making arrows (line 23). Presumably *qn* can refer not only to the material of arrows but to arrows themselves. The translation of *qn* as 'arrow' here accords with a scene in which Anat's desire for the bow might particularly be aroused if she saw it cocked for action. It also accords with the Near Eastern custom of making arrows from reeds (Sukenik, "Composite Bow," 13). Margalit (*UPA* 303–4) discusses the materials used in constructing a composite bow. He says that the reeds must be for part of the bow, not for arrows. It is not certain, however, how they would be used in constructing the bow.

39. Restoration following *CAT*, based on line 13.

40. Following *CARTU* 161 (see *ARTU* 237: "just as the lightning makes the Flood shudder"); *SP* 167; *MLC* 606 *ǵḏ* 'dispararse, saltar'. See 1.4 VII 41, where Baʿl's hand, with an *arz* pole in it, shakes; the pole is equivalent to the thunderbolt (*SP* 167).

41. Perhaps lines 11–13 described how the bow shot. Dijkstra and de Moor ("Passages," 185) restore line 13a to read: [ʿnt . tnḫtn . q]n 'ʿAnatu would lay an arrow on'. This provides a parallel to line 13b–14a.

42. Following *ARTU* 237. Otherwise the bow could be the subject of the verb and the line would form an inclusion, with line 10, around the apparent description of the bow's function.

43. Basing the meaning of *yqr* on Arab. *qwr* '(II) to make a round hole . . . cut out in a round form; (V) to coil (of a snake)' (*DMWA* 796; so the meaning taken by *ARTU* 237; cf. *MLC* 620). For the shape of a composite bow, see *UPA* 291. Others read 'whistle, hiss' (*MLC* 620; *CML* 108).

(18) [ḫrṣ . w aš]lḥ*k* .	[Gold, and I will im]part (it) to you.
w tn . *qš*tk . ʿm (19) [btlt .] ʿn[t .]	Just give your bow to [Virgin] Ana[t],
qṣʿ*tk . ybmt . limm*	your arrows to the Sister-in-law of the nations."[44]
(20) w *yʿn . aqht . ǵzr .*	Aqhat, the hero, answered:
adr . ṯqbm (21) b *lbnn .*	"The ash-trees[45] from the Lebanon are excellent,[46]
adr . gdm . b rumm	the tendons from wild oxen are excellent,
(22) *adr . qrnt . b yʿlm .*	the horns from mountain goats are excellent,
mtnm (23) *b ʿqbt . ṯr .*	the sinews from the hocks of a bull,
adr . b ǵl il . qnm	the reeds from the vast reed-bed[47] are excellent–
(24) *tn . l kṯr . w ḫss .*	give (these) to Kothar-wa-Ḫasis,
ybʿl . qšt . l ʿnt	he will fashion[48] a bow for Anat,[49]
(25) *qṣʿt . l ybmt . limm .*	arrows for the Sister-in-law of the nations."
w tʿn . btlt (26) *ʿnt .*	Virgin Anat answered:
irš . ḥym . l aqht . ǵzr	"(Then) request life for Aqhat, the hero,
(27) irš . *ḥym . w atnk .*	request life and I will give (it) to you,
bl mt (28) w *ašlḥk .*	immortality and I will impart (it) to you.
ašsprk . ʿm . bʿl (29) *šnt .*	I will make you count the years with Baʿl,
ʿm . bn il . tspr . yrḫm	you will count the months with the son(s) of Il.
(30) *k bʿl . k yḥwy . yʿšr .*	Just as Baʿl, in the way that he lives,[50] preparations are made,[51]

44. On Anat's epithet as *ybmt limm*, see Walls (*The Goddess Anat*, 94–107), who ends inconclusively. The interpretation here is not certain.

45. Cf. J. C. de Moor, "The Ash in Ugarit," *UF* 3 (1971) 349–50 (so also *ARTU* 237; *CML* 108; *MLC* 644 "fresno").

46. *Adr* in this and the following line is taken as a 3d-person plural suffixing verb (masculine or feminine, depending on the context), according to Dijkstra and de Moor, "Passages," 186–87. J. Sanmartín ("Zu ug. *adr* in KTU 1.17 VI 20–23," *UF* 9 [1977] 371–73) argues the word is an adjective in construct state. So also Watson, "Delaying Devices," 211; *GUL* 45.

47. For *ǵl MLC* 606 gives 'cañaveral'; Arab. *ǵîl* 'thicket' (*DMWA* 691); for *qnm* 'reeds' as the material for arrows, see Sukenik, "Composite Bow," 14.

48. For problems with associating Ugaritic *bʿl* with Heb. *pʿl*, see L. Grabbe, "Hebrew *pāʿal* / Ugaritic *bʿl* and the Supposed *b/p* Interchange in Semitic," *UF* 11 (1979) 307–14; Margalit, *UPA* 275. Margalit reads *yb*{ }*l* 'he (= Kothar-wa-Ḫasis) will produce' and compares 1.17 V 2 *abl . qšt*. Grabbe thinks the semantic range of Ugaritic *bʿl* (= Semitic **bʿl*) may have changed to include the meaning 'make' (p. 310). Cf. *GUL* 28.

49. Watson ("Delaying Devices," 210–11) has noted the literary effect of placing the instruction at the end of the list of materials.

50. This translation was suggested by my student, David Bernat. The point is that Anat is offering Aqhat not just immortality but divinity too. Otherwise, the verb *yḥwy*

ḥwy . yʿš(31)*r . w yšqynh .*	preparations are made for the living one and he is given drink,
ybd . w yšr . ʿlh	(and) one recites and sings about[52] him,
(32) *nʿ*m[n . w y]*ʿnynn .*	a kindly [one], he responds to him,
ap ank . aḥwy (33) *aq*ht [. ǵ]zr .	So I will make Aqhat, the hero, live."
w . yʿn . aqht . ǵzr	Aqhat, the hero, answered:
(34) *al . tšrgn . y btltm .*	"Do not lie to me, O Virgin,
dm . l ǵzr (35) *šrgk . ḫḫm .*	for to (this) hero your lie is sputum.[53]
mt . uḫryt . mh . yqḥ	What does a man obtain as his destiny?[54]

may be a D passive (so Dijkstra and de Moor, "Passages," 187–88), parallel to the apparent D active in line 32b. In this case, the line can be translated: 'Just as Baʿl, as he is revived . . .'. It may thus be an allusion to Baʿl's resuscitation. See Il's exclamation: *k ḥy . aliyn . bʿl k iṯ . zbl . bʿl . arṣ* 'for mighty Baʿl lives, the prince, master of the earth, exists!' (1.6 III 20–21). Another possibility is to take *k bʿl . k yḥwy* as a simple comparison: 'As Baʿl, so shall he [i.e., Aqhat] live . . .' (cf. *RTU* 273). Some interpreters take the verb *yḥwy* in line 30 as transitive, with Baʿl as the subject: "And Baal when he gives life gives a feast, / Gives a feast to the life-given and bids him drink; / Sings and chants over him, / Sweetly serenad[es] him: / So give I life to Aqhat the Youth" (*ANET* 151b; M. Dahood, "Review of de Moor, *Seasonal Pattern*," *Or* 41 [1972] 137–38); "Ebenso wie Baal fürwahr am Leben erhält und bewirtet, / den Belebten bewirtet und ihm zu trinken gibt, / —es spielt und singt vor ihm / der Liebliche und er antwortet ihm— / so kann auch ich am Leben erhalten, Aqht, junger Mann!" (Dietrich and Loretz, "Baal *rpu*," 180–81; they connect the text with the image of feasting and music in 1.108:1–5 and identify *rpu mlk ʿlm* with Baʿl, who, at such a feast, vivifies the *rpum*); "As Baal revives, then invites, / Invites the revived to drink, / Trills and sings over him, / With pleasant tune they respond; / So I'll revive Aqhat the Hero" (*UNP* 61). The problem with these interpretations is the unlikelihood that Baʿl is the subject of all or part of the verbs after *yḥwy*, in view of the similarly described feast in the Baʿl cycle, 1.3 I 2–22 (see the discussion of parts of this text in the main discussion below). In this pericope, Baʿl is feasted by *another* being, who makes preparations (*yšʿr*) and gives him drink (*w yšqynh*; 1.3 I 9) and who, as a 'kindly one' (*nʿm*) chants (*ybd*) and sings (*yšr*) over Baʿl (*ʿl . bʿl*; lines 18–21)—all terms that appear in the present passage from Aqhat (lines 30–32). Spronk (*Beatific Afterlife*, 151, 155) takes *yḥwy* as a transitive with the proper change of subject in the following verbs.

51. An impersonal use of a singular active verb (*yʿšr*), construed as passive. So the verbs in the next poetic line. On the meaning 'prepare' rather than 'serve', see *SP* 71; Dijkstra and de Moor, "Passages," 189. Margalit (*UPA* 311–14) says that the precise meaning of *ʿšr* is 'to serve' and that here the sense is metaphorical: life is being served to Baʿl.

52. The word *ʿl* is often taken as 'before' rather than 'about'. For the latter, see *UPA* 305 n. 12; *CML* 112; *TO* 1 432. This interpretation is possible even in the parallel, 1.3 I 21 (see below).

53. Compare *ḫḫm* to Akk. *ḫaḫḫu* (CAD H 28b) 'spittle, slime; cough (as a disease)'. Alternatively, 'thorns' (*UPA* 306 n. 14). See the discussion of M. Held on *ḫaḫḫu* as 'spittle' in Akkadian ("Pits and Pitfalls in Akkadian and Biblical Hebrew," *JANES* 5 [1973] 189).

54. Margalit (*UPA* 151, 313–15) reads the emended *mt*! . *uḫryt* (so CTA) as the apparently written *mm . uḫryt* and translates 'a spiked-shaft (in) the posterior'. For this

(36) *mh . yqḥ . mt . aṯryt .*	What does a man obtain as his lot?
spsg . ysk (37) [l] *riš .*	(A) *spsg*(?)[55] will cover[56] the head,
ḥrṣ . l ẓr . qdqdy	(a) *ḥrṣ*(?),[57] on top of my pate.
(38) [ap]m*t . kl . amt .*	[Yes,] the death of all I will die,[58]
w an . mtm . amt	I will surely die.
(39) [ap . m]*ṯn . rgmm . argm .*	[Yet a sec]ond thing I must say:
qštm (40) [kl[59].]m*hrm .*	A bow is [a weapon(?) of] warriors,
ht . tṣdn . tinṯt	now, will womenkind[60] hunt [with it]?"
(41) [xxx g]mx *. tṣḥq . ʿnt .*	[. . .] Anat laughed out [loud],
w b lb . tqny (42) [xxx] .	and in her mind she forged [a plan(?)[61]]:
ṯb . ly . l aqht . ġzr .	"Turn to me, Aqhat, hero,
ṯb ly w lk (43) [aṯb .]	turn to me, and [I will turn] to you.[62]
hm *. l aqryk . b ntb . pšʿ*	Should I encounter you on the path of rebellion,
(44) [xxxxx]x *. b ntb . gan .*	[. . .] on the path of insolence,
ašqlk . tḥt (45) [pʿny . a]*n*[!]*k .*	I [my]self will fell you beneath [my feet],

reason (as well as prosodic considerations), he does not see *mt . aṯryt* in the next line as parallel.

55. For the term, see the discussion on pp. 148–53, below. It is doubtful that this means 'glaze'.

56. *Ysk* is from the root *skk* 'cover, screen' rather than *nsk* 'pour' (cf. *UPA* 318–19 n. 22; M. Dietrich and O. Loretz, "Einzelfragen zu Wörtern aus den ugaritischen Mythen und Wirtschaftstexten: Zur ugaritischen Lexikographie [XV]," *UF* 11 [1979] 195).

57. See the discussion of the term on p. 152. It is doubtful that this means 'potash, lime, plaster'.

58. Cf. Num 16:29.

59. *CAT* apparently (it has a space between the letters–two prepositions?) restores kl 'weapon' (Heb. *kĕlî*; so also *ARTU* 239; *CARTU* 107); Margalit (*UPA* 126) restores *nṯq* with a similar meaning.

60. Margalit (*UPA* 310 n. 27) says that *tinṯt* is chosen, instead of *aṯt* 'woman', in order to stress the *weakness* of women because of the resonance with the root *ʾanāšu* 'be weak'.

61. Dijkstra and de Moor ("Passages," 190) and de Moor and Spronk (*CARTU* 107) restore *ḫnp* 'viciousness', and de Moor (*ARTU* 239) translates 'but in her heart she devised [a vicious plan]'. Margalit (*UPA* 126, 152) takes the break at the beginning of line 42 with the next poetic line and restores hln 'Now, then'. He translates the phrase *w b lb . tqny* by itself as 'But inside, she was scheming'.

62. Margalit's interpretation (*UPA* 152) of *ṯb l-* as 'take leave of' makes good sense in the context: Anat would be suggesting severance of ties and cessation of hostilities. And it is not impossible, since in Hebrew *šwb* can have a separative preposition with the sense of 'leave' or 'turn away' (for example, Gen 27:45; Josh 22:16; Ezek 3:20; 18:24, 26, 27; 33:11, 18, 19; etc.). But the parallel in 1.3 IV 54–55 (Anat also speaking, with context of personal attack following) does not seem to indicate separation (and cf. Zech 1:3, Mal 3:7, 2 Chr 30:6). The phrase seems to indicate reconciliation (cf. Mal 3:24). Pardee ("The Preposition in Ugaritic [I]," 374) renders the lines 'Reconsider, Hero Aqht, reconsider for your own sake' (he does not read the restoration of [aṯb]).

nʿmn . *ʿmq* . *nšm*	kindly one, strongest[63] of men."
(46) [tdʿṣ . pʿ]n*m* . *w tr* . *arṣ* .	[She lifted her fe]et and the earth shook,
idk (47) [l ttn . p]n*m* . *ʿm* . *il* .	[then she s]et out toward Il. . . .

This is a case of what might be called ritual failure. The banquet proceeds properly until Anat spies Aqhat's bow. She asks him for it—twice. The first time, she offers him silver and gold.[64] Aqhat refuses the offer and tells her to have her own bow made. Anat then offers him something of greater worth: eternal life, the kind that Baʿl has. Aqhat also rejects this by calling her offer a filthy lie, since death for humans is inevitable. Anat breaks off negotiation with a threat: if Aqhat does not reconcile but remains rebellious, she will destroy him. She then leaves, apparently abruptly, and travels to Il, from whom she requests indulgence to punish Aqhat. The ritual snarl lies in the tension and animosity that has been generated and in cutting the banquet short.

One of the problems in the study of ritual has been how to account for these sorts of cases. Various functionalist and related approaches have viewed the task of ritual as reinforcing social ties and promoting solidarity among the participants,[65] channeling or deferring aggression and conflict,[66] providing individuals with psychological stability over against external chaos, integrating various principles or abstract phenomena (for example, the social and the cultural[67] or the domestic and the wild[68]). These approaches have been formulated to account for what ritual does when it is carried through to completion and to the satisfaction of those involved, without what might be viewed as unnecessary conflict. However, they have not been able fully to analyze or explain ritual when it does not work in positive directions. Other approaches that take into account the negative characteristics in ritual are also necessary, not only because these characteristics exist, but because they are common.

Part of the reason that analysis of ritual from this perspective is difficult is that there are several ways that a ritual performance might manifest problems. These need to be sorted out and studied independently,

63. Cf. Greenfield, "Ugaritic Lexicographical Notes," *JCS* 21 (1967) 89. Or perhaps 'wisest' (*UPA* 152).

64. This is reminiscent of the offers of riches made to Kirta, which he also refuses (1.14 I 51–II 3; III 22–40, etc.).

65. Burkert, "Problem of Ritual Killing," 169–70.

66. Mack ("Introduction," 31) notes that Burkert sees ritual as being mainly determined by the problem of aggression and the need for resolution.

67. C. Geertz, *The Interpretation of Cultures* (New York: Basic, 1973) 87–125, 142–69.

68. Burkert, as summarized by Mack, "Introduction," 52–53.

because they may have different explanations. Another reason for the difficulty in this approach is that problems are not always objectively determinable. One person's success may be another's failure. This becomes especially complicated when an external observer is the one making the evaluation.

A study that goes a long way in solving the first problem and recognizes the second is Ronald Grimes's comprehensive typology of problematic ritual.[69] He bases it on the analysis of speech acts by J. L. Austin.[70] He uses Austin's distinction between felicitous and infelicitous speech acts to analyze ritual. This allows Grimes to avoid the narrow functionalist implications of viewing problematic ritual as having simply succeeded or failed (though these terms are still useful for description of some cases). More importantly, the categorization allows him to include much more than what might be termed "failed" ritual. It also allows him to recognize problems even within what might be viewed as successful ritual.

Grimes posits nine categories of infelicitous ritual. The first two are based on Austin's analysis. The first involves *misfire*, which includes the subcategories *misinvocation* and *misexecution*. Misinvocation involves cases in which a practice is considered illegitimate or ineffectual (a *nonplay*: for example, the use of the ritual of other groups) or in which a practice is legitimate but the persons involved or circumstances are not (a *misapplication*: for example, female administration in a religion where males are thought to be the only ones suitable for the clergy or not performing a rite at the proper time). Misexecution occurs when a legitimate act is impaired by a *flaw*, a procedure that uses ambiguous or incorrect words, gestures, or materials (for example, Aaron's sons' using illegitimate coals for their incense offering, Lev 10:1–3), or by a *hitch*, a procedure left undone within a larger ritual performance (for example, the priests' not eating the purgation offering in Lev 10:16–20).

The second category is *abuse* (this refers to the treatment of the rite, not individuals in the rite; see "violation," below, for the latter). Abuse includes cases of: *insincerity*, where intentions or feelings do not correspond with the demands of ritual (see the prophetic criticism in Isa 1:10–17); a *breach*, when a ritual involves a consequent activity that is left undone (for example, Kirta's not fulfilling his vow); a *gloss*, the unsuccessful covering of problems and contradictions (Grimes notes a case in which a bride was visibly pregnant, despite the camouflage of a wedding

69. R. Grimes, "Infelicitous Performances and Ritual Criticism," in his book *Ritual Criticism*, 191–209.

70. J. L. Austin, *How to Do Things with Words* (2d ed.; ed. J. O. Urmson and M. Sbisà; Cambridge: Harvard University Press, 1975) 12–24.

dress); a *flop*, when a rite does not produce the expected atmosphere or psychological effect (the lack of proper effect can often be specifically attributed to one of the other instances of infelicity listed here, though it may happen even when specific causes cannot be identified).

To the main categories of misfire and abuse, derived from Austin, Grimes adds seven others: (3) *ineffectuality*, when expected observable effects are not achieved (for example, unsuccessful healing rites); (4) *violation*, when ritual is demeaning or threatening (for example, human sacrifice or ritual cliterodectomy); (5) *contagion*, when a rite has an unexpected effect (for example, when the burning of an effigy leads to a riot not originally intended); (6) *opacity*, when a performance is not intelligible (to the extent that it should be; for example, a rite performed in a language that is not understood sufficiently well for the purposes of the rite or when symbolism is complex); (7) *defeat*, when one rite invalidates another (for example, a ritual against sorcery);[71] (8) *omission*, when an (entire) act is left unperformed (for example, nonobservance of a prescribed festival; contrast a "hitch," above); and (9) *misframe*, when the nature or genre of a ritual is misunderstood (for example, this might happen when an outsider views the ritual of others; notice the "criticism" of sacrifice in the apocryphal Bel and the Dragon).

Some of the categorizations may be made relatively objectively, if one knows what to have expected in a ritual situation, especially in the cases of flaw, hitch, breach, and omission. Other judgments depend on the points of view of various ritual agents, as in cases of misapplication, flop, defeat; or on the analyst's ethical perspective, as in cases of violation. This difficulty notwithstanding, the different categories and their subdivisions are useful as an analytical tool. This is especially true because they allow us to perceive the nuances of infelicity. The present feast in the Aqhat story is not simply a failed ritual. It is infelicitous in *five* ways. One can see in it nonplay, hitch, insincerity, flop, and violation.

Anat's request for the bow is a nonplay, an unconventional procedure, because it is extraordinary. It is true that ritual in general and feasting in particular are often concerned with giving and receiving. But Anat's request for the bow goes beyond the normal expectations for a feast. It certainly exceeds the expectations provided by the paradigm of felicitous feasting in the first part of the story. In those feasts, the gods, as good guests, receive what is given to them and do not ask for more.

71. To this category, or parallel to it, may be added cases of ritual competition, such as Cain and Abel's sacrifices (Genesis 4) or the sacrifices offered by Elijah and the prophets of Baal (1 Kings 18).

The feast involves a hitch because it apparently breaks off without completion. As has been noted, Anat is so angry that she abruptly leaves to complain to Il.

Abuse is evident in the animosity that arises between Anat and Aqhat in bargaining for the bow. Aqhat's disdain and Anat's consequent threat are cases of insincerity. A flop is visible in that the ritual fails to produce the proper mood.

Violation is apparent in the threat that Anat makes against Aqhat's life. As noted above, violation is often a matter that is a function of the eye of the beholder and can arise from a judgment not based on the cultural context in which a rite occurs. Western observers may, for example, consider a clitoridectomy a violation, even though performers and even the patients may not view it this way. Sometimes a judgment of violation can be made on the basis of a rite's culture and background. This is surely the case in the feast we are considering in the Aqhat story. The value of life is in fact admitted by Anat in her offer of eternal life to Aqhat. When he does not yield the bow, she tries to take away the remaining life that he has as a mortal. Aqhat would understand this as a violation, and Anat apparently intends it to be so understood.

Anat's violation is egregious. This, however, should not mask the fact that Aqhat also commits an act of violation. He shows contempt for the goddess when, rejecting the offer of eternal life, he calls the offer a phlegmy lie and then tells her that she has no need for the bow because she is a woman.

In addition to Grimes's approach to ritual infelicity, Clifford Geertz's well-known essay on ritual and social change points up a feature in the Aqhat ritual that should not be overlooked.[72] In his essay, he argues that the disruption of a funerary ritual that he observed in Java was due to "incongruity between the cultural framework of meaning and the patterning of social interaction."[73] That is, the social situation in which the participants found themselves had changed and did not match the cultural forms of ritual activity. Therefore, the ritual did not transpire smoothly. Though this argument may be criticized from a theoretical point of view,[74] it is an indication to us that social differences of one sort or another between the previous feasts and this one with Anat and Aqhat may partly account for the problems this time.

72. Geertz, "Ritual and Social Change: A Javanese Example," in his *Interpretation*, 142–69. On ritual change, see Bell, *Perspectives*, 210–52.

73. Geertz, "Ritual and Social Change," 169.

74. Cf. Bell, *Ritual Theory*, 33–35.

The feasts prior to this one involved mainly males or operated at their behest. The initial feast involved only males: Daniʾil, Baʿl, and Il, and the third feast involved mainly Daniʾil and Kothar-wa-Ḫasis. When females appeared, they did so in support of the wishes of the males: the Kotharat presumably came, not of their own volition, but to make good the promise of Il; and Danatay obediently prepared a meal according to Daniʾil's request. In contrast to this, Anat is a rather independent female deity who has a liminal character, as Walls has argued, and stands in some opposition to "the patriarchal institutions of marriage and the social expectations of feminine behavior."[75] She thus appears as an incalculable wild card in the feast, which, especially if it is part of Aqhat's passage to manhood, grows out of the male-oriented context in which the initial feasts have occurred. This point of difference is manifested in Aqhat's statement that bows are for men, not women.[76] Anat's exceptional character is noted again when she goes to Il to complain about Aqhat, and the god responds: "I know, my daughter, that you are manlike" (*ydʿtk . bt . k anšt*; 1.18 I 16; see chapter 9). The only other female who seems to act independently in the story is Pughat, who kills Yaṭupan. However, she actually operates according to patriarchal interests: she asks her father for a blessing to aid her in avenging her brother's death. Because she dresses up like Anat and avenges the murder that Anat orchestrated, one could say that she restores the social pattern found before the appearance of Anat in the story. At any rate, one of the reasons that the present feast fails is that Anat does not share the social presuppositions and larger interests of Aqhat, his family, and the supporting deities.[77]

A third perspective on ritual infelicity comes from Catherine Bell's work. She does not deal with this topic in a primary way, but her understanding of ritual sheds light on it. She sees ritual as a means of establishing social structure and relationships, not merely being a reflection of

75. Walls, *The Goddess Anat*, 217 and passim.

76. Burkert ("Problem of Ritual Killing," 165, referring to other scholars) notes, by the way, "what seem to be practically universals in human civilizations: the hunt as men's business, and men feeding the family."

77. There is another level on which gender may play a part in the conflict between Anat and Aqhat. The bow may be taken as a symbol of virility. Thus, Anat is either seeking Aqhat's maleness or seeking him as a lover, much as Ishtar sought Gilgamesh (Gilgamesh VI). While it is true that Aqhat claims that the bow is not women's equipment, this sort of interpretation may go too far in finding psychological meaning in the text, especially since it is not clear that the feast at which Aqhat is killed is a marriage feast (see chapter 10). For discussion of this issue, see D. Hillers, "The Bow of Aqhat: The Meaning of a Mythological Theme," in *Orient and Occident* (ed. H. A. Hoffner; AOAT 22; Neukirchen-Vluyn: Neukirchener Verlag, 1973) 71–80; H. H. P. Dressler, "Is the Bow of Aqhat a Symbol of Virility?" *UF* 7 (1975) 217–20; Walls, *The Goddess Anat*, 186–206.

them. At the heart of this creative operation is the negotiation of power. In the process, even someone who is subordinate is empowered in some way (in other words, the process achieves "redemptive hegemony"). In her analysis, power is not to be understood in terms of coercion or violence but, following Michel Foucault, a concession in the negotiation between a superior and inferior. A superior has power only to the extent that an inferior is *willing* to become dependent. Similarly, the superior needs to relinquish his or her demands to some extent so that the inferior will consent to be ruled. In the ritual negotiation of power, much of what is given up is hidden to the eyes of the agents. This facilitates the process of negotiation and makes it successful. This perspective shows, by the way, that inherent in much of ritual is a potential for conflict. It should make us wary of simple classification of a rite as felicitous or infelicitous and keep us from a purely functionalist approach. The study of ritual should seek, when evidence permits, an analysis of the negotiation of power and the way that the interests of the agents evolve.

In any case, it is possible in the ritual negotiation of power for one or both parties to demand too much, to the point that compromise is not possible and the ritual cannot be consummated. Bell notes that "a power relationship undoes itself when, pushing to quell completely the insubordination necessary to it, it succeeds in reducing the other to total subservience or in transforming the other into an overt adversary."[78] This is essentially what has happened in the banquet scene with Aqhat. The two agents have failed in their negotiations, and the relationship between the two has completely broken down. The failure is emphasized by Anat's making, not just one, but two offers, and Aqhat's rejection of both.

Who is to blame for the failure in the ritual give and take? The text is not entirely clear. Anat seems culpable inasmuch as she interrupts her feasting to make a request for the bow. Note that upon seeing the bow she casts her cup to the ground. This looks as though she is refusing the feast that is presumably offered to her (among other gods; see above, on which gods may or may not be present) in the hope of obtaining a better gift. Moreover, her request runs counter to the way that requests have operated during feasting up to this point. Humans have been making requests; now a deity is making a request. Hence, she seems to be going beyond the bounds of proper behavior, even for a deity.

Aqhat for his part seems to be acting in a reasonable manner at first. Inasmuch as a deity has given him the bow, he may not want to yield it lest he bring upon himself another god's anger. He also responds politely and constructively to Anat's first request. He tells her how to go about

78. Bell, *Ritual Theory*, 201.

having a facsimile made. Anat's second offer does not show anger and confirms that Aqhat's first response was not accompanied by scorn. Yet Aqhat seems to lose his temper in his second response, perhaps in part because of his youth. Instead of offering a reasoned reply, he calls her offer a despicable lie and tries to put her in her presumed womanly place. There is thus a development in the assertion of wills during the scene. Anat is the first to act on her desire, which leads to a contravention of convention. Aqhat remains civil at first but angrily asserts his will in the end. Their mutual recalcitrance and loss of tempers prevent resolution.[79]

Structure and Participants

The basic structure of the rite is fairly clear from what is visible in the Aqhat text, along with restorations. First there is an invitation to eat, which is then followed by a description of the feast. In it, the description of eating precedes the description of drinking, and the preponderance of the description centers on the drinking. This correlates with the structure of the examples from the Baʿl cycle adduced above. They also put eating before drinking and they devote more attention to drinking than to eating, except for (b), which breaks off but may have had the same emphasis. Daniʾil's feasting of Baʿl and Il, the Kotharat, and Kothar-wa-Ḫasis in the Aqhat story also places eating before drinking.

A similar pattern is found in other texts. In 1.22 II 12–27, one of the *rpum* texts, the slaughtering of animals is described first (line 12–17), then wine, of various sorts, is presented (17–20). During the six days of offerings, eating comes before drinking (21–22, 23–24). Il's *mrzḥ* has eating before drinking (1.114:2–3), with a focus on drinking (2–3, 15–16, 18, 21–22), though eating is not unimportant (lines 6–13). In Kirta's feasts, the slaughtering of animals precedes the mention of wine (1.15 IV 4–5, 15–16; V 1–2), and eating is mentioned before drinking (1.15 IV 27; V 10; VI 2, 4). In Kirta's sacrifice (1.14 II 13–19; III 56–IV 2), the animal is slaughtered before the wine libation.

The placement of solid food first indicates that it is primary, but the space devoted to drink shows that it is an important "recreational" or socializing supplement. The presence of both of these elements marks a

79. Margalit (*UPA* 299, 301, 303) sees Aqhat as quite cleverly responding to the goddess and even showing off. Aqhat is not guilty of hubris but instead "is . . . something of a Promethean figure who naively, and suicidally, challenges an immoral and unscrupulous goddess who would abuse her divine privilege and shame her divine birth by depriving a mortal lad of a cherished birthday present" (p. 301). On the use of contrasts in the development in the passage, see W. G. E. Watson, "Antithesis in Ugaritic Verse," *UF* 18 (1986) 417–18.

feast as socially important and complex. In the present feast, especially if it is part of a celebration of Aqhat's passage to manhood, it is likely that we are to imagine that his larger family and perhaps the family's friends are in attendance. Though the high gods are probably not present, as noted above, it is likely that other lesser gods in addition to Anat are present.[80] The other feasts inside and outside the Aqhat narrative, which have been noted above, are similarly complex with the appearance of family, friends, and gods as participants. These contrast with the scene involving Pughat and Yaṭupan at the end of the story, in which only wine is served. In that scene, the recipient is not a friend, a superior, or a god. Pughat is disguised as Anat, a goddess, and Yaṭupan is apparently a human. More particularly, Yaṭupan is Anat's *employee*; Anat is Yaṭupan's and his troops' *agrt* 'she who hires' (see chapter 18 on this term). This perhaps explains why only wine is being served. Yaṭupan is not worthy of a greater meal. (For a reason that Anat would be serving Yaṭupan in the first place, see chapter 18.)

These observations correlate with an observation made by Mary Douglas in her study of the social meaning of meals in Britain. Though she studies a completely different culture, and though she has much more evidence for pressing her point than we have available in the Ugaritic texts, what she says is nonetheless applicable here. She notes that the complexity of a meal is a sign of social intimacy, import, and engagement. She distinguishes between complete meals and simple drinks and observes:

> Drinks are for strangers, acquaintances, workmen, and family. Meals are for family, close friends, honored guests. The grand operator of the system is the line between intimacy and distance. Those we know at meals we also know at drinks. The meal expresses close friendship. Those we only know at drinks we know less intimately.[81]

Yaṭupan is Anat's "workman." The two have a relationship in which the former provides services for the latter; it lacks the dimensions that are found between family members and friends or between humans and the gods, such as responsibility, obligation, love, and honor.

Looking closely at the individuals who participate in meals instead of just drinks leads to discovering another possible reason for the tension between Aqhat and Anat. Douglas says that meals are for "family, close friends, honored guests." These participants are not all in the same social

80. Margalit (*UPA* 299) says that the guests include family, friends, and perhaps the *rpum*, but not Il and Baʿl.

81. Douglas, *Implicit Meanings*, 256. She goes on to note that hot meals involve closer friends than cold meals.

category, which makes us wonder if meals (as opposed to drinks) are a simple marker of intimacy. An individual might be intimate with family and friends at a meal but not necessarily with an honored guest. It is true that the inclusion of a guest at a meal is a means of honoring the guest as if he or she were one of the host's intimates. The honor sends a message to the guest and even places him or her in a new relationship to the host: the guest is now like family and friends. Nevertheless, the guest may remain at a distance, either because the meal is a single or infrequent event (in which case the guest in fact is not being treated as a family member or friend) or because the guest has another social relationship to the host that is inconsistent with being a family member or friend (for example, if the guest is one's employer). The elaborateness of a meal may actually be a marker of distance in some cases. For example, many types of meals that one would serve to family and perhaps friends would never be served to one's employer.

Some of the tensions between Aqhat and Anat can be analyzed as problems of intimacy and distance. Anat is an honored guest. Therefore, even though she may be included symbolically as a family member or friend, she is still superior to the humans, and they can never treat her simply as family or friend. At the same time, a god invited to a feast sponsored by humans cannot assume a position of familiarity with them. In the feast under discussion, the distance that should be observed in a feasting situation of this type seems to have been compromised by both host (Aqhat) and guest. Anat seems to behave with too much familiarity in asking for the bow, despite the fact that gods may ask for anything they wish. Aqhat also spurns Anat almost as though she were his sibling. The controversy between them appears juvenile. Their fight is reminiscent of Cain and Abel; and the consequences are similar.

Contrasts

As I have already shown, this scene acquires much of its significance by diverging from the initial pattern of successful rituals. A deity makes a request here, not a human. Anat casts down her cup, in contrast to Il's taking his up to bless Daniʾil. A reversal of relationships has also taken place: a human now essentially rejects the superiority of a deity. Aqhat's activity also fails to fulfill the ideals expressed for a son in the filial duties. Duty E suggests that the son was to be a successful feaster of divinities. Here he does not measure up. Notably, however, only male divinities appear in duty E. Nothing is said about a son's ability to handle Anat, which illustrates again the fact that feasting in the first part of the story functions according to male lines of interest.

The negotiations between Aqhat and Anat themselves portray an ideal, with which the failed feast clashes. In Anat's second offer, for instance, the one to which Aqhat responds with anger, the specific point at which the feast irretrievably deteriorates, Anat promises eternal life such as Baʿl has. She also tells Aqhat that he can be feasted and celebrated with song like Baʿl (lines 30–32). The passage uses the same language found in the feasting of Baʿl in 1.3 I, the first part of which was presented above (example [a], p. 101):

ndd (9) *yʿšr . w yšqynh*	Having stood, he made ready and gave him drink.
. . .	. . .
(18) *qm . ybd . w yšr*	Having arisen, he recited and sang,
(19) *mṣltm . bd . nʿm*	cymbals in the hand of the kindly one.
(20) *yšr . ǵzr . ṭb . ql*	The youth with pleasant voice sang[82]
(21) *ʿl . bʿl . b ṣrrt* (22) *ṣpn .*	about Baʿl on the heights of Ṣaphon.

Several terms are common to this and the Aqhat passage: *yʿšr,* specifically *yʿšr w yšqynh*; *ybd w yšr*; *nʿm* and *nʿmn*; and *ʿl* with respect to Baʿl. Moreover, we have seen that the description of the feast in the Aqhat text is otherwise similar to the feast scene in this Baʿl text. From the comparison, we infer that Anat is saying that Aqhat can be the recipient of the type of feast that she and presumably the other gods present are being given just then.[83]

This offer contrasts two types of bodies, mortal and immortal. Mortal bodies provide an offering and immortals receive it. Anat's offer allows Aqhat to obtain a new body, so to speak, and pass from offerer to recipient. Aqhat's possible transformation to an immortal being is balanced by Anat's symbolic move to the human side: Anat, a god, now makes a request. In these ways, there is a symbolic or literal mixing of the divine and human spheres, which have been kept separate to this point.

The negative consequences of this role confusion or boundary crossing is elucidated by René Girard's observation that violence is associated with the loss of "cultural distinctions" (which include social distinctions).[84] These distinctions serve as a "dam against violence." If they are obliterated, malice floods in. In reverse relationship, violence can serve to erode these distinctions. It is doubtful that we should go as far as Girard

82. On singing for Baʿl, see 1.101:15–18, in which Anat sings of Baʿl's love with a lyre. Cf. de Moor, "Studies in the New Alphabetic Texts," 180–83.

83. It is not clear that this should be taken as evidence that Baʿl is present at the feast with Aqhat and Anat.

84. Girard, *Violence*, 49–52 (see more comprehensively, pp. 39–69).

might, to say: (1) that the feast here involves a case of purifying (or sacred) violence, or sacrifice, which stands in the place of impure (profane, savage, uncontrolled) violence; (2) that because of the blurring of cultural distinctions, however, it does not have a sublimating effect and therefore ends in antagonism, leading ultimately to murder (which also occurs, arguably, in a "sacrificial" context). As I noted in the discussion about the initial petition feast, there is little in the descriptions of the feasts throughout the Aqhat story about the killing of the animals to provide meat for the feasts; the act seems unimportant. The animals are offerings, not necessarily sacrifices. Nevertheless, this feast is a case in which expected patterns of behavior are disregarded and upset. Custom and etiquette have been laid aside. With no boundaries for behavior, the confrontation escalates to violence. This observation and the observation made above that Anat does not serve the interests of male-oriented feasting demonstrate that infelicity can be a function of a "sociocultural" situation that differs from normal or traditional expectations.

In the treatment of the initial offering above (chapter 1), I made the observation that the present feast is the second most elaborate in the story. This is necessarily so because at this point the dynamics of the entire story change; the complexity of the ritual scene is a correlate, even a signal, of this change. To invoke the metaphor of movement again, it takes more energy to change course than to maintain travel in the same direction. This feast provides that energy. The expenditure of energy then continues into the next feast, when Anat kills Aqhat.

Chapter 9
Anat's Complaint to Il

A brief scene involving ritualized activity appears before Anat consummates her plan against Aqhat. Besides giving a fuller characterization of Anat, it structurally parallels the foregoing infelicitous feast.

As soon as she leaves Aqhat, the goddess goes to Il, to whom she expresses her contempt for the mortal. In her approach she prostrates herself before him. This places the following words of her petition in a ritualized context (1.17 VI):

(50) [l pʿn . il . t]h*br* . *w tql* .	[She] lowered herself and fell [before Il],
tštḥ (51) [wy . w tkbd]n*h* .	she bow[ed and honored] him.[1]

Her obeisance not only reflects but is a means of demonstrating anew her relationship to the high god.[2] It involves the symbolism of placing her body low in relation to Il, who remains unbowed. The subordinate action is a means of establishing or reestablishing the relationship illustrated by the action. The subordinate relationship, however, is challenged and contradicted as Anat continues her petition.

As or after she prostrates herself, she begins her criticism of Aqhat. Unfortunately, because of breakage, we really only know about this from the introduction to the complaint (1.17 VI):

tlšn . aqht . ǵzr	She slandered[3] Aqhat, the hero,
(52) [tqll[4] . kdd . dn]i*l . mt . rpi*	[she cursed the child of Dan]iʾil, the Rapiʾan.
w tʿn (53) [btlt . ʿnt .]	[The Virgin Anat] said,
[tšu .] g*h . w tṣḥ .*	[she raised] her voice and cried:
*h*wt (54) [xxxxxxxx]	"Him [. . .]

1. For restorations, see 1.4 IV 25–26; 1.6 I 37–38.

2. On Anat's subordiantion to Il, see Walls, *The Goddess Anat*, 108–9.

3. So *UPA* 152; similarly *ARTU* 240: 'railed at'. Cf. W. G. E. Watson, "More on Preludes to Speech in Ugaritic," *UF* 24 (1992) 362. This verb appears in the section on Pughat's visit to Yaṭupan.

4. So the restoration in *CAT*; Margalit (*UPA* 126, 152) restores *l tmk* 'Verily does she deprecate'.

[xxxx] *aqht* . yšm[ḫ][5]	[. . .] Aqhat rejoi[ced(?)],
(55) broken	[. . .]"

The remaining eleven lines are lost.

The next tablet (1.18) continues with Anat's visit to Il. The first half dozen lines of this are also broken, but apparently she is still complaining about and plotting against Aqhat. We find the verb *aṯ*br 'I will break' in line 4, which is logically something Anat might say about Aqhat or his concerns. But it is doubtful that she is saying she will break his bow; the bow is something she wants–whole and functional–for herself. Nevertheless, the verb might play contextually at a more abstract level with the breaking of the bow (*ṯṯ*br *qšt*; 1.19 I 3-4) and/or, later on, Baʿl's breaking the wings of the vultures (1.19 III 2, 8, etc.; see chapter 14).

Il probably gives a short response to Anat around lines 4b-6a.[6] This is indicated by what appears to be the angry counter-response from Anat that follows, which is much like the one she gives in the Baʿl text, 1.3 V 19-25 (which aids in the restoration of the Aqhat text). The Aqhat text reads (1.18 I):

w tʿn [btlt . ʿnt]	And [Virgin Anat] answered:
(7) [bnt . bh]*tk* . *y il*m [.]	"[In the building[7] of] your [man]sion, O Il,
[bnt . bhtk] (8) [al . tšmḫ .]	[in the building of your mansion, do not rejoice],
al . *tš*[mḫ . b rm . hklk]	do not rej[oice in the height of your palace.]
(9) [ank . al .] a*ḫdhm* . [bymny .]	[I will certainly] seize them [with my right hand],
[ank] (10) [amḫṣ . b] g*dlt* . *ar*[kty .]	[I will smite (them) with my lo]ng mighty arm,
[amḫṣ] (11) [l qdq]d*k* .	[I will smite] your h[ead],
ašhlk [. šbtk . dmm]	I will make [your white hair] flow [with blood],

5. Margalit (*UPA* 152, 319) restores the line [aḥl . an .] *aqht* . yš[pl] '[I ask that] Aqht be br[ought low]'.

6. De Moor and Spronk (*CARTU* 108) reconstruct lines 4-6a: [ ]h . *aṯ*br [. qšth . w yʿn] (5) [ṯr . il . a]b*h* . *ap* . a[nšt . btlt] (6) [ʿnt . bt] . *w tʿn* . [btlt . ʿnt]; de Moor (*ARTU* 241) translates: '"[ ] his [ ], I shall break [his bow]!" [And the Bull Ilu,] her fa[ther, answered:] "Are [you] an]gry, Virgin Anatu, my daughter?"] And [the Virgin Anatu] answered' (the restoration is based in part on the idiom in 1.2 I 38, 43; 1.6 V 21; cf. 1.169:15).

7. The reconstruction in lines 7-8 follows Margalit (*UPA* 127) and is based on the legibility of *b* rm in the parallel 1.3 V 21 (so *CAT*). Dijkstra and de Moor ("Passages," 192-93) argue that 'building' does not fit the context here; they read *bnm btk/hklk* 'sons of your house/palace'. De Moor and Spronk (*CARTU* 7, 108) and de Moor (*ARTU* 17, 241) modify this reading in both passages and have it refer to sons and daughters.

(12) šb[t . dq]n*k* . *mmʿm* .	your wh[ite bea]rd with gore.
w [xxxxxxx] (13) *aqht w ypltk* .	And [. . .][8] Aqhat, and he will rescue you,
bn [dnil . xxxx] (14) *w yʿḏrk* .	the son [of Daniʾil], and he will save[9] you,
b yd . *btlt* . [ʿnt . xxx]	from the hand of Virgin [Anat . . .].

Apparently, in the broken portion, Il does not respond in accord with Anat's initial criticism or request, so she threatens him in this manner.

This threat runs counter to her show of reverence at the beginning of her complaint and involves substantial irony. This is enhanced, if the restoration of [b rm] 'in the height of' in line 8b is correct. The lowness (subordination) of Anat in body ironically plays against the institutional height (superiority) of Il. It seems that the humility she demonstrates in gesture is either not sincere or is only conditional, genuine only as long as the power to whom she bows agrees to her demands. This illustrates how important words, and not just actions, are in ritual activity.[10] The mouth may contradict the body.

Though infelicity may be present, the encounter is not necessarily a failure, because Il finally concedes and tells Anat to act according to her intentions:[11]

(15) *w yʿ*n . *lṭpn* . *il d* p[id]	Lṭpn, the merc[iful] god, answered:
(16) *ydʿ*k . *bt* . *k anšt* .	"I know, my daughter, that you are manlike,[12]
w i[n . b ilht] (17) *qlṣ*k .	and the contempt you have is [not found among goddesses].
tbʿ . *bt* . *ḫnp* . *lb*[k xxxxx]	Go, my daughter, the evil(?) of [your] heart [do(?)],
[a](18)*ḫd* . *d iṯ* . *b kbdk* .	[se]ize what is in your bosom,
tšt . d[iṯ b] (19) *irtk* .	accomplish what [is in] your breast.
dṯ . *ydṯ* . *mʿqbk*	May the one who obstructs you be smashed(?)."[13]

8. Margalit restores (*UPA* 153, 320) *w*[tqra] 'Then [you can call on] Aqht for help'. De Moor and Spronk (*CARTU* 108) and de Moor (*ARTU*, 241) restore, read, and divide: *w*[yṯʿk . l il] *aqht* . / *w ypltk* . *bn* . [dnil . aby] / *w yʿḏrk* . *b yd* . *btlt* . [ʿnt . l il] 'Then let Aqhatu [save you, O Ilu], / and let the son [of Daniʾilu] deliver you, [my father], / and let him help you from the hand of the Virgin [Anatu, O Ilu]!'

9. Cf. B. Q. Baisas, "Ugaritic *ʿḏr* and Hebrew *ʿzr* I," *UF* 5 (1973) 41–52.

10. Contra Bell, *Ritual Theory*, 110–14.

11. Margalit (*UPA* 153) does not take this as a concession but a warning to Anat.

12. On the supposed androgyny of Anat, see Dijkstra and de Moor, "Passages," 193–94; Walls, *The Goddess Anat*, 83–86. Walls (pp. 84–85) understands *anšt* as 'incorrigible'; *UNP* 63 renders 'desperate'; *GUL* 97, 114, 'you are meek'.

13. Aistleitner, *Wörterbuch*, 83: 'niederschlagen, niedertreten'; *MLC* 539: 'aplastar'.

The entire passage has similarities to the feast with Anat and Aqhat. In both, Anat makes two requests (explicit or implicit), and in both, the person petitioned makes two responses.[14] The communication with Il can therefore be seen as structurally recapitulating the prior feast scene. But there are differences. The persons petitioned, Aqhat and Il, are heterogeneous, mortal and divine. And they are the mortal and divine figures who, so far in the story, stand at opposite ends of the hierarchy. Il is the high god—at least he is the one to whom Baʿl needs to appeal to bless Daniʾil. Aqhat is the son, subordinate to his father and presumably to his mother. Anat is like a pin-ball, bouncing between these two extreme posts. In her movements to and from these individuals, as well as in making requests of them, she stands out as an active figure; they appear as relatively passive. This strengthens the observation made above that the failure of the feast involving Anat and Aqhat may be due to the goddess's unconventional social position. Anat is intermediate between the high gods and humans; she is dependent on both of them for her success and fulfillment. The traditional hierarchical structure, established in part by ritual, does not fully suit her needs. She therefore has to subvert it. This subversion—and therefore a close brush with ritual failure—appears in her petition of Il. She has to threaten him as she did Aqhat. Il saves himself by conceding. A feature of his concession that stands out vividly against the rejection of Aqhat is the affirmation of Anat's masculine character (even though it is formulaic; see 1.3 V 23).

14. One difference is that in the Anat-Aqhat feast, Anat has the last word by threatening Aqhat.

Chapter 10
Anat's Killing of Aqhat

After visiting Il (1.18 I 20–32), Anat pursues plans to kill Aqhat , in the context of a feast (1.18 I 20–22). Among other things she tells him to go to the city (or fortress[1]) of Abilum. This conversation is followed by a break of about 150 lines between the end of column I and the beginning of column IV.[2] These lines probably recounted Aqhat's journey and arrival at Abilum. It is also likely that the break included information about his preparations for the upcoming fateful feast (see below). When the text resumes in column IV, Anat approaches Yaṭupan, her hired mercenary. She apparently tells him that Aqhat is staying (*yṯb*) in Abilum (see 1.18 IV 7).[3] It is not clear whether Anat intended to kill Aqhat at this time, but she readily accepts Yaṭupan's recommendation that she do so, and decides to take advantage of Aqhat's feast as the occasion for the killing. She succeeds, thus providing another example of ritual infelicity.

The Text and the Feast's Purpose

The text, beginning with Yaṭupan's advice to kill Aqhat, reads as follows (1.18 IV):

1. See Margalit (*UPA* 327 n. 13, 350), who derives *qrt* from *qwr* 'be round'. The word may refer to a 'walled-in area'.

2. De Moor (*ARTU* 243) estimates that "about 173 lines" are missing. Margalit (*UPA* 154, 205 n. 28) argues that col. IV is the direct continuation of col. I and that the tablet had only two columns. This judgment is made on the basis of the context of cols. I and IV.

3. Since Anat is addressing Yaṭupan, the verb in the fragmentary *yṯb* . *yṭp* [. . .] of 1.18 IV 7 would most easily refer to someone other than Yaṭupan—that is, Aqhat (so *CML* 112; *ARTU* 244). Margalit (*UPA* 129, 154–55) has Anat address Yaṭupan with the verb *yṯb*, telling him to stay at Abilum and then, before *w y*ʿ*n* of line 11, Margalit inserts seven lines of text, which he supposes have fallen out, some of which come from 1.19 I 14b–17a and some of which are conjectural expansion. In the inserted lines, Anat says that Aqhat is coming to Abilum.

(11) *w yʿn . yṭpn* . m[hr . št]	(11) Yaṭupan,[4] the warrior of the Lady(?),[5] answered:
(12) *šmʿ . l btlt . ʿnt .*	(12) "Hear, O Virgin, Anat:
at . ʿ[l . qšth] (13) *tmḫṣh .*	F[or his bow] you (13) should smite him,
qṣʿth . hwt . l tḥ[wy .xxx]	(for) his arrows, do not let him l[ive[6] . . .].
(14) *nʿmn . ǵzr . št . ṯrm .*	The kindly hero has prepared a meal
w[xxxxx] (15) *ištir . b ḏdm .*	and [. . .] remain(s)/*ištir*-substance(??) in the camp/teat(??)
w nʿrs[. xxxx]	and is ground/we rejoice(??) [. . .]."[7]
(16) *w* t*ʿn . btlt . ʿnt .*	The Virgin Anat answered:
ṯb . yṭp . w [xxx] (17) *lk*	"Pay attention, Yaṭup, and [ ] for you.
*aštk . km . nšr . b ḥ*b[šy]	I will put you in [my belt]-pouch[8] like a vulture,
(18) *km . diy . b tʿrty*	in my bag[9] like a kite.
aqht . [km . yṯb] (19) *l lḥm .*	[When] Aqhat [sits down] to eat,
[[b]] *w bn . dnil . l ṯrm*	the son of Daniʾil to dine,
[ʿlh] (20) *nšrm . trḫpn .*	vultures will hover [over him],
ybṣr . [ḥbl . d](21)*iym .*	[a group of k]ites will watch.[10]
bn . nšrm . arḫp . an[k .]	I [my]self will hover among the vultures,
ʿl (22) *aqht . ʿdbk .*[11]	(and) set[12] you over Aqhat.
hlmn . ṯnm . qdqd	Strike him twice on the head,
(23) *ṯlṯid . ʿl . udn .*	thrice on the temple.

4. The vocalization is uncertain. W. G. E. Watson connects the name with Akk. *naṭāpu* 'tear out' and gives it the meaning 'Render, Ripper' ("Puzzling Passages in the Tale of Aqhat," *UF* 8 [1976] 371–78; cf. *ARTU* 244 n. 135). Margalit (*UPA* 296, 333, 339–40) connects it with Arab. *ṭāfa* 'wander', referring to the soldier's nomadic character.

5. On *št*, see chapter 18.

6. Margalit (*UPA* 155, 331, 335) interprets this verb 'dispossess' (with emphatic *l*-). With this, he emends the text by adding *tmḫṣh . ʿl* before *qṣʿth* (perhaps on the basis of 1.19 I 14–16) and redividing the line into a tricolon: *at . . . tmḫṣh* / ⟨tmḫṣh ʿl⟩ . . . *hwt* / *l tḥ*[wy . . .] *nʿmn ǵzr*. I agree with Margalit that *l tḥ*[wy] should not be interpreted as meaning 'you shall bring (him) back to life'.

7. See below for a discussion of lines 14b–15a.

8. Cf. 1.3 II 13. Discussions include *SP* 91–92; *UPA* 340–41. Other translations: 'wristlet' (*CML* 112; cf. W. G. E. Watson, "The Falcon Episode in the Aqhat Tale," *JNSL* 5 [1977] 72); 'arm' (cf. Dietrich and Loretz, "Zur ugaritischen Lexikographie [V]," 30); 'game-bag' (*TO* 1 438; *ARTU* 245).

9. So *SP* 91–92. See 1.19 IV 45. Margalit (*UPA* 341) suggests that this word comes from the root *ʿry* 'be naked' and refers to an "article of clothing which concealed the area of one's 'nakedness.'"

10. Compare Arab. *baṣura/baṣira* 'look, understand' (*DMWA* 60).

11. On the form *ʿdbk*, an infinitive, see Dijkstra and de Moor, "Passages," 195.

12. For this meaning, see Dietrich and Loretz, "Debatte über die Lautentwicklung," 125–26. Cf. M. Dietrich and O. Loretz, "*ʿdb* und *ʿḏb* im ugaritischen," *UF* 17 (1985) 106; Pardee ("The Preposition in Ugaritic [I]," 362) has 'position over' for *ʿdb ʿl* here.

špk . km . šiy (24) *dm*	Shed (his) blood like a smasher(?),[13]
km . šḫṭ . l brkh .	like a slaughterer, to his knees.
tṣi . km (25) *rḥ . npšh .*	Let his breath escape like wind,
km . iṯl . brlth .	his soul like an *iṯl*-plant(?),[14]
km (26) *qṭr . b aph .*	like smoke[15] from his nostrils.
u[!] *ap . mprh .*	Indeed, his heart(?),[16]
ank (27) *l aḥwy .*	I will not let live!"[17]
tqḥ . yṭpn . mhr . št	She took Yaṭupan, the warrior of the Lady,
(28) *tštn . k nšr . b ḥbšh*	placed him in her belt like a vulture,
km . *diy* (29) *b tʿrth .*	in her bag like a kite.
aqht . km . yṯb . l lḥ[m]	Aqhat was sitting down to ea[t],
(30) *bn . dnil . l ṯrm .*	the son of Daniʾil, to dine.
*ʿlh . nš*rm (31) *trḫpn .*	Vultures hovered over him,
ybṣr . ḥbl . diy[m]	a group of kite[s] watched.
[bn] (32) *nšrm . trḫp . ʿnt .*	Anat hovered [among] the vultures,
ʿl[. aqht] (33) *tʿdbnh .*	she set him over [Aqhat].
hlmn . ṯnm[. qdqd]	He struck him twice [on the head],
(34) *ṯlṯid . ʿl . udn*	thrice on the temple.
š[pk . km] (35) *šiy . dmh .*	He sh[ed] his blood [like] a smasher,
km . šḫ[ṭ . l brkh]	like a slaughter[er, to his knees].

13. Compare *šiy* to Heb. *šāʾâ* 'make a din or crash, crash into ruins' (BDB 980). Dijkstra and de Moor ("Passages," 195–96) take the word to mean 'criminal', from a metathesized form of the root *šwʾ* (compare Arab. *sāʾa* [*swʾ*] 'be bad, evil'). The *il šiy* in 1.12 I 22 may be related. Other translations: 'murderer, assassin' (*ARTU* 245; *MLC* 626); 'water' (*UPA* 341 = Hur. *šiye* 'water'; this unique word for water was chosen because of alliteration). W. G. E. Watson ("Two Similes in Aqht," *UF* 23 [1991] 359–60) takes the Ugaritic term as a cognate with Akk. *šâʾu* 'fly' and translates this and the next lines '(in order to) spill his [= Aqhat's] blood like a certain bird, like a falcon (?) [lit., attacker or leaper] over his knees'.

14. Arab. *aṯl* 'tamarisk'. Perhaps this simile is based on the shape of the plant. The connection with Hittite *iššalli* 'spittle' (Puhvel, *Dictionary*, 380–81) is questionable (cf. J. C. de Moor, "Frustula ugaritica," *JNES* 24 [1965] 363–64; Dijkstra and de Moor, "Passages," 196; *ARTU* 246; *CML* 112). Margalit (*UPA* 343) relates this word to the root *ʾṯ(ṯ)*, meaning in Arabic 'be luxuriant, thick', with the *-l* morpheme denoting potentiality; hence, *iṯl* is perhaps a "plant in bud but not yet in bloom."

15. The simile 'like smoke' *kqṭr* with the verb *yṣʾ* appears in an incantation in 1.169:3.

16. On this meaning of *mpr*, see de Moor and Spronk (*CARTU* 152) Other meanings: 'prostration' (*MLC* 385); 'death convulsions' (R. M. Wright, "Egyptian *npꜣpꜣ*: A Cognate for Ugaritic *mpr* 'Convulsion'," *UF* 26 [1994] 539–41; *UPA* 156). The word probably also appears in line 38 (*mhrh* to be read *mprh*; so *ARTU* 246; *UPA* 130; for the reverse emendation, see *TO* 1 440 and see 339 note f; *CML* 113; Dijkstra and de Moor, "Passages," 196). It is doubtful that *ṣmt* of 38 should be inserted before *mprh* in line 26 (so *UPA* 130).

17. Line 26c–27a is certainly to be construed negatively (Dijkstra and de Moor, "Passages," 196–97), as in line 13 (contra *MLC* 385; *TO* 1 439).

(36) *yṣat* . *km* . *rḥ* . *npš*[h .]	[His] breath escaped like wind,
[km . iṯl] (37) *brlth* .	his soul [like an *iṯl*-plant],
km . *qṭr* . b[aph(?)]	like smoke from his nostrils.

Because of breakage and difficulties in terminology, the purpose and nature of this feast is not clear. It has been suggested that it is a marriage feast for Anat and Aqhat.[18] This is based in part on Anat's comment to Aqhat: *at* . *aḫ* . *w an* . a[ḫtk] 'You are my brother, and I am [your sis]ter' (1.18 I 24). It is also based on *nʿrs* in 1.18 IV 15 which, on the basis of Arabic, is understood as meaning 'we shall celebrate the marriage'.[19] Moreover, the term *ṯirk* (1.18 I 25), in a broken passage just after Anat states her sisterly relation to Aqhat, has been understood to mean 'your (Aqhat's) groomsmen'.[20]

How Anat and Yaṭupan act in carrying out their plot, however, seems to contradict this conclusion. Neither of them is on the scene as a participant in the feast. They hide among vultures, waiting for the right opportunity to strike Aqhat. Aqhat seems to be holding the feast without Anat, the supposed bride. It is already underway when Yaṭupan and Anat plan specifically how to kill him. Unless this is some prenuptial feast involving only the groom (a Late Bronze bachelor party?), it would have to be taken as part of the marriage festivities, and thus one would expect Anat to be a participant. To have Anat clearly present, feigning to be a participant, would not have been conceptually difficult. The story does have Pughat employ this strategy later on, when she serves wine to Yaṭupan.

The evidences for a wedding feast therefore must be understood otherwise. The phrase "You are my brother, and I am [your sis]ter" may also be a more general attempt to seduce the boy, as Ishtar tried to do to Gilgamesh,[21] but here with the goal of killing him.[22] On the other hand, the

18. Cf. Dijkstra and de Moor, "Passages," 194; de Moor, "Frustula" 361; idem, "Seasonal Pattern in the Legend of Aqhatu," 65–66; M. Pope, *Song of Songs* (AB 7C; Garden City, N.Y.: Doubleday, 1977) 480–81; compare the use of "sister" and "brother" in Cant 4:9–5:1, 8:1. For some of the difficulties with this interpretation, see Walls, *The Goddess Anat*, 193–94.

19. In Arabic, the verb *ʿarasa* means 'to marry' and in form IV 'to arrange a marriage' (*DMWA* 602). For the interpretation, see *ARTU* 242–43, 245; Dijkstra and de Moor, "Passages," 195.

20. Ibid., 194; de Moor, "Seasonal Pattern in the Legend of Aqhatu," 65; *ARTU* 242 n. 129 (here the root *ṯʾr* is equivalent to *ṯʿr* 'arrange'). Gibson (*CML* 25) says that Anat is disguised as a woman to entice Aqhat.

21. *UPA* 324–28. On this passage, which has often been compared to the Anat-Aqhat interchange, see T. Abusch, "Ishtar's Proposal and Gilgamesh's Refusal: An Interpretation of *The Gilgamesh Epic*, Tablet 6, Lines 1–79," *History of Religions* 26 (1986) 143–87.

22. Dressler ("The Metamorphosis of a Lacuna: Is *at.aḫ.wan* . . . a Proposal of Marriage?" *UF* 11 [1979] 211–17) shows that Anat's addressing Aqhat as "brother" is not

line may be a pretense of reconciliation. The term *nʿrs* may refer to general rejoicing or may refer to a type of meal used in the feast.[23] The term *ṯirk* could refer to 'relatives' or 'preparers' and not necessarily have a marriage context.[24]

If it is not a marriage feast, it may be connected with the hunting that is fragmentarily mentioned in 1.18 I 27, 29. In these lines Anat appears to tell Aqhat to go hunting and that she is going to teach him how to hunt.[25] The gap in the text that follows would provide plenty of room for describing this activity in some detail. This of course must remain in the realm of speculation.

In the lines that remain, the feast is not described in any detail. It is described only with the verb *ṯrm* (noun and verb, lines 14, 19, 30), which is used elsewhere of human and divine dining.[26] The general verb *lḥm* is also used (19, 29). The presence of vultures and kites (*nšrm, diym*) indicate that flesh is present. These birds seem to be the same type as the scavenging *nšrm* flying around Daniʾil's house when the drought takes hold (1.19 I 32–33) and the *nšrm* that Daniʾil conjures and that presumably or actually eat Aqhat's remains (1.19 II 56–IV 45). The birds may be flying over Aqhat in this feast to obtain any scraps discarded after slaughtering and feasting.[27] The obscure phrase *ištir . b ḏdm* in the broken line 15, if it does not refer to Aqhat's companions staying in the camp apart from the place where Aqhat is holding the feast,[28] may also indicate that

connected with marriage. He takes it as part of the introduction to Anat's invitation to hunt.

23. Other meanings proposed include: 'be tired' (*CML* 155; this refers to Arab. *ʿarisa*); 'barley-groats' (*UPA* 210; compare Heb.*ʿarîsâ* 'coarse meal'); 'rejoice' (*MLC* 605, based on a generalization of the Arab. verb *ʿarasa*); 'make cakes' (*TO* 1 438; based on Mishnaic Hebrew *ʿērēs* [denominative from *ʿărîsâ* 'dough'] 'to start dough; knead' [cf. M. Jastrow, *A Dictionary of the Targumim, the Talmud Babli and Yerushalmi, and the Midrashic Literature* (New York: Judaica, 1971) 1120]).

24. Compare Heb. *šĕʾēr* and Arab. *ṯāʾr-*. The interpretation 'preparers' admits the connection of the term with the root *ṯʿr*; see p. 130 n. 20 above. See *UPA* 328.

25. So *ARTU* 243.

26. Cf. 1.2 I 21; 1.16 VI 20–21; 1.92:15. On *ṯrm*, see *SP* 130.

27. Therefore, it is doubtful that we should think of the *nšrm* as falcons, even though the image of hunting with a falcon may lie behind Yaṭupan's attack on Aqhat. See *UPA* 332, 335–36, 340–41 and n. 4 (Margalit here suggests that a *nšr* "in Aqht, perhaps in the Ugaritic literary texts generally, . . . denotes the relatively small peregrine falcon favoured for hunting," though on pp. 358–59 he recognizes that the creatures flying over the place where Daniʾil is judging after Aqhat's death are "carnivorous birds").

28. See the reconstruction in Dijkstra and de Moor, "Passages," 195: *w*[ǵlmh] *ištir . bḏdm* 'and [his lads] stayed behind in the encampment'. This is more likely if the *gprm* below are Aqhat's companions who mourn him immediately after his death and if they are the ones who bring the message back to Daniʾil and Pughat.

flesh is present, if *ḏd* means 'teat' or the like.[29] Instead of a verb meaning 'remain(s)', *ištir* may be a noun referring to a substance.[30] In 4.290:3, the item appears as something that may be placed in a *kd* 'jug', in the context of *šmn* 'oil'.[31] These hints indicate that the meal was not simply for nourishment or a "lunch-break"[32] but was an elaborate or even ritualized occasion.

Infelicity

This feast complements or extends the effect of the failed feast at which Aqhat and Anat dispute the bow. That engagement broke down, with the two losing their tempers and with Anat threatening Aqhat. Here Anat carries out her threat against Aqhat. In a way, then, the two feasts are unified in purpose—at least from the point of view of Anat.

The type of ritual infelicity here is different from the type identified in the earlier feast. Anat is not a direct participant in the feast, nor does she seem to be expected to participate. The meal is apparently not dedicated to her or offered to her. She stands outside the structure of the feast, and she keeps herself hidden. She, or more specifically Yaṭupan, her mercenary, only becomes a visible participant by crashing the party, literally.

In Grimes's categories, this occasion involves a violation, the killing of Aqhat, as well as a hitch, because the event is never completed. It also involves *deceit*, a category that should be added to Grimes's list alongside "violation" or "insincerity," if it is not a separate category. Aqhat has no idea that he will be violated as he eats. The goddess with whom he had

29. So *UPA* 155, 'teat'; Margalit, *Life and Death*, 100–101; *CARTU* 135. Other suggestions for *ḏd* in the passage are: 'cavern' (*MLC* 384, 540 [*ḏd* II]; G. del Olmo Lete, "Notes on Ugaritic Semantics IV," *UF* 10 [1978] 43–44; based on *zdh* in the Siloam inscription); 'camp, tent' (*TO* 1 438 and 121 note d; an allograph to *šd* and parallel to *ahlm* 'tents'; *ARTU* 245; see Dijkstra and de Moor in the previous note; see *CARTU* 135; R. J. Clifford, "The Tent of El and the Israelite Tent of Meeting," *CBQ* 33 [1971] 221–27); 'mountain' (*CML* 112, 145; Akk. *šadû*; Heb. *šadday*; perhaps connected to *ṯd, žd* 'breast'). Also possible is 'flock' (cf. Arab. *ḏwd* 'scatter, drive away'; *ḏaud* 'defense, protection'; *miḏwad* 'manger, crib' [*DMWA* 315]; M. Dietrich and O. Loretz, "Ug. *ʿbš, *ṯbš*, heb. **šbš* [Am 5,11] sowie ug. *ṯšy* und *šbš*," *UF* 10 [1978] 435; *CARTU* 135).

30. J. Hoftijzer ("A Note on G 1083^3: *ʾištʾir* and Related Matters," *UF* 3 [1971] 363) translates *ištir b ḏdm w nʿrs* 'he [Aqht] stays behind (alone) in the fields and has made a halt'. He argues that *ištir* cannot be a substance. *Nʿrs* is to be connected with Classical Arab. *ʿrs* 'to make a short pause during the night'. On *ištir* as a Gt and its vocalization, see J. Tropper, "Zur Vokalisierung des ugaritischen Gt-Stammes," *UF* 22 (1990) 373.

31. Those who take the term as a verb include: *MLC* 384; *CML* 112; *ARTU* 245. *TO* 1 438 takes it as a substance, specifically 'honey'. De Moor ("Frustula," 361) suggests 'wild honey'. Margalit does not translate but renders "IŠTIR in a teat" (*UPA* 155).

32. So *UPA* 336.

ceremonial struggle in the past is not present, as far as he is concerned. She uses the situation set up by Aqhat to launch a surprise attack. Doing this, she imposes an alternative agenda on the rite. She is thus a ritual parasite, one whose goal is not simply to subsist by means of another's ritual but to destroy the host.

Ritual deceit as a narrative motif is not uncommon. The Bible, for example, contains several examples. Some cases involve the death of participants. A case with a banquet theme is Jehu's Baʿal fest (2 Kgs 10:18–31). He gathers the god's worshipers from around Israel into the Baʿal temple to make offerings. He then has his men kill the worshipers, and the temple with its specific cult fixtures is destroyed. Another case is found in the story about the slaughter of Shechem, Hamor, and their associates (Genesis 34). Jacob's sons accept a treaty offer from these people but ask them to be circumcised. The sons then take advantage of their weakness to destroy them. Jezebel, in another example, plots the death of Naboth by having him falsely accused at a gathering associated with a feast (1 Kgs 21:8–16).[33] Ritual deceit in one form or another is also found in Jacob's obtaining the blessing of his brother Esau (Genesis 27), the Benjaminites' stealing wives at the annual feast at Shiloh (Judg 21:19–25), and Samson's destruction of the temple at a sacrificial feast of Dagon (Judg 16:23–31).

These cases raise an important analytical distinction that must be made in treating ritual infelicity. Not every case can be called ritual failure. Indeed, failure is a relative judgment and depends on a particular agent's point of view. New practice may unfold in the doing of the ritual. In terms of these considerations, Jehu's festival was a success for him, the circumcision of Shechem and associates was a success for Jacob's sons, and obtaining the blessing was a success for Jacob. In a similar way, Aqhat's last feast is a success for Anat.

But in her success she fails. As noted earlier, one of the ways that a ceremony may be judged successful is if it helps to construct a relationship of power between the participants. This requires a measure of compromise. Clearly there has been no compromise in Aqhat and Anat's case. Anat did not put herself in a position in which the two might work toward this goal, and she imposed complete domination over Aqhat by killing him. Though she exercised power to annihilate him, the power that she had over him ceases to exist when Aqhat ceases to exist.

The two cases of infelicitous feasts therefore stand at opposite ends of a continuum, as it were. In the first, in which Anat seeks the bow, *the two*

33. It is not clear whether this is a feast to conclude the fast (or maybe to introduce it) or perhaps a gathering for some other purpose.

parties fail to go far enough in constructing a relationship of power. Neither will compromise. In the second, in which Aqhat dies, *Anat goes too far* by completely dominating Aqhat. She does not concede anything, and Aqhat is never given the opportunity to negotiate. Effective ritual can be seen as standing somewhere between these two poles; the parties agree, but coercion is limited and balanced with a degree of freedom.

There is yet another way in which this feast is a failure for Anat. It is evident in the broken and otherwise very difficult passage describing Anat's reaction to the murder (discussed more fully in the section on mourning; see chap. 12). As soon as Aqhat is dead, Anat begins to mourn for him. Perhaps as part of cleansing herself after the murder, the bow is broken (1.19 I):[34]

(2) *tkrb* . x[xxxxx]x .	She was grieved(?) [. . .],
*l qr*b[. x]m*ym* (3) *tql* .	in the middle o[f] the water she fell,
ʿ[nt . xxxx]x *lb* .	A[nat . . .] in the midst (??).
*t*t̲b*r* (4) *qšt* . w(?)[xx]	The bow [. . .] was broken,
[kk(??)]n*r* . *y*t̲br (5) *t̲mn* . [kt̲r(?) .]	[like a ly]re(??) the precious thing(?) [of Kothar(?)] was broken.

Just a few lines later, she reflects on the loss of the bow:

(13) *k apʿ* . *il* . *b* g*drt* .	Like a mighty viper in a rock-fence,
*kl*b *l* (14) *ḫṭh* . *imḫṣh* .	a dog (going) for his stick, I smote him;
kd . *ʿl* . qš*th* . (15) *imḫṣh* .	thus, for his bow I smote him,
ʿl . *qṣʿth* . h*wt* (16) *l* . *aḥw* .	for his arrows I did not let him live,
ap . *qšth* . l tt*n* (17) *ly* .	yet his bow has not been given to me.

The last phrase may refer to the fact that Aqhat did not give the bow to Anat in the feast when she demanded it. On the other hand, because of the conjunction *ap* and the passive construction that place Aqhat in the background, the phrase may refer to the fact that she failed to maintain possession of the bow after his death.

Anat's failure to retain the bow intact can be analyzed according to Grimes's schema as a case of ineffectuality. To be sure, this category mainly involves cases in which "magical" causation has not been achieved (for example, when rain does not come after supplicating a deity for relief from drought). Anat's attempt to acquire the bow is different from this sort of case because she hopes to obtain it directly and physically, by violence and theft, not by supernatural means. But it can be reckoned as part

34. See the more detailed notes on this passage in chapter 12.

of this category, because ritual seeks to achieve concrete as well as metaphysical results. A sacrificial ritual can be the means of dividing up and distributing meat to offerers and priestly officiants. The participants can go away enriched, physically and economically, not just spiritually. If Anat's and Aqhat's negotiations in the first banquet had proceeded properly, Anat would have obtained the bow and Aqhat would have obtained riches and even immortality. In Aqhat's last supper, Anat resorts only to vicious means to obtain what she could not otherwise. She is nonetheless disappointed.

Chapter 11
Conclusion to Part 2

It is clear from the preceding analysis that the ritual practices in the story up to the death of Aqhat have a dynamic interrelationship with one another that contributes significantly to the sense and development of the story. The ritual activities up through the blessing of Aqhat are positive, successful, and felicitous. The most prominent of these are the three feasts: to the high gods, to the Kotharat, and to Kothar-wa-Ḫasis. In all of them, humans honor the gods, and the gods respond to the benefit of the humans. The other ritual practices performed or alluded to in this part of the story are also positive: the cultic activities, some of which include feasting, as well as the ideal duties of a faithful son as well as the blessings given by Il to Daniʾil and by Daniʾil to Aqhat. The effect of these scenes and motifs on readers and hearers is similar to what happens in real-life ritual. As Bell has explained it, members of a group gain what can be called a *sense of ritual* through the experience of ritual in their social context. By this sense, they become adept and "know how to improvise a birthday celebration, stage an elaborate wedding, or rush through a minimally acceptable funeral."[1] Similarly, readers and hearers develop a sense of what ritual is and should be through the "experience" of felicitous ritual performances and motifs at the beginning of this story. They come to know the parts played by humans and the gods, how they interact, the attitudes that should prevail, the types of gifts that one group gives to the other, the care that should be taken in performing ritual activities, and so forth.

Just when this paradigm is clearly in mind, the story undermines it by introducing ritual performances that are negative, unsuccessful, and infelicitous. Feasts constitute the main examples, as in the preceding section, which involved positive ritual activities. The negative feasts include the feast during which Anat seeks possession of Aqhat's bow and the feast at which Anat slays Aqhat. These are complemented by Anat's complaint about Aqhat to Il, which involves ritualized behavior to some extent. These negative cases run counter to the earlier positive cases in their

1. Bell, *Ritual Theory*, 80.

manifestation of insincerity and deceit, the creation of animosity between the parties (Anat and Aqhat, and Anat and Il), and the failure to consummate ritual performance.

The cases of positive and negative ritual, specifically the feasts, are not incidental to the telling of the story. They are integral to setting up the story's concerns and articulating its plot. The positive feasts introduce the main characters: Daniʾil, Aqhat, Il, and Baʿl. They also introduce less central but still important supporting characters: Danatay, the Kotharat, and Kothar-wa-Ḫasis. The only main characters not introduced in this part of the story or by positive ritual are Anat and her mercenary extension, Yaṭupan. The positive performances, in particular, are the means by which Daniʾil obtains his son Aqhat, about whose life and death the story is mainly concerned. The negative feasts introduce Anat and Yaṭupan (as well as the vultures) and, more importantly, depict the decisive turn in the plot: the death of Aqhat. We are able to sense the effectiveness of the later negative feasts because they contrast with the preceding positive feasts. More than a son—and his bow—have been lost in the botched ceremonies. A whole *system*, one that makes it possible for humans and gods to communicate and to benefit each other, has been upset. This is observable not only in the tensions manifested between Aqhat and Anat but also in the striking fact that Daniʾil does not engage in feasting again until after the family has recovered from Aqhat's death.

The contrasts in the rituals are supported by structural characteristics. The initial feast is the most complex. It begins modestly and with vagueness but builds to a climax with the revelation of the gods and the promise of a son. This forms an effective introduction to the whole section in which feasting is prominent. The ensuing feasts that are positive become less and less complex. This can be explained by Daniʾil's needing less and less from the gods, once Aqhat is born and then comes to maturity. However, it also possesses significance that is brought to bear on the infelicitous feasting that follows. The decrescendo in activity might be viewed as ominous: the less elaborate the ritual activity, the fewer the contacts with the gods. The reader receives the impression that something is about to happen to alter the story's course. More importantly, the decrease in ritual activity creates a pianissimo, after which the failed feast between Anat and Aqhat, the second most elaborately described feast in the text, creates a loud crash. This is followed up ritually in two ways: in Anat's complaint to Il, which imitates the structure of the feast preceding it, thus underscoring its significance as a major turning point in the story; and in the feast at Abilum, at which Anat actualizes her threat.

Ritual's capacity to operate in the ways described above is partly due to its ability to establish relationships and articulate emotions, thus creating a social world in real life. Many of these effects persist in ritual in story—in this story in particular and in story generally. Even though readers and hearers do not personally perform the ceremonies, they are not unattached observers. They become engaged in the story's world and become participants. In this way, ritual in narrative becomes meaningful. Indeed, the image-world created in the minds of the hearers by the description of a ritual performance can be more meaningful than any direct description. As a symbol, ritual can concentrate much meaning in a limited space and add nuances that direct verbal description cannot provide. For example, we were able to see the hierarchical structures and attitudes of the agents implicitly displayed in the performances and see how they shifted as the rituals shifted from felicitous to infelicitous.

Part 3

Mourning and Retaliation

With the death of Aqhat, the mood changes and, with it, the nature of the ritual activity. Instead of feasts, we find rites of mourning, distress, and retaliation. We have already briefly referred to Anat's mourning after killing Aqhat. Her response anticipates Daniʾil's mourning rites, to which the story soon turns. Daniʾil engages in two series of rites, which have two different tendencies or goals. The first series, before he learns of Aqhat's death, seeks to rectify the agricultural woes resulting from the murder. The second series flows from the revelation of Aqhat's death. The rites in the latter series are indirectly punitive, attacking not Anat, who killed Aqhat, but the vultures and locales associated with Aqhat's death.

Despite the difference in goals, the rites in this portion of the story hold together as a unity because they display an intensifying and focusing structure throughout. The rites become more and more complex as the passage unfolds. Further, as Daniʾil gains knowledge about his son's death, the goal of the ritual action narrows. The whole section provides a counterpoint to the course of feasts at the beginning of the story. The feasts started out properly and prosperously but ended in collapse and tragedy. These rites recover from that misfortune as much as possible.

Chapter 12

Anat's Mourning

Anat, surprisingly, is the first to mourn for Aqhat, and she does so immediately after she kills him. Unfortunately, the tablets are damaged in this part of the story, and several terms are obscure.[1] This makes it the most difficult passage in the entire text. I must admit at the outset that much of it remains opaque and that the interpretation here is tentative. Nevertheless, it is possible to see in it a structure of intensification. Anat's initial response is rather reserved. When the bow breaks, she enters into a much more labored lament.

Text and Structure

In terms of basic structure, there seem to be two sections of direct speech in which Anat mourns. The second of these speeches is much more elaborate than the first. The passage begins right after Aqhat expires (1.18 IV–1.19 I):

[xxxxxx] (38) *ʿnt . b ṣmt . mp!rh .*	[. . .] Anat at the silencing[2] of his heart(?),[3]
[xxxxx] (39) *aqht .*	[. . .] Aqhat,
w tbk . yl[d . xxxx]	and she wept for the la[d . . .].
[xxx] (40) *abn . ank .*	"[. . .] I create/understand(?),[4]
w ʿl . q[štk . mḫṣtk(?)]	and for [your bo]w [I smote you(?)],

1. On the strangeness of the terminology, see *UPA* 345, 352–54, 356; A. Caquot, "Une nouvelle interpretation de KTU 1.19 I 1–19," *SEL* 2 (1985) 93. The language is so different from what we find in other places that it leads Margalit to suppose that the section "originates in a poem other than Aqht into which it has been incorporated secondarily (with minor alterations as required by the narrative context)." Parker (*UNP* 67, 79 n. 24) leaves much of the section untranslated.

2. Arab. *ṣamata* 'be silent'; compare Heb. *ṣmt* 'exterminate'. Compare *tṣmt*, used of Anat when fighting in 1.3 II 8.

3. See p. 129 nn. 16–17 on line 26. Caquot ("Nouvelle interpretation de KTU 1.19 I 1–19," 94) reads *mhrh* 'son champion'.

4. If we are to understand this as 'create', it is doubtful that it means that Anat is going to recreate (*bny*) Aqhat. For taking the term from the root *b(y)n*, see Caquot, "Nouvelle interpretation de KTU 1.19 I 1–19," 94.

[ʿl] (41) *qṣʿtk . at . l* ḥ[ytk x]	[for] your arrows, you,[5] I could not [let you live . . .].
[xxxxxx] (42) *w ḫlq . ʿpt .* m[ḫṣk . . . .]	[. . .] the birds that [smote you] have fled(?)[. . .]."[6]
. . .[7]	
(2) *tkrb* . x[xxxxx]x .	She was grieved(?) [. . .],[8]
l qrb[. x]*mym* (3) *tql* .	in the middle o[f] the water she fell,[9]
ʿ[nt . xxxx]x[10] *lb* .	A[nat . . .] in the midst (??).
*ṯ*br (4) *qšt* . w(?)[xx]	The bow [. . .] was broken,
[kk(??)]nr . *y*ṯbr (5) *ṯmn* . [kṯr(?) .]	[like a ly]re(??)[11] the precious thing(?)[12] [of Kothar(?)] was broken.
b*tlt* . ʿnt (6) *ṯṯb* . [ ]	The Virgin Anat sat(?) [ ].[13]
[t]š*a* (7) *tlm* .	[S]he lifted the quiver (saying):
k mr [k mr(?)] .	"How utterly [bitter(?)]![14]
ydh . k šr	His arms were like a flash(?),[15]

5. For this use of the independent pronoun for emphasis, see 1.2 IV 11–12, 19.

6. This line may be part of Anat's speech. If so, and if it refers to the *nšrm* that were involved in Aqhat's death, then it may anticipate Daniʾil's search among the birds to find Aqhat's remains. *UPA* 343 reads here: [lqṭp ?] *w ḫlq . ʿpmm* '[plucked?] and perished like the leaves'.

7. 1.19 I, because of the larger context, directly continues 1.18 IV (Caquot ["Nouvelle interpretation de KTU 1.19 I 1–19," 18] is not certain about the connection). It has a title *l aqht* 'Pertaining to Aqhat' in the first line, which is not represented here.

8. Arab. *karaba* 'oppress, distress, worry' (see *ARTU* 247). Del Olmo Lete (*MLC* 386) sees *tkrb* as referring to the cumbersome nature of the bow. Margalit (*UPA* 156) takes the verb as 'hasten' (of Anat; cf. Margalit, "Lexicographical Notes [II]," 119–20).

9. Some take the verb *tql* with the previous phrase referring to the bow falling in the water (*MLC* 386; *UPA* 131, 156).

10. This is the space that seems available according to the photograph.

11. The word [k]nr is restored by *CARTU* 111 and [kk]nr by *UPA* 131. Margalit's restoration (in *UPA*) makes the best sense because it does not require us to wonder why a lyre comes into the picture alongside the bow, and the lyre as a stringed instrument is similar to a stringed bow in a general way.

12. For *ṯmn* compare Arab. *ṯammana* 'appraise, estimate'; *ṯamīn* 'costly, precious'. See A. Cooper, "Two Exegetical Notes on Aqht," *UF* 20 (1988) 20. See *UPA* 131, 157 which has "prize" and restores *kṯr* in the following lacuna ('prize [of Koshar]'). Del Olmo Lete (*MLC* 387) understands the line as 'eight [arrows] were broken'. De Moor (*ARTU* 247) takes *ṯmn* as 'there'.

13. In the break, de Moor and Spronk (*CARTU* 111) restore [l arṣ]. The word *ṯb* may be understood as 'respond' (*MLC* 387). Margalit (*UPA* 157) translates it 'return' and with restoration reads: '(Anat did) return [to (Mt.) Inbb]'.

14. Dietrich and Loretz ("Einzelfragen," 196) restore *k* m[r k mr]. On the expression (and the one in line 12), see the discussion below.

15. For šr compare Akk. *šarūru* 'Strahlen(glanz)' (AHw 1193–94; *UPA* 347 n. 9). It has also been rendered 'singer' (Dijkstra and de Moor, "Passages," 198; *ARTU* 248; *MLC* 387). One might seek to find a negative description in these lines by reading *šr* as 'umbilical cord' (Arab. *surr*-).

(8) k *nr* . *uṣbʿ*⟨t⟩*h* .	like a flame,[16] his fingers.[17]
k *ḥrṣ* . *abn* (9) *ph* .	like a cutter,[18] his mouthstones.[19]
tiḫd . *šnth* .	His teeth would lay hold,[20]
w akl . *b* q*mm* .	and consume[21] among/against the enemies,[22]
(10) *tšt* . *ḥrṣ* .	they would (be) set (as) a/the cutter,
klb[23] . *ilnm*	(like) a divine/chthonic dog.[24]
(11) *w ṯn* . *gprm* . *mn* .	The *gprm* have repeated, have recited,[25]
gprh . *š*r (12) *aqht* . *yʿn* .	his *gprm* have recited, have sung(?)[26] (about) Aqhat, saying,[27]
k mr . *k mrm*	'How utterly bitter!'
(13) *k apʿ* . *il* . *b gdrt* .	Like a mighty[28] viper in a rock-fence,[29]
*kl*b *l* (14) *ḫṭh* . *imḫṣh* .	(like) a dog (going) for his stick,[30] I smote him;[31]
kd . *ʿl* . q*šth* . (15) *imḫṣh* .	thus, for his bow I smote him,

16. This is also translated 'musician' (Dijkstra and de Moor, "Passages," 198; *ARTU* 248; compare Akk. *nāru*); 'like a (wild-)fire' (*UPA* 157). Some take *knr* to be a single word, 'lyre', with the previous word: *kšr* kn*r uṣbʿ*⟨t⟩*h* 'his fingers like strings of a lyre'.

17. After Anat battles in 1.3 II 32–35, she washes her hands (*ydh*) and fingers (*uṣbʿth*); one therefore wonders whether the same terms in the Aqhat passage may refer to her rather than to Aqhat.

18. See the discussion of *ḥrṣ* below.

19. A metaphor for teeth.

20. On the words in this line, see below. Gibson (*CML* 113) takes *abn ph* with the verb that follows as 'The stones of her mouth she clenched'.

21. An infinitive absolute of *akl*.

22. See below on *qmm*.

23. That *klb* here refers to a dog is supported by the term in 13b, where it is apparently part of the complaint over the loss of Aqhat. Dijkstra and de Moor ("Passages," 198) and de Moor (*ARTU* 248): 'like the heart of old trees'. For Margalit's still different interpretation, see below.

24. Alternately, Anat is calling him the dog of the gods. This may be opprobrium or it may be a positive attribute, something like the gods' watchdog.

25. See below for the meaning of this line.

26. Other interpretations of šr include: *MLC* 387: 'prince'; *UPA* 157: 'to behold' (Aqhat is the subject). For the verb *š(y)r* 'sing' without a following preposition in the sense of sing about, see Dijkstra and de Moor, "Passages," 199.

27. For construing *yʿn* thus, see *ARTU* 248. Other interpretations: 'Aqhat was humbled' (*MLC* 387; *CML* 114); 'perceive' (*UPA* 157; Aqhat is the subject).

28. For *il* as an indication of greatness, see *CARTU* 127 ('might'); *UPA* 157 ('giant', though Margalit takes the *k*- as an asseverative, not a comparative particle); *ARTU* 248: 'dangerous viper'.

29. Cf. 1.169:3.

30. Akk. *ḫaṭṭu* 'scepter, staff, stick, branch' (CAD H 153b). Similarly, *CML* 114. Del Olmo Lete (*MLC* 387) sees the dog tied to a stake; *ARTU* 248 translates 'like a dog deserving the stick' (or according to n. 165 there, with emendation, 'for his sin'; cf. Dijkstra and de Moor, "Passages," 199); Margalit (*UPA* 157, 349–52) translates the two lines

ʿl . qṣʿth . hwt (16) *l . aḥw .*	for his arrows I did not let him live,
ap . qšth . l tt*n* (17) *ly .*	yet his bow has not been given to me.
w bmth . *ḥmṣ* ṣrr	By his death the *ṣrr*[32] is spoiled,[33]
(18) *prʿ . qẓ . yḥ .*	the firstfruits[34] of summer wither(?),[35]
*šbl*t (19) b *ǵlph*	the ear in its husk."

Anat's first speech in lines 40–42 is relatively easy to set off. The verb *tbk* 'she wept' (line 39) provides an introduction. The speech itself is characterized by a first-person verb and pronoun referring to Anat (line 40) and second-person pronouns referring to Aqhat (41). The only real question is whether line 42 is part of the speech or part of the description. Here I follow *CAT*, which restores m[ḫṣk], with a second-person pronoun, thus making it part of the speech.[36]

The second speech is more problematic. Lines 2–6a are narrative description. They are broken but tell, at least, that the bow that Anat apparently gained possession of was broken. Perhaps it broke when she fell (line 2b–3a) into a body of water.

It is not clear whether the lines after this should all be taken as Anat's speech, whether they contain description interwoven with speech, or whether they are all description. Anat seems to be speaking in at least lines 13–17a. These lines have first-person verb forms that recount the killing of Aqhat. Margalit excises the lines with these verbs (14 *imḫṣh* to 17 *ly*) because he thinks that they do not fit the context.[37] This allows him to read the remaining lines 2–12 + 17b–19 as pure narrative description. This excision seems overly conjectural, and it is hard to argue that

'Verily a giant viper (stood) by a wall-barrier, a dog (stood) at his scepter(-side)' (the dog and snake are sentries to the underworld, by whom Aqhat must pass).

31. For the stichometry here, see Dijkstra and de Moor, "Passage," 199. On Margalit's emendation, see below.

32. Probably a plant of some sort (*CARTU* 165 'young ear of corn'; see the note in *ARTU* 248 n. 166). Otherwise, this may be a verb, with *ḥmṣ* being the noun referring to vegetation. Compare Arab. *ḍrr* 'to harm, damage'. *UPA* 131, 156 reads: *w*bm*t*[h . y]*ḥmṣ* (.) ṣr[ḥ] 'and behind there loom[ed] a to[wer]'.

33. Arab. *ḥmḍ* 'become sour' or *ḥmṣ* II 'roast, fry'. De Moor ("Seasonal Pattern in the Legend of Aqhatu," 66–67; *ARTU* 248 n. 166) reads 'dry up, be parched', from Syrian Arabic.

34. For *prʿ* as 'firstfruit(s)', see *MLC* 612; *ARTU* 248; Dijkstra and de Moor, "Passages," 199; cf. 182. Note the occurrence of *prʿm ṣdk* 'firstfruits of your hunt' (1.17 V 37; see p. 94 n. 2 above on this); and perhaps *tlḥmn . . . tštyn . . . bprʿ* 'they ate . . . they drank of firstfruits' (1.22 I 23–24).

35. De Moor and Spronk (*CARTU* 154) take the root of *yḥ* as *nḥy* 'droop'. Compare Arab. *nḥw* 'move, go, walk' (also Heb. *nḥh*).

36. So also *ARTU* 247; *MLC* 386. Gibson (*CML* 113) leaves it outside the quotation.

37. *UPA* 219 and n. 22; cf. 131, 334–35, 345.

the context supports it, because the context is extremely difficult to establish in the first place.[38] I proceed on the assumption that the lines belong to the context and that therefore lines 13–17a contain words that Anat speaks.

Speech in this section seems further indicated by the phrase *k mr . k mrm* (line 12b). This can be understood as an interjection of lament, 'How bitter! How bitter!'[39] The same phrase may also appear in the broken line 7b. The occurrence in 7b can be viewed as part of Anat's speech (see below on the introduction to this speech in 6b–7a). But the occurrence in 12b is not simply attributable to Anat. The phrase in 12b is preceded by the verb *yʿn*. While this may mean 'spoke, answered' instead of 'saw' or 'was humbled', it is not a third-person feminine singular form, and thus Anat is not the direct speaker of what, at least immediately, follows. The subject of the verb may be either Aqhat or the *gprm/gprh* (a dual? see below) of line 11. The former option does not seem likely, since Aqhat is dead. Though the dead are vital entities in Ugaritic religion (see the discussion of the first filial duty, chapter 2), it is not clear why his ghost would be an active participant at this point. One might expect him to have a larger speaking or acting part than just this speech. Additionally, the context of Anat's speech in lines 13–17a, by using third-person pronouns of Aqhat, seems to treat him as remote rather than on the scene.

By elimination, then, the subject of *yʿn* in line 12 appears to be *gprm*. Because the term ends in *-m*, it is presumably dual or plural, and because it appears to be the subject of the verb, it presumably refers to beings of some sort. They do not appear elsewhere in the story or in Ugaritic texts. Some have understood that there are specifically two of them, either taking *ṯn* in line 11 as a number defining the quantity or seeing *gprm* as a dual. This would allow them to be connected with the *ġlmm* 'two youths' who bring Daniʾil and Pughat word of Aqhat's death (1.19 II 28).[40] That

38. One might say, however, in view of the apparent suffixing form in 1.18 IV 41 that Anat uses to describe her killing of Aqhat, that the prefixing forms here are out of place. One might also say that speaking about Aqhat in the third person rather than the second, as in 1.18 IV 41, may indicate that the passage does not belong here.

39. Dietrich and Loretz, "Einzelfragen," 196; Dijkstra and de Moor, "Passages," 197–198; *ARTU* 247–48. Other interpretations of the terms include: 'like a valiant one' (*MLC* 387, 566); 'priest' (compare Heb. *kmr*; Virolleaud, *Danel*, 137); 'pile of grain' (Gordon, *Ugaritic Textbook*, #1260, referring to Akk. *kamru* 'sorted [dates] ready for transport', CAD K 126); 'the heart of darkness' (*UPA* 157; cf. 349 n. 20).

40. Cf. *ARTU* 248 n. 161; Dijkstra and de Moor, "Passages," 199. Margalit (*UPA* 157, 348, 353) takes the two instances of the term in different ways: '(in accordance with) the instruction of the Nethergods [*gprm*]. From [m*n*] his grave pit [*gprh*], Aqhat beheld'. It is etymologically connected with Arab. *jafr* 'divination' and *jufrat* 'pit, hole'.

Aqhat had comrades or servants in the vicinity of his death may be indicated by the obscure *w*[xxxxx] *ištir . b d̲dm*, which is part of Yaṭupan's description of Aqhat's situation before his and Anat's fatal attack (1.18 IV 14–15; see p. 131). This could be expansively rendered 'And (his servants/associates?) remained in the encampment'. Support for this basic understanding of *gprm* is found in the form *gprh* (also line 11), which presumably is the same as the former, except with a suffix. The suffix probably refers to Aqhat, given the context, where the singular referent before and immediately after is Aqhat (see below). The etymology of the term is not clear.[41]

Since the *gprm* are the subject of *yʿn*, they are also the subject of *šr* 'sing'. There may be two more verbs denoting their speech and marking it specifically as ritual speech: *t̲n* 'repeat'[42] (*t̲ny*; if this is not a number) and *mn* 'recite' (*mny*).[43] How much of their recitation and singing is cited? Since a first-person verb whose subject is Anat appears in the poetic line 13b–14, and since line 13a is parallel to it, Anat must be speaking there. Consequently, the *gprm* can only be speaking the phrase *k mr . k mrm* 'How utterly bitter!' This brief citation seems out of proportion to the space devoted to introducing it (line 12b versus lines 11a–12a). However,

---

The preceding term *ilnm* (line 10b), if referring to chthonic deities (so Dietrich and Loretz, "Einzelfragen," 196), could support this interpretation (a difficulty with his interpretation is taking the term *mn* as the preposition 'from'; cf. Dietrich, Loretz, and Sanmartín, "Zur ugaritischen Lexikographie [VII]," 92–93). Cooper ("Two Exegetical Notes," 20–21) on the basis of Arabic takes the term as 'carcass' (referring to Aqhat's corpse). Anat in lines 8b–12a is splitting Aqhat open and ritually dismembering him (but not burying him, according to Margalit's view; for this, see below). The advantage to this interpretation is that it allows Aqhat to have been more easily consumed by Ṣamal. Aistleitner (*Wörterbuch*, 68) connects the term with Akk. *gipāru* (a place of residence for cultic functionaries; meadow, pasture; cf. CAD G 83) and renders it 'umfriedeter Raum?' Del Olmo Lete (*MLC* 387, 534) renders 'atacar' (based on Akk. *gapāru* [=? *gubburu* 'overpower'; CAD 118]) and translates *w t̲n . . . šr* 'y por dos veces atacó, a quien [m*n*] le atacaba, el Príncipe'. Similarly, Caquot, Sznycer, and Herdner (*TO* 1 442 and note m) translate 'Qui l'a subjugué, subjugué, le prince Aqhat?' Virolleaud (*Danel*) takes it as 'tree' (Heb. *gōper*). Gibson (*CML* 114) does not translate the terms, and Gordon (*Ugaritic Textbook*) does not give a meaning.

41. See the previous note. A connection with Semitic **gbr*, for example, Heb. *gibbôr* 'hero, warrior' (so Dijkstra and de Moor, "Passages," 199), is doubtful phonologically. A change of /*b*/ to /*p*/ seems possible only when the /*b*/ is followed by an unvoiced consonant, as in *lpš* /*lvpš-*/ for **lbš* /*lvbš-*/ (cf. Gordon, *Ugaritic Textbook*, §5.28); also cf. *špš* = /*šapš-*/ ← /*šampš-*/ ← /*šamš-*/.

42. *ARTU* 248 takes *t̲n* as a verb, 'repeat'. *MLC* 387 has 'por dos veces'. Margalit takes (*UPA* 157, 348 and n. 17) *w t̲n . gprm* 'and (according to) the instruction of the Nethergods' as parallel with *k lb . ilnm* 'In accordance with the wish of the chthonics'.

43. So *ARTU* 248. See n. 40 (above) for construing m*n* either as a pronoun or a preposition.

the phrase *k mr . k mr*m may be the incipit or title of a dirge that would have been understood as being much longer than one line. The text as it stands may be an abridgement of the scene to shift the focus more onto Anat's own words, because after all she is the one who, ironically, had Aqhat killed but is now reacting with mourning and who, also ironically, lost the very thing that she sought from Aqhat.

Another reason that the speech of the *gprm* is abbreviated is that the introduction to their speech in 11a–12a as well as their speech appears to be spoken by Anat herself.[44] She describes what they are saying. The reason for this conclusion is that the first-person speech whose subject is Anat, as just noted, appears immediately after *k mr . k mr*m, with no clue that there is a change in speakers. The break seems too abrupt to be explainable as an implicit change in speakers. It is also doubtful that the *gprm* are speaking for Anat in the first person or citing her words. We are left with assuming that Anat is describing the reaction of the *gprm*.

The question then becomes: where, exactly, does Anat's speech begin? Line 5b–6a reports that Anat sits down after the breaking of the bow. Some have taken the *ša* of 6b as an imperative verb, with an object, *tlm*, meaning 'furrow'.[45] If this be the case, Anat calls on an agricultural entity to undertake mourning.[46] This interpretation would mean that Anat does not speak either of the 'How utterly bitter!' clauses in 7b or 12b; she is citing what someone or something else should say or has said.[47] While this is structurally attractive, it is simpler to take the verb as [t]*ša* 'she lifted', with Anat as the subject, and to read *tlm* as the object, meaning 'quiver'.[48] The quiver can be seen as metonymically representing Aqhat as well as the bow. The goddess speaks her following words of mourning to the quiver, referring to both the lad and the weapon.

44. So Dijkstra and de Moor, "Passages," 197; *ARTU* 247–48.

45. Compare Arab. *talam* and Heb. *telem* 'furrow' (de Moor, *SP* 99; M. Dietrich and O. Loretz, "Ein ug. Fruchtbarkeitsritus [KTU 1.16 III 1–11]," *UF* 10 [1978] 425). Some connect *tlm* with Arab. *lwm* 'to blame, censure, rebuke'; *talwīm* 'censure, rebuke'. In this case, Anat is calling for some sort of censure (of herself?). Another interpretation is *tl* 'weapon' (*MLC* 636; compare Heb. *tĕlî* 'quiver'). *MLC* also indicates that 'hills' (*tel*) is possible. Margalit reflects this interpretation with his reading [t]*ša* (→) *tlm . km* (.) r[u]m 'She climbed the mountain like a wi[ld-bu]ll' (*UPA* 131, 157, 347 n. 8).

46. So Dijkstra and de Moor, "Passages," 197; *ARTU* 247; Dietrich and Loretz, "Einzelfragen," 196.

47. For an earlier explanation along this line, see my article "The Play of Ritual in the Aqhat Narrative," in *Crossing Boundaries and Linking Horizons: Studies in Honor of Michael C. Astour on His 80th Birthday* (ed. G. D. Young, M. W. Chavalas, and R. E. Averbeck; Bethesda, Md.: CDL, 1997) 594.

48. So, for example, Cooper, "Two Exegetical Notes," 20; Walls, *The Goddess Anat*, 196. This, by the way, would give support to the idea that the gift to Daniʾil and Aqhat was of both a bow and arrows, not simply a bow.

Based on the context established in the foregoing argument that Anat begins to speak in line 7b and is found speaking also in 11a–17a, the intervening lines (7c–10b) also must be part of Anat's speech.

A Funerary Rite?

Before defining further the full outlines of Anat's speech, an interpretation of lines 8b–11a that has ramifications for the study of ritual in the text of Aqhat must be examined. Baruch Margalit has argued, as noted already, that lines 2–19 contain only narrative description. He interprets lines 8b–11a as referring to funerary activity that Anat performs on Aqhat's corpse. He renders these lines as follows:[49]

p *ḥrṣ . ad*(!)*n* (.) *ph*	Then she incised the gums of his mouth,
tiḫd . šnth . p! *t*!*n*!*kl*	she grasped his teeth and extracted (them).
b qmm (.) *tšt . ḥrṣ*	She plastered (his) crown with lime,
k lb . ilnm	in accordance with the wish of the chthonics,
w ṯn . gprm	and the instruction of the Nethergods.

This correlates with Aqhat's rejection of Anat's offer of eternal life, in which he says that immortality is impossible but that (1.17 VI 36b–37; Margalit's translation):

spsg . ysk (.) (37) [l] r*iš* .	a coating will cover (my) head,
ḥrṣ . l ẓr . qdqdy	lime-plaster (will deck) the top of my skull.[50]

According to Margalit's argument, these passages may be correlated to the Pre-Pottery Neolithic B practice of plastering skulls, evidenced in remains from the Jordan Valley, Transjordan, and Huleh regions. This burial custom apparently was intended to reconstitute the natural contours of the person while alive. Strikingly, some of the skulls have had the lower teeth removed as part of this preparation.[51] If this interpretation is correct, it

49. *UPA* 157; cf. B. Margalit, "Studia Ugaritica II: Studies in Krt and Aqht," *UF* 8 (1976) 169–72.

50. Margalit's translation (*UPA* 151). Cf. B. Margalit, "Lexicographical Notes on the Aqht Epic (Part I: KTU 1.17–18)," *UF* 15 (1983) 84–86. For my translation and discussion, see chapter 8.

51. Cf. *UPA* 307–10, 344–49. Authors who see a connection between the plastering of skulls and either the passage under study here or Aqhat's response to Anat earlier in the text include: E. Good, "Two Notes," 72–74; A. S. Kapelrud, *The Violent Goddess: Anat in the Ras Shamra Texts* (Oslo: Scandinavian University Books, 1969) 74–75; Gordon, *Ugaritic Textbook*, 543 (notes on pp. 399 and 451).

constitutes an interesting play of ritual themes in the story. The mortality that Aqhat predicted for himself has come to pass, and he receives the specific last rites that he described. He also receives them from the deity who promised him eternal life. By performing these rites, Anat emphasizes his mortal end and his loss of the opportunity for immortality. This, to some degree, completes the circle that began with the argument between Anat and Aqhat and helps, from a structural point of view, to mark the end of the conflict per se. While it closes off one part of the story, however, it opens another: Daniʾil's mourning rites and responses begin, culminating, more or less, in the discovery of Aqhat's remains. Thus, Anat's supposed funerary activities point backward and forward in the story at the same time.

On the other hand, several objections render Margalit's interpretation doubtful.[52] First of all, in 1.17 VI 36b–37, the interpretations of *spsg* and *ḥrṣ* are disputed. The meaning 'coating' depends on an emendation in Prov 26:23, *kesep sîgîm* being read as *k-spsg* to produce the simile *k-spsg mĕṣuppeh ʿal-ḥāreś śĕpātaim dōlĕqîm wĕleb-rāʿ* 'Like *spsg* overlaid on fired clay, so are burning lips with an evil heart'. Ginsberg, who proposed this emendation and the connection with Ugaritic *spsg*, understood the term to mean 'glaze(?)'. The question mark is his.[53]

While this emendation is reasonable, it is not absolutely certain.[54] Therefore, one should not base a definition of the Ugaritic term on it, especially since there are other attestations of the term in Ugaritic texts and several instances of an apparently related term in Hittite texts that provide information about the meaning of the term. These more certain

52. The objection that is mainly brought against this type of interpretation is that the finds are from the Pre-Pottery Neolithic B (ca. seventh millennium B.C.E.) period, while the Aqhat text dates from the Late Bronze Age (cf. Rainey, "Observations," 154). Margalit (*UPA* 309–10, 336) has responded by saying that some of the skulls may have, through erosion, become visible to people in a later period and that the Aqhat passages report not the funerary practice of the time of its writing but speculation based on these finds in later antiquity. For objections in general, see: *TO* 1 432–33 note b; Dijkstra and de Moor, "Passages," 190; Dietrich and Loretz, "Einzelfragen," 195; Rainey, "Observations," 154.

53. H. L. Ginsberg, "The North-Canaanite Myth of Anath and Aqhat II," *BASOR* 98 (1945) 21. Many recognize the legitimacy of emending *kesep sîgîm* in Prov 26:23 to *k-spsgym* (cf. J. Barr, *Comparative Philology and the Text of the Old Testament* [repr. with additions and corrections; Winona Lake, Ind.: Eisenbrauns, 1987) 219–20; BHS; *HALAT*[3] 722; W. McKane, *Proverbs: A New Approach* [OTL; Philadelphia: Westminster, 1970] 603–4; *GUL* 5).

54. See M. Dietrich, O. Loretz, and J. Sanmartín, "Die anagebliche ug.-he. Parallele spsg || sps(j)g(jm)," *UF* 8 (1976) 37–40. They see *sygym* as a gloss and read the verse: *ksp mṣph ʿl ḥrś / śptym dlqym w lb rʿ* 'Gehämmertes Silber über einer Tonscherbe, "glatte" Lippen und ein böses Herz!'

occurrences should occupy the central place in the study of the term's meaning.

In the Ugaritic texts, the term appears as [ś]*pśg* . *iqni* '*śpśg* of lapis lazuli' in a list of clothing and other items (*CAT* 4.182:8).[55] It occurs next to other items: *allm* . *lbnm* 'white *all*-clothing'; *all* . *šmt* '*all*-clothing of red dyed wool(?)';[56] *all* . *iqni* '*all*-clothing of lapis color' (see lines 4–6). It would seem that [ś]*pśg* . *iqni* is a '*spsg* of lapis', and therefore an object of some sort that is made wholly or partly of lapis lazuli or has the same color as lapis lazuli.[57] It may be a textile, a type of clothing, or it may be a type of stone. The latter is not to be discounted, especially in view of the *abn* . *ṣrp* 'stones of *ṣrp*' that appears a few lines later as well as later in the text (lines 10, 27).[58] The term also appears in *CAT* 4.205 (a record), again a text containing mostly textiles and clothing (note the terms: *kdwṯ*, *pld*, *pṯt* 'linen'; *šʿrt* 'wool'; *lpš*/*lbš* 'clothing').[59] Line 14 includes the term *sbsg*.

The apparently related Hittite word is *zapzagi-* (plural: *zapzagaya*).[60] This also refers to an object. In an evocation ritual (CTH 485), sweet oil cake, coarse meal, and *zapzagaya* (plural)—all mentioned in series in the same sentence—are 'scattered/poured out down' (*kattanda isḫuwanzi*) in an offering on top of other materials previously set out as offerings.[61] The

55. See the description of the tablet in *CAT*. D. Hillers ("Book Notices," *BASOR* 206 [1972] 49) takes it as '(blue) glaze' and perhaps a lapis lazuli imitation in glass.

56. Cf. W. H. van Soldt, "Fabrics and Dyes at Ugarit," *UF* 22 (1990) 338 and 343.

57. The term *iqnu*/*iqni* occurs throughout the text. In the line just before [. . . ś]*pśg* . *iqni*, one finds *ʿšrm* . *ǵprt* '20 *ǵprt*-pieces of clothing' (cf. Gordon, *Ugaritic Textbook*, #1980; Arab. *ǵufrat-* 'cover, lid'; *ǵifārat-* 'kerchief for covering the head, headcloth'; *miǵfar* 'helmet'). It is not clear if this has a connection with *śpśg*.

58. Gordon (*Ugaritic Textbook*, #2197) notes that these are stones "used for adorning jewelry and garments." Greenfield ("Lexicographical Notes," 92) calls this a bead that resembles semi-precious stone (cf. Hillers, "Book Notices," 49). Van Soldt shows that *abn* . *ṣrp* is to be understood as 'alum' ("Fabrics and Dyes," 324–25).

59. See the description in *CAT*. Additionally, note the following: for *kdwṯ*, Gordon, *Ugaritic Textbook*, #1198; for *pld*, ibid., #2045; for *šʿrt* 'wool', van Soldt, "Fabrics and Dyes," 333–35; cf. Gordon, *Ugaritic Textbook*, #2460; for *lpš*/*lbš* 'clothing', ibid., ##1738, 2074. On other garments, see also ibid., ##118, 1546.

60. The connection was first made by W. F. Albright, "A New Hebrew Word for 'Glaze' in Proverbs 26:23," *BASOR* 98 (1945) 24–25; cf. C. Rabin, "Hittite Words in Hebrew," *Or* 32 (1963) 139; H. A. Hoffner, "Ugaritic pwt: A Term from the Early Canaanite Dyeing Industry," *JAOS* 87 (1967) 300–301 n. 5; Watson, "Non-semitic Words," 543. On the word's stem and singular and plural forms, see E. Neu, "Hethitisch *zapzagi-*," *UF* 27 (1995) 395–402, esp. pp. 395–96.

61. IBoT 148 iii 9 (V. Haas and G. Wilhelm, *Hurritische und luwische Riten aus Kizzuwatna* [AOATS 3; Kevelaer: Butzon & Bercker / Neukirchen-Vluyn: Neukirchener Verlag, 1974] 222–23, 288, translate 'Fritte'). The Akkadian term *zabzagû*, which appears in a lexical text, is not definable in and of itself (see CAD Z 10a, which bases the definition on the study of the Ugaritic term).

word *zapzagaya* is preceded by the determinative NA$_4$, which indicates that the objects are a type of stone or objects made of stone or a stone-related material.[62] A similar impression is made by another evocation ritual (CTH 484), where a ^{NA_4}AŠ.TUR^{TIM}-stone and *zapzagaya* (plural) are 'scattered/poured out on' (*anda isḫuwai*) in offering.[63] On this (or on something previously stated), coarse meal (*memal*) and a sweet oil cake (NINDA.Ì.E.DÉ.A) are then scattered (*anda isḫuwai*).[64] The proximity of *zapzagaya* to ^{NA_4}AŠ.TUR^{TIM} is consistent with the view that the former are stones or objects of stone or related material. The character of *zapzagaya* as object and stone is further seen in several texts where they are placed in a balance (^{GIŠ}ÉRIN ["NUNUZ"] ZI.BA.NA).[65] The sorts of things put in a balance according to other texts include silver, gold, lead, and (precious) stones (NA$_4$.ḪÁ).[66] In a ritual for building a palace (CTH 414), the king offers a *zapziki* to the throne.[67] This is something *by* or *with* which (*zapzikit*, instrumental case) eating is done.[68] Later on in the text, a *zapziki* is set out before female weavers.[69] Figs are apparently scattered out on it (*šuḫḫai*). Here the *zapziki-* is an object, perhaps a dish or tray of some sort that could be made of stone or related material. In the Papanikri ritual (CTH 476) "two *zapzagaya*" are listed among things to obtain for the ritual.[70] Again, these are objects. Interestingly, the list in which they occur includes several clothing items, which reminds one of the context of *śpśg/sbsg* in Ugaritic. But the list places "two shekels of silver" just before the *zapzagaya*, so the latter may not be connected with textiles.

62. Cf. $^{[N]A_4}$*za-ap-za-aq-qa-ya* (VBoT 37:3).

63. KUB 15.31 iii 40–41 (cf. Haas and Wilhelm, *Riten*, 164–65).

64. See the distribution of these materials in CHD under *memal*.

65. KUB 30.19+ i 32 (cf. H. Otten, *Hethitische Totenrituale* [Deutsche Akademie der Wissenschaften zu Berlin, Institut für Orientforschung 37; Berlin: Akademie, 1958] 32–33): *A-NA* ^{GIŠ}ÉRIN ZÉ.PA.NA-*as-sa*[*-an za-ap-za-ga-a-ya ki-it-ta-ri*]; KUB 30.24a+ i 7 (cf. Otten, *Totenrituale*, 58–59): [*A-NA* ^{GIŠ}ÉRIN ZI.B]A.NA-*ya-as-sa-an za-ap-za-ga-a-ya* [*ki-it-ta-ri*]; KUB 7.37:10–11: [. . .]-*TUM* ^{GIŠ}ÉRIN *ZI-PA-NI-TUM* [. . .] *za-ap-za-ga-ya ki-it-ta-ri*. The first two texts may be translated '*zapzagaya* lie in the balance' (the latter is too broken). *HW*^{2} E 37a translates the first text 'auf der Waage [liegt Glas (Pl. N. n)]'. On the ritual use of balances, see the discussion in Otten, *Totenrituale*, 131–33.

66. See the text cited in *HW*^{2} 36–37.

67. KUB 29.1 i 14 (cf. B. Schwartz, "A Hittite Ritual Text [KUB 29.1 = 1780/c]," *Or* 16 (1947) 23–55; *ANET* 357); *zapziki* is singular.

68. Line 15, *zapzikit*, instrumental.

69. CTH 414 ii 14, *zapziki*, singular object of the verb *dai*. CHD L 58a summarizes the passage: "A glassware bowl [= *zapzaki*] of figs is placed before a group of female weavers and a pottery (?) bowl [*kenupi*] of raisins and *ḫašigga* is placed before a group of male weavers and someone says 'Soothe the king! Soothe his eyes! Take sickness from him!'"

70. KBo 5.1 i 52 (cf. F. Sommer and H. Ehelolf, *Das hethitische Ritual des Papanikri von Komana* [Bogazköi-Studien 10; Leipzig: Hinrichs, 1924]); the noun is plural.

The Ugaritic and Hittite evidence taken together–not taking the Aqhat story into consideration for the moment–indicates that the term refers to stone material. It seems to be precious or semiprecious, as well as decorative and attractive, and consequently might be used on clothing and even as a material for offerings alongside food and other gifts. It comes in different sizes, because a single one (*zapziki/zapzaki*) may be employed as a tray large enough to hold food or an indefinite number might be scattered out (*zapzagaya*). Except for Aqhat, none of these occurrences allows for the meaning 'plaster' or even 'glaze'.[71] The meaning 'glass (bowl)'[72] or 'frit' (glass ingredients)[73] is likewise not suggested by these occurrences. In a recent detailed study of Hittite *zapzagi-*, E. Neu has come to a similar conclusion. He rejects the interpretation that the Hittite term refers to a type of vessel or glaze and concludes that it "um eine Materialangabe (wertvolles Gestein/Mineral) handelt."[74]

Given this evidence, it is unlikely that the attestation of *spsg* in the Aqhat text means 'glaze' or 'plaster', even if the emended Proverbs passage is considered relevant. Indeed, the weight of the evidence requires reevaluation of the meaning of the emended **spsg* in the Proverbs passage.[75]

71. Contra H. Hoffner, "An English-Hittite Glossary," *RHA* 25 (1967) 46, which gives 'glaze'.

72. *HW*[1] 260a, which gives the meaning 'Glas (als Material und Gefäß); Glasschüssel' for *zapzagai-/zapzaki-/zapziki-*, notes that "unter diesem Ansatz lassen sich die Bedeutungen 'Glasure' (Albright . . .) und 'kostbare Schale' (Goetze . . .) wohl miteinander in Einklang bringen."

73. Haas and Wilhelm (*Riten*, 165, 223, 288) translate 'Fritte'.

74. Neu, "Hethitisch *zapzagi-*," 402; The features of *zapzagi-* summarized in his article (pp. 401–2) are: (1) it is determined generally with NA_4 'stone'; (2) it is mentioned with precious metals and stones; (3) it is used as stone of some weight; (4) it is found in a mountain; (5) it is a neuter noun, often plural; (6) it can be counted; (7) it can be taken in small pieces; (8) it can be poured out; (9) it is placed with precious metals and stones in the foundations of the building in a building ritual; (10) it is "sealed" in a magical ritual context.

75. One wonders if, given the emendation, *spsg* could not be the *object* that is overlaid rather than the *material* being used to overlay another object. This is supported by *ʿammudê šiṭṭîm mĕṣuppîm zāhāb* 'acacia posts covered with gold' (Exod 26:32), in which the participle modifies the object covered. If so, the emended Proverbs line could be translated: "Like an object made of *spsg* overlaid, upon the clay." The *ʿal-ḥereś* phrase specifies the material out of which the *spsg*, presumably an attractive vessel, is made in order to set up the contrast of outside–comely/inside–evil. The material with which the *spsg* is overlaid is not mentioned. This is not a problem, however, in view of the possibility of leaving the material of overlay unstated (2 Kgs 18:16). If *spsg* is the material of overlay and not the object overlaid, it may be that it refers to decorative stone that is somehow attached to a clay pot rather than a glaze. On overlaying (*ṣph*!) with stone, see 2 Chr 3:6. If **spsg* in Proverbs does mean 'glaze', then it may be a secondary meaning developed from the term that primarily referred to decorative stone or stone objects (perhaps even glass).

Therefore, it cannot provide a definition for the Ugaritic or Hittite terms.[76] On the basis of Ugaritic and Hittite evidence, one must imagine that Aqhat is telling Anat, not that plaster or glaze will be poured on or will cover his head, but that (valuable) *spsg*-stone/stones will be poured on or cover his head. If this refers to a funerary activity, it is not the Neolithic practice connected with the skulls found in the areas of the Jordan and Galilee.

Part of the interpretation of *spsg* as 'plaster' or 'glaze' has come from viewing the parallel word *ḥrṣ* as connected with Arabic *ḥuruḍ* 'potash, gypsum, quicklime(?)',[77] but this is not certain. If *spsg* is a valuable stone rather than a coating material, *ḥrṣ* defined as 'potash, gypsum, quicklime(?)' may not be acceptable. It may itself refer to an object or objects.[78] M. Dietrich and O. Loretz analyze the various occurrences of *ḥrṣ* in Ugaritic texts together.[79] They connect the word in Aqhat's speech with the *ḥrṣ* in economic tablets,[80] and they render it 'Beigaben' or, as G. del Olmo Lete paraphrases it, 'objetos complimentarios'. This they derive from the root *ḥrṣ*, meaning 'to cut (off)'. It is possible, however, to associate this noun with Arabic *ḥaraṣa* 'desire, covet' and think of the noun as referring to a desired or precious object (or objects). This would provide a good parallel to *spsg* as a precious and attractive stone. In any case, the disposition of *ḥrṣ* in 1.17 VI 37 is not exactly the same as the attested plastered skulls: here it is placed *on top of the head*, not around the whole head. This is one of the reasons why, if *ḥrṣ* does mean 'potash, gypsum, quicklime', it may be a metaphor for the whitening of the hair, which in turn metonymically denotes aging, though this interpretation itself is not really convincing because of the oddness of the metaphor.[81]

76. On the methodological need to avoid using biblical obuscurities to interpret obscurities in Ugaritic, see Dietrich and Loretz, "Rāpiu und Milku," 123 (and cf. pp. 129–30).

77. This is the meaning offered by Ginsberg ("North Canaanite Myth II," 22 and n. 58), which yields the translation 'plaster' for the Ugaritic term. Those accepting a meaning along this line for the term in this passage (besides Margalit) include: Gordon, *Ugaritic Textbook*, #900; *TO* 1 433 (cf. note c); *CML* 109; *CARTU* 139; *ARTU* 239. Aistleitner (*Wörterbuch*, 107) takes it as 'Furche, Runzel'—wrinkles from old age, apparently.

78. Again, see Dietrich and Loretz, "Einzelfragen," 194–96. They associate all occurrences of the root *ḥrṣ* in the Aqhat story as well as in economic tablets with the same basic root meaning 'to cut off'. Dijkstra and de Moor ("Passages," 190) equate *ḥrṣ* with *ḫrṣ* 'gold'; this is doubtful. *RTU* 274–75 n. 115 sees *ḥrṣ* as a *mistake* for *ḫrṣ* and suggests *spsg* might even be emended to ⟨*k*⟩*spsg*, to provide a better parallel.

79. Dietrich and Loretz, "Einzelfragen," 194–96 (cf. *MLC* 549). They apparently lay aside their earlier interpretation of the Aqhat passage, which followed A. Goetze: "Gießt man eine *spsg*-Schale über meinen Kopf, / Feinöl [*ḥrṣ*] auf meinen Scheitel" (in Dietrich, Loretz, and Sanmartín, "Die angebliche ug.-he. Parallele," 39).

80. Cf. 4.145:8; 4.169:4; 4.368:2, 5, 7, 8, 15; 4.377:5–6; 4.384:11.

81. For those taking this meaning, see *CML* 109: 'glaze'; *TO* 1 432: 'quelque chose de blanc' (see there).

In addition to the foregoing questions about the terms *spsg* and *ḥrṣ*, several more difficulties are evident in Margalit's interpretation of 1.19 I 8b–11a. The reading *p tnkl* is unlikely. The photograph that accompanies Margalit's edition makes it rather clear that *w* must be read rather than *p t*: the horizontal lines of the supposed *p* are too short for a *p*, to judge from this letter elsewhere in the column; they are consistent, however, with the letter *w*.[82] Furthermore, this reading gives the two instances of *ḥrṣ* (8b, 10a) different meanings: 'she incised' and 'lime'.[83] One might expect them to be the same or come from the same root. Moreover, this interpretation of the passage does not explain why Anat prepares Aqhat's head but does not do anything with the body, which is later found by Daniʾil and is buried. One would think if she is undertaking rites for Aqhat, she would care for his body too.

In sum, the review of the evidence demonstrates the unlikelihood that a funerary rite such as proposed by Margalit exists here. To be sure, one could still interpret lines 9b–10b as having to do with some funerary activity: Anat in some way "seizes" Aqhat's teeth and puts in place a *ḥrṣ* object, perhaps by/on his head. But this does not have the archaeological precedent that Margalit presupposed for his interpretation, and it is very difficult to make sense of it in the larger context. Therefore, another interpretation of the lines must be sought.

The Meaning of 1.19 I 8b–11a and the Scope of the Speech

Even if the funerary interpretation is not satisfying, and if in fact the problematic lines (1.19 I 8b–11a) are to be read as part of Anat's speech as argued above, the meaning of the section is nevertheless far from clear. The starting point of any interpretation seems to lie in noting several words in lines 8b–10b that can be associated: *šnth* 'his teeth' and *akl* 'eat', and with these *abn ph* 'mouthstones', which appears to be a metaphorical reference to teeth. It may be imagined that the teeth are eating or consuming in some way. The term *ḥrṣ*, if connected with Akkadian

82. Further, the verb *nkl* 'to extract' is unusual and does not exactly conform to the Arab. cognate *nakala* 'recoil, shrink, desist, draw back, withdraw', on which Margalit depends. The notion of "drawing back" appears to be something that the subject of the verb does; the verb's object does not draw back.

83. Margalit explains (*UPA* 348 n. 13) that *ḥrṣ* 'lime' was chosen rather than *spsg* because of similarity to *ḥrṣ* 'incise'. Yet *ḥrṣ* is a very unusual root in Ugaritic, and one expects the two proximate occurrences to have a similar meaning. See the next note. On the care that should be taken in proposing homonyms in Ugaritic lexicography, see J. C. de Moor, "Ugaritic Lexicography," in *Studies on Semitic Lexicography* (ed. P. Fronzaroli; QS 2; Florence: Istituto di Linguistica e di Lingue Orientali, Università di Firenze, 1973) 85.

ḫarāṣu 'to cut down, to cut off; . . . incise', as has been suggested,[84] can be associated with or compared to the action of molars, cuspids, and incisors. The verb *tiḫd* 'seize' then fits as the biting or grasping of the teeth. These words indicate that the lines carry a connotation of violence, not of neutral mastication. Taking *klb ilnm* as 'dog of the *ilnm*' (see p. 142 n. 23), with the latter term referring either to gods in general or specifically chthonic deities, would correlate nicely with a context of oral hostility. In such a context, *qmm* may be understood as 'enemies' (literally, 'those who rise against').[85]

Putting these terms together in a sensible concatenation, lines 8b–9a could be understood as the continuation of the comparison begun in 7c–8a. In the earlier lines, *šr* and *nr* could be taken as 'flash (of lightning)'[86] and 'flame', respectively. These suit a context of intimidation better than 'singer' and 'musician'. And they may even have anatomical echoes, since the arm (*yd*) has a jointed form much like lightning (one thinks of Phoenician-alphabetic *yod*), and fingers may be imagined as flames. (Interestingly, in American Sign Language the noun *fire* and the verb *burn* are signed by holding the fingers of both hands up and moving the hands in forward-directed alternating circles.) In a context of comparison, *ḥrṣ* in line 8b–9a could be understood as some sort of cutting agent or instrument, which cannot be further defined because of lack of context.[87] The teeth are being compared to such a cutter.

84. Dietrich and Loretz, "Einzelfragen," 193–97; see *MLC* 387, 'to bite' for both instances of the word (lines 8b and 10a); Aistleitner (*Wörterbuch*, 107) takes the occurrence in line 8b as 'Dreschschlitten o[der] Egge' (he translates: 'wie ein Dreschschlitten mit Steinen ist sein Maul'). Cooper ("Two Exegetical Notes," 20–21) takes it as 'split'. For the Akkadian, see the CAD Ḫ 92b. Compare also Heb. *ḥāraṣ* 'cut, sharpen, decide'; Ethiopic *ḥaraṣa* and *ḫaraṣa* 'cut into, engrave' (A. Dillmann, *Lexicon Linguae Aethiopicae* [Leipzig: Weigel, 1865] 89, 590; see W. Leslau, *Ethiopic and South Arabic Contributions to the Hebrew Lexicon* [University of California Publications in Semitic Philology 20; Berkeley: University of California Press, 1958] 22, which compares Geez *ḥaraṣa* and *ḥaraḍa* 'grind' to the Hebrew). Other interpretations of the two occurrences of *ḥrṣ* in the passage (lines 8b and 10a): both as 'decay' (Dijkstra and de Moor, "Passages," 197; connected with Arab. *ḥaraḍa* 'become corrupt, decay'); the first as 'potash' and the second as 'rotting' (*ARTU* 248). Gibson (*CML* 113) leaves the words untranslated.

85. Compare Heb. *qām*. *TO* 1 441 (and note i): 'adversaires'. Various solutions include: 'stalks' (Dijkstra and de Moor, "Passages," 198; compare Heb. *qāmâ* 'standing grain'); 'crown (of head)' (*UPA* 157; compare Arab. *qimmatu* 'top, summit; crown of head' [*DMWA* 789]); 'entrails' (*MLC* 387, 618; this reads [m]*ʿmm*); 'whole body' (*ARTU* 248 and *CARTU* 159, reading *b ʿmm*; compare Arab. *ʿmm*). *RTU* 290 n. 181 reads m *ʿmm* 'entrails' here and understands lines 9b–12a as referring to Anat's consumption and dismemberment of Aqhat.

86. See pp. 141–42 nn. 15–16.

87. Dietrich and Loretz ("Einzelfragen," 196) define it as a 'Schneideinstrument'. Compare Heb. *ḥărîṣê habbarzel* 'cutting instruments made of iron' (2 Sam 12:31 // 1 Chr 20:3).

This tricolon of comparison (7c/8a/8b–9a) gives way to two bicola (9b/9c; 10a/10b),[88] expanding the description of dental action. The teeth seize and consume enemies, and they metaphorically dispatch or place a "cutter."[89] This cutter is either being defined as the 'divine/chthonic dog', or it is being implicitly compared to one.

The description in 7c–10b, especially 9b–10b, seems to refer to Aqhat's potential. Aqhat at this stage in the story is still a youth and has only recently, it seems, received his bow. He is not a fully formed or experienced hunter or warrior. But Anat is in a position to appreciate Aqhat's capabilities. She is a warrior herself,[90] who employs other warriors (for example, Yaṭupan) to do her bidding. She can judge the lad's character. Occasion for making this judgment might have been hunting activities that the two undertook together (1.18 I 27–28). Certainly his courage in standing up to her with clever ripostes[91] unveils an assertive personality necessary to conduct battle. Her mourning is thus not merely over the loss of a fine weapon but over the loss of a future hero.

One last question regarding the scope of Anat's second speech is whether lines 17b–19a, the lines just before the scene turns to Daniʾil and his various responses in the wake of Aqhat's death, are part of the same speech. These lines, though difficult in certain particulars, deal with the agricultural failure attending Aqhat's death. They could be read as a passing comment, setting up the next scene, in which Daniʾil and Pughat show their awareness of the drought. The *w*- conjunction and the continuation of the third-person pronoun in b*m*th, however, create the sense that 17b is part of Anat's speech.

Thus, Anat's second speech covers all of lines 7b–19a.

Intensification

Anat's mourning—her actions and speeches—shows an increase in intensity. Just after Aqhat's murder, she weeps (*tbk*, line 39b). She adds four or five lines of lament (lines 39b–42), which seem in part to attempt to justify her action. She does not, therefore, show complete remorse. One wonders if her tears are partly for joy in obtaining the bow. At any rate, the lament is followed by further narrative description detailing the

88. It might also be analyzed as a tricolon: *tiḥd . šnth . w akl . / b qmm tšt . ḥrṣ . / klb . ilnm*. But here *w akl* seems syntactically awkward and one might expect three terms, not two, in the last line.

89. Dietrich and Loretz ("Einzelfragen," 196) divide lines 9b–10 as *w akl b qmm tšt / ḥrṣ klb ilnm* and translate 'Und doch: Den Fresser setzte man in die Ähren, / den Biß des Hundes der Toten'.

90. See Walls, *The Goddess Anat*, 161–215.

91. So judged by *UPA* 310–11.

breakage of the bow (lines 2-5a). Now Anat can show remorse more fully, partly because she recognizes the futility of her anger and violence. The speech that follows is much more elaborate and has two parallel parts (7b-10b // 11a-19a). In each part she cites or refers to the mourning cry: *k mr k mr*(*m*) 'How utterly bitter!' (7b, 11a-12b). After each of these, she adds words of lament. In 7c-10b she describes the loss of Aqhat as a potentially powerful warrior/hero. This is the "thou" of what abstractly can be called an "I-thou" relationship (but certainly not in the Buberian sense!). In 13a-19a she deals with other pronominal referents, first the "I" (13-17a)—her part in the killing, which echoes what she said in lines 40b-41a—and then the "it" (17b-19a)—the natural world and how it is affected.

The passage, understood this way, entails two larger contextual ramifications. First, it provides a dynamic transition to Daniʾil and his situation. Not only does the theme of agricultural failure prepare for the next scene, but the development in Anat's response provides contrast with the more mundane and normal activities in which Daniʾil is involved. That scene begins with the stereotypical notice (see 1.17 V 4-8) of Daniʾil's judging (1.19 I):

(19b) *ap*nk . *dnil* (20) [m]t . *rpi* .	Now, Daniʾil, [the R]apiʾan,
*aph*n . *ġzr* (21) [mt . h]rnmy .	then, the hero, [the Ha]rnamiyyan,
ytšu (22) [yṯb . b ap . ṯ]ġr [.]	got up, [sat in front of the g]ate,
[t]*ḥt* (23) [adrm . d b grn .]	[be]fore [the distinguished one on the threshing floor].
ydn [dn . almnt .]	He judged [the widow's cause],
[y]*ṯpṭ* (25) [ṯpṭ . ytm]	[He] decided the [case of the fatherless].

Nothing is out of the ordinary here, when compared to what Anat has expressed. In musical terms, the dynamics of the movement from Anat's mourning to Daniʾil's judging are that of a *subito piano*.

The second significant aspect of Anat's mourning is that the pattern of intensification found in it is duplicated in Daniʾil's responses that follow. As Anat did, Daniʾil will multiply his responses to Aqhat's death and its consequences. The multiplication will consist of piling up parallel reactions. Anat's mourning thus anticipates Daniʾil's reaction. A major difference, however, is that Daniʾil's responses are more numerous and sustained.

Chapter 13
Dani'il's Agricultural Rites

After Anat's recitation, the text immediately turns to Dani'il. He is at the gate judging the cause of the widow and fatherless, as we just saw (1.19 I 19–25). Thus the situation for him is much the same that it was when Kothar-wa-Hasis brought the bow to him (see 1.17 V 6–8). As the passage unfolds, however, we find that he is aware of a drought, though not of its cause. Dani'il undertakes a series of rites, seeking to remedy the agricultural failure. The presentation of rites builds to a climax at the revelation to Dani'il of the death of his son.

Pughat's Response

Just after Dani'il is reintroduced, his daughter, Pughat, appears on the scene (1.19 I):

(24) [. . .y]*t̠pṭ*	[. . . he d]ecided
(25) [t̠pṭ . ytm . tmǵy . bt]h	[the case of the fatherless.] His [daughter arrived,]
(26) [pǵt . t̠kmt . my . ḥsp]t![1]	[Pughat,[2] who shoulders water, who gat]hers[3]
(27) [l šʿr . ṭl . ydʿt]	[dew from the fleece, who knows]
(28) *h*lk . [kbkbm . b n]ši	the course [of the stars.[4] As (she) lif]ted
(29) *ʿnh . w tphn* . . .	her eyes, she saw . . .

1. The average length of the lines before this as well as the place of the -t! on the tablet (according to the photo in Margalit) indicate that twelve signs could precede.

2. Perhaps meaning simply 'girl' (*UPA* 251).

3. On the meaning of the verb *ḥsp*, referring to the gathering of water and dew (though not necessarily for a libation), see M. Dietrich and O. Loretz, "'Wasser- und Tauschöpfen' als Bezeichnung für Regenmagie," *UF* 17 (1985) 98. Gordon (*Ugaritic Textbook*, #884) has 'to pour water (water)' (he notes Arab. *ḥasafa* 'pour water' [of a cloud]); similarly, *MLC* 548. For *ḥsp* with dew, see 1.3 II 38.

4. This epithet should probably be interpreted in view of the idea that there was a connection between dew (*ṭl* and *rbb*) and the heaven and the stars (1.3 II 38–41; IV 42–44; see Dietrich and Loretz, "Wasser- und Tauschöpfen," 96–97). It is less certain that it refers to Pughat's diligence in rising early and turning in late (cf. *ARTU* 251 n. 182;

The breakage in these lines has generally been filled in using either (a) the formula describing the approach of someone from afar, to describe Pughat's approach (mainly based on *CAT* 1.17 V 8–11 because of the larger contextual similarity of judgment at the gate, but also 1.3 IV 38–40), or (b) the epithets of Pughat, as found in 1.19 II 1–3, 6–7; IV 28, 36–38. The first of these solutions, as followed, for example, by *CAT*, is not satisfactory. It reads: (25) [ṯpṭ . ytm . xxxx]h (26) [b alp . šd . rbt . km]n (27) [tdrq . pǵt . k yʿn] (28) *h*lk . [pǵt . yʿn . b n]ši (29) *ʿnh* . *w tphn*. . . .[5] This requires reversing the order of the nouns *hlk* and *tdrq*, contrary to the order in which they appear in the other examples. It does not leave room for the introductory phrase *b nši ʿnh w yphn*, found in 1.17 V 8–11.[6] It is also not clear that Pughat would need to travel the distances apparently indicated by the words *alp šd* and *rbt kmn* to reach her father.[7]

The second of the foregoing solutions is preferable, partly because it has fewer complications than the first and partly because this may be the first time Pughat is introduced in the story (at least it is the first time in what we have). If this is not the first time she is introduced, she is at least being reintroduced after not appearing on the scene for a while.[8] Listing her epithets here then makes perfect sense. Margalit as well as Dijkstra and de Moor restore the text along this line.[9] Their solutions are not satisfactory, however, because they need to introduce another line into the text.[10] A simpler solution can be achieved if the *n*-sign at the end of line

---

TO 1 445 note m). It may be specifically connected with water-gathering, since knowing astronomical data helps predict the seasons (so *ARTU*), and rising early is necessary before the dew evaporates (*UPA* 366–67).

5. See also, in part, CTA 87 n. 8

6. Some have tried to restore this at the end of line 25 with the -h at the end being the suffix on *ʿnh* (cf. Virolleaud apud CTA; *CML* 114). This, however, requires omitting the line containing the term *tdrq*.

7. Cf. *ARTU* 14 n. 68; Gordon, *Ugaritic Textbook*, #1256.

8. Margalit (*UPA* 250) supposes that the birth of Pughat was told in a tablet that may have come before 1.17.

9. Margalit (*UPA* 132, 157) reads and translates: [y]*ṯpṭ* (25) [ṯpṭ . ytm pht . bt]*h* (26) [pǵt . pǵt . šibt . ʿ]n (.) (27) [w ṯkmt . mym ḥspt .] (27 bis) [l šʿr . ṭl wydʿt] (28) *hlk* . [kbkbm b n]ši (.) (29) *ʿnh* . *w tphn* 'He adjudicates [the case of the orphaned]; / [Now present is] his [daughter, Pughat]. / [A lass (who) draws (from) the spr]ing [and shoulders water], / [Wrings dew from the wool(-fleece)], / [Knows] the course of [the stars]. / Lift[ing] her gaze, she observed'; Dijkstra and de Moor ("Passages," 200) read: (25) [ṯpṭ . ytm . bnš]i (26) [ʿnh . yphn . pǵ]t (27) [ṯkmt . my . ḥspt] (27 bis) [l šʿr . ṭl . ydʿt] (28) *h*lk . (kbkbm . b n]ši. Margalit's solution introduces a fourth epithet for Pughat and is thus more speculative than Dijkstra's and de Moor's.

10. Even though recognized as a possibility by CTA 87 n. 9. Note line 27 bis in the foregoing note.

26 (so *CAT*) is read -t$^{!}$.[11] This *-t* could belong to the participle *ḥspt* in her epithet. The rest fits easily in the space, without requiring an extra line, as can be observed in the passage cited and translated above. A few words are all that need to be supplied to make a transition from Daniʾil's judging to Pughat. One might suppose that the text noted her arrival on the scene in some way. Hence the conjectured tmǵy in line 25. Otherwise, the verb *yʿn* 'He (Daniʾil) saw (his daughter)' could be restored.

Determining how Pughat is introduced here bears on what she sees and the general mood of mourning to which Daniʾil will respond. Pughat notices various evidences of a drought (1.19 I):

(28) [. . . b n]ši (29) *ʿnh . w tphn*	[As (she) li]fted her eyes, she saw,
[. šʿr] (30) *b grn . yḫrb*	[the fleece (?)[12]] on the threshing floor was dry,
[. xxxx] (31) *yǵly .*	the [. . .] had drooped,[13]
yḫsp . ib . krmm	the blossom[14] of the vineyards sagged.[15]
(32) *ʿl . bt . abh .*	Over the house of her father,
*nšrm . trḫ*pn .	vultures hovered,
(33) *ybṣr . ḥbl . diym*	a group of kites watched.
(34) *tbky . pǵt . b*m . *lb*	Pughat wept in[16] (her) heart,
(35) *tdmʿ . bm .* kbd	tears flowed in (her) soul.

This augments the drought introduced already in Anat's lament (1.19 I 17–19). Anat commented there on the withering of vegetation. Pughat notices this too. The vegetation she refers to is different from the vegetation in Anat's list. These two passages, taken together, paint a wide-ranging picture of languishing nature.

---

11. CTA, *CAT* read [. . .]n. Dijkstra and de Moor, "Passages," 200 read a -t (but as part of the name [pǵ]t).

12. De Moor and Spronk (*CARTU* 111; cf *ARTU* 249) restore *šʿrm* 'barley'. Margalit restores (*UPA* 158, 358) šʿr and takes it as 'wool-fleece', pertaining to Pughat's epithet as *ḥspt l šʿr ṭl* 'who draws dew from the wool'. See the discussion below.

13. For the verb, see 1.2 I 23 (contrast 29); 1.3 I 1; 1.19 III 54; *SP* 68; *UPA* 358 n. 4.

14. So *UPA* 358 (*CML* 144: 'blossom'; Gibson notes Job 8:12). Alternatively, *ib* may be understood as 'fruit' (compare Heb. *ʾēb*; Akk. *inbu*).

15. Compare Arab. *ḫasafa* 'sink down'; Dijkstra and de Moor, "Passages," 201.

16. For inner weeping, see Watson, "Preludes," 365; *UPA* 363. D. Pardee ("Attestations of Ugaritic Verb/Preposition Combinations in Later Dialects," *UF* 9 [1977] 208) notes *bky b* + body part means 'weep in' (also "The Preposition in Ugaritic [I]," 341; "The Preposition in Ugaritic [II]," 217–18). Contrast internal laughing in 1.12 I (12), *il . yẓḥq . bm* (13) *lb . w ygmd̲ . bm kbd* 'Il laughed in his heart, chuckled in his soul' (compare Sarah in Gen 18:12). Less likely is the translation 'from' in this and the next line (cf. *ARTU* 250 and n. 172).

A unique observation that Pughat makes (so it seems, if the restoration of *šʿr* in line 29 is correct) is that there is no dew. The events in this story appear to take place around May, when the rains have ended and dew becomes a source of water for some plants and even for humans.[17] The types of plants involved and the description of their stage of growth are part of the indications of this season.[18] The cool nights and moist air lead to the deposit of dew on plants and on the ground. One of the ways to collect water apparently was to set out a wool-fleece and then to wring the water out. This is what Pughat's epithet apparently refers to in the phrase *ḥspt l šʿr ṭl* 'who pours dew from the fleece'. This procedure is also found in Judg 6:36–40, where Gideon asks for a sign of his election by having Yahweh manipulate the way in which a fleece becomes wet with dew. Not to be missed is Gideon's placing his fleece out on the threshing floor (*grn*), the same place where Pughat observes that something is dry in line 30. This background from the story of Gideon, along with Pughat's epithets, suggest that Pughat has come to check a fleece for water and finds it dry.[19]

After this observation, she looks beyond the fleece and the threshing floor. She first sees, on a horizontal plane, that plants have withered. Then, in the vertical dimension, she sees vultures flying over her father's house. These birds probably indicate that animals are dying from lack of water.[20] But they also connect the drought with Aqhat's death, because the vultures were earlier associated with his feast and then provided cover for Anat and Yaṭupan as they killed him. This connection is made by the reader, but it is not something that Pughat knows. She has much of the empirical evidence but not enough to formulate a hypothesis, or the right hypothesis.

Her reaction is to mourn, but she keeps this inside. As the text says, "Pughat wept in her heart." Her mourning is thus informal. It anticipates a more elaborate ritual response.

---

17. De Moor (*SP* 99) notes that dew occurs in the fall as well as the summer and that the *rb(b)* (dew drizzle) falls from mid-September to mid-October.

18. The season appears to be early spring (cf. *UPA* 358–59, 361; de Moor, "Seasonal Pattern in the Legend of Aqhatu," 66–68; *ARTU* 249 n. 170): grain is green in the husk (1.19 I 18–19); grain is in the field (II 13); grapes are still growing (I 31); summer fruit, even their firstfruits, are still to come (I 17–18, 41); the heat is explainable as the effect of the sirocco, which occurs in the spring (I 40). For the view that the time is near harvest in the fall, see M. Dietrich and O. Loretz, "*ṣrk* im Kontext der Rede Danils in KTU 1.19 i 38–46," *UF* 18 (1986) 98 (cf. their "Wasser- und Tauschöpfen," 97).

19. Thus, it is unlikely that her epithet means 'pour water on the dew' or that, further, this refers to some magical rain rite (cf. *SP* 99–100; Dietrich and Loretz, "Wasser- und Tauschöpfen," 96), similar to the water libation on Sukkot (*Mishna Sukka* 4:9; compare what is perhaps ritual water-drawing in Isa 12:3).

20. Cf. Hos 8:1, Jer 12:9, Job 39:30.

Daniʾil's First Prayer

As the text continues, we find that Daniʾil has apparently already reacted to the drought in a more formal manner by rending his clothing. He then utters a prayer that refers to the drought and Baʿl's fertilizing moisture (1.19 I):

(36) *tmzʿ . kst . dnil . mt* (37) *rpi .*	The cloak of Daniʾil, the Rapiʾan, was torn,
al⟨l⟩ *. ǵzr . mt hrnmy .*	the garment of the hero, the Harnamiyyan.
(38) *apnk . dnil . mt* (39) *rpi .*	Then Daniʾil, the Rapiʾan,
yṣly . ʿrpt . b(40) *ḥm . un .*	prayed the clouds in the afflicting[21] heat:[22]
yr . ʿrpt (41) *tmṭr . b qẓ .*	"Let the clouds bring precipitation on the summer-fruit,
ṭl . yṭll .(42) *l ǵnbm .*	let dew distill on the grapes![23]
šbʿ . šnt (43) *yṣrk . bʿl .*	Baʿl could be missing[24] for seven years,
ṯmn . rkb (44) *ʿrpt .*	eight, the cloud-rider![25]
bl . ṭl . bl rbb	Without dew, without rain,
(45) *bl* . šrʿ *. thmtm .*	without the surge[26] of the deep waters,
bl (46) *ṭbn . ql . bʿl .*	without the sweetness of Baʿl's voice!"[27]
k tmzʿ (47) *kst . dnil . mt .* rpi	Indeed,[28] the cloak of Daniʾil, the Rapiʾan, was torn,
(48) *all . ǵzr .* mt . hr[nmy]	the garment of the hero, the Harnamiyyan.

A small problem in the passage is the meaning of *tmzʿ kst dnil* in line 36 and the parallel in line 46b–47. Despite some arguments to the contrary,

21. *Un* is a noun; compare Heb. *ʾāwen* 'trouble, sorrow'; also possible is a connection with Heb. *ʾānâ* (I) 'mourn' (compare the nouns *ʾăniyyâ* and *taʾăniyyâ*, both 'mourn'). For discussion of views, see *UPA* 370–71 (Margalit here takes it as a precative particle introducing Daniʾil's prayer).

22. Margalit argues that *ḥm* does not referr to heat but instead to Daniʾil's emotional state (*UPA* 359 n. 5). It may still be taken as climatic heat, if it is not seen as the cause. W. G. E. Watson also takes it as referring to heat in his "Puzzling Passages in the Tale of Aqhat," *UF* 8 (1976) 377.

23. "[S]ummer dew on the mountains greatly helps the swelling of the grapes" (D. Baly and A. D. Tushingham, *Atlas of the Biblical World* [New York: World, 1971] 30).

24. See the discussion of *yṣrk* below.

25. The reference to the length of agricultural failure perhaps alludes to the myth of Baʿl, in which Baʿl appears to be subject to Mot for seven years (1.6 V 8–9; cf. *SP* 32–33).

26. For *šrʿ*, I rely on Arab. *saraʿa* 'be quick, fast'. Cf. Gordon, *Ugaritic Textbook*, #2488; *MLC* 633; *ARTU* 251. For another suggestion, see *UPA* 377.

27. Compare *ǵzr . ṭb . ql* 'sweet-voiced youth' (1.3 I 20). Margalit (*UPA* 378–80) argues that this is not thunder (cf. Dijkstra and de Moor, "Passages," 202) but the sound of flooded brooks and rivers after rain.

28. For the emphatic *k*-, see Dijkstra and de Moor, "Passages," 201.

the verb *tmzʿ* seems best explained on the basis of Arabic *mazaʿa*, which can mean 'tear, rip'.[29] The real question is whether Pughat is the subject of the verb, the one who tears her father's clothing,[30] or whether the verb describes a rending already done by Daniʾil.[31] The former option is unlikely because tearing of another's clothing is odd and because the phrase is repeated in lines 46–48, without Pughat as an immediate referent. The verb is either to be understood as stative in sense or passive in form. In either case, *kst* is the subject.[32] The repeated mention of cloak-rending in lines 46–48 is not to be understood to mean that the action takes place twice. This is repetition for literary effect, either as an inclusio with the first occurrence in 36–37 around Daniʾil's prayer, or as a resumptive repetition to introduce the other ritual responses in 1.19 I 46–II 25.

Some have seen Daniʾil's torn clothes as part of the series of things that Pughat observes. Were this so, one might expect the description of Daniʾil's clothing to come just after the observation about the vultures (lines 32–33) and before the description of her response (lines 34–35). Because it comes after her response, it must instead be an introduction or transition to Daniʾil's prayer. It gives a basis for that prayer. What the seemingly unimportant passing comment reveals is that, despite the fact that Daniʾil appears to be socially and emotionally whole at the beginning of the passage, which described his judging the widows and orphans, he has apparently already observed and reacted to the drought.

A greater difficulty in the passage is the structure and sense of Daniʾil's prayer. The main structural problem lies in determining the prayer's beginning and the poetic line division in 38–42a. Depending on how the passage and specific words have been understood, the introduction to

29. *DMWA* 906. Margalit (*UPA* 359–60) has argued that 'bound, leap' rather than 'tear, rip' is the base meaning of Arab. *mazaʿa* (cf. J. G. Hava, *Arabic-English Dictionary* [Beirut: Catholic Press, 1951] 718) and that therefore the phrase is to be translated: 'The garment of Danʾel, the Rapian, fluttered'. This is what happens when Pughat tells him the bad news about the climate. The problem with this is that one expects a response that displays more personal effect or agency, not clothes fluttering without specific reference to Daniʾil as the agent (and it is not clear that *tgṣ kslh* refers to clothes shaking, either; see 1.3 III 32–35; 1.4 II 16–20; 1.19 II 44–47). Another problem with this view is that it assumes that Pughat tells her father about what she has seen. Margalit thinks that the passage has been telescoped and that Pughat's report is not described. A solution might be to understand *bm* in lines 34–35 as 'from' rather than 'in' (see p. 159 n. 16 above), in which case Pughat would be vocal in her response and Daniʾil would perceive it. This, however, seems to be an awkward way of understanding the use of *lb* and *kbd* in the context. These, one expects, are organs of thought; the weeping seems to be internalized.

30. So *CML* 114, line 36–37; *RTU* 295.

31. *MLC* 388; *ARTU* 250–51.

32. Dijkstra and de Moor, "Passages," 201.

the prayer has been defined as extending through *yṣly*, *ḥm*, *yr*, or even *ǵnbm*.[33] The starting point for a solution seems to be a recognition of the parallel between *tmṭr* 'let (them) produce rain/precipitation' and *yṭll* 'let (it) condense' (both line 41). Because the latter precipitation is produced with respect to grapes (*l ǵnbm*), we suspect that the first verb refers to precipitation for other produce, *b qẓ* 'on summer fruit'. It is possible to see *b qẓ* as parallel to *b ḥm un yr*, as do Dietrich and Loretz–'in der Sommerhitze' // 'in der Gluthitze zum Frühregen'.[34] That the preposition *b-* accompanies both of these words appears to support this solution instead of the solution that I have offered, since *b qẓ* and *l ǵnbm* have two different prepositions. But a three-member construct phrase, *ḥm un yr*, literally, 'the heat of the strength of the early rain', appears somewhat awkward or overwrought, if not conceptually difficult. Thus, taking *b qẓ* as 'on the summer fruit' seems reasonable. The term *b qẓ* clearly ends the poetic line in which it appears; the question remains, however, where this line begins: does it begin with *ʿrpt*, or does it include the term *yr*? Since the following line has the word *ṭl*, it is reasonable for the line to begin with *yr*. This is apparently related to Hebrew *yōreh* 'early rain', but in view of the indications that this scene is set approximately in May (see above), it should be understood more generally, as 'precipitation' or 'moisture', which could include dew. Thus, two lines are well defined: (40b–41a) *yr* . *ʿrpt* (.) *tmṭr* . *b qẓ* . / (41b–42a) *ṭl* . *yṭll* . *l ǵnbm* 'Let the clouds bring precipitaton on the summer-fruit, / let dew distill on the grapes!'

The way these lines are formulated makes it reasonable, furthermore, to suppose that they are not part of a description that introduces Dani'il's speech but part of the speech itself. Where does this begin? Certainly the verb *yṣly* '(Dani'il) entreated' (on the meaning, see below) must be part of the introduction. This leaves only *ʿrpt b ḥm un* ambiguous–either being part of the introduction or part of the prayer itself. That it is part of the introduction seems clear because of its lack of substantial parallels with the following line. It is true that *ʿrpt* appears here as in line 40b–41a, but *ʿrpt* can be an object of *yṣly* and *b ḥm un* an adverbial 'in the afflicting heat', describing the environmental condition in which Dani'il speaks.

With the lineation understood thus, we can ask the larger contextual questions about the passage. The foregoing interpretation of lines 40b–42a forms an ostensible contradiction with lines 42b–46a. The former section is positive in drift while the latter, if read in the indicative mood,

33. For the terminus of the clause with *yṣly*, see Dietrich and Loretz, "*ṣrk*," 98–99; *ḥm*, *UPA* 132; *yr*, *ARTU* 250; *ǵnbm*, *CML* 114. For Gibson, everything from *ʿrpt* (first occurrence) to *l ǵnbm* is indirectly presented as the gist, apparently, of the prayer that is cited in 42b–46a.

34. Dietrich and Loretz, "*ṣrk*," 98–99 and n. 19.

is negative, opposite of the former wish. This has led to several solutions: reading lines 42b–46a (1) as a curse, with the preceding positive lines describing the circumstance in which Daniʾil uttered the curse;[35] (2) as an oracular or divine response to lines 40b–42a, Daniʾil's prayer, telling him that drought will prevail for seven/eight years;[36] (3) as a rhetorical question;[37] or (4) as a statement of feared potentiality.[38]

The first solution largely depends on lexical lists in which Ugaritic *ṣly* is defined in Akkadian as 'curse'.[39] This equation, however, cannot be confidently assumed for all, or even the majority, of attestations of *ṣly*. The specific context of the term appears must be the guide; lines 40b–42a make it appear to be a prayer or entreaty more than a curse. This is not unfounded in view of other texts. *CAT* 1.119, for example, after a sacrificial schedule in the month of *ibʿlt*, a recitation is appended promising offerings to Baʿl if he will defend against an enemy (see pp. 76–78). The summary says, *w šmʿ* [. b]ʿl . *l* . *ṣlt*[km] 'Baʿl will hearken to your prayer'. The root *ṣly* can therefore indicate a petition for help.[40] This is close to the meaning it has in the Aqhat passage. Observe that, at this point in the story, there is no reason to utter a curse, because Daniʾil does not know that Aqhat is dead.

The second solution is difficult, because a switch in speakers is not evident. Furthermore, Daniʾil's subsequent rites performed for the benefit of the crop do not seem to be aware of a prediction of a lengthy drought (1.19 II 12–25). Moreover, the repetition of the cloak-rending bicolon in 46b–48 is a structural indication that lines 40b–46a are to be seen as a unit spoken by Daniʾil. As already noted, this resumptively encloses Daniʾil's prayer. It describes what Daniʾil has already done. Therefore, lines 40b–46a appear to belong together as part of Daniʾil's response, which includes the rending of his clothes. The last statement about rending clothes certainly does not appear to be a reaction to anything in lines 40b–46a. Margalit, who argues for the second solution to these lines, did so in large part because of his interpretation of the verb *yṣrk* (line 43a),

35. Cf. Watson, "Puzzling Passages," 377; *ANET* 153; Pardee, "The Preposition in Ugaritic [I]," 357.

36. *UPA* 158.

37. Cf. *CML* 115.

38. Dietrich and Loretz, "*ṣrk*," 98–99.

39. Ug. 5 §130 III 16′ (pp. 234–35) and §137 II 46′ (pp. 244–45): *ṣilya* = [*arāru*] and *arratum*.

40. For the meaning 'pray, entreat', see M. Dietrich and O. Loretz, "Zur ugaritischen Lexikographie (VI): Das Verb *ṣlj* 'bitten, beten' und das Nomen *ṣlt* 'Bitte, Gebet'," *UF* 5 (1973) 273–74; *UPA* 368–70. For the interpretation 'adjure' (and a different division of the poetic lines), see J. C. de Moor, "A Note on CTA 19 (1 Aqht): I.39–42," *UF* 6 (1974) 495–96.

which he understood as coming from the root *ṣrr* 'to be hostile to, afflict' plus suffix *-k*.[41] While there is no linguistic difficulty in this, derivation from the root *ṣrk* is not impossible. True, meanings given to it such as 'fail' may go beyond the semantic range suggested by cognates, but the basic meanings 'to be in need, to be lacking, to be decrepit, poor' suggest that the meaning 'be lacking' in our text is possible.[42] The phrase *bl ṭbn ql bˁl* 'without the sweetness of Baˁl's voice' (lines 45–46) supports the interpretation of a missing Baˁl or, more specifically and naturally, the missing *effects* of this deity.

The third and fourth solutions are relatively similar: rhetorical questions can be read as statements of anxiety. Both of these are satisfactory possibilities. Since questions are not clearly indicated,[43] reading them as modal statements referring to something that is feared is a reasonable solution.

The foregoing observations lead to the following conclusions about Daniʾil's utterance: It is a prayer (*yṣly*), not an incantation or adjuration.[44] It begins with a bicolon containing two wishes in the jussive (lines 40b–42a). This is followed by another bicolon posed as a modal statement of apprehension (42b–44a). Then a tricolon appears (44b–46a) with a series of *bl* clauses, which continue and define the previous bicolon. The clauses develop from simple to more complex expressions: *bl* with one word (twice), then with two words, then with three words. This foreshadows the larger overall structure of intensification in Daniʾil's reaction.

A larger climactic development is visible in the overall description in lines 1.19 I 19–48. This parallels the unfolding of the feast scene at the beginning of the story. That feast, it will be recalled, is described at first without words: Daniʾil is silent as he makes his offerings over six days. A climax and clarification of his activity comes when the gods begin to speak on the seventh day. Similarly, in 1.19 I 19–37 the characters are silent; only actions or the result of actions are described. Daniʾil's subsequent prayer in lines 38–48 caps this description and adds definition. It therefore heightens the level of description.

41. *UPA* 374–75. On the derivation from *ṣrr* 'afflict' (Arab. *ḍarra*), see also Gordon, *Ugaritic Textbook*, #2200. Cf. Watson ("Puzzling Passages," 377 n. 50), who takes it from *ṣrr* 'bind' (Arab. *ṣarra*).

42. See Dietrich and Loretz, "*ṣrk*," 97, for an etymological discussion; note the cautions in *UPA* 374–75. Compare Heb. *ṣōrek* 'need'; Arab. *ḍaraka* 'be needy'; Akk. *ṣarāku* 'be fragile' or the like (AHw 1083); compare (possible borrowings) Aram. *ṣrak* 'need, want'; Syr. *ṣrak* 'lack, want, be poor'.

43. Dietrich and Loretz, "*ṣrk*," 99.

44. See *UPA* 368–70.

This passage is similar to Dani'il's offering at the beginning of the story in another way: both involve lamentation. Here, to be sure, the mourning in Dani'il's and Pughat's reactions is not the same as the mourning at the beginning. The father and daughter are not here responding to the lack of a family member; they are ignorant of Aqhat's death. They are reacting only to a lack of moisture. But Dani'il is again making a petition for a remedy and, notably, again he employs clothing symbolism. In the first rite he wears a *mizrt* and *ṣt*-clothing to signal his need; here he wears torn clothing for the same purpose. In some measure, then, the story has gone in a cycle and is returning conceptually to its beginning.

Finally, the observations made by Anat, Pughat, and then by Dani'il in regard to the drought become progressively more intense. Anat and Pughat refer to *symptoms*: withering plants and the lack of moisture. Dani'il's prayer notes the lack of water as well but moves beyond this to the theological *cause*: the absence of Baʿl. This constitutes another element in the intensification of description. Another point of interplay with the initial feast increases the intensity, this one a matter of contrast. Dani'il's initial petition led to Baʿl's presence: "Baʿl drew near in his compassion" (1.17 I 16). In the present case, Baʿl is feared to be absent.

Dani'il's Double Prayer

Dani'il's response to the drought continues in a more aggressive form than before. He has Pughat harness an ass to carry him around his fields. Her faithfulness is reminiscent of the duties of an ideal son. She helps her father to move about, just as a son might help his father after a drinking bout. Her presence and activity on behalf of her father stress the absence of Aqhat.

It is not clear if her preparations are accompanied by mourning on her part. The term *bkm* accompanies the description of her actions and may be interpreted as an infinitive absolute of the root *bky* 'to weep', with enclitic *mem* (1.19 II):

(8) bk*m* . *tmdln* . *ʿr*	Weeping(?), she roped[45] the ass,
(9) *bkm* . *tṣmd* . *pḥl* .	weeping(?), she harnessed the donkey,
*b*km (10) *tšu* . *abh* .	weeping(?), she lifted her father,
tštnn . *l* [b]*mt* *ʿr*	placed him on the [b]ack of the ass,
(11) *l ysmsm* . *bmt* . *pḥl*	on the proper spot on the donkey's back.[46]

45. See the considerations of W. G. E. Watson, "Unravelling Ugaritic *mdl*," *SEL* 3 (1986) 73, with reference to R. M. Good's observation.

46. On the passage, see the parallel in 1.4 IV 7–18 and see W. G. E. Watson, "Parallels to Some Passages in Ugaritic," *UF* 10 (1978) 398–99.

If this is a correct interpretation, then she is augmenting her response with what appears to be open weeping. Her explicit sadness would provide a pivot to the more expressive action by Daniʾil that is about to come. However, this interpretation is not indisputable. Margalit, for example, offers the exact opposite interpretation. He takes *bkm* in connection with Arabic *bakima/bakum* 'be dumb; be silent'.[47] The reserve that Pughat showed earlier is maintained here, according to his reading. Dijkstra and de Moor do not even translate the term as a verb but as a particle meaning 'thereupon'.[48] The question of Pughat's psycho-ritual state at this point must be left open.

The rite in which Pughat aids her father is clear for the most part. It displays a compounding in ritual response that continues the intensifying development that we have noted so far (1.19 II):

A

(12) *ydnil* [49]. *ysb . palth*	Daniʾil went about his dry land,[50]
(13) *bṣql . yph . b palt .*	he saw a shoot[51] in his dry land,
bṣq[l] (14) *yph . b yǵlm .*	he saw a shoot in the *yǵlm*-soil.[52]

47. *DMWA* 70; R. Blachère, M. Chouémi, and C. Denizean, *Dictionnaire Arabe-Français-Anglais (Langue classique et moderne)* (Paris: Maisonneuve et Larose, 1967–) 776; *UPA* 360–61 n. 13. For the interpretation 'weeping', see *GUL* 103, 125; *RTU* 298.

48. Dijkstra and de Moor, "Passages," 203; cf. *ARTU* 252.

49. Line 12 begins *ydnil* and 19, *ydnh* (cf. CTA; KTU^{1}). In view of the parallelism between 12–18 and 19–25, they should probably read the same. *CAT* suggests reading *ydn dnil* in both cases; Gibson (*CML* 115–16), *ydn dnil* and *ydnh*, respectively (*ydn*[*h*], a verb, 'he approached'; compare Arab. *dnw* 'be close, come near'); de Moor and Spronk (*CARTU* 112), *ydnh dnil* and *ydnh*, respectively (a verb with suffix: 'he urged it on', apparently connected with Arab. *wadana* 'beat [with a stick]'; cf. Dijkstra and de Moor, "Passages," 203); and Margalit (*UPA* 223–24), *ydnil* in both cases (a prefixed form of the name *dnil*).

50. The etymology of *palt* is unknown. For attempts, see Greenfield, "Lexicographical Notes," 90 n. 13; Dijkstra and de Moor, "Passages," 203; Margalit, "Lexicographical Notes [II]," 137–39; J. Tropper, "Ugaritisch *palt* und hebräisch *poʾrôt*," *UF* 26 (1994) 483–86; Sapin (apud *UPA* 388 n. 2). By parallelism with *ḥmdrt* in line 21 and larger context, a meaning like 'dry land' is possible. For a discussion of the terms, see *UPA* 388–89.

51. In terms of the chronological flow of the story and the season, *bṣql* must be a young plant, but it is difficult to define the word more precisely (the occurrence 1.85:5 does not help). On the basis of the Aramaic translation of 2 Kgs 4:42 (where in Heb. *bṣqlnw* appears), as well as Deut 8:4, Neh 9:21, Margalit (*UPA* 389–92) takes it as a "'would-be' sheaf of grain whose kernels are still encased in husk." Cf. Barr, *Comparative Philology*, 294. Dijkstra and de Moor ("Passages," 203–4; de Moor, "Ugaritic Lexicography," 93 n. 3) take it as 'shoot', root *bṣq* with *-l* affix (so Margalit).

52. It is not clear if this is connected to Arab. *ǵulla* 'burn with thirst' and refers to dry land (*DMWA* 679; see Cassuto, *Biblical and Oriental Studies II*, 196) or with Arab. *waǵala* 'penetrate deeply' (*wāǵil* and *mūǵil* both mean 'deep-rooted') and refers to a type

*bṣql . yḥ*bq (15) *w ynšq .*	He embraced and kissed the shoot:
aḥl .an . bṣ[ql] (16) *y*{*n*}*pʿ .*	"I pray that[53] the shoot may grow,[54]
b palt . bṣql . ypʿ .	in the dry land the shoot may grow,
*b yǵ*lm (17) *ur .*	in the *yǵlm*-soil the plant.[55]
tispk . yd . aqht (18) *ǵzr .*	May the hand of Aqhat the hero gather you,
tštk . b qrbm . asm	place you inside the granary."

B

(19) *ydni*⟨l⟩ *. ysb . aklth .*	Daniʾil went about his clodded-land,[56]
yph (20) *šblt . b ak*⟨l⟩*t .*	he saw an ear in the clodded-land,
*šblt . yp*ʿ (21) *b ḥmdrt .*	he saw an ear in his parched land.[57]
šblt . yḥ[bq] (22) w *ynšq .*	He embraced and kissed the ear:
aḥl . an . š[blt] (23) *tp*ʿ *.*	"I pray that the e[ar] may grow,

of soil (deep soil?) (*DMWA* 1083; cf. Aistleitner, *Wörterbuch*, 133; *UPA* 393–94; Margalit's interpretation of this as '"buried" plant bulbs' does not fit the context of the other three parallel terms, *palt*, *aklt*, and *ḥmdrt*, unless the last, as Greenfield says ["Lexicographical Notes," 90], refers to 'dried grain'). Dijkstra and de Moor ("Passages," 204) define it as 'languishing stalks' connected with Arab. *waǵl/waǵil* 'undernourished, miserable'. They prefer to connect it with the crop rather than the field. *RTU* 299 has 'wilted plants'.

53. Margalit (*UPA* 392–93) and (apparently) de Moor (*ARTU* 252) and de Moor and Spronk (*CARTU* 138) understand *aḥl* as a D-stem first-person common singular verb, similar in meaning to Heb. *ḥlh* II 'to entreat (for favor)', followed by a first-person common singular pronoun. Other interpretations: Dijkstra and de Moor, "Passages," 204: an interjection *aḥl* plus demonstrative *an* 'O that this shoot'); Cassuto, *Biblical and Oriental Studies II*, 196: interjection *aḥl* plus request particle *an*.

54. The root of *yp*ʿ, by context, appears to be the same as Akk. *(w)apû*, Heb. *yp*ʿ. The forms in lines 20 and 23 indicate that the *-n-* in 16b may be a mistake (so *CAT*; it is doubtfully an N-stem [cf. Dijkstra and de Moor, "Passages," 205], nor is it a nasalized form similar to Aram. *manda*ʿ ← *madda*ʿ).

55. Here I follow Margalit's division of the lines (*UPA* 134, 394–96), which includes the term *ur* in a tricolon that begins with *aḥl an*, rather than placing it at the beginning of the next bicolon as a vocative (cf. *ARTU* 252–53). Margalit's definition of *ur* as plants that grow in arid soil, however, seems to contradict the implication that the *bṣql* here and the *šblt* in the parallel passage are plants that do not do well in arid soil. I translate the term 'plant' for want of a more specific definition. A connection with Arab. *ʾuwār* 'scorching heat' is not certain. The *ʾōrōt* of 2 Kgs 4:39 may be plants in general, such as one might put in a soup, not specifically those that grow in drought (despite v. 38).

56. Perhaps to be connected with Akk. *akkullāt*, which CAD (s.v.) defines as 'clods or similar undesirable formations on a field' or 'a field or terrain characterized by such a feature'. *DLU* 22: 'tierra cosumida, rastrojo?'

57. For *ḥmdrt*, compare with Akk. *ḫamadīru* 'shrivelled or withered'; *ḫamadīrūtu* 'shrivelling (said of trees)' (CAD Ḫ 58; cf. *CML* 116, 146; Gordon, *Ugaritic Textbook*, #873; Aistleitner, *Wörterbuch*, 104; *UPA* 388–89; Margalit, "Lexicographical Notes [II]," 137–39). It is possible that, instead of referring to land, it may refer to withered plants (Greenfield, "Lexicographical Notes," 89–90; cf. *RTU* 299).

b aklt . šblt . tpʿ	in the clodded-land the ear may grow,
[. b ḫ]*mdrt* (24) *ur*[58] .	[in the par]ched land the plant.
tispk . yd . aqht . ǵz[r]	May the hand of Aqhat the hero gather you,
(25) *tštk . bm . qrbm . asm*	place you inside the granary."

Daniʾil here travels about his land. The action indicated by the verb *sbb* is not necessarily ritualized activity (for example, circumambulation) but simply indicates movement to various parts of the field.[59] Ritualized activity, however, is evident in the way he treats the plants he finds, which are in their early stages of development.[60] He undertakes two performances (A and B), which are parallel to one another (lines 12–18 and 19–25). Each contains an unusual action and a verbal recitation. The action involves embracing and kissing a plant. Because it is a drought and every plant counts, and also because he hopes that Aqhat will harvest these particular plants, we have to assume that he leaves the plants in the ground. Therefore, he must be bending low to the earth to caress them and kiss them. One thus gets the impression that he is kneeling down or even lying on the ground beside them. The recitations are formal and prayer-like, especially with the introductory phrase *aḫl . an* 'I pray/make entreaty that'. Certainly this is not "high ritual" or liturgy. But it is clearly ritualized activity, not simply eccentric behavior or simple dramatization.

The prayers deal with the whole life of the plant's hoped-for existence: growing in the land, being harvested, and ultimately being placed in storage. In charting this natural history, Daniʾil brings in Aqhat as an agent. This creates a picture of irony, in which readers and hearers know of Aqhat's fate, but Daniʾil and his daughter go about blind to the ultimate cause of the drought.

The dual rite creates a climax to the activities of Daniʾil in 1.19 I 36–II 25. The feeling of rising climax is achieved in several ways. In terms of structure, the progression moves from Daniʾil's reaction and a rite with a single prayer to a rite with two prayers. Ritual action increases as well. The first rite is accompanied by the rending of garments. This is incidentally told. The pair of prayers, in contrast, involves the actions of embracing and kissing, which are an integral part of the ceremony. The sites of the rites are also different. Daniʾil performs the first at home but takes to

58. For resolution of the grammatical problem of masculine *ur* with preceding feminine *tpʿ*, see *UPA* 395: nouns in lines where verbs are supplied conceptually from preceding lines do not necessarily need to agree with the foregoing verbs.

59. The *sb* in 1.16 III 3, however, an agricultural rite where *šmn* [šlm] 'oil [of well-being(?)]' is poured out, may be ritualized action.

60. Margalit (*UPA* 382) discounts the idea that Daniʾil is performing a ritual here. His judgment may be due to the difficulties in defining ritual in anthropology and religious studies. See the introduction to this work.

the road for the dual prayer over the plants and moves to different fields or different parts of the same field. There is also a transition in mood. The first prayer expresses hope with jussive verbs, accompanied by a modal statement that shows anxiety about whether Baʿl has forsaken the land. The rite with the two prayers is more assertive and focused. Each prayer begins with jussive verbs, which are followed by personification of the plants and a second-person address to them.[61] The tenor of the two prayers is determination, not fear or anxiety. The climax is also felt in the themes treated. In the examination of the single prayer, I noted that Pughat recognized the symptoms of drought in her inspection and that Daniʾil in his first prayer moved to the cause, the possible absence of Baʿl. The double prayer advances the subject matter again by bringing in Aqhat.

By these means, the description focuses on Aqhat; the revelation of Aqhat's death to Daniʾil, which immediately follows, is then able to achieve a sharp dramatic effect.[62] Readers and hearers, who know that Aqhat is dead, see Pughat and Daniʾil moving about somewhat blindly in their reactions. Daniʾil almost embarrasses himself—he unquestionably looks pathetic—in the eyes of readers and hearers, hoping for nature to heal itself and praying for Aqhat to reap the harvest. Daniʾil's emotional and ritual investment is in an impossible hope. He moves down a path that is a patent dead end. Thus, the cognitive dissonance he feels and our perception of it are even greater when he learns the truth. This is one of the reasons for his intense anger, which we sense in the retaliatory rites that follow (see below).

Daniʾil's responses to agricultural failure and the other rites that follow the death of Aqhat (see below on these) are related to *rites de passage*, transition rites. Arnold van Gennep is the author of the classic delineation of these transition rites. He notes that these rites have three stages: (1) separation, (2) marginality or liminality, and (3) aggregation or incorporation.[63] Another rite with these three stages is found in the biblical ritual for priestly consecration in which the priests are separated from society on the first day of the rite, exist in a liminal state (not fully part of the community, yet not fully enabled as priests) for seven days, and then are brought back into the community on the eighth day.[64] Of course, as in this example, in many rites of transition the people do not return to the

61. See W. G. E. Watson, "Apostrophe in the Aqhat Poem," *UF* 16 (1984) 323–26.

62. Margalit (*UPA* 389 n. 11) notes that the dual rite correlates with the *two* messengers that quickly appear on the scene, confronting another pair, Daniʾil and Pughat.

63. A. van Gennep, *The Rites of Passage* (Chicago: University of Chicago Press, 1960) 10–11 and passim.

64. See Leach's analysis in his *Culture*, 89–91 (cf. 77–79).

same position that they previously held. They are often reintegrated at a higher level, or at least their status has changed and may even involve an element of perpetual liminality, as in the case of the Israelite priests. They are part of society but at the same time are above or outside it.

Victor Turner has developed van Gennep's model, paying particular attention to the middle stage vis-à-vis the nonliminal stages at either end.[65] Liminality sometimes leads to or is concomitant with a state of communitas, a new pattern of social relationships in which preexisting social differences and roles are minimalized or disregarded. In Near Eastern ritual, the slapping of the king during the Babylonian *akītu* festival may be considered a sample of this rearrangement, if not inversion, of the social pattern.[66] The social situation that liminality and especially communitas contrast with is structure. The new pattern in the liminal stage constitutes antistructure.

The rites we are examining in this part of the of the Aqhat story are similar to *rites de passage*. Dani'il and his associates are in a state of liminality. Structure has been upset in various ways. The relationship of humans to the gods has been disturbed. The son promised by the gods has been killed. Nature, in a more cosmic definition of structure, has also been disturbed by the killing. The rites that Dani'il performs are attempts to return to structure. But there is a difference between these rites and *rites de passage* proper. In the *rites de passage*, liminality is induced by ritual means; in Dani'il's story this is not the case. Yes, Aqhat's death does come about through two instances of ritual failure. But these feasts are not calculated to bring about a liminal state. Liminality is an accidental development, and therefore the rites cannot count as rites of separation. Thus, the ritual performances after the death of Aqhat deal with only the last two elements of van Gennep's categorization: the states of liminality and aggregation. Performances with only these elements may be called *rites of crisis*, to distinguish them from *rites de passage*.

Rites of crisis generally have a goal different from the goal of regular *rites de passage*. Instead of altering the status of the ritual patient or the environment, they seek to restore an individual or environment to the status prior to crisis. For example, purification rites, in any society, remove pollution, which is often accidental. They return the individual to the state that existed before contamination.[67] They do not advance or modify the social status of the individual.

65. V. Turner, *The Ritual Process: Structure and Anti-structure* (Ithaca: Cornell University Press, 1969) and his *Dramas* (passim).

66. Cf. *ANET* 334a, lines 415ff. (F. Thureau-Dangin, *Rituels accadiens* [Paris: Ernest Leroux, 1921] 127–54). See K. van der Toorn, "The Babylonian New Year Festival," 333.

67. See my "Spectrum," 173–75.

Dani'il's agricultural rites have this goal. They seek a return to the state of fertility that existed beforehand. By referring to the god Baʿl in the first prayer, Dani'il also indirectly expresses the need for the deity to resume his beneficial role on behalf of humans. By mentioning Aqhat in the later prayers, he calls to mind and reinforces the patterns of social relationships that lie behind agricultural labor. He is not seeking an alteration in the status or role of any of the individuals or powers involved.

This analysis of rites of crisis in contrast to *rites de passage* is helpful, beyond clarifying the intent of the two types of ritual. It provides a basis for a contrast that we will see in dealing with the rites that are performed, after Dani'il finds out about Aqhat's death. When he learns of his death, Dani'il cannot continue to perform rites of restoration. Aqhat cannot be brought back. The father needs to move to another type of ritual, which seeks to remedy the crisis in another manner. Instead of restoration, he will seek retaliation.

Note that the rites that Dani'il performs for the land and the ensuing announcement by messengers that Aqhat is dead stand counter to the ritual development at the beginning of the story. Dani'il performed rites there that achieved a positive result. He was promised a son, and the son was born. In the agricultural section here, the rites are done in propriety; there is no misexecution or abuse, to use Grimes's categories of ritual infelicity. However, the result is ineffectiveness. Nature remains impaired. Ritual failure is the result of ignorance.

Chapter 14

The Messengers and Conjuration of the Vultures

The responses to Aqhat's death after Daniʾil is informed of it become more complex. The messengers who bring the dire news are themselves engaged in mourning behavior that is more complex than any in which Daniʾil or Pughat has been engaged. In his response, Daniʾil performs a rite with, not just one or two, but three parts, and a fourth, summarizing and capping element is even added to those. At the same time, Daniʾil, having better intelligence, changes the aim of his responses.

The Messengers

As soon as Daniʾil finishes the second of his two prayers in the field, Pughat looks up and sees messengers coming (1.19 II):

(27) b *nši* ʿ*n*h . *w tphn* .	As (Pughat) lifted her eyes, she saw:[1]
in . š[lm] (28) b *hl*k . *ǵl*mm .	There was no calm in the approach of the two lads,
bddy . *y*ṣa	they came separately,[2]
(29) [x] *yṣa* . *w l* . *yṣa* .	(and?) they came with hesitation.[3]
hlm . ṯ[nm] (30) [q]*dqd* .	They struck (their) [h]ead tw[ice],
ṯlṯid . ʿ*l* . *ud*[n]	three times on the ea[r].[4]
(31) l [a]*sr* . *pdm* . *rišh*[m]	They had not tied up (their) hair,[5]
(32) ʿ*l* . *pd* . *as*r . ḥǵ[xx] .	on the hair on their temples they had tied a . . . ,
l gl[ḥ]t (33) *mḫlpt* .	their braids had been clipped.

1. There seems to be no real difficulty in taking the subject of the verb as Pughat, contrary to Dijkstra and de Moor, "Passages," 205–6.

2. Cf. *ARTU* 253 n. 195; *UPA* 159, 383.

3. Literally, 'they came and they did not come'. See *UPA* 159. *ARTU* 253: '. . . they came back, but he (Aqhat) did not come back!'

4. This is probably not something that the heralds are saying (for example, *MLC* 391).

5. For *pd* compare Arab. *fawd* 'temple; hair around the temples' (*DMWA* 731).

w l . *ytk* . dmʿt [.]	Tears poured forth,
k*m* (34) *rbʿt* . *t̠qlm* .	like quarter shekels . . . [. . .],
*tg*x[xxxx] *bm* (35) *yd* .	. . . [. . .] in/by the hand.
ṣpnhm . *tliy*m[6]	Their secret was overpowering,
[xxx . ṣ]*pnhm* (36) *nṣḥy* .	[. . .] their secret was subduing,[7]
*š*rr . mʿ[xxx] xxa*y*[8]	“. . .
(37) n*bšrkm*(?)[9] . *dn*il .	Can we bring good news to you, O Daniʾil . . .
m b *h*xx (38) *riš* . rqth .	. . . head, his temple(?),[10]
tḥt ʿ*nt* y*q*l . *l* . *tš*ʿly *hwt* .	under Anat he fell, she could not raise him.
[š]*ṣat k rḥ* . *npšhm*	She made his breath escape like wind,
(39) *k it̠l* . *brl*thm .	his soul like an *it̠l*-plant,
[k qṭr . b aph]	[like smoke from his nostrils.]”
(40) *tmǵyn* . *tša* . ghm . w[tṣḥ]	They arrived and lifted their voice, [crying]:
(41) *šm*ʿ . *l dnil* . mt . [rpi]	“Hear, O Daniʾil, [Rapiʾan].
(42) *mt* . *aqht* . *ǵz*r .	Aqhat, the hero, is dead.
[šṣat] (43) *btlt* . ʿ*nt* . k r[ḥ . npšh]	The Virgin Anat [made his breath escape] like wi[nd],
(44) [[i]]*k it̠l* . *brlth* .	his soul like an *it̠l*-plant,
[k qṭr . b aph]	[like smoke from his nostrils.]”

This passage is difficult because of damage to the tablet. It is mainly troublesome in lines 34–37, where the messengers' mourning behavior is obscure. From what remains of the text, however, their general actions and words are relatively clear. As they come, they walk erratically. This is a signal of their dismay. This contrasts with the smooth approach of Kothar-wa-Ḫasis earlier in the story, when he brought a favorable message.[11] They also strike themselves on the head and ear. This is perhaps a semaphore, visually announcing in advance the bad news that they will relay

6. *CAT* and Dijkstra and de Moor (“Passages,” 207) read *nliy*m. KTU[1], Margalit (*UPA* 134), and de Moor and Spronk (*CARTU* 113) read the first letter as *t*-.

7. For this rendition of the lines with *ṣpn*, see *UPA* 134, 160, 396–98. The interpretation of the word as Ṣapan does not fit the context well, either as a geographical place or as a metonym for a deity (for example, Dijkstra and de Moor, “Passages,” 207). Cooper's interpretation ('Pughat struck their scrota with her hand'; in his “Two Exegetical Notes,” 24) is unlikely, though it has the virtue of making sense of the double report in the passage. Still, the meaning of *tliy*m and *nṣḥy* is not certain.

8. The text follows *CAT*. Dijkstra and de Moor (“Passages,” 206) reconstruct and read *šrr* . *m*[lakny] 'Hard is our message!'

9. *CAT* and KTU[1] have a*bšrkm*; CTA and *UPA* 228 have n*bšrkm*.

10. De Moor and Spronk (*CARTU* 113) and de Moor (*ARTU* 254 and n. 206) read and translate: m b h[lm] *riš* rq[t]h 'what (news) now that the head has been struck on the temp[le]?'

11. For this and other contrasts, see *UPA* 384–86.

by mouth to Dani᾿il. Other visible signs of mourning are described: they have clipped part of their hair and not tied up the rest.[12] They are also wailing.

One of the difficulties in the text is the messengers' speech in lines 37–39. The speech precedes the notice of their arrival (line 40) and another announcement of the bad news (lines 41–44). This might be an indication of disarray in the text.[13] If one wants to make sense of the text as it stands, it may be that the preliminary speech in lines 37–39 should be read as a soliloquy that augments and explains the visible signs of mourning described before it. If the messengers are indeed acting out the murder of the son as they approach, it is not impossible that they add words, even though they have not yet reached Dani᾿il.

Setting verbal responses temporarily aside, we can see that this is the most complex mourning behavior so far displayed in the aftermath of Aqhat's death. Prior to this point, Pughat has mourned, but only internally, and Dani᾿il has only torn his clothing. In contrast, a dense series of actions describes the messengers' mourning. Their knowledge of the real reason for mourning complements this. Their compounded behavior prepares for the more extensive ritual actions performed by Dani᾿il.

The Conjuration of the Vultures

When Dani᾿il finds out the bad news, after a brief description of his physical reaction (for this, see p. 194 below) and a short break of about nine lines in which he responds verbally (1.19 II 47–55), he engages in a threefold conjuration concerning the vultures that are flying overhead, in an effort to find his son's remains. This is capped by a prospective curse against them should they disturb Aqhat's remains (1.19 II–III):

A

(56) *b nš*i[. ʿnh . w yphn .]	As (he) lifted [his eyes, he saw,]
[yḥd] (55) b ʿrp*t*[. nšrm .]	[he observed vultures] in the clouds.
[yšu] (1) [gh .]w *yṣḥ* [.]	[He raised his voice] and cried,
kn[p . nšrm] (2) bʿ*l* . *yṯb*⟨r⟩ .	"May Baʿl break the [vultures' wi]ngs,
bʿ*l* . *y*ṯbr [. diy . hmt]	may Baʿl break [their pinions]!
(3) *tqln* . *tḥ*⟨t⟩ *p*ʿ*ny* .	May they fall at my feet,
*ibq*ʿ [. kbdthm . w](4) *aḥd* .	so I can cleave [their viscera and] observe!

12. For hair disheveling, see Lev 10:6; 21:10. For shaving or tearing out hair in mourning or grief: Judg 16:19; Isa 22:12; Jer 16:6; 41:5; 47:5; 48:37; Ezek 7:18; Amos 8:10; Mic 1:16; see also the literature listed in *SP* 193.

13. *RTU* 302. One of Margalit's rather extensive modifications to the text (*UPA* 134–35, 226–31) is placing lines 40–41 before line 37.

hm . iṯ . šmt . hm . i[ṯ] (5) *ʿẓm* .	If there is fat, if there is bone,
ab[[p]]*ky . w . aqbrnh*	I will weep and bury him,
(6) *ašt . b ḫrt . ilm . arṣ*[!]	I will place (him) in a cavern of the underworld gods."[14]
(7) *b ph . rgm . l y*[[x]]*ṣa* .	The utterance had barely left his mouth,
b špth . hwt[h]	his word from his lips,
(8) *knp . nšrm . bʿl . yṯbr*	(when) Baʿl broke the vultures' wings,
(9) *bʿl . ṯbr . diy hmt* .	Baʿl broke their pinions.
tq[!]*ln* (10) *tḥt* . p*ʿnh* .	They fell at his feet.
ybqʿ . kbdthm . w [yḥd]	He cleaved their viscera and [observed]:
(11) *in . šmt . in . ʿẓm* .	there was no fat, there was no bone.
yšu . gh (12) w *yṣḥ* .	He raised his voice and cried,
knp . *nš*rm . ⟨bʿl⟩ *ybn*	"May ⟨Baʿl⟩ mend the vultures' wings,
(13) *bʿl . ybn . diy . hmt* .	may Baʿl mend their pinions!"
nšrm (14) tp*r* . w *du* .	He sewed[15] up the vultures, and they flew off.

B

b nši . ʿnh . w yp⟨h⟩n	As (he) lifted his eyes, he saw,
(15) *yḥd . hrgb . ab* . nšrm	he observed Hargab, the father of the vultures.
(16) *yšu . gh . w yṣḥ* .	He raised his voice and cried,
kn*p* . hr[g]b (17) *bʿl . yṯb*⟨r⟩ .	"May Baʿl break the wings of Hargab,
*bʿl . yṯ*br . *diy* [.] hwt	may Baʿl break his pinions!
(18) *w yql . tḥt . pʿny* .	May he fall at my feet,
i*bqʿ* . kbd[h] (19) w *aḥd* .	so I can cleave his viscera and observe!
hm . iṯ . šmt . hm . iṯ [. ʿẓm]	If there is fat, if there is [bone,]
(20) abky . w *aqbrn* .	I will weep and bury him.
ašt . b ḫr*t* (21) ilm [. arṣ .]	I will place (him) in a cavern of the [underworld] gods."
[b ph . rgm . l yṣa .]	[The utterance had barely left his mouth,]
[b šp] (22) th . hwth .	his word from his li[ps,]
kn*p* . hrg*b* . *bʿl . ṯbr*	when Baʿl broke the wings of Hargab,
(23) bʿl . ṯbr . *diy . hwt* .	Baʿl broke his pinions.
*w y*ql (24) tḥt . *pʿ*nh .	He fell at his feet.
ybqʿ . k*bdh* . w yḥd	He cleaved his viscera and observed:
(25) in . šmt . *in . ʿẓm* .	there was no fat, there was no bone.
*y*šu . gh (26) w *yṣḥ* .	He raised his voice and cried,
knp . hrgb . bʿl . ybn	"May Baʿl mend the wings of Hargab,

14. Or 'grave'; compare *ḫrt ilm arṣ* in 1.5 V 5–6; on the meaning and syntax of the phrase, see *SP* 184.

15. Baʿl is apparently the one who sews up the vultures. On the meaning and morphology of *tpr*, see *UPA* 408 n. 11.

(27) bˁl . *ybn . diy . hwt* .	may Baˁl mend his pinions!"
hrgb (28) t*pr* . w *du* .	He sewed up Hargab, and he flew off.

C

b n*ši* . *ˁnh* . (29) w *yphn* .	As (he) lifted his eyes, he saw,
yḥd . *ṣml* . *um* . *nš*rm	he observed Ṣamal,[16] the mother of the vultures.
(30) yšu . *gh* . w y*ṣḥ* .	He raised his voice and cried,
knp . *ṣml* . (31) *bˁl* . *yṯbr* .	"May Baˁl break Ṣamal's wings,
bˁl . yṯ*br* . diy (32) *hyt* .	may Baˁl break her pinions!
tql . *tḥt* . *pˁny* .	May she fall at my feet,
ibqˁ (33) kbdh . *w aḥd* .	so I can cleave her viscera and observe.
hm . *iṯ* . šmt . ⟨hm⟩ *iṯ* (34) *ˁẓm* .	If there is fat, if there is bone,
abky . *w aqbrnh* .	I will weep and bury him,
aštn (35) b *ḫrt* . *ilm* . *arṣ* .	I will place (him) in a cavern of the underworld gods."
b ph . *rgm* . *l* y[ṣ]a (36)	The utterance had barely left his mouth,
b *špth* . *hwth* .	his word from his lips,
knp . *ṣml* . bˁ[l] ⟨ṯbr⟩	when Baˁl ⟨broke⟩ Ṣamal's wings,
(37) b*ˁl* . *ṯbr* . *diy* . *hyt* .	Baˁl broke her pinions.
tql . tḥt (38) *pˁnh* .	She fell at his feet.
ybqˁ . *kbdh* . *w* y*ḥd* .	He cleaved her viscera and observed:
(39) *iṯ* . *šmt* . *iṯ* . *ˁẓm* .	there was fat, there was bone!
w yq*ḥ* . b*hm* (40) a*qht* .	He took Aqhat from her,[17]
yb⟨ky⟩[18] . *l lqẓ* .	he we⟨pt⟩(?), yes, gathered(?),[19]
ybky . w yqbr	he wept and buried.
(41) *yqbr.nn* . *b* m*dgt* . *b knrt*	He buried him in a tomb(?) in *knrt*.[20]

16. The etymology of Ṣamal's name is unclear. Greenfield ("Lexicographical Notes," 90; Aartun, "Neue Beiträge," 17) suggests a connection with Mishnaic Heb. *ṣemel* 'hard, ripe fig' and Arab. *ṣamala* 'be hard'. Her name may indicate hardness and maturity. Cooper ("Two Exegetical Notes," 23 n. 16) says it may mean 'striker' (he notes the existence of Arab. *ṣamala* 'strike someone with a stick').

17. Taking b*hm* as *b*+*h*+enclitic *-m*. It is possible that b*hm* means 'from them', referring to the fat and bone, which did not all derive from Aqhat. It may also be possible to understand b*hm aqht* as 'the remains of Aqhat' (cf. *UPA* 408 n. 12).

18. This is the reconstruction of *CAT*.

19. Compare Arab. *laqaṭa* 'gather, collect'; Heb. *lāqaṭ* 'pick, gather up' (cf. Dijkstra and de Moor, "Passages," 208). See also Segert, *Grammar*, 191a and 35; §37.1; *MLC* 573. On the syntax of affirmative *l-*, see Segert, *Grammar*, §65.24.

20. So the reading in *CAT* and rendered 'Kinneret' by Margalit (*UPA* 163) and de Moor (*ARTU* 258). Cf. H. H. P. Dressler, "The Evidence of the Ugaritic Tablet CTA 19 (*CAT* 1.19): A Reconsideration of the Kinnereth Hypothesis," *VT* 34 (1984) 216–21. His collation yielded the reading *bṯugt* . *bkn*h, which he translates 'he buried him with the howling of his lament' (the final *-h* may be a *-p*). Parker (*UNP* 74) translates the line 'Buries him in MDGT, in KNRT'. *RTU* 306 translates *ad sensum* 'he buried him in a tomb in a cemetery'. See p. 180 n. 25, below.

D

(42) *w yšu . gh . w yṣḥ .*	He raised his voice and cried,
knp . nšrm (43) *bˁl . yṯbr .*	"May Baˁl break the wings of the vultures,
bˁl . yṯbr . diy (44) *hmt .*	may Baˁl break their pinions,
hm . tˁpn . ˁl . qbr . bny	if they fly over my son's grave,
(45) *tšḫṭa.nn . b šnth .*	and disturb[21] him in his sleep."

The first three conjurations form a coherent group with a common goal. Daniʾil is looking for his son's remains. He makes the assumption that the vultures that are flying overhead, which had been present when Pughat realized that there was a drought (1.19 I 32–33), may have consumed Aqhat. He therefore calls upon Baˁl to fell them so that he can inspect them. He makes three attempts and succeeds, charmingly, the third time.

The threefold progression creates a sense of culmination similar to the way that counting off seven days of offering created a sense of culmination in Daniʾil's petition feast and the feast for the Kotharat at the beginning of the story.[22] A passage through time or through a series naturally creates an expectation of climax or resolution. The third attempt and climax in the present rite is marked by the discovery of Aqhat's remains in the third vulture, Ṣamal. The variation in wording in this case emphasizes the find. The first two cases are worded in exactly the same way, except for differences pertaining to the bird being addressed. The third case begins just like the first two, but when Aqhat's remains are found, the rhythm is disrupted. But even as it disrupts the pattern, it echoes it. The failure to find Aqhat's remains in the first two cases is described with a line containing internal parallelism that acts as a refrain:[23] *in . šmt . in . ˁẓm* 'there was no fat, there was no bone'. When the remains are found, at the point where the third case begins to diverge from the first two cases, a similarly patterned phrase occurs, but with positive terms: *iṯ . šmt . iṯ . ˁẓm* 'there was fat, there was bone!' This upsets the pattern established by the first two instances of the negative phrase and thereby draws attention to itself.

The order in which the birds are called down does not at first appear to correlate with the intensification just observed. Thinking that plurality

21. An Š-stem of *ḫṭʾ*; or with emendation, 'awake (from)' (compare Akk. *ḫâṭu* 'watch over, . . . search', CAD s.v.; Dijkstra and de Moor, "Passages," 209). Margalit (*UPA* 422–24) connects it with *tḫṭa* 'shake' in 1.169:5. On warnings against disturbing the dead, see the Phoenician texts in *KAI* 1:2, 9 A 5, 13:3–5.

22. Cf. *UPA* 406. He notes patterns of threes in 1.4 III 17–18; Gen 22:4; 31:22; Exod 19:11, 16.

23. Cf. W. G. E. Watson, "Internal Parallelism in Ugaritic Verse," *SEL* 1 (1984) 56–57, 59.

marks climax and knowing that earlier in the story females are subordinated to males, one might instead expect this order: Ṣamal, Hargab, and then the group of vultures. Or perhaps, thinking that the vultures in the group are considered children of the other two, one might expect to find the group, then Ṣamal the mother, and then Hargab the father. But no, the final examination is of the single female. Even though her third-place appearance does not immediately effect intensification, there is logic in her appearance at this point. She correlates in gender with Anat. These two females are responsible for the death and disappearance of Aqhat.[24] They are the ones who subvert the male-oriented pattern and promise. Thus, it is entirely reasonable for Ṣamal to appear in third position. Her appearance may after all contribute to the sense of culmination in the third conjuration.

The conjurations are rites of crisis, as were the agricultural rites that Daniʾil performed prior to learning about Aqhat's death. In comparing rites of crisis to *rites de passage* above, we noted that, instead of advancing a person's or the environment's status or quality, rites of crisis seek simply to restore the previous existing order. The vulture rites have a different goal. Since they cannot hope to return to the preexisting order of things, they can only partially effect restoration by helping Daniʾil find Aqhat's body.

Once Aqhat's remains are found, the intent of the rites changes. In the first two conjurations, Daniʾil brings down various birds, but they appear only to be anesthetized. He asks Baʿl to mend them; the god does so, and the birds fly off, apparently not much worse for the experience. Ṣamal, in contrast, is never repaired. She is left dead, a disemboweled carcass. The performance therefore goes beyond recovery and restoration and turns punitive. This same goal is also found in the capping curse: Baʿl is to break the wing of any vulture that disturbs Aqhat's interred remains.

Contacts with Earlier Parts of the Story

The rites here recall and form contrasts to earlier parts of the narrative. For example, the deities Baʿl and Anat are both associated with the vultures–Baʿl in the present passage and Anat in the scene where Aqhat is killed. Their relation to the birds is not the same. Here Baʿl has power over the birds. In the killing of Aqhat, Anat and Yaṭupan only fly among the vultures, using them for cover, but they do not appear to control

24. Margalit (*UPA* 406–7) notes that the absence of explanation for Ṣamal's ending up with Aqhat's remains inside her, after murder instigated by Anat, leads to (symbolic?) identification of the two females.

them. It may be that this is indicative of the tensions between the male-oriented structure of the natural and social worlds, which Anat is subverting. Though the birds are in Baˁl's control, Anat uses them to her advantage to carry out a plan that cancels the promises and blessing made by the high gods. Perhaps Ṣamal's ingestion of Aqhat is a sign of Anat's ability to obtain or assert power within the male-structured world. If so, Daniˀil's killing of Ṣamal, carried out with the help of Baˁl, is a symbolic attempt to reestablish traditional structure.

Ironic contrasts are found in Daniˀil's burial of Aqhat. First it should be noted that Daniˀil puts the remains in a tomb, perhaps in the Kinneret area, where the story may have taken place.[25] Margalit argues that this interment was in Lake Kinneret itself.[26] This is doubtful, because Daniˀil earlier says that he wanted to put his son's remains *b ḫrt ilm arṣ* 'in a cavern of the underworld gods' (lines 6, 20–21, 35).[27] This implies an earthly, not watery, burial. The term m*dgt* in line 41 probably does not mean 'fishpond', a supposed reference to the lake. It is better explained as a term for 'grave' or 'tomb', which would be consistent with placement in a *ḫrt* 'cavern, cavity'. Its cognate root may be Arabic *djj* or *djw*, having to do with darkness.[28]

Daniˀil's activities are reminiscent in a general way of the burial customs that Aqhat mentions in his rejection of Anat's offer of eternal life. There the son says that a *spsg* and a *ḥrṣ* will cover or be placed in proximity to the head of the dead (1.17 VI 36–37). Daniˀil's actions, even though they do not include these particular activities, reflect a similar care for the dead. They bring to completion Aqhat's "prophecy" of his death where he, in connection with his refusal of Anat's bid for the bow, says, "[Yes,]

25. On the Kinneret hypothesis for the story, see *UPA* 296, 327–28, 329–30, 333, 337–40, 345–49, 405, 408–22 (also Margalit's discussion of *spsg*; see above; cf. Margalit, "The Geographical Setting of the *AQHT* Story and Its Ramifications," in *Ugarit in Retrospect* [ed. G. D. Young; Winona Lake, Ind.: Eisenbrauns, 1981] 131–58; idem, "Observations on the Jael-Sisera Story (Judges 4–5)," in *Pomegranates and Golden Bells: Studies in Biblical, Jewish, and Near Eastern Ritual, Law, and Literature in Honor of Jacob Milgrom* [ed. D. P. Wright, D. N. Freedman and A. Hurvitz; Winona Lake, Ind.: Eisenbrauns, 1995] 629–41). The geographical and archaeological specificity that Margalit proposes in many cases is speculative. See also p. 177 n. 20 above.

26. *UPA* 404. Margalit says that this may be an act of expiation to counteract the drought (p. 408).

27. Even Margalit (*UPA* 162) construes this as '(earth)-cavities of the chthonic gods'. This is where Anat places Baˁl: *tštnn . b ḫrt ilm . arṣ* (1.6 I 17–18). This is at the heights of Ṣapan.

28. Arab *dujjat* 'intense darkness' (*DMWA* 271); *dajā* 'be dark, gloomy' (*DMWA* 272); accordingly, it is rendered 'dark chamber/place' (*CML* 150); 'mausoleum' (*CARTU* 149). Margalit (*UPA* 163) renders 'fishpond' (see the objection to this in *ARTU* 258 n. 220).

the death of all I will die; I will surely die" (1.17 VI 38) and where he refers burial practices *to himself*, saying that "(a) *ḥrṣ* (will cover) the top of my pate" (line 37).

Daniʾil's care for his dead son also contrasts with the filial duties (1.17 I 26–33). There the son is to care for the father. An implication in the list is that the son will continue to serve the father into his declining years and outlive the father. Now the father is performing duties for the son. The ideal and the blessing have been completely defeated.

Chapter 15
The Curse on the Locales

The threefold conjuration of the vultures with its capping curse is followed by curses on three locales, perhaps all towns. This series structurally echoes the vulture rites. But it is wholly devoted to cursing, is tactically offensive in character, and involves traveling to the different sites. The series thus intensifies further the force of Daniʾil's reaction and constitutes the apex of his reaction.

The Text and Textual Problems

This series directly follows the conjuration of the vultures (1.19 III–IV):

A

qr . my[m] (46) *mlk* . *yṣm* .	The king(?) (then) damned Qor-Mayi[m]:
y lkm . *qr* . *mym* .	"Woe to you,[1] Qor-Mayim,
d ʿ[lk] (47) *mḫṣ* . *aqht* . *ǵzr* .	for [you are responsible for][2] the murder of Aqhat, the hero!
amd . *gr bt il*	(You shall) always (be) an alien[3] in Il's house![4]

1. The context demands a meaning like 'woe to you', though it is unclear if the interjectory particle consists of *y-* or *yl* (for the latter, compare Arab. *wayl* 'distress, woe'). Cf. *UPA* 427.

2. So Dijkstra and de Moor, "Passages," 209. Alternately: 'For close to you was Aqhat murdered' (so *UPA* 163; Pardee, "Preposition in Ugaritic [I]," 356).

3. Margalit (*UPA* 163) takes this phrase as an imperative directed to Aqhat: 'Dwell (Aqhat) forever in the House of El'. Parker (*UNP* 74) takes *grbt* as a single word and translates 'May El clothe you in leprosy(?)'.

4. This may be a cultic curse, similar to Deut 23:2–9, which does not allow persons with certain defects and certain foreigners in the congregation (*qāhāl*). On this as the temple of Il, see Niehr, "El-Tempel." Gibson (*CML* 119) takes this line as a reference to refuge: "be continually a seeker of sanctuary." Others take it as a mythological notion. Margalit (*UPA* 412, 428–31) suggest that this shows where Il's abode (*bt*) is, or at least the way of access to it, in the Kinneret Sea (for different assessments of Il's abode, see Cross, *Canaanite Myth*, 36–39; Smith, *Baal Cycle*, 186–89; M. Pope, *El in the Ugaritic Texts* [VTSup 2; Leiden: Brill, 1955] 72–81).

(48) *ʿnt . brḥ . p ʿlm.h .*	Now a fugitive[5] and forever,
ʿnt . p dr . dr	now and for all time!"

B

(49) *ʿ*db *. uḫry mṭ . ydh*	He put down the end of his staff,[6]
(50) *ymǵ . l mrrt . tǵll . bnr*	he arrived at Mrrt-Tǵll-Bnr.
(51) *yšu . gh . w yṣḥ .*	He raised his voice and cried:
y lk . m*rrt* (52) *tǵll . bnr .*	"Woe to you, Mrrt-Tǵll-Bnr,
d *ʿlk . mḫṣ . aqht* (53) *ǵzr .*	for you are responsible for the murder of Aqhat, the hero!
*šrš*k *. b arṣ . al* (54) *ypʿ .*	May your root not sprout from the ground,
riš . ǵly . bd . nsʿk	(your) head droop[7] in the hand of the one that uproots you!
(55) *ʿnt . brḥ . p ʿlmh .*	Now a fugitive, and forever,
(56) *ʿnt . p dr . dr .*	now and for all time!"

C

ʿdb . uḫry . mṭ ydh	He put down the end of his staff,
(1) *ymǵ . l qrt . ablm .*	he arrived at Abilum city,[8]
*ab*lm (2) *qrt . zbl . yrḫ .*	Abilum, the city of exalted Yariḫ.
yšu . gh (3) *w yṣḥ .*	He raised his voice and cried:
y lk . qrt . ablm	"Woe to you, Abilum city,
(4) *d ʿlk . mḫṣ . aqht . ǵzr*	for you are responsible for the murder of Aqhat, the hero!
(5) *ʿwrt . yštk . bʿl .*	May Baʿl make you blind,[9]
l ht (6) *w ʿlmh .*	from now and forever,
l ʿnt *. p dr . dr*	from now and for all time!"
(7) *ʿdb . uḫry . mṭ . ydh*	He put down the end of his staff,
(8) *dnil . bth . ym . ǵyn .*	Daniʾil arrived at his house,
yšt (9) *ql . dnil . l hklh .*	Daniʾil entered his palace.

The meaning and stichometry of line 45b–46a have been disputed. Many have taken the line as I have construed it.[10] Margalit has made a strong

5. Margalit (*UPA* 163) translates this line 'through time and eternity'.

6. Margalit (*UPA* 163): 'Stooping, he picked up his walking-stick'. Cf. Dijkstra and de Moor, "Passages," 209: 'He put down the tip of his walking stick'. Dietrich and Loretz, "*ʿdb* und *ḏb*," 108: 'Er machte gleich danach seinen Wanderstab bereit'.

7. Taking *ǵly* as an infinitive absolute with a jussive sense.

8. Margalit (*UPA* 163) takes *qrt* as 'fort'.

9. Margalit (*UPA* 164, 416), 'May Baal stop-up thy well-spring(s)'. His rendering is partly determined by the assumption that the curse of Qor Mayim has to do with damming the outlet of the Sea of Galilee.

10. *CML* 119, 'The king cursed Qor-[mayim]'; *ARTU* 259, 'The king struck Qor-Mayima'; *MLC* 396, 'A Qiru-Mayima el Rey maldijo'.

argument that *mlk* should not be understood as 'king'.[11] There is no other indisputable evidence that Daniʾil is a king. He is never called a king elsewhere. He is in fact more like a biblical patriarch or elder than a king. The filial duties contain activities that seem out of place for a king's son (taking care of his father's house and cleaning the father's clothes). As for the term *mlk* in line 46 of the curse on the locales, its meaning as 'king' is suspicious, because proper names always accompany epithets; epithets referring to individuals do not occur alone. Moreover, lines 45b–46b may not be an introduction to the curses that follow. These lines may be governed by the introduction that precedes the final vulture curse in line 42. The term *yṣm* is not found to introduce the second and third curses, and therefore a meaning 'curse' or the like is suspicious; it may not refer to speaking at all.

On the basis of prosodic analysis, Margalit divides lines 45–46 differently: *tšḫṭann . b šnth qr . my*[m] / *mlk . yṣm . ylkm . qr . mym*. He takes the *mlk yṣm* phrase as part of the curse spoken about Qor-Mayim. *Mlk* for him is a noun *ml* with the pronominal suffix *-k*. *Ml* is explained by the Arabic root *m(y)l* 'bend down, slope'. He takes *yṣm* from the root *ṣmm* 'to stop, plug'. This yields the translation: 'If they disturb him from his sleep (in) the lake. / May your down-course be blocked, cursed lake . . .'.[12]

His arguments, especially about not taking *mlk* as 'king', are nearly persuasive. However, the customary understanding seems to be required by the structure of the passage. The second and third curses begin with the term *ylk* (= *ylkm*; lines 51b, 3b) 'Woe to you!' This makes it reasonable to assume that the first curse also begins with this term. This too shows that Margalit's line division is doubtful, since *ylkm* in the first curse comes in the middle of a poetic line. The second and third curses, furthermore, have introductions that mention the name of the locale that Daniʾil is about to defame (49–51a, 56b–2a). These are not part of direct speech but part of narrative description. We would expect a similar introduction to the first curse. Line 45b–46a, as I and most scholars divide it, provides this introduction.

11. See Margalit, *UPA* 424–27; also 253, 274, 278, 279, 292, 361. For him, Daniʾil is a "well-to-do landowner belonging to the patrician class known as *adrm* charged with the public administration" (p. 251). For others not viewing him as a king, see Gibson, "Myth, Legend, and Folklore," 66–67. For Daniʾil as king, see de Moor, "Seasonal Pattern in the Legend of Aqhatu," 61, 75 n. 7 (partly based on 1.20 and 1.22, but in 1.17 I 25 Daniʾil appears to own a palace and in 1.17 V 4–8 [and parallel] Daniʾil judges). See also Dressler, "Identification," 153; J. F. Healey, "The Immortality of the King: Ugarit and the Psalms," *Or* 53 (1984) 249.

12. *UPA* 138, 163 (and discussion).

The reason that the terminology is different from the terminology in the introductions to the second and third curses is in part due to a feature of the text recognized by Margalit. The phrase *w yšu . gh . w yṣḥ .* 'He raised his voice and cried' in line 42 (see the text in chapter 14) is the main introduction to this curse. Daniʾil is apparently near or at Qor-Mayim for the burial of his son. He does not move about here, as in the case of the second and third curses. Thus, an introduction with a different formulation is necessary, one that does not mention travel and that does not repeat *w yšu gh w yṣḥ*, but one that nevertheless introduces the place that will be cursed and the fact that Daniʾil is making an utterance. Consequently *yṣm* 'he cursed' is used, related to Arabic *waṣama* 'disgrace, tarnish, blemish' (in other words, 'damn' instead of 'dam').[13] This particular verb provides color, not only for the first curse, but for the second and third.[14]

If these structural considerations have force, then one is compelled to take *mlk* as 'king', if for no other reason than lack of a better alternative. It may be here that we have an exception (barring scribal error as a solution) to the considerations about the appearance of an epithet listed by Margalit. The epithet *mlk*, to judge from the Kirta story, need not be placed immediately next to the individual's name. The term can appear in the a- or b-line of a strophe, paralleled by the name Kirta in the other line (1.14 III 26–28; VI 14–15; 1.16 I 39–40, 56–57). The poetic distancing of *mlk* and an explicit referent in the Kirta text, as well as the observation above that line 45b–46a in Aqhat briefly resumes the fuller introduction of line 42 may explain the lack of a proper noun with *mlk* in line 46. Line 42 introduces Daniʾil as the speaker (even though his name is not mentioned, it is clear from the context). Line 45b–46a carries on this introduction and perhaps picks up on one of his epithets instead of using his name.

Support for taking *mlk* as 'king' is found in the blessing of Aqhat (see p. 94). There Danʾil is said to have a *hkl* 'palace'. His palace is also mentioned in the description of the *dbḥ* ceremony (see p. 201).

The line *ʿdb . uḫry . mṭ . ydh*, which appears after the three curses, is also difficult (lines 49, 56b, 7). It has been taken as the last phrase spoken in the curses.[15] It seems better taken as part of Daniʾil's actions described in the narrative, being paralleled by the following lines describing his arrival at a certain place. In this case *uḫry* means the 'end' of the walking stick (*mṭ ydh*), and the verb *ʿdb*, which means 'prepare' but also 'place,

13. *DMWA* 1074. De Moor (*ARTU* 259 n. 222) says that the Arabic means 'to strike'.

14. Watson ("Preludes to Speech," 361) places *qr* . my[m] *mlk* . yṣm in his catalogue of preambles introducing speech.

15. *CML* 120: 'let every last one make ready a staff for his hand'; *MLC* 396: 'cuyo báculo sea colocado el último'.

put',[16] refers to what Daniʾil does to the stick. It is not clear if this is simply a way of indicating that he set out on his way, if setting down the stick is a ritual action, or if it indicates that he did something with the rod, perhaps raising it while uttering each curse, after which he lowered it.[17]

A larger question concerns exactly what is cursed. The last of the three objects cursed is the town Abilum, which we know as the place to which Aqhat was invited by Anat and where he was killed. It is not immediately clear if the first two are towns or other geographical or natural entities or phenomena. Qor-Mayim means literally 'Well/Source of Water'. Margalit has taken this to refer to the Sea of Galilee where, in his view, Aqhat was interred. For him, the last line of the summary and prospective vulture curse include *tšḫṭa.nn . b šnth . qr* . my[m], which he translates 'if they disturb him from his sleep (in) the lake'.[18] The curse of Qor Mayim is thus simply a curse of the lake. As noted above, he takes *mlk* as 'your downcourse', referring to the lake's outlet. The curse refers to "estuarial blockage."[19] The last part of this "curse" (*amd . . . dr . dr*, lines 47b–48), in his view, is addressed to Aqhat in the lake: 'Dwell (Aqht) forever in the House of El, / Through time and eternity, / Now and for (all) generations'.[20]

One difficulty with this interpretation is having lines 47b–48 addressed to Aqhat. If it is a curse spoken against the son, then it goes against the whole tenor of the story and Daniʾil's reaction up to this point.[21] If it is not a curse, but a statement of blessing or even a neutral statement, then it is out of line with the curses that appear in the same position in the words against Mrrt-tǵll-bnr and Abilum.[22] By the logic of the context, the words have to be directed against Qor-Mayim and, because of the nature of the curse involving *gr* 'dwelling' or being in the status of a *gr* 'alien', Qor-Mayim must be animate. This is true all the more so if *brḥ* in line 48a (see also 55) means 'flee' or 'a fugitive'. Consequently, Qor-Mayim either must be the lake addressed as a mythological being, or it must be a town that is attacked. The latter is contextually justified because of the parallel with the town Abilum.

16. On the verb, see Dietrich and Loretz, "Debatte über die Lautentwicklung," 123–32; Dietrich, Loretz, and Sanmartín, "Lexikographie (VII)," 94–95; *UPA* 431–32.

17. Compare the use of rods in ritual actions in the Bible (Exod 4:2–4, 17, 20; 7:8–12, 15–22; 8:1–3, 12–14; 9:23; 17:5–6, 8–13; Num 20:8–9).

18. *UPA* 138, 163.

19. *UPA* 410.

20. *UPA* 163.

21. Margalit (*UPA* 409) refers to the passage as a curse.

22. Margalit (*UPA* 412) says that Daniʾil's putting Aqhat in the lake is "demonstrative if not defiant." By it, "Danʾel seems to be saying: 'Let El who gave Aqht to me now take and keep him.'" Later on (428) he says that in the line *amd . gr. bt . il*, "one hears here the faintest echo of a protest."

Concerning Mrrt-tǵll-bnr in the second curse, it is true that the accompanying denunciation dealing with roots and head (of a plant) befit a tree.[23] But tree imagery is often used of people.[24] The context with the city Abilum allows the supposition that this is a town as well.[25]

Purpose and Structure

The basic outline of the series of curses is clear: Daniʾil moves about uttering them against three different locales. This has been compared to other Near Eastern ritual or legal texts that describe the ascertaining of administrative responsibility for homicide when the identity of the murderer is not known. The *ʿeglâ ʿarûpâ* rite in Deut 21:1–9 designates the city nearest the victim's body as responsible. The elders of this city are to perform a rite that reenacts the murder and thus transfers the blood guilt to an uninhabited area. In this way, the debilitating effects of blood guilt on agricultural concerns is avoided.[26] In Hammurabi's Laws (§§23–24), a city and its governor (*rabiānum*) in whose district a robbery or loss of life occur are to make recompense. Under Hittite law (§IV), when a person is found dead in land that does not belong to anyone, any town found within a three-"mile" (DANNA) radius makes compensation to the victim's heir.

Michael Heltzer has noted the phenomenon of collective responsibility at or around Ugarit.[27] In PRU 4 17.299, which is poorly preserved, it appears that an individual brought a claim against the citizens of *Ḫalbi rapši* because his brother died there. In RS 20.239 (Ug. 5, 52), a man named Madaʾe complains to the *sākinu* (vizier) of Ugarit that the people of the town Rakba had stolen his oxen. These people either need to pay or take an oath in a sanctuary to free themselves from obligation. It appears that the plaintiff is holding Rakba responsible for the oxen that disappeared in its jurisdiction. Heltzer concludes that

> the data available from the various texts shows us that every theft, murder, or other crime committed by people of a certain village, or inside the

23. So *UPA* 405.

24. For example, Ezek 17:5–10, Ps 1:3, Daniel 4.

25. Margalit (*UPA* 418) attempts to connect *mrrt* with *ʾilān* 'be strong'. This is doubtful in view of Pardee, "Semitic Root *mrr*." Dijkstra and de Moor ("Passages," 209–10) offer meanings for the words that lead to construing the name as 'The bitter/mourning one, who brings under the yoke'.

26. For an argument for this meaning of the rite and for the effects of blood guilt on agricultural concerns, see my "Deuteronomy 21:1–9 as a Rite of Elimination," *CBQ* 49 (1987) 387–403.

27. M. Heltzer, *The Rural Community in Ancient Ugarit* (Wiesbaden: Reichert, 1976) 63–65.

territory of a village, was the collective responsibility of the citizens of that village. Perhaps this occurred only in cases where no criminal was named or apprehended by the authorities.[28]

Daniʾil moves from place to place attributing liability for Aqhat's death by means of his curses, in a spirit similar to these texts. But the endeavor is not legal in nature. Daniʾil is not seeking compensation. He is not approaching town or district leaders for aid and adjudication. Nor is his performance a means of relocating blood guilt, as in Deuteronomy 21, even though there is a concern about agricultural failure running throughout this part of the Aqhat story.[29] Daniʾil's ritual performance has a different purpose: it is retaliatory and punitive. As such, it can condemn a number of supposed culprits, in contrast with a legal process, in which one town would be responsible.

Daniʾil caps his series of curses with the censure of Abilum. It is doubtful that Daniʾil knows exactly where Aqhat was killed. When the messengers come in 1.19 II to tell him that his son is dead and that Anat is responsible, they do not say where Aqhat died. And, though the text describing the messengers announcement is somewhat broken, there is no room for restoring this as part of their message. The story probably presupposes that Daniʾil knew that Aqhat was staying in Abilum. Anat had invited him there, and his father would logically have known this. Consequently, he curses the various towns in the area of Abilum. But if Daniʾil is searching with a blindfold, he is finally able to pin the donkey's tale on the closest city. Readers and hearers recognize his success because they are familiar with the narrative's geography. This success creates a climax, parallel to the threefold curse of the vultures. Daniʾil called down the birds until he found, the third time, the one with Aqhat's remains. He curses the cities until the third time, when he comes to the one at which Aqhat was killed.

It should be noted, of course, that from Daniʾil's point of view the second series operates differently from the first. In the second, he is not cursing various locales with the hope of finding the one that is guilty for Aqhat's death. All of the towns are in the same general area: Daniʾil does not seem to go far from where Ṣamal was felled to bury Aqhat near Qor-Mayim, and Ṣamal seems not to have been far from Abilum where Aqhat is killed. What Daniʾil is doing, from his perspective, is cursing all of the towns or areas in the proximity of Aqhat's death.

28. Ibid., 65.

29. The curse on Mrrt-ǵll-bnr involves motifs of agricultural blight (53b–54), but it is metaphorical, referring to the inhabitants, not their land, just as all of the curses are directed against the people.

This contextual climax that readers and hearers perceive is paralleled by a rough increase in structural complexity. The basic outline of the rites and words are similar to one another. This is summarized in the table below. Each curse begins with an introduction naming the locale and noting that Daniʾil is speaking (register I), which is followed by a statement of woe and an accusation that the locale is responsible for Aqhat's death (register II), after which comes a curse specific to the area (register III), followed finally by adverbial clauses indicating that the curse will endure (register IV).

A	*B*	*C*
	Register I	
qr . my[m] (46) *mlk* . *yṣm* .	(49) *ʿdb . uḫry mṭ . ydh* (50) *ymǵ . l mrrt . tǵll . bnr*	*ʿdb . uḫry . mṭ ydh* (1) *ymǵ . l qrt . ablm .* *a*blm (2) *qrt . ẓbl . yrḫ .*
The king(?) damned Qor-Mayim:	He put down the end of his staff,	He put down the end of his staff,
	he arrived at M.-T.-B.	he arrived at Abilum city, Abilum the city of exalted Yariḫ.
	(51) *yšu . gh . w* y*ṣḥ* .	*yšu* . gh (3) *w yṣḥ* .
	He raised his voice and cried:	He raised his voiced and cried:
	Register II	
y lkm . qr . mym .	*y lk* . *mrrt* (52) *tǵll . bnr .*	y lk . qrt . ablm
"Woe to you, Qor-Mayim,	"Woe to you, M.-T.-B.,	"Woe to you, Abilum city,
d ʿ[lk] (47) *mḫṣ . aqht . ǵzr .*	d *ʿlk . mḫṣ . aqht* (53) *ǵzr .*	(4) *d ʿlk . mḫṣ . aqht . ǵzr*
for [you are responsible for] the murder of Aqhat, the hero!	for you are responsible for the murder of Aqhat, the hero!	for you are responsible for the murder of Aqhat, the hero!
	Register III	
amd . gr bt il	*šr*šk *.b arṣ . al* (54) *ypʿ . riš .* *ǵly . bd . nsʿk*	(5) *ʿwrt . yštk . bʿl .*
You shall always (be) an alien in Il's house!	May your root not sprout from the ground, (your) head droop in the hand of the one that uproots you!	May Baʿl make you blind,
	Register IV	
(48) *ʿnt . brḥ . p ʿlm.h . ʿnt . p dr . dr*	(55) *ʿnt . brḥ . p ʿlmh .* (56) *ʿnt . p dr . dr .*	*l ht* (6) *w ʿlmh .* *l ʿnt . p dr . dr*
Now a fugitive, and forever, now and for all time!"	Now a fugitive, and forever, now and for all time!"	from now and forever, from now and for all time!"

Despite the similarity in the three passages, there is variation, indicative of the heightening of intensity over the course of the series. The first curse consists of six lines, and the second and third have nine lines each. Compared to A, passage B is more complex in having a three-line introduction (register I) and a four-line curse (register III). Passage C is the same overall length as B, but it has a longer introduction and a shorter curse. The longer introduction correlates with focus on the city Abilum as the specific locale where Aqhat was killed. The shorter curse in C may create the impression that there is a decrease in intensity. This, however, is partially offset by the variants in the adverbs (register IV). The words of register IV are exactly the same in A and B but have a variant formulation in C, with *l-* prepositions and *ht* instead of *ʿnt*. Even though *brḥ* is missing in the third case, the variety of the third case vis-à-vis the first two may convey a sense of heightened expression.

At the same time that the curses internally display an evolution in force, they as a group heighten the sense of intensity vis-à-vis the conjurations of the vultures. The conjurations are performed in situ. We do not know where Daniʾil was, but he did not move about; the vultures were over him in one place. The curses, however, are pronounced over various locales, and Daniʾil needs to move about to do this. This movement adds fervor to the malediction. He is out searching for responsible parties.

Intensification in the rites appearing after the announcement of Aqhat's death is found also in the purposes of the rite. As retaliatory rites, the last series extends the force of the preceding vulture conjurations. Those rites begin with the goal of discovering Aqhat's remains: they are rites of restoration. But the conjuration of Ṣamal and then the following curse on birds who might disturb Aqhat's remains are punitive. The curses against the towns, which it should be remembered follow in the same breath as the final vulture curse, pick up on this change in orientation and fully embrace it.

Chapter 16
Conclusion to Part 3

The foregoing analysis has revealed features of intensification on the micro and macro levels, as it were, throughout the middle part of the Aqhat text. Each subsection–Anat's mourning, Pughat's and Daniʾil's responses to agricultural failure before finding out about the death of Aqhat, Daniʾil's conjuration of the vultures, and then his curse of the three towns–exhibits a contextual or structural evolution in complexity. These individual developments join together, along with a larger overarching development in the complexity of form and content, to reach a consummation in the responses to Aqhat's death.

Anat's mourning begins immediately after she kills Aqhat. How this passage is to be understood is not certain. But it seems that her reaction sets the pattern for what is to come. She begins with a short lament and then, after the bow she desired is broken, she enters into a longer dirge with two parts. This dirge mourns the potential heroic stature of Aqhat, her loss of the bow, and the drought that has begun.

After the text's notice of Pughat's internal mourning, Daniʾil begins his various performances. Before he finds out about Aqhat's death, he performs two rites. The first rite is a single prayer, for moisture. It has minimal ritual action: the rending of the cloak, which the text describes indirectly with a passive verb. The narrative does not portray Daniʾil as actually performing this action. Next, Daniʾil performs his complex rite. For this, Daniʾil is on the move, not at home. He also performs the gesture of cradling and kissing plants. In his prayers he brings Aqhat into the picture, hoping that the son will be able to harvest the crops.

Messengers then come with news about the death of Aqhat. They are mourning as they approach. When Daniʾil hears the news, he amplifies his response by having Baʿl bring down the vultures for inspection. Daniʾil does this three times while in one place. To be sure, the number of these rites seems to be a matter of chance; that is, if he had spied Ṣamal first and brought her down, there would have been only one conjuration. But we are dealing with narrative structure and effect here, not simply with what might happen in real life. The story narrates three occurrences, and these poetically heighten the degree of ritual activity. Daniʾil follows the conjuration by cursing the vultures as a group and prospectively: they are not to upset the remains of his son whom he has just buried. This provides a transition to the curses of the three locales that immediately follow. The description in these curses shows a structural compounding to some degree. Contextually, the curses culminate in an attack on the city Abilum, the specific place where Aqhat died. Compared to the vulture conjuration, these curses portray intensification, in that the scenes involving them are ambulatory not stationary.

Schematically, the developmental structure of all of these performances can be portrayed in this way:

$$1 \rightarrow 1(2) \mid\mid (m) \rightarrow 1rs \rightarrow 2i \mid\mid m \rightarrow 3s + 1s \rightarrow 3i$$

Here the first || separates Anat's responses from Pughat's and Daniʾil's, and the second || marks Daniʾil's finding out that Aqhat is dead. The numbers refer to the number of parts in the rites; for example, the 1(2) for Anat's prayer indicates a single prayer with two parts and the 3s + 1s refers to the threefold conjuration of the vultures with its capping curse. The letter *m* with parentheses refers to Pughat's inward mourning, and without parentheses to the mourning of the messengers; *r* to Daniʾil's wearing rent clothing; and *s* to a stationary rite as opposed to *i*, which designates an itinerant rite.

This figure allows the development to be comprehended in a glance. One of the features to note is that the second and third segments both reflect elements of the segment that precedes. Daniʾil's agricultural rites (in the middle segment) include two rites, the first with one prayer and the second with two prayers. This parallels Anat's response, which contains a simple, one-part lament, followed by a longer lament with two parts. The final segment parallels the middle segment in two ways. Daniʾil's responses are prefaced by the mourning of others: the middle segment begins with Pughat's internal mourning, and the last begins with the messengers' mourning. The second parallel is the locus of Daniʾil's performance of his rites. Daniʾil's first rites (or ritual complexes) in each segment are performed while he is stationary (the first prayer for rain and the conjuration of the vultures), and the second rites (or complexes), while he is moving about (the prayer for the plants in the field and the curses of the towns).

A larger correlation between the various segments is visible. Anat's first and second laments are separated by an event that gives rise to the second, more complex lament: the breaking of the bow. Daniʾil's responses in the second and third segments are separated by an event that gives rise to Daniʾil's more intense response in the third segment: the revelation of Aqhat's death. Thus, Anat's mourning not only anticipates the form of Daniʾil's agricultural rites, it also anticipates the whole of Daniʾil's ritual responses.[1]

Development of the rituals also underscores the development of the structure. First, we should recall that all of these performances are rites of crisis comparable to transition rites, which are characterized by separation, liminality, and aggregation stages. The rites of crisis in Aqhat differ in that the liminality stage is caused, not by ritual plan, but by unexpected violence and—a fact that cannot be unimportant—by a liminal deity, Anat. Liminality is evident in the natural, psychological, social, and theological spheres. Crops are failing because of a drought. Pughat, Daniʾil, the messengers bearing bad tidings, and even Anat are distressed and grieving. Daniʾil's curses on the various locales indicate a breakdown in human relationships to some extent. The gods' promise to Daniʾil has been annulled. Except for Daniʾil's call for Baʿl to help in felling the vultures, a scene in which Baʿl is notably silent,[2] gods and humans do not interact with one another. And, quite remarkably, there are no feasts to sustain and re-create beneficial relationships with the gods. The structure-creating activities of the first part of the story have ceased. Daniʾil and his associates are now in a situation that is, if not an instance of Turnerian antistructure, at least a situation evidencing unstructure or destructure.

Daniʾil's rites attempt to recover structure to some degree. They evolve in their purpose as he advances through the situation of liminality. When he is ignorant of Aqhat's death, he performs rites of restoration, whose goal is the cure of nature. This impresses the reader/hearer as misguided and pitiable because Daniʾil is addressing the symptom, not the cause. As various ritual texts from the ancient Near East show, the cause must be treated in order for a solution to be achieved.[3] As Daniʾil finds out the true reason for the drought, his ritual goals change. He addresses the cause more directly—the death of his son. He seeks partial restoration through the discovery of Aqhat's remains. Then he turns to retaliation in the curses on the vultures and the towns. Admittedly, he has stopped short of going after the true cause, Anat. He appears not to want to curse the goddess, which might result in his own death. He can only address

1. A relatively minor parallel between two of the rites, if it is in fact a parallel, is Daniʾil's rending of his clothes in the middle segment and the rending of the vultures in the final segment.

2. So noted by *UPA* 405.

3. See Shurpu, tablet II (and dingir.šà.dib.ba incantations: W. G. Lambert, "DINGIR.ŠÀ.DIB.BA Incantations," *JNES* 33 [1974] 267–322; and the *lipšur*-litanies: E. Reiner, "*Lipšur* Litanies," *JNES* 15 [1956] 129–49). See K. van der Toorn, *Sin and Sanction in Israel and Mesopotamia* (SSN 22; Assen/Maastricht: Van Gorcum, 1985) 94–97.

the cause metonymically, attacking the agencies indirectly associated with Aqhat's death. In any case, the movement from ignorance, distress, and an attempt at restoration to knowledge, anger, and retaliation correlates with and buttresses the literary-structural development.

The intensifying concatenation of ritual activity is what gives this section of the narrative much of its power. As Daniʾil becomes aware of his personal tragedy, his ritual responses multiply. This fact, in addition to what is explicitly said about his emotional state, allows the reader/hearer to sense the depth of his grief. The closest the tale comes in this section to describing his emotional state directly is in presenting his reaction to the announcement of Aqhat's death (1.19 II):

(44) [bh . pʿnm] (45) *tṭṭ* .	[(His) feet] jerked,[4]
ʿl[n . pnh . tdʿ .]	ab[ove (his) face sweated],
[bʿdn] (46) *ksl* . yṯ[br .]	[behind] (his) loins we[re broken],
[yǵṣ . pnt . kslh]	[the vertebrae of his back trembled],
(47) *anš* . d[t . ẓrh]	the nerves o[f his back].[5]

This formulaic description (restorable from 1.3 III 32–35; 1.4 II 16–20)[6] is brief and occurs only at one point, a very crucial point, in the whole scene: when the messengers announce the death of Aqhat. It is significant in the course of the story because it forms a perfect contrast to Daniʾil's reaction of joy upon hearing Il's blessing (1.17 II):[7]

(8) *b d*ʾ*n*i*l* (9) *pnm . tšmḫ* .	On Daniʾil his face brightened,
*w ʿl . yṣhl pi*t	above, his brow glowed.[8]
(10) *yprq . lṣb . w yṣḥq*	He smiled and laughed,
pʿn . l hdm . yṯpd .	he set (his) feet on the footstool.

4. Arab. *naṭṭa* 'spring, jump, leap' (*DMWA* 973).

5. Margalit's interpretation of the last two lines as 'The corners of his vestment fluttered, in unison with tho[se of his back]' is problematic (*UPA* 399–400). Since the text is concerned with body parts (*pʿnm, pnh, ksl* [in the third line], and *ẓr*), one expects the second *ksl* also to refer to a body part. It is not exactly the same body part as in the third line, which has only *ksl*. *Pnt ksl* refers to a related but apparently distinguishable body part (*SP* 137 suggests 'vertebrae, joints'). The interpretation of *anš* as a preposition, 'in unison with', from the root *anš* 'be friendly' (compare Arab. *ʾanisa*) also seems stretched. Again a body part of some sort is possible, and Heb. *nāšeh* 'sciatic nerve' provides a suitable cognate (cf. *SP* 132).

6. Cf. D. Hillers, "A Convention in Hebrew Literature: The Reaction to Bad News," *ZAW* 77 (1965) 86–90.

7. Noted by *UPA* 385.

8. Margalit (*UPA* 174) notes the problem of disagreement between the nouns and their verbs in lines 8–9. He proposes to switch their position.

But the ritual procedures that precede and follow Daniʾil's reaction have the definite purpose of displaying the evolving dimensions and nuances of his grief and anger.

A description of the general mourning that took place for seven years follows Daniʾil's flurry of ritual activity (1.19 IV):

(9) *ʿrb* . *b* (10) bt⟨h b⟩*kyt* .[9]	⟨We⟩eping women entered into his house,
b hklh . *mšspdt* .	into his palace, lamenting women,[10]
b ḥẓrh . (11) *pẓǵm* . *ǵr* .	into his court, men lacerating[11] (their) skin.
ybk . *l aqht* . (12) *ǵzr* .	They wept for Aqhat, the hero,
ydmʿ . *l* kdd . *dnil* (13) *mt* . *rpi* .	they mourned for the child of Daniʾil, the Rapiʾan.
l ymm . *l yrḫm*	Days became months,
(14) *l yrḫm* . *l šnt* .	months became years.
ʿ*d* (15) *šbʿt* . *šnt* .	For seven years,
ybk . *l aq*(16)*ht* . *ǵzr* .	they wept for Aqhat, the hero,
*ydm*ʿ . l *kdd* (17) d*nil* . *mt* . rp[i]	they mourned for the child of Daniʾil, the Rapiʾan.

The mention of seven years here echoes Daniʾil's fear that the drought will last seven (or eight) years, stated in his first response to the catastrophe following Aqhat's death. These two references to seven years constitute an inclusio around Daniʾil's own responses to Aqhat's death. They help to define his reactions as a unit.

The seven-year mourning, of course, is not the first case of mourning. Words referring to weeping or descriptions of mourning activities are found throughout this section. Anat weeps and is apparently grieved (*tbk*, 1.18 IV 39; *tkrb*[?], 1.19 I 2), the *gpr*-beings lament his loss (1.19 I 12–13), Pughat weeps and mourns in her heart (*tbky, tdmʿ*; 1.19 I 34–35), Daniʾil tears his garment (1.19 I 36–37, 46–48), the hair of the messengers is disheveled and clipped and they walk erratically (1.19 II 27–44), and Daniʾil weeps for and buries his son (*ybky*; 1.19 III 39–41; cf. 5-6, 20-21). The statement about seven-year mourning is the last and, though briefly related, the most comprehensive account of mourning because of its duration, the number of people involved, and the inclusion of both genders.

9. So *CAT* 60 n. 2.

10. Compare the lamenting women in Jer 9:16–20. For professional female mourners in various cultures, see *UPA* 435 and the bibliography in n. 1 there.

11. Many connect this term with Heb. *pāṣaʿ* 'wound, bruise' (*MLC* 610; *CML* 155). See Dijkstra and de Moor, "Passages," 210 on cognates. On the custom in the Bible, compare Lev 21:5, Deut 14:1, Jer 41:5.

Thus the father, family, and friends, despite the vigor of Daniʾil's ritual performances, do not escape liminality for a significant period of time. The rites preceding the seven-year mourning have clarified a significant amount of chaos but have not cured it. These rites, rather than providing a return to structure, appear to stop short, only achieving a modicum of stability so that normal liminal rites may proceed. That is, Aqhat's death has so upset the status quo that normal mourning, such as one might find in the case of a natural death, cannot proceed without some prior remedy.

Against this, the minimal affirmation of sociocultural structure in the rites is understandable. In Daniʾil's agricultural rites, the gods are not invoked at all. Only third-person jussive expressions of hope—what form-critics of the Psalms would call *Wünsche*—are found. The gods are of course in the background of such expressions. But the narrative chooses not to mention them explicitly, except to express fear that Baʿl might be absent for seven/eight years. In the conjuration of the vultures, Daniʾil directly calls on Baʿl. This affirms his supremacy in control over Daniʾil's life and in control over nature. But there is no interaction between the man and god, as in the beginning of the story. Daniʾil speaks to the god and the god acts, almost mechanically. In the cursing of the towns, Daniʾil mentions two deities: Il (1.19 III 47) and Baʿl (IV 5).[12] In this way, he reaffirms the supremacy and power of these two gods, who granted blessing at the beginning of the story. But Daniʾil does not speak to them here, nor do they speak to him. In all of this, Daniʾil acts according to relationships presupposed and/or established in the successful feasts at the beginning of the story. But he does not perform rites that are directed primarily at reestablishing those relationships.

He does not even present an offering in connection with the burial of Aqhat. This might be expected from the Baʿl cycle, in which Anat slaughters a great quantity of different types of animals as a *gmn*-offering for Baʿl after she buries him (1.6 I):[13]

tṭbḥ . šbʿm (19) *rumm .*	She slaughtered seventy wild oxen,
k gmn . aliyn (20) [b]*ʿl*	as a *gmn*-offering for mighty Baʿl.
tṭbḥ . šbʿm . alpm	She slaughtered seventy oxen,
(21) [k] *gmn . aliyn . bʿl*	[as a] *gmn*-offering for mighty Baʿl.
(22) [tṭ]b*ḥ . šbʿm . ṣin*	[She sl]aughtered seventy flock animals,
(23) [k g]mn *. aliyn . bʿl*	[as a g]*mn* offering for might Baʿl.
(24) [tṭ]b*ḫ . šbʿm . aylm*	[She slaugh]tered seventy stags,

12. Yariḫ is mentioned in the narrative in passing (IV 2).

13. The meaning of *gmn* is not clear, though it is understood by several to refer to a type of funerary offering (*MLC* 224, 533; Walls, *The Goddess Anat*, 69).

(25) [k gmn .] *aliyn . bˁl*	[as a *gmn*] offering for mighty Baˁl.
(26) [tṭbḫ . š]bˁ*m . y*ˁ*lm*	[She slaughtered se]venty goats,
(27) [k gmn . al]iyn *. bˁl*	[as a *gmn* offering for mi]ghty Baˁl.
(28) [tṭbḫ . šbˁm . y]*ḥmrm*	[She slaughtered seventy] antelopes,
(29) [k gm]n . *aliyn* [.] *b*ˁl	[as a *gm*]*n* offering for mighty Baˁl.

The lack of a sacrifice in connection with Aqhat is particularly noticeable because Daniʾil's and Anat's burial procedures are otherwise quite similar. Both weep (*bky*) and bury (*qbr*), and the burial is achieved by 'placing' the body in 'a cavern of the underworld gods' (*šyt b ḫrt ilm arṣ;* see 1.6 I 16–18 and 1.19 III 5–6, 20–22, 34–35). After burying Baˁl, Anat immediately performs the offering, the description of which was just cited. Daniʾil, in contrast, does not perform a sacrifice but proceeds to curse the areas near where Aqhat was killed.

Daniʾil's various mourning rites are reminiscent of his position in the beginning of the story. There he had no son; now he is in the same position. We saw that he donned mourning garb (a *mizrt* and *ṣt*-clothing) in his seven-day lament petition. This was compared to Il's mourning for Baˁl's death in which Il descended from his throne and, among other things, began gashing his skin, something we now find Daniʾil's mourners doing. The fact that Daniʾil took seven days for his petition rite and now takes seven years in mourning Aqhat signals similarity between the scenes. Moreover, the presence of mourning women in Daniʾil's house for seven years reflects, after a fashion, the seven-day visit of the Kotharat to Daniʾil's house.[14]

The fact that the mourning lasts seven years, not days,[15] may be part of a folkloric motif for periods of famine[16] and mourning,[17] but within the story, it signifies that the loss of a promised son is more unbearable than not having one in the first place. The loss of Aqhat has exacerbated Daniʾil's misfortune, making it more severe than it was at the beginning of the story.

14. This last point observed in *UPA* 438–39.

15. The length of the period for mourning and/or impurity in the Bible: Gen 50:10; Num 19:11–12, 14, 16, 19; 31:19, 24; 1 Sam 31:13; Ezek 44:26.

16. See the Pharaoh's dreams in Genesis 41.

17. Note the seven-year mourning by wailing-women in the Elkurnirša myth (*ANET* 519; noted in *UPA* 437, though I doubt that Elkurnirša is the origin for the motif in Aqhat).

Part 4

Renewal and Revenge

After seven years of mourning, Dani'il and his household can begin to return to normal life and a normal course of ritual activity. The presentation of offerings, which is missing during the entire period of distress and mourning, resumes. At the same time, Aqhat's death is not yet fully recompensed. In the preceding rites, Dani'il moves closer to attacking the cause of his misfortune, but even in the curses he deals with entities that are only indirectly associated with his son's death. His daughter proposes retaliation closer to the cause. She uses a feasting situation to accomplish her plan by deceit. Unfortunately the text breaks off, and we cannot be certain what she does or how ritual plays a part in the rest of the story.

Chapter 17

Daniʾil's dbḥ *and the Blessing of Pughat*

The mourning for Aqhat lasts for seven years (as noted above), but the poet spends only a few lines describing it. The story moves quickly to the sequel, where Daniʾil resumes his offerings to the gods. This becomes the occasion for Pughat to avenge her brother's death. After the description of the sacrifice, Pughat asks her father for a blessing so that she may be successful in slaying the one who slew her Aqhat.

The dbḥ

The sacrifice described here is different from the foregoing feasts, having different accompaniments. It incorporates elements of joy, which have been missing since the conflict between Aqhat and Anat arose (1.19 IV):

(17) [m]k . *b* šbʿ (18) *šnt* .	In the seventh year,
*w y*ʿn [. dnil . m]t [.] rp*i*	Daniʾil, the Rapiʾan, answered,
(19) *yṯb* . *ǵzr* . m[t . hrnmy.]	the hero, the [Harnamiy]yan, responded,
[y]šu (20) *gh* . *w yṣḥ* .	[he l]ifted his voice and cried:
t[bʿ . b] b[t]y (21) b*kyt* .	"De[part from] my hou[se], weeping women,
*b hk*ly . mš*spdt*	from my palace, lamenting women,
(22) *b ḥẓry* . *pẓǵ*m . *ǵr* .	from my court, men who lacerate (the) skin."
*w yq*r[y] (23) *dbḥ* . *ilm*	He ma[de] an offering[1] to[2] the gods,[3]
*yš*ʿly . *dǵṯ*hm (24) *b šmym* .	he made his[4] incense rise to the heavenly beings,

1. De Moor (*SP* 103) understands the verb in this context to be a D-stem of *qry*, which in the G-stem means 'to meet'.

2. See the preposition *l-* in line 29, below.

3. Parker ("Ugaritic Deity Rāpiu," 101) suggests reading *il-m*, singular noun with enclitic *-m*. A plural is suggested, however, by *b šmym* and b [k]bkbm in the next lines, words that appear to refer to deities. Making an offering of Rpu (= Hrnmy, according to Parker) to the various sky-gods, however, creates a complex if not awkward cultic picture.

4. Restored as *dǵṯ*hm, in *CAT. CARTU* 116 and CTA 91 read only *dǵṯ*h. The *CAT* reading may be explained as singular possessive suffix *-h* plus enclitic *-m*. See *dǵṯ*h in line 30. If this is a singular pronoun, the referent is not entirely clear. If *il-m* rather than

dǵṯ hrnmy [.] b[5] [k](25)bkbm .	Harnamiyyan incense to the astral beings.[6]
ʿlh . yd . d[nil . xx]xx	Upon it the hand of D[aniʾil . . .] . . . (??),
(26) ʿ*lh . yd . ʿd .*	upon it the hand again (??).[7]
l hklh xxx mṣ(27)*ltm .*	To his palace cymbals (were brought??),
*mrqdm . d*šn . l bt[h]	clappers(?) of ivory to [his] house.

To end the period of mourning, Daniʾil simply dismisses those who have been mourning in his house. He then makes an offering consisting of three parts. He offers a *dbḥ* 'sacrifice' to the gods. This is presumably a ritual meal, to judge from other uses of the term. In 1.114:1, Il has a *dbḥ* that includes flesh and plenty of wine. *CAT* 1.23:27 uses the term in a context of feasting (line 6) and divine engorgement (62–76). The *dbḥ* in 1.161 (compare line 1) contains a series of offerings (28–30), including a bird offering (30). Though it is described in only one line in our text, we are to imagine that a ritual meal is being given to the deities.[8]

The *dbḥ* includes or is accompanied by an offering of *dǵṯ*. Since the *dǵṯ* is made to rise among the celestial beings and stars (see lines 24–25), it appears to be an offering or a part of an offering that is burned, perhaps

---

a plural *ilm* is to be read in line 23, the suffix may refer to that deity (so Parker, "Ugaritic Deity Rāpiu," 101). The suffix may also refer to the *dbḥ* (so *UPA* 164, 257). But one might expect it to be a semantic (though not necessarily syntactic) parallel to *hrnmy* in the next line. Since Daniʾil is a *mt hrnmy* 'a Hrnmy man', the incense may be called "his" or "Hrnmy" incense. On *hrnmy*, see p. 21 n. 5.

5. The preposition *b-*, rather than a relative *d-* (*UPA* 139, 256–57), is suggested by *b šmym* in the previous line.

6. Star deities; cf. 1.43:2–3; 1.10 I 4; see de Moor, "Frustula Ugaritica," 356.

7. Lines 25–26 are extremely broken. De Moor and Spronk (*CARTU* 116) read the same consonants as *CAT*, which is reproduced here, though they do not offer anything for the unreadable signs that *CAT* marks with x. De Moor ("Seasonal Pattern in the Legend of Aqhatu," 69; *ARTU* 262) translates 'He praised [his] child, [Daniʾilu] praised his child'. If the text given by *CAT* is correct as far as it goes, one wonders if Daniʾil performs some gesture here. I am reminded of hand placement in cultic rites in the Bible and in Hittite literature (see my "Gesture of Hand Placement in the Hebrew Bible and in Hittite Literature," *JAOS* 106 [1986] 433–46) and wonder if something similar is going on here (though otherwise unattested in Ugaritic texts as far as I know). The passage could be read ʿlh . yd . d[nil . yš]t | ʿ*lh . yd.* ʿ*d*⟨b⟩ 'Da[niʾil se]t (his) hand upon it (i.e., the incense), he placed his hand upon it'. This speculation is not completely unfounded, because in one Hittite text, a substance called *tuḫḫueššar* (perhaps incense), to which *dǵṯ* is perhaps related (see the discussion below), receives hand placement (QĀTAM *dai-*; see my "Gesture of Hand Placement," 442 and n. 57; this note indicates that other Hittite texts show that apparently the substance was used for purifying the hands). Purifying the hands may be part of what Daniʾil is doing with the *dǵṯ*. The ʿ*d* may otherwise go with the next poetic line and be an adverb (or conjunction).

8. On *dbḥ*, see also de Tarragon, *Culte*, 56–58; del Olmo Lete, *Canaanite Religion*, 34; Margalit (*UPA* 438) says that the participants may have eaten this offering.

even incense. The presence of the term *dǵṯt* in 1.23:15 supports the last meaning. There the material is burned seven times over a basin (*agn*). It is probably borrowed from or at least related to a Hittite term whose stem is manifested in the Hittite word *tuḫueššar*, which is some sort of purifying material and/or perhaps incense.[9] If *dǵṯ* is incense, it may be a sign of the relatively joyful nature of the occasion. The incense that accompanies some of the offerings in the Bible marks rejoicing (see Lev 5:11; Num 5:15). Olfactory pleasures are as important as gustatory pleasures in making offerings. Other Near Eastern literatures indicate that the gods enjoy the smell as well as the taste of sacrifices.[10]

A clear indication of joy is the presence of *mṣltm* and *mrqdm d šn*. Since *mṣltm* are presumably instruments (cymbals), *mrqdm dšn* appear also to be instruments. This seems confirmed by the list of instruments in 1.108:4–5. After *knr* 'lyre', *ṯlb* 'shawm', and *tp* 'drum', the terms *mṣltm* and *mrqdm dšn* appear. This context makes the last term appear to be an instrument.[11] The term *dšn* is to be understood as the determinative pronoun *d* plus *šn* 'tooth' or 'ivory'. It is doubtful that it means 'ointment'[12] or is related to the Hebrew root *dšn*, which has to do with fat. The term *mrqdm dšn* may in fact refer to clappers made of hippopotamus ivory.[13]

Though the feasts earlier in the Aqhat story do not include incense and music, we recall that filial duty B appears to do so. Dani'il was to have a son (1.17 I):

l arṣ . mšṣu . qṭrh	who brings forth his (father's) incense/ smoke from the earth,
(28) l*ʿpr . ḏmr . aṯrh .*	the song of his (father's) place from the dust.

9. See S. Alp, "Zum Wesen der kultischen Reinigungssubstanz *tuḫḫueššar* und die Verbalform *tuḫša*," *Or* 52 (1983) 14–19; H. Güterbock, "Lexicographical Notes II," *RHA* 22/74 (1964) 107; A. Kammenhuber, "Hethitisch *tuḫḫueššar*," *MSS* 1 (1956) 63–70; H. Hoffner, "An Anatolian Cult Term in Ugaritic," *JNES* 23 (1964) 66–68; Margalit, "Lexicographical Notes [II]," 164–66; de Moor, "Frustula Ugaritica," 355–56; *UPA* 270, 342; Watson, "Non-Semitic Words," 542; Wright, "Gesture of Hand Placement," 442 n. 57. Recently, *DLU* 131 renders *dǵṯt* as 'ofrenda de perfumes(?)' and compares the Hittite root.

10. See Gilgamesh XI 155–65; Atrahasis III v 34–37; Gen 8:21 (and compare P's term *rêaḥ niḥōaḥ*).

11. The following *b ḥbr . kṯr . ẓbm* may refer to persons (see, for example, de Moor, *ARTU* 188, who translates 'the merry companions of Kothar'). It is still not clear whether this requires the preceding phrase to refer to persons and not instruments.

12. *CARTU* 135. Dijkstra and de Moor ("Passages," 211) translate 'anointed dancers'.

13. For clappers of hippopotamus tooth from the area of Ugarit, see A. Caubet, "La musique à Ougarit: Nouveaux témoignages matériels," in *Ugarit, Religion, and Culture: Proceedings of the International Colloquium on Ugarit, Religion, and Culture–Edinburgh, July 1994* (ed. N. Wyatt, W. G. E. Watson, and J. B. Lloyd; Ugaritische-Biblische Literatur 12; Münster: Ugarit-Verlag, 1996) 11, 29.

These lines are not connected with any primary offering, such as a *dbḥ*; it seems we have only the music and incense. The description may be skirting poetically around the direct description of a larger sacrificial complex by listing only the peripheral or supplementary elements.

The presence of joy is a sign that the liminal period introduced by Aqhat's death has essentially passed. Daniʾil's condition has regained structure. Yet the detail of the description does not match the import of the feast. Only eight lines are devoted to outlining this complex feast. There is an editorial notation that may have sought to extend or expand the description. To the side of line 23, which mentions the *dbḥ*, the phrase *w hndt . yṯb . l mspr* is written. De Moor translates this 'the recitation of this (passage) should be repeated'.[14] He says that the scribe Ilimilk "probably . . . meant to instruct the reciting priest to extend the sacrifices of Daniʾilu over a period of seven days." He notes that this would constitute a clear parallel to the beginning of the story, where Daniʾil's first offering essentially lasts for seven days. However, this interpretation of the added phrase is not indisputable, given that the story has such simple narrative here. There are no words cited in the text (such as an incantation) that could be repeated. Moreover, repeating the description (in lines 22b–26) seven times does not necessarily imply a seven-day feast. Even if de Moor's interpretation is correct, this description is cut short by Pughat's request for a blessing so that she can successfully avenge her brother's death. Thus, the realization that the balance pans of justice are not yet even tempers the joy of the occasion.

The Blessing of Pughat

As part of or a supplement to Daniʾil's feast, Pughat comes to her father and asks for a blessing so that she will be able to exact vengeance for her brother's death. Here she may be following the duty of an unmarried sister, not only to mourn for her dead brother, but also to seek vengeance.[15] This transforms Daniʾil's feast into a launching pad for aggression instead of a simple rite of aggregation (1.19 IV):

(28) w *tʿn . pǵt . ṯkmt .* my*m*	Pughat, who shoulders water, answered:
(29) *qrym . ab . dbḥ .* l *ilm*	"My father has made an offering to the gods,

14. *ARTU* 262 n. 242; compare pp. 265 and 56 n. 251. A similar phrase (**w ṯb l mspr*) appears in an incantation in the middle of a text at the head of an incantation (1.40:35); see J. C. de Moor, "An Ugaritic Expiation Ritual and Its Old Testament Parallels," *UF* 23 (1991) 287. This instruction is found in another text (1.4 V 42; cf. de Tarragon, *Culte*, 93).

15. See Walls, *The Goddess Anat*, 79–80; here he also discusses Ṯtmnt in Kirta and Anat in the Baʿl story.

(30) šʿly . *dǵṯ*h . b š*mym*	he made his incense rise to the heavenly beings,
(31) *dǵṯ* . *hrnmy* . b *kb*kbm	Harnamiyyan incense to the astral deities.
(32) *l tb*rk*n* . *a*lk . br*k*tm	Bless me so that I may go (forth) blessed,
(33) *t*mrn . al*k* . *nm*rrt	benefit[16] me so that I may go (forth) supported.
(34) *imḫṣ* . *mḫṣ* . *aḫy* .	I will slay the slayer of my brother,
*a*kl [.] m(35)*k*ly [. ʿ]*l* . um*ty* .	I will destroy the one who destroyed the child of my mother."[17]
w yʿn . dn(36)*i*l . *mt* . *rpi* .	Dani'il, the Rapi'an, answered:
npš . tḥ [.] pǵ[t] (37) ṯkmt . *mym* .	"By my life, may Pughat, who shoulders water, live,
ḥspt . *l šʿr* (38) ṭl .	who extracts dew from the fleece,
ydʿt [.] *hlk* . *kbkbm* [18]	who knows the course of the stars,
[ap] (39) *n*pš . *hy* . *mḫ* .	[even (?)] by my(?) life, (that) is my(?) vitality![19]
tmḫṣ . *mḫṣ*[. aḫk]	You shall slay the slayer of [your[20] brother!],
(40) *tkl* . *mkly* . *ʿl* . *umt* .	you shall destroy the one who destroyed the child of (your) mother." (??)

This blessing has already been compared to the one that Il gives to Dani'il at the beginning of the story (1.17 I 34–47; see pp. 72–73 above). As in that blessing, a request for a blessing precedes this one. After the request, the blessing begins with an oath, wishing life on the one blessed. The person's full name is used, as it were, by listing epithets. The specific blessing appears at the end, which accords with the substance of Pughat's request. Apart from these structural similarities, the two blessings are also similar in that they deal with Dani'il's son in some way: the first blessing helps Dani'il produce a son, and the second helps avenge the son's death. Furthermore, since the seven-day petition offering at the beginning of the story has the function of leading Dani'il out of distress in a way similar to the *dbḥ* here, both blessings occur in the context of rites of integration.

This is not the first blessing that Dani'il gives in the story, however. Just after receiving the bow from Kothar-wa-Ḫasis, Dani'il apparently blesses Aqhat and gives him the bow (1.17 V 33–39; see above). That blessing

16. See p. 39 n. 79 above.

17. Margalit (*UPA* 165) reads 'mother's suckling'. That Pughat describes Aqhat by reference to the mother may be significant for understanding male-female issues in the narrative.

18. So KTU, CTA, *UPA* 140. *CAT* has *kbkm*.

19. See the discussion on Il's blessing of Dani'il, pp. 72–74.

20. Second person, following *UPA* 140. KTU restores aḫh 'her brother' and apparently takes the verbs as third-person feminine singular (so *ARTU* 263).

does not display the same structure found in the blessings that Il gives Daniʾil and that Daniʾil gives Pughat; for example, it lacks an introduction containing an oath. But despite its distinct form, it shares the same spirit as these other blessings, anticipating prosperity and success. It serves with Il's blessing at the beginning of the story to distinguish the felicitous feasts and ritual from what follows. Those initial blessings and the blessing of Pughat here can now be seen to frame the middle section of mourning and retaliation. This is more than just a structural observation. The lack of blessing in the middle section and the lack of feasts contribute to the sense of misfortune and gloom. Pughat's blessing, along with the *dbḥ*, transform the foul mood into a happier one.

Even though the blessing is not necessarily a planned part of Daniʾil's *dbḥ*, it and the *dbḥ* constitute another case in which the ritual action described turns into a speech. Pughat's speech and Daniʾil's consequent blessing, however, do not give definition to his *dbḥ* in the same way that Baʿl's words help define the significance of Daniʾil's six-day petition rite. Rather, the words spoken here change the orientation of the *dbḥ*. Daniʾil is simply recovering from mourning by offering his *dbḥ*. Now Pughat uses this occasion for setting out to remedy blood guilt and restore family honor.

Chapter 18

The Wine Service for Yaṭupan

The tablet that records the extant story's final scene, in which Pughat visits Yaṭupan to avenge her brother's death, ends before the scene is over, and the tablet containing the sequel has not been found. For this reason, we are not absolutely certain what happens. However, in view of the blessing that Pughat receives from her father and because Yaṭupan is the specific individual who killed Aqhat, we assume that Pughat must have killed Yaṭupan. To do this, she employs deceit to infiltrate his camp. She serves him a drink, apparently to get him drunk, and then dispatches him. In this way the scene juxtaposes infelicity and felicity, deceit and success.

Pughat's Preparations

As soon as she receives her father's blessing, Pughat prepares for encountering Yaṭupan (1.19 IV):

[xx] (41) *d* . *txxl* . b *ym* .[1]	. . . she . . . in/from the sea,
trtḥ[ṣ] (42) w . tad*m* .[2]	she washed and rouged herself,
tid[!]*m* . *b ǵ*lp *y*m	with rouge[3] from a sea-shell,[4]
(43) *d alp* . *šd* . *ẓuh* . *b ym* .[5]	whose source is a thousand *šd*-measures, in the sea.

1. CTA reads *d. ttql* . b *ym* (*TO* 1 456: 'Elle se la[ve] (à l'eau) qui descend dans la mer'). Margalit (*UPA* 140, 165) restores and translates: [td]d . *ttql* . by*m* '[She went] forth; she plunged into the sea (of Galilee)'. Virolleaud reads: *dgt* (?) *t* (?) [ ] *l*(?) *b* (?)*ym* (cf. CTA 91 n. 7). De Moor and Spronk (*CARTU* 116–17) have: *dg*t tšʿ*l* . *b ym* . 'She made a fish come up from the sea' (translation in *ARTU* 263).

2. So *CAT*; J. C. de Moor, "Murices in Ugaritic Mythology," *Or* 37 (1968) 212–15; *CARTU* 117; *CML* 121. Margalit (*UPA* 140, 165) reads *trtḥ*[ṣ . ydm] (.) w{.}ṯk*m* 'She wash[ed (her) hands] and shoulder(s)'.

3. Taking the word as a noun (cf. *CML* 121), in distinction from the preceding verb, tad*m*.

4. That is, from an animal with a shell. Compare *ǵlp* as 'husk' in 1.19 I 19.

5. For line 43 I follow *CAT*; *CARTU* 117. Margalit (*UPA* 140) restores and divides differently: [ṣdp ?] (.) (43) *d alp* . *šd* / *ẓuh* . *b ym* . *t*[šlp(n) ?] '[Whelks] from a thousand ŠIDDU away; / She [remov]ed her tunic in the sea'.

t[ḥt] (44) *tlbš . np*ṣ *. ǵzr .*	Underneath she put on clothing of a hero,
tšt . ḫ[lpn] b (45) *nšgh .*	she put a b[lade][6] in her *nšg*,[7]
*ḥrb . tšt . b t*ʿr[th]	a knife she put in her bag.
(46) *w ʿl . tlbš . npṣ . aṯt .*	On top she put the clothes of a woman.

Other mythic texts display the washing activity found here. Kirta cleansed as Pughat does, prior to making his sacrifice (1.14 III 52–54; cf. 1.14 II 9–11) just after waking from a dream-revelation:

(52) *yrtḥṣ . w yadm*	He washed and rouged himself,
(53) *yrḥṣ . ydh . amth*	he washed his hands, his forearms,
(54) *uṣbʿth . ʿd . ṯkm*	from his fingers to (his) shoulder.

Anat performs similar washings in the Baʿl cycle. One example is found after *tmtḫṣ b bt tḫtṣb bn ṯlḥnm* 'she fought in the house, slaughtered among the tables' (1.3 II 38–III 2):

(38) t*ḥspn . mh . w trḥṣ*	She collected water and washed,
(39) *ṭl . šmm .*	(with) the dew of heaven,
šmn *. arṣ .*	the "oil" of the earth,
rbb (40) [r]*kb ʿrpt .*	the precipitation of the Cloud [R]ider.
ṭl . šmm . tskh	The dew the heaven poured on her,
(41) [r]b*b . nskh . kbkbm*	the precipitation that the stars poured on her.
(1) *ttpp . anh*b[m .]	She beautified herself(?) with *an*[*hb*-stone/shell(?)[8]]
[d alp . šd] (2) *ẓuh . b ym*	[who]se source is [a thousand *šd*-measures] in the sea.

She also washes in this manner when she goes to Baʿl at Ṣaphon, and he gives her an ox as a meal (1.3 IV):

(42) *tḥspn . mh . w trḥṣ*	She collected water and washed,
(43) *ṭl . šmm .*	(with) the dew of heaven,

6. A restoration such as *ḫ*[lpn] (so *CAT; CARTU* 117; Gaster restores *ḫ*[*lp.b*] apud apparatus in *CML* 121) is justified because of the parallel following line and possible cognates from: Biblical Hebrew *maḥălāp*, Rabbinic Hebrew *ḥallîp*, and Syriac *ḥlūptāʾ*; all meaning 'knife'. *TO* 1 457 restores 'couteau'. On possible phonological problems, see Dijkstra and de Moor "Passages," 121; *HALAT* 308.

7. The meaning of *nšg* should be similar to *tʿrt* in the next poetic line (on *tʿrt*, see p. 128 n. 9 above). Several take this to be 'sheath' or the like (*CML* 121; *MLC* 593). It might also be connected with Arab. *nasaja* 'to weave, knit' (cf. *CARTU* 156; *ARTU* 264: 'plaited bag'). The connection with Heb. *nśg* (*hiśśîg*) is doubtful (*TO* 1 457 note y).

8. CAD I/J 322: *janibu/ajanibu* 'a stone'.

šmn . arṣ .	the "oil" of the earth.
*ṭl . š*m[m . ts]*kh*	The dew of hea[ven pou]red on her,
(44) *rbb . nskh . kbkbm*	the precipitation that the stars poured on her.
(45) *ttpp . anhbm .*	She beautified herself(?) with *anhb*-stone/shell(?),
d alp . šd (46) ẓuh . b y[m]	whose source is a thousand *šd*-measures in the s[ea].

All of these cases, including Pughat's washing, include bathing followed apparently by a cosmetic reddening of the arms (if not more of the body). That this is a cosmetic and not simply a hard scrubbing that turns the arms red is indicated by Pughat's washing, which connects the reddening (*tid!m*) with a sea shell (*ǵlp ym*), "whose source is a thousand *šd*-measures in the sea," and by Anat's toilet, which includes beautifying with the *anhb*, "whose source" also "is a thousand *šd*-measures in the sea." This all points to the use of a dye from a marine animal, specifically, *Murex trunculus*.[9]

A question that arises about Pughat's washing, especially in consideration of these other examples, is whether it is a case of ritual washing.[10] Kirta's washing before his sacrifice certainly must be viewed as an ablution. It prepares him for the sacrifice he is to make. Anat's washing and use of *anhb* can be seen as ritual performances: in the first example she cleanses from having done battle, and in the second case she prepares for a ritual meal.[11]

It is reasonable, then, to view Pughat's washing and reddening as ritual activities. But for what purpose? It is not clear that the acts are associated with Pughat's recovery from mourning, since in this case we would expect them to precede Daniʾil's *dbḥ* and blessing of Pughat. They might be in preparation for the feasting that will take place with Yaṭupan, but it seems that, in view of her intentions and deceit (see below), she would hardly bother with the etiquette of the occasion.

Another fragmentary and briefly recounted use of *anhbm* by Anat may hold the key. *Before* she goes to the battle after which she washes and applies the dye from *anhbm* (as observed above in 1.3 II 38–III 2), she apparently puts on dye from *anhbm*: *kpr . šbʿ . bnt . rḥ . gdm w anhbm*

9. *UPA* 453 and n. 1; de Moor, "Murices," 212–15; *SP* 85–87.

10. On purity and purification at Ugarit, see H. Cazelles, "Pur et impure aux origines de l'Hébreu et a Ugarit," in *Festschrift R. P. Fleisch* (2 vols.) = *Melanges Université Saint Joseph* 49 (1975–76) 2.443–49; de Tarragon, *Culte*, 79–91.

11. The difficult text 1.13 also has Anat washing (dyeing is not mentioned) prior to visiting Il (line 18). On ablutions, see B. Levine, "Ugaritic Descriptive Rituals," *JCS* 17 (1963) 105.

'henna . . . seven girls, and the smell of coriander and *anhbm*-dye' (1.3 II 2–3). The context before this is broken, but it seems that Anat puts the various materials on herself, unless the seven girls are aiding in the application.[12] This passage may indicate that dyeing and, presumably along with it, washing are part of preparations for going out to battle.[13] This fits the context of Pughat's activity, especially since the following lines tell how she arranges the dagger under her clothing. Purification makes sense as a transition from common status to warrior status. It correlates with customs found in the Bible, for example, where battle is to be conducted in a state of purity (Deut 23:10–14, 1 Sam 21:3–7).[14]

Pughat's Deceit

Pughat's encounter with Yaṭupan follows her preparations, including dressing (which will be discussed in more detail below). This encounter again involves the motif of feasting (1.19 IV):

[lm] (47) *ṣbi* . *nrt* . *ilm* . *špš* .	When the lamp of the gods, the Sun, set,
ʿr[bt] (48) pǵ*t* . *minš* . *šdm* .	Pughat entered the place of encounter[15] in the fields,
*l m*ʿr[b] (49) *nrt* . *ilm* . *špš* .	when the lamp of the gods, the Sun, declined,
mǵy[t] (50) *pǵt* . l *ahlm* .	Pughat arrived at the tents.
rgm . *l y*ṭ[pn . y](51)*bl* .	Word [was br]ought to Yaṭ[upan]:
agrtn . *bat* . *b ḏdk* .	"The one who pays us has come to your dwelling(s),
[ʿnt (?)] (52) *bat* . *b* ⟨a⟩*hlm* .	[Anat(?)][16] has come to the tents."
*w y*ʿ*n* . *yṭpn* . m[hr] (53) št .	Yaṭupan, the wa[rrior] of the Lady, answered:
qḥn . *w tšqyn* . *yn* .	"Take it (the cup) and give me wine to drink;
t[q]ḥ (54) *ks* . *bdy* .	ta[k]e the cup from my hand,

12. The relationship between the henna and the seven girls is not clear; *ARTU* 5 has the seven girls placing it on Anat, whereas *CML* 47 sees Anat putting on the amount of henna that seven girls would put on. Since the text before this is missing, we do not know if Anat washes.

13. Margalit goes so far as to (apparently) refer to the dye as "war-paint" (*UPA* 322).

14. Cf. my "Holiness, OT," *ABD* 3.244a.

15. Arab. *ʾanisa* 'be sociable, friendly; like to be together' (cf. *ARTU* 264: 'meeting-place'; *CML* 121: 'gathering-place'; *MLC* 574: 'campamento'). Margalit (*UPA* 165) renders 'comrade-of-the-fields'. *TO* 1 457 and note z give 'lieux peuplés', literally, 'les (endroits) peuplés des champs'.

16. *CARTU* 117 and *UPA* 141 restore ʿnt. *CAT* restores pǵt. See the discussion below.

qbʿt . b ymny .	the goblet from my right hand."[17]
tq(55)*ḥ . pǵt . w tšqynh .*	Pughat took (it) and she gave him drink;
tq$^!$ḥ [. ks .] b*dh*	she took [the cup] from his hand,
(56) *qbʿt . b ymnh .*	the goblet from his right hand.
w yʿn . yṭ[p]*n*[. mh]*r* (57) *št .*	Yaṭu[pa]n, [the warri]or of the Lady, answered:
b yn . yšt . ila .	"By (this) wine, O lady(?), I can prevail,
*ilš*n[18] [.] il (58) *d yqny . ḏdm .*	I could (even) slander(?) Il, who created the dwellings.
yd *. mḫṣt . a*q[ht] . *ǵ*(59)*zr .*	The hand that slew Aq[hat], the hero,
tmḫṣ . alpm . ib *. št*[.]	will slay two thousand enemies of the Lady(?)."
[t]*š*t (60) ḥ*ršm* [19]*. l ahlm .*	[She] set an incantation(?) over the tents,
p x[x .] ḥ*km* (61) *ybl . lbh .*[20]	and her heart brought forth a clever (?) [. . .].
km . b ṯn . yn[. t]ml*ah .*	Yes, again [she] poured out wine for him,[21]
(62) *ṯnm . tšqy msk . hwt .*	a second time she gave him spiced-wine to drink,
tšqy [ ]s[ ][22]	she gave him . . . to drink.

Pughat uses deceit to kill Yaṭupan, just as Anat used it to kill Aqhat. The question here is what is the extent of her deceit. It is clear from her preparations that she hides a weapon under her clothing (lines 44–45) to be used, perhaps not just for defense, but in accomplishing her plan. She also wears male clothing under her female clothing (line 44). This may be to allow herself to get away more easily, perhaps for disguise so that she can slip through crowds and slip by guards unnoticed. In these various ways, at least, she conceals her true motives.

17. In the context, this speech works better when directed to Pughat (so *UPA* 165), not to messengers describing what Pughat is to do (so *ARTU* 264). See the discussion below.

18. So *CARTU* 117. *CAT* reads *il š*xn or, in the note, *ilš*xn(?).

19. *UPA* 141 reads ʿ$^!$*ršm* 'double couch'. This is a venue for his drunkenness and eventually his death (cf. p. 454).

20. So *CAT*. *CARTU* 117 reads *p*[tgm]r*m* (61) *ybl . lbh*; *ARTU* 265 translates 'Then [she carried] out the wish of her heart'. *UPA* 141 reads and renders pm[la .] *km* (.) (61) *ybl . lbh* 'And his chest fi[lled up] (with wine) like a rivulet'. *MLC* 401 reads and translates *p*[ ]*km* (61) *ybl* | *lbh . km . bṯn y*-[ ]*ṣ*/*lah* 'Entonces [sus entrañas] como las de un carnero, | su corazón como el de una serpiente se le [hinchó]'.

21. *UPA* 141, 166 reads *km . bṯn . y*[mk .] l*ah* 'His strength eb[bed level] with a snake'.

22. *UPA* 141, 166 reads for the last part of line 61, *tšqy* [. m]s[k . (m)škr ?] 'She served him (*hwt*) spirits a second time, / She served him [the intoxicating bevera]ge'. *CARTU* 117 has *tšqy*[h .] s[m] 'she gave [him] a d[rug] to drink'.

Her deceit apparently also involves disguising herself as Anat.[23] The main evidence for this is the designation of Pughat as *agrtn* 'our *agrt*'. This can be interpreted by recourse to the Arabic root *ʾajara*, which means 'to reward, recompense' and in stem II 'to hire out'. The Ugaritic term, taken as an active participle /*ʾāgirt-*/, would consequently define the visitor as one who has engaged, paid, or hired the group led by Yaṭupan.[24] Since the story has few lacunae in the part that introduces Yaṭupan and describes his counsel to kill Aqhat (1.18 IV 5ff.), there is no reason to believe that Pughat has had any relationship with Yaṭupan or that he or his comrades recognize her for any reason. Therefore, she herself cannot be called *their ʾāgirt-* . However, the goddess Anat has had a relationship with Yaṭupan in which he could be considered her employee. This indicates that Yaṭupan's group understands Pughat to be Anat.

An alternative interpretation is to take *agrt* as 'our hired woman',[25] presumably a passive participle, /*ʾagīrat-*/. Since Anat would not be depicted as a hired woman, this would mean that Pughat is not necessarily in disguise. The problem with this interpretation of *agrt* is the accompanying pronoun *-n* 'our', which seems to indicate that Pughat as a "hired woman" has some prior relationship to Yaṭupan and his group. But as already noted, this is unlikely.[26] This difficulty is not entirely solved by postulating that she, as a "hired woman," is to be viewed as a prostitute. This assumes some prior relationship to or arrangement with Pughat, unless of course there is a coincidence in her coming as a harlot and Yaṭupan's expectation of such a woman or unless Pughat somehow knew about his expectation and preempted or waylaid the real prostitute. Even if, despite these difficulties, *agrt* is taken specifically to mean 'prostitute', deceit is still present. However, Pughat's appearance would then be worldly rather than divine.

A more debatable piece of evidence that Pughat is disguised as Anat is the phrase *b yn . yšt . ila* (line 57). Many have solved the problems of this line by emending *ila* to *iln*! to refer to Il, as suggested by the context of the

23. Those who accept this include: de Moor, "Murices," 212; *ARTU* 264; *CML* 121; *UPA* 452 (and his restoration of ʿnt at the end of line 51 on p. 141); Watson, "Puzzling Passages," 375–76. Margalit (*UPA* 322) thinks that the *npṣ ǵzr* 'hero clothing' (line 44) that Pughat wore is what Anat wore, something that marked her "manly" nature, to which Il referred when she threatened him (1.18 I 16).

24. *UPA* 165, 'She-who-engaged-us'; *ARTU* 264, 'our employer'; *TO* 1 457, 'Celle qui nous engage'.

25. Cf. Walls, *The Goddess Anat*, 208; Parker, *Pre-biblical Narrative Tradition*, 131; *CML* 121 n. 2.

26. Walls's translation 'a hired woman' instead of 'our hired woman' hides the difficulty (*The Goddess Anat*, 207).

next line. The line then becomes a toast to him: 'May our god drink of the wine'.[27] This interpretation is valid only insofar as the emendation is correct. Margalit has interpreted the line quite differently. He takes *ila* as a divine name that is attested in Amorite and Sutean names and he argues that this divine name is the cultural forerunner of Ugaritic Il.[28] The line is to be read *byn . yšt . ila . il* (.) št and is to be translated 'From (this) wine shall drink ILA, god of the Suteans'. His interpretation is difficult, because the final *ʾalep* of *ila* is not satisfactorily explained and, as he admits, other extant Ugaritic texts do not attest this god.[29]

Another line of interpretation is that *ila* may be interpreted as a first-person verb from the root *lʾy*. Thus *b yn . . . ila* means 'I will prevail . . . by means of (this) wine'; it is a boast rather than a toast. This is a reasonable rendering of the text, but the problem is in understanding the sequence of letters *yšt*, which appears between *yn* and *ila*. Recently Parker has taken it as a verb: *byn.yšt.ila.il š*[ ] 'By the wine that is drunk I'll defeat the god . . .'.[30] The difficulty with this is that a third-person passive—or at least impersonal—reference to wine, 'that is drunk', is conceptually flat; that it is drunk seems to go without saying. More fitting would be a phrase such as **b yn ašt ila* 'by the wine that I drink I will prevail'.

The rendition of *yšt* by de Moor, who also takes *ila* as a verb 'I become strong', seems preferable, and it supports the idea that Pughat is disguised as Anat.[31] He construes the sequence as a vocative particle *y-* plus the epithet *št*. This epithet presumably refers to Anat, and the line could be rendered, without a decision as to the exact meaning of the epithet, 'By wine, O *št*, I can prevail'.

The evidence that *št* is an epithet is not conclusive but is relatively strong. *CAT* 1.23:60-61 appears to support this interpretation. In this passage, Il has fathered the gods Shahar and Shalim. The text describes them as *ilmy* . nʿ*mm agzrym . bn ym .ynq*m . b *ap . d̲d̲ . št* 'the two kindly (and) ravenous gods, born on the same day, sucking at the breast-nipples of the *št*'.[32] While *št* may be read as a verb with the following ('They placed [*št*] a lip to the ground, and a lip to the sky . . .'),[33] lines 23-24,

27. *CML* 121 and the note there; *TO* 1 457 and note c.

28. *UPA* 462-64 (cf. p. 281).

29. *UPA* 339 says that "the phonetic complement *ʾa* very likely [reflects] the speaker's 'Amorite' dialect."

30. *UNP* 78.

31. *ARTU* 264.

32. Cf. *CML* 126; *MLC* 446 (in his glossary, p. 633, del Olmo Lete says that this is an epithet of Anat or Athirat); *ARTU* 126 and n. 58 (reference is to Anat). In his recent translation, T. Lewis takes the term as an epithet in this text: 'Who sucks the teats of the Lady's breasts' (*UNP* 213).

33. *TO* 1 377; *UPA* 337 n. 2.

which are parallel to line 61, suggest that a proper noun or its equivalent should follow the words *ap . d̲d̲* 'breast'. Those earlier lines read: *ilm . nʿmm* [. agzrym . bn]*ym ynqm* . b *ap zd (= d̲d̲)* . *at̲rt* 'the kindly [(and) ravenous] gods, [born] on the same day, sucking at the breast-nipples of ʾAthirat'. Though this appears to make *št* in this text an epithet of ʾAthirat instead of Anat, it may be an epithet that could be used of other divine females. In fact, in 1.23:13, 28, the divine beings *ʾt̲rt w rḥmy* 'ʾAthirat and Raḥmay' appear together. The latter may refer to Anat.[34]

Moreover, Yaṭupan is referred to as *mhr št* in both of his appearances in the Aqhat story (in making plans to kill Aqhat, 1.18 IV 5, [10], 27; and in the present wine-drinking scene, 1.19 IV 52–53, 56–57). This has generally been taken to mean 'warrior of the *št*' (I leave the term untranslated for now). Margalit and Parker (Margalit in part because of difficulties with a proposed etymology; see below) take the phrase to mean 'Sutean warrior'.[35] Walls, however, has marshaled evidence from Egypt in support of *št* as an epithet. The Egyptian phrase *mhr ʿnt*, used of Ramses II, "can mean either 'suckling of Anat' or 'warrior of Anat.'" If the latter rendering is correct, it provides an exact parallel to the Ugaritic phrase, in which case *št* would be an epithet, not just of any goddess, but of Anat in particular.[36]

This contextual evidence suggests that *št* may be taken as an epithet of Anat. The question is: what is its meaning? Those who take it as an epithet generally compare Arabic *sitt-* 'lady' and so translate the Ugaritic term. Margalit has questioned this equation, because the Arabic term is a dialectal form that may not have great antiquity (hence his attempt to find an alternative interpretation, noted above).[37] But even if Arabic *sitt-* is not entirely reliable as a precedent, it is still possible to compare the Arabic root *swd* 'to be master, head, lord'.[38] The Ugaritic term may be a noun in which the final *-d-* of the root has assimilated to the *-t-*, the feminine nominal augment: *šV̄dt-* → *šV̄tt-*; thus the consonantal writing *št*.

34. *CML* 123 n. 10; cf. *ARTU* 120 n. 18. Walls (*The Goddess Anat*, 79–82) is not certain that *rḥmy* is to be identified with Anat but allows it as a possibility. Walls does accept the interpretation of *št* as 'Lady', referring to Anat (p. 153).

35. *UPA* (337–38) and *UNP* (65, 66, 78).

36. Walls, *The Goddess Anat*, 153. The word *št* in the phrase *tmḫṣ . alpm . ib . št* 'it (Yaṭupan's hand) shall slay two thousand of the enemies of (the) *št*' (line 59b) also makes sense as an epithet. The previous line speaks of his killing Aqhat, one of Anat's foes; this b-line would continue that idea and generalize it.

37. It is questionable, since it may be a reflection of a dialectal form (so the marking in *DMWA* 397), even a contraction or development from **sayyidati* (so *UPA* 337–38).

38. *DMWA* 440.

One advantage of this interpretation of *št* should not be overlooked. It does not require interrupting the one-to-one encounter of Pughat and Yaṭupan with a libation or toast to another god, either Il or Amorite/Sutean Ila. Yaṭupan receives his drink and then goes directly to boasting, providing readers and hearers, in case they had forgotten, with the reason for which Pughat is about to kill him. The next line (57c–58a) can be read as part of this bravado. I follow de Moor again: the partially broken *ilšn* can be taken as a first-person verb from the root *lšn*, meaning something like 'calumniate, slander'.[39] This verb was used to describe Anat's condemnation of Aqhat to Il (1.17 VI 51). Here Yaṭupan glories that he would even be powerful enough to tell off Il. This fits the wild and unconventional spirit of Anat's side in this whole affair very nicely. It also symbolically recapitulates Anat's lambasting threat of Il as she set about to kill Aqhat, which, interestingly, is the next subject of Yaṭupan's boast (line 58b–59a).

The Wine Service

The foregoing considerations make it clear that Pughat's encounter with Yaṭupan involves deceit and that she is probably disguised as Anat. This deceit occurs in a ritual feasting context that has two parts, one coming before and the other after Yaṭupan's boast: (1) the drinking of wine, in lines 53b–56a, and (2) consequent ritual activity that also includes wine-drinking, in lines 59c–61. What is going on in either of these parts is somewhat opaque. In the first part, the problem is just who the subjects of the verbs are. The subject of *qḥn* (53) and its parallel tq*ḥ* (54–55) has been understood to be Yaṭupan's servants or Pughat. The subject of the verb *tšqyn* (53) and its parallel *tšqynh* (55) has been understood as Yaṭupan's servants or Pughat and, when Pughat, the verb has been taken with either a simple ('she drinks') or a causative sense ('she gives drink'). The subject of the verb t[q]ḥ (53) and *tq*⸢ḥ (55) has been understood as either Yaṭupan's servants or Pughat.[40] A similar problem exists in the sec-

39. Cf. Ps 101:5, Prov 30:10.

40. See *CML* 121: '"Bring her and give her wine to drink; take the cup. . . ." They brought Pughat and gave her (it) to drink; they too [the cup] . . .'. *TO* 1 457: '"Prenez-la, et qu'elle boive du vin. Prenez une coupe. . . ." Pughat prend (du vin) et le boit elle pren[d une coupe] . . .'. *ARTU* 264: '"Bring her in and let her give me wine to drink! Let her take the cup. . . ." They brought Pughatu in and she gave him drink. She took the cup . . .' (and so *CML* 121 n. 3). *UPA* 165–66: '"Take (the cup) and serve me wine, take the cup from my hand. . . ." Pughat took (the cup) and served him drink, she took the cup . . .'. *UNP* 78: '"Take and drink the wine, take the cup from my hand, the goblet from my fingers." Paghit takes and drinks it, tak[es the cup from] his hand, the goblet from his fingers'.

ond part of the ritual activity in line 61c, which describes the consumption of wine. The subject of the verb *tšqy* there may be construed as Yaṭupan's servants or Pughat and, in Pughat's case, with a simple or a causative sense. Depending on how the verb is construed, the pronoun *hwt* in line 61c is taken either as a genitive modifying *msk* ('his spiced wine')[41] or as an object of the verb.[42]

The logic of the situation suggests that Pughat-as-Anat is being given wine rather than being asked to serve wine. After all, Anat is Yaṭupan's *agrt* 'employer', and there is no immediate reason to think that she is now to be his waiter. It also seems odd, if Pughat were serving the wine, for the text to describe her as taking the cup from Yaṭupan's hand.

On the other hand, the reasonable restoration of [t]mlah 'she filled/poured out for him' in line 61b,[43] parallel to *tšqy* in the next poetic line, points to Pughat as the subject and the server.[44] It may be that, despite the hierarchy of goddess over her hired warrior, Yaṭupan is bold enough, perhaps out of drunkenness, to ask Anat to serve him. After all, if the interpretation of line 57c–58a is correct, he would challenge even Il. This inversion of relationships plays against the hierarchical picture set up at the beginning of the story, especially by the hospitality feasts in which Daniʾil serves visiting divinities (the Kotharat and Kothar-wa-Ḫasis). It also plays against the challenges to hierarchy in Anat and Aqhat's failure to agree with each other. Yaṭupan vaunts himself over the goddess, having her serve him rather than his serving her. He, symbolically, becomes an offender, like Aqhat. This constitutes a measure-for-measure turning of the tables. Yaṭupan is now—at least theoretically—rejecting Anat's authority, as Aqhat did. And just as Aqhat suffered, we now expect Yaṭupan to suffer.[45]

The problem of Pughat's taking the cup from Yaṭupan's hand is not great if the description is seen as telescoped: the verbs *tšqyn* and *tšqynh* refer to her presentation of the wine, and the taking of the cup from the hand refers to her removing the cup after it was drunk. Thus, the text indirectly portrays Yaṭupan as draining the cup by reference to setting out the table and clearing it.

41. So *CML* 122, 'his mixture'; *TO* 1 458, 'le vin mêlé (de Yaṭupan)'.

42. So *ARTU* 265; *UPA* 166; Segert (*Grammar*, §61.1) gives this very line as an example of the objective use of the genitive-accusative pronoun.

43. So *CAT*; *CARTU* 117; Dijkstra and de Moor, "Passages," 213–14 (they note that the suffix is to be understood as a dative).

44. On the meaning of *šqy* as 'to give drink', not 'to drink', see chapter 1 above.

45. Otherwise, perhaps because of Yaṭupan's service to the deity, Anat promised to feast him in some way, and thus Yaṭupan's request is simply making good on this promise. Margalit takes it further: Anat had promised sexual favors too.

The second part of the feast includes drinking, as we have already seen (lines 61b–c). But other activities take place in lines 59c–61a. What these are is unclear. The word ḥ*ršm* in line 60a may mean something like 'incantation, spell', as in the term *ḥăkam ḥărāšîm* in Isa 3:3, which likely means 'expert in spells; magician'.[46] But this cannot be verified because of problems in the next, parallel line of the Aqhat text and because of the missing end of the text.[47] Also problematic is what person the verb preceding this word in line 59c should be and what its referent is. The restoration [t]š*t* may have as subject: (a) Yaṭupan's hand, which makes it a continuation of his boast;[48] (b) Pughat, which makes it the resumption of narrative description;[49] or (c) an impersonal plural, 'they set', which also would be a resumption of narrative description. The restoration [y]š*t* is also possible, part of a resumption in narrative description and referring either to Yaṭupan or some undefined individual.[50]

Any conclusion must be tentative, decided by process of elimination. Since line 59c–60a does not form a clear parallel to 59b, it probably resumes narration and is not part of Yaṭupan's boast. The best interpretation of ḥ*ršm* is something to do with the magical arts. As a magical act within narrative description, it is an offensive, not defensive, act. In the context, an offensive act makes best sense with Pughat as agent.[51] For these reasons, I render 59c–60a '[She] set an incantation (?) over the tents'.

The meaning of the line that follows (60b–61a) must also remain wholly tentative. The line probably begins with *p* x[x] and ends with *ybl* . *lbh*.[52] Restorations and readings vary. De Moor restores *p* [tgm]r*m* . *ybl* . *lbh* and translates 'Then [she carried] out the wish of her heart'.[53] Margalit reads and translates: *p*m[la .] *km* (.) *ybl* . *lbh* 'And as his chest fi[lled up] (with wine) like a rivulet'. *CAT*'s restoration of ḥ*km* at the end of line 60 may provide a parallel to ḥ*ršm* in the previous line, especially if in the break before it (*p* x[x .]) there is a noun that ḥ*km* may modify as an attributive adjective. I translate 'her heart brought forth a clever [. . .]'.

46. *HALAT* 344a; H. Wildberger, *Isaiah 1-12* (Minneapolis: Fortress, 1991) 124.

47. *TO* 1 458 note f says that these are perhaps "objets manufacturés" used to bribe Yaṭupan. The problem with this is that it appears to require the root *ḥrṯ* (Arab. *ḥaraṯa* 'plow'; Heb. *ḥāraš* 'engrave, plow', whence *ḥārāš* 'artisan'; Syriac *ḥrat*; Ethiopic *ḥarasa*). *UPA* 141, 166 reads: [y]š*t* (.) (60) ᶜ'*ršm* . *l ahlm* 'a double-couch (was) set up inside the tent'.

48. So *CML* 122; *MLC* 400.

49. So *TO* 1 458; *ARTU* 265.

50. An undefined individual in *UPA* 166, 243–44.

51. An emendation to ᶜ'*ršm* is speculative (*UPA* 242–43).

52. So *ARTU* 265, *UPA* 141. *CML* 122, *TO* 1 458, and *MLC* 401 take *lbh* with the following.

53. *CARTU* 117; *ARTU* 265.

The next line (61b), which begins a new bicolon, is relatively clear. The end of the line has already been discussed above: Pughat is pouring out wine again for Yaṭupan. The question is whether *km . bṯn* means 'like a snake'[54] or whether the *ṯn* element is parallel to the *ṯnm* in the next, parallel line and means 'again; a second time'.[55] 'Like a snake' would nicely fit the context of deceit, but the latter interpretation provides the best parallel. I would interpret *km* as the affirmative particle *k-* plus enclitic *-m*. The term *b ṯn* is a preposition plus ordinal number, synonymous with *ṯnm* in the next line.

The last line (61d) is too broken to restore. Apparently Pughat is pouring out some other drink for Yaṭupan. Margalit restores: *tšqy* [. m]s[k . (m)škr ?] 'She served him [the intoxicating bevera]ge'.[56] De Moor restores *tšqy*[h .] s[m] 'she gave [him] a d[rug] to drink'.[57] Though a confident restoration cannot be ventured, at least it is clear that Pughat continues to give him intoxicating drink.

From this discussion, the outlines and many of the details of the wine feast are clear. Yaṭupan has Pughat (thought to be Anat) serve him wine. Pughat does this. Yaṭupan then boasts to her of his boundless prowess and, while doing so, even confesses to killing Aqhat. Then Pughat does some magic, perhaps recites an incantation, which is to affect Yaṭupan's whole camp (see *l ahlm* 'for/on the tents' in 60a; compare 52a). She then has Yaṭupan drink some more wine. The tablet ends here, but presumably there was a sequel, in which, like Judith, Pughat killed the drunk oppressor. Rather than cutting off his head, as in the case of Holofernes, Pughat would have executed him by drawing her concealed dagger and stabbing him, as Ehud stabbed Eglon (Judg 3:15–30).

Infelicity

This scene resonates with Anat's killing of Aqhat. Both females use disguises. Pughat covers her warrior clothes with female dress and otherwise appears to dress up as Anat. Anat hides among the vultures, perhaps even making herself appear like one so as not to be noticed. Both hide their respective weapons, a dagger and Yaṭupan, in their bags or belts, to be used on their victims. They both execute their plans in the context of feast situations. The only significant *strategic* difference is that Anat plans on using a feast situation from the beginning, whereas Pughat encounters

54. So the majority (*UPA* 166; *TO* 1 458; *MLC* 401; *CML* 122).
55. So *ARTU* 265, 'When for a second time [she po]ured w[ine] for him'.
56. *UPA* 141, 166.
57. *CARTU* 117; *ARTU* 265.

hers by accident. In other words, Pughat apparently does not contemplate the serving of wine before meeting Yaṭupan; he is the one who initiates the wine service. Pughat may just as well have executed her plan in a nonritual context, as did Ehud or Jael (Judges 3, 4–5).

Of course, the presence of deceit, akin to Grimes's categories of insincerity and violation, marks this as another case of ritual infelicity. As in Anat's killing of Aqhat, participants in the ritual have conflicting agendas, and only one will be able to consider the performance a success. But Pughat has the advantage, because she is feigning participation in the ceremony. Yaṭupan does not know that this is an occasion for ambush. For all he knows, he is renegotiating and expanding his relationship with Anat. He thinks that his status is being raised nearly to a divine level. Pughat also has the advantage, because she apparently uses a magical incantation. She thus brings supernatural power into play. Anat by nature also had access to supernatural power and apparently used it deceptively, in order to place herself and Yaṭupan in a position to kill Aqhat.

Another of Grimes's categories can be seen in Pughat's wine service: competition. She seeks to cancel, to the greatest possible extent, what Anat achieved in a ritual context earlier in the story. To be sure, this is not pure ritual competition, in which a rite is performed to annul the direct effect of another rite, such as rites performed to counteract sorcery; or two groups/individuals performing rites to determine which is effective or which has the most satisfactory result, as in the sacrifices offered by Elijah and the prophets of Baʿl (1 Kings 18) or the offering of incense by Korah and his band (Numbers 16). Nevertheless, Pughat and her activities can be seen as competitive because, from a technical point of view, she dresses up as the goddess and uses magic to accomplish her goal and, from a judicial point of view, she attacks the perpetrator of the initial ritual crime.

Pughat's wine service should be viewed as the ultimate culmination of the recuperation rites begun by Daniʾil after the death of Aqhat. The development of this series of rites parallels the development of rites at the beginning of the story up to the son's death. In both series, we first have rites that are performed properly, capped by a rite involving deceit (here one can count the two infelicitous feasts involving Anat as a unit; the first feast provides the basis for what Anat does in the second). The first part of this study showed how the felicitious feasts preceding the infelicitous feasts with Anat emphasize the latter and give them meaning. In a similar way, at the end of the story, the properly proceeding mourning and restoration rites performed by Daniʾil provide a backdrop against which Pughat's deceit stands out. It is the climax of the long sequence of recovery rites. But the significance of Pughat's wine service lies not so much in contrasting with the preceding mourning rites but in rectifying the problem created by the original instance of deceit. One wrong rite corrects another.

It should be noted that, though Pughat seeks to avenge Anat's attack on her brother, neither she nor her other family members–as far as we know–ever go after the goddess. They do not even lodge a complaint against her, as Job does against Yahweh and Gilgamesh against Ishtar. Her father's responses before her action against Yaṭupan became more and more focused on the cause of Aqhat's death, turning from responding to symptoms (the drought) to responding to the characters indirectly involved in the killing (first the vultures–specifically the female vulture, Ṣamal, who consumed Aqhat's remains and is symbolically associated with Anat–and then the nearby regions). Pughat's response provides a culmination to her father's responses in her attack on the specific instrument of Aqhat's death. But this is as far as she or the family goes. Anat escapes. Perhaps Yaṭupan is as far as the family dares to go without bringing further misfortune upon itself.

The individuals that are primarily involved in the pinnacle ritual feasts at the beginning of the story and here at the end are females. It is not clear, however, that this is a sign that the text is mainly interested in conflict between males and females, or more precisely, male and female aspects of society. Certainly Anat and Pughat, viewed in contrast to the males in the story, appear to be creative, intellectually able, relatively independent, and daring. Ṣamal, the mother of vultures, apparently sides with Anat and is almost a reflection of her. But not all of the females appear this way. The Kotharat and Danatay act in accordance with the wills of the dominant males. Pughat, for all her talent and initiative, acts in support of the social and family structure in which the father is dominant. After all, she receives the blessing of her father and avenges her brother. The gender dynamics in the story are, therefore, more complicated than simply female versus male.

One thing to note in solving this question is that, despite their similarities, Anat and Pughat are opposed to one another. Anat kills Aqhat and upsets the promises made to Daniʾil. Pughat redresses the problems. Anat is thus destroyer and Pughat is restorer. These actors' female character comes into play in regard to these negative and positive capacities. The high gods, who in the story are responsible for the way the world is constructed, physically and socially, grant blessing to Daniʾil. A lesser god, Anat, voids these promises. She is perceived as a lesser deity, according to the historical-social context of the story, because she is feminine. Her bowing before Il to receive his permission to go after Aqhat demonstrates her lower "social" position. In almost measure-for-measure fashion, ultimate recovery for Daniʾil and his family comes through an individual in a similarly subordinate position–in fact, through the one who is least of all in the entire divine-human social world of the story: a *human female daughter*. The story, to put it abstractly, embodies the idea that structure can be upset as well as mended by marginal agencies and forces. The powerful are not always powerful enough to control the world or to heal it from catastrophe.

Chapter 19
Conclusion to Part 4

The *dbḥ* leads Daniʾil and his family out of mourning. During the seven years of mourning, Daniʾil did not make offerings to the gods—at least, the text does not tell us about any offerings. He makes an offering only after this period is completed. This does not mean that at this point he has fully recovered from the loss. Though his *dbḥ* involves joy, he does not have a son, and vengeance has not been taken. Pughat offers to kill Aqhat's killer to restore judicial equilibrium. She employs the same strategy that Aqhat and Yaṭupan used against Aqhat.

But if the *dbḥ* allows Daniʾil to offer to the gods again, it is noteworthy that, in the *dbḥ* and in the aftermath involving Pughat, the gods take no active part. They are not listed or described as participants in the *dbḥ* in any fashion. The lack of the gods is most keenly felt when Pughat is blessed. One would expect them to bless her as they did Daniʾil at the beginning of the story, especially since the tragedy had come at the hands of one of the gods. But the deities are silent. A suitable alternative would perhaps be for Daniʾil to invoke the blessings of the gods upon his daughter. But he does not do this. He does not mention any god, and he gives a guarantee of his blessing by swearing by his own life, not by the life of the gods. In the entire final section of the story, the sphere of action is solely human. This creates the impression that even though Daniʾil has returned to sacrificing, there is still some strain between the human and the divine.

But Pughat succeeds admirably (so we guess), despite the lack of explicit divine help and despite the greater risk facing her than what faced Anat, whose basic strategy she employs. In her use of deceit, Pughat is much more daring than Anat. Anat stays outside Aqhat's feast, hiding until the opportunity is right to send an emissary to commit the deed. Pughat, however, enters the presence of her victim and plays along with him until, presumably, she finds occasion to kill him. Pughat thus subjects herself to detection and danger for a sustained period. Once committed she cannot turn back. Anat, in contrast, can withdraw at the last minute without her victim's ever knowing that he was a target of attack.

As has been noted, the slaying of Yaṭupan is perhaps the most that Daniʾil and his family could hope for in seeking redress for the crime.

Neither he nor Pughat could successfully assail Anat directly. It is also doubtful that Aqhat is resurrected in some way to reestablish the promise of the gods. His burial seems definitive. The seven years of mourning place too much time between the crime and a possible resuscitation–one might expect him to be revived immediately if he was to be revived. Furthermore, to be able to kill Yaṭupan and then receive the son back seems to tilt the resolution too much in Daniʾil's favor. This does not mean that Daniʾil did not have another son, or that Pughat did not turn out to be an effective replacement for Aqhat, much as the daughter Thitmanat has a special place in the Kirta story. These, nevertheless, are only surmises, in view of the missing text.

Chapter 20
General Conclusion

Figures 1 and 2 graphically summarize the results of the contextual study of ritual in the Ugaritic narrative of Aqhat. The first figure shows the overall contours of the story. Daniʾil appears in the beginning without a son. His situation rapidly changes for the better through a series of three feasts that he performs on behalf of various deities. The initial feast, the most elaborate and offered to the high gods Baʿl and Il, brings with it a blessing that promises Daniʾil a son and forecasts in the list of filial duties that the son will continue and aid the father in feasting the deities. The son that is to be born, therefore, will be pious, as his father was—at least that is what we expect. Daniʾil's ascendancy continues with the visit of the Kotharat, whom he feasts. This insures the birth of the son that follows soon afterward. Daniʾil's blessing is fully realized when Aqhat comes of age and receives what seems to be a token of that occasion, the gift of a divinely made bow brought by Kothar-wa-Ḫasis. Daniʾil feasts this deity and then gives the bow to Aqhat with a blessing.

Just as the story reaches the acme of covenantal fulfillment, Daniʾil's world crashes. Feasts that had hitherto brought good fortune now bring calamity. Anat desires the boy's bow, perhaps at the very feast where Aqhat's maturation is being celebrated. Neither she nor he is able to concede enough to complete negotiations successfully. The feast ends unconsummated, and the two are angry at each other, especially Anat at Aqhat. After receiving Il's consent to go after Aqhat—also by using a threat against the god—Anat kills Aqhat at another feast. Contextualizing the blessing of Daniʾil and the demise of Aqhat in feasting contexts allows the contrast between the two events to be acutely perceived. The felicitous feasts prepare readers to sense just where and how far the infelicitous feasts have gone wrong.

The undoing of the promise does not simply bring Daniʾil back to the default position at which he was found at the beginning of the story. He descends below it. This is signaled by his mourning and by the drought that ensues. Nature commiserates with the father. A further sign of

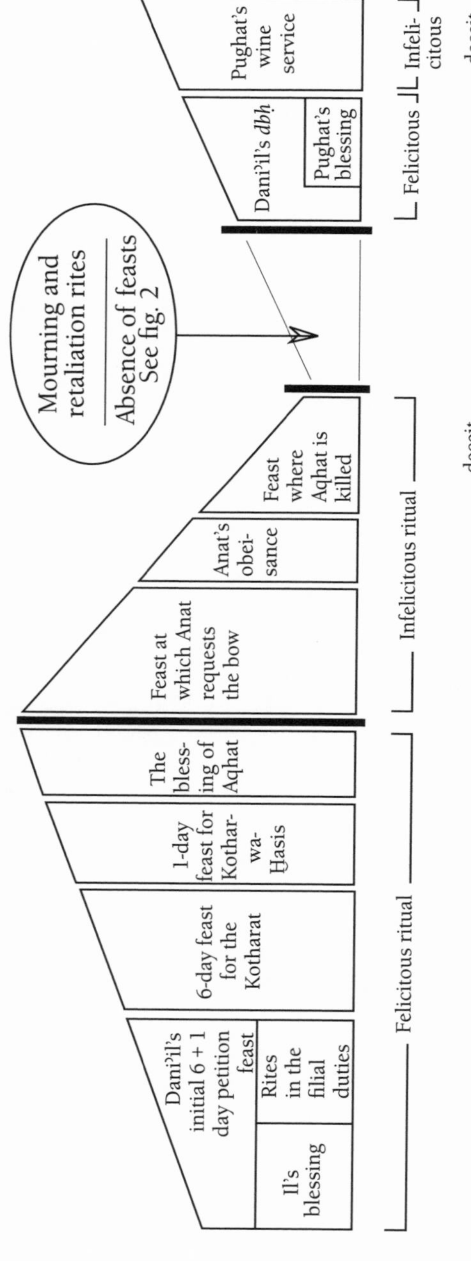

Figure 1. The Dynamics of Feasts in the Aqhat Story

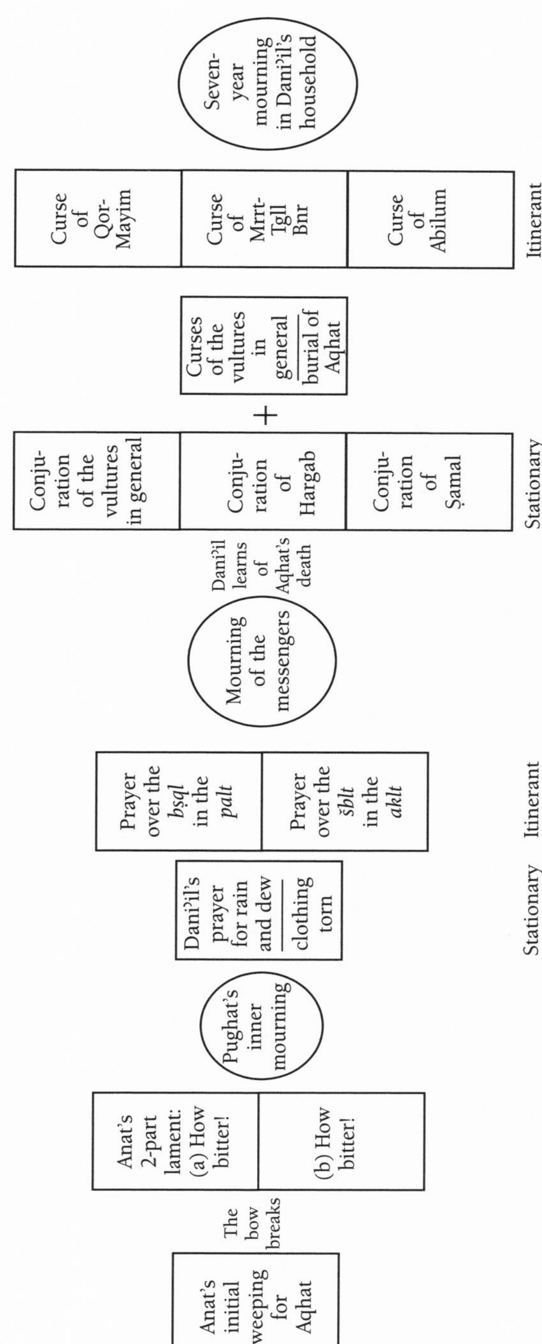

Figure 2. The Dynamics of Mourning and Retaliation Rites

Dani'il's humiliation is that, during the seven years of mourning, he is not represented as making offerings to the gods. Except for mentioning Baʿl indirectly in a prayer for rain and then calling on the god to ground the vultures so that he can look for his son, Dani'il has no commerce with the gods. It is not until the end of the seven years that he returns to offerings by sending away the mourners and making his *dbḥ*. Even at this point, he has not fully recovered. Pughat still needs to exact vengeance from Yaṭupan. Only when she does this can Dani'il be said to have fully recovered. It is not surprising then that, despite the offering of the *dbḥ*, the gods never appear on the scene in the last part of the story.

This recovery, it should be noted, is only a return to Dani'il's position at the beginning of the story. The missing end of the story may have contained a scene in which he receives another son, thus raising him to the position he was in when Aqhat was alive and flourishing. But this is not certain. Even more doubtful is the supposition that Aqhat was resurrected in some way. Pughat's revenge may have provided the resolution of the conflict in the tale, by her taking the preeminent position over the male child, much as Thitmanat is the favored child in the Kirta story. In other words, the poet may have been satisfied to tell about the tragic reversal of divine promise, with Dani'il having to be content with his daughter.

The tale is effective because of contextual and structural contrasts and because of similarities between ritual activities throughout. We have already touched on the contextual contrast between felicitous and infelicitous feasting at the beginning of the story. We should also note here that the last two feasts recapitulate the initial sequence of felicitous and infelicitous feasts: Dani'il's *dbḥ* proceeds properly, but Pughat's wine service involves deceit. Anat's deceit leads to loss for Dani'il; however, Pughat's produces gain, relatively speaking. Additionally, Dani'il's blessing of Pughat at the end of the story echoes the idiom of Il's blessing of Dani'il at the beginning of the story. On the one hand, this is a function of the story's social hierarchy, in which a subordinate is blessed by one who is immediately superior. On the other hand, Dani'il's blessing of Pughat is an indication that the family must resort to self-help to avenge the death of a family member.

The middle section of mourning and retaliation rites (in figure 2) displays an intensifying configuration of structural contrasts and echoes. The primary intensification occurs in Dani'il's own rites, in between and around which are placed brief scenes of mourning (by Pughat, the messengers, and then Dani'il's household). Dani'il's performances include first a single prayer for moisture, then a double prayer for the field, a threefold conjuration of the vultures with a capping curse, and then a threefold curse of the towns. In these scenes, Dani'il alternates between being stationary and being mobile. This alternation continues in the final feasts of the story. Daniʾil's *dbḥ* is presumably at or near home: just before the rite, he sends mourners away from his house. Pughat's vengeance also occurs away from home, at the camp of Yaṭupan. Another mimicking pattern occurs in Daniʾil's initial prayers for moisture and the fields. These have a 1 + 2 structure and echo the mourning of Anat, if our interpretation of that troublesome passage (in chapter 12) is essentially correct. She appears to have initially uttered a short lamentation and then a longer lamentation, which is divisible into two parts. A comparison between Anat's mourning and Daniʾil's rites also reveals another similarity: an event, the breaking of the bow, motivates Anat's compounded response; another event, the announcement of Aqhat's death, motivates Daniʾil elaborate threefold rites. An intensifying structure is also found at the beginning of the story. In the initial feast, Daniʾil appears to go about his activities in silence, after which Baʿl speaks and makes known to the hearers/readers the specific reason for Daniʾil's activity and induces Il to bless him. This anticipates the later structure of climax (see figure 1).

All of these factors reveal just how integral and central ritual is to the narrative. Ritual elements do not simply provide a stage for events in the story; they largely determine the very meaning of the story. The different rites convey much of what we know about the relationships of the characters. The characters' emotions and ethics—love, anger, hate, frustration, piety, a sense of duty and honor—are revealed through their various performances. Ritual's expressive nature suits well this descriptive task in narrative. While ritual is not the same sort of communication as language and expressiveness is not its defining characteristic, ritual's actions and objects are symbolic. This is true, perhaps not in the more direct ways suggested by scholars such as E. Leach, C. Geertz, S. Tambiah, and V. Turner, but at least in the more subtle and indirect ways suggested by C. Bell and F. Staal. Ritual as symbol in real life defines the status of individuals, marks transitions, celebrates joy, makes the endurance of misfortune possible, and otherwise creates "reality" for participants. These functions of ritual also come to bear in narrative. The main difference is that, instead of being participants in the rites, readers and hearers are observers. Story does draw readers and hearers into its world, however, until they become virtual participants through sympathetic identification with characters.

Several times above, I have referred to ritual texts from Ugarit that recount or reflect actual practice. They have helped to elucidate the Aqhat text. These parallels are few, however, and the ones that do exist are phenomenologically loose. This may be in part because the customs in the story reflect a time prior to the period of the actual ritual texts from

Ugarit,[1] or they may reflect a different sociocultural background. These conclusions are difficult to verify, however. The differences may reflect the fact that relatively few ritual texts have been discovered in and around Ugarit. It is also possible that the differences are simply a function of narration: just as ritual in real life contributes to and constructs a particular reality for the participants, so ritual in narrative seeks to create a world for its characters. This requires that the ritual, even though it depends to some extent on real-world models, be molded to the needs of its narrative.

Nevertheless, the story of Aqhat does appear to contribute indirectly to our understanding of ritual in the ancient Near East, especially in the kingdom of Ugarit, where the story presumably was produced and certainly where it was preserved. First of all, the fact that ritual in story could be modeled to the wishes of the authors/poets afforded them the opportunity to compose from an ideal perspective. In actual ritual, humans are the only visible participants. The gods, who are often of interest in actual ritual, are hidden. In story, however, they are observable participants and are as active as the human beings. Interpretation of the rituals embedded in narrative allows us to estimate the way a particular society viewed the effect and purpose of their ritual practices. Narrative thus provides indirect access to the manifest native interpretation of ritual. What is interesting is that the tale of Aqhat does not present a simple, positive ideal throughout, with humans performing a rite and gods responding with blessing. The story is interested in negative aspects of ritual as well. While it shows us how ritual might succeed, it is just as concerned to show us how it might fail. This is presumably a manifestation of real experience, in which rites did not always proceed smoothly and did not always have the effects desired. The story, in other words, reveals what according to participants' perspectives can go wrong in ritual. The Aqhat story indicates that ritual infelicity can be attributed to the competing and contrary desires of the gods, to ignorance in performing rites, and the need to assert and acquire power.

The story, particularly Pughat's revenge, also indicates that humans are not necessarily at the mercy of the gods in ritual situations. They can draw on their own power in blessing: note that Daniʾil blesses his daughter by his life and virtue, not by the gods or by their power. Note also that it is Pughat who employs deceit in ritual to exterminate Yaṭupan. It is not unimportant that in this example she is the least powerful character in the story, the *female child* of Daniʾil, going after the most powerful or at

1. For example, some have argued that the Baʿl cycle or portions of it are older than their written attestation or version (see the discussion in *SP* 48–54; Smith, *The Ugaritic Baal Cycle*, 29–58, esp. pp. 33–36).

least the most violent human (?) character. Ritual is not simply the tool of the dominant for constructing relationships of power over inferiors. Beings of low status can subvert it to gain an advantage. In any case, the purpose of many of the rituals in the story—not only the feasts but also the rites of mourning and retaliation—is to modify relationships of power.

One question arises naturally out of our discussion: why is ritual so prevalent and important to this text? One response is that the text may have had a cultic use or origin that left an imprint on the story. However, this is doubtful. The nature of the ritual in the text does not correlate with such a purpose. The ritual elements included are not solely cultic (that is, dealing with temple, priesthood, sacrifice, and/or purity). Many are performed outside of a cultic milieu, especially the mourning and retaliation rites. The ritual events in the story also have a private or domestic rather than communal, official, and high-liturgical orientation. Furthermore, the story seems to concentrate on what can be called "dark ritual"—that is, infelicitous performances or those that involve negative emotions and situations. This does not coordinate well with cultic use, in which ritual is expected to be proper and celebrative.

Other factors are probably responsible for the concentration of ritual in the story. The tale is primarily about the interaction of humans and deities. In the cultural world of the ancient Near East, these interactions were largely viewed as occurring in and being facilitated by ritual events. Thus, it would be natural for an author to employ ritual to describe the interaction of gods and humans in narrative. This hypothesis is supported by the similar preponderance of ritual in the Kirta tale, which also treats commerce between the human and divine spheres. This hypothesis also explains the more limited occurrence of human-divine ritual in the Baʿl cycle, which deals with matters only on the divine plane (though we often find deities interacting with each other there in ritual contexts). Another reason for the concentration of ritual in the Aqhat story may have been the symbolic force that ritual has, as noted above. With an economy of words it is thus able to communicate much to readers and hearers. Finally, ritual may also play a large role because of the power that dark ritual has in a narrative context. Positive, ideal ritual is relatively static; it exhibits or brings about an equilibrium. It is therefore not very stimulating. Dark ritual, in contrast, has a dynamic character. It either undoes ideal ritual or it embodies a struggle to return to an ideal situation. In doing so, it engages the imagination.

Indexes

Index of Subjects

Index of Authors

Index of Ugaritic Texts

Texts published in CAT

Index of Other Ancient Near Eastern Texts

Index of Biblical Passages